International Perspectives on Intercultural Education

႘ ◆ ႄ

International Perspectives on Intercultural Education

෨ ◆ ෪

Edited by

Kenneth Cushner
Kent State University

LEA LAWRENCE ERLBAUM ASSOCIATES, PUBLISHERS
1998   Mahwah, New Jersey   London

Lawrence Erlbaum Associates, Inc., Publishers
10 Industrial Avenue
Mahwah, NJ 07430

Cover design by Kathryn Houghtaling Lacey

Library of Congress Cataloging-in-Publication Data

International perspectives on intercultural education /
edited by Kenneth Cushner.
    p. cm.
Includes bibliographical references and indexes.
ISBN 0–8058–2745-5 (cloth : alk. paper). —
ISBN 0–8058–2746–3 (pbk. : alk. paper)
    1. Multicultural education--Cross-cultural studies.   I.
Cushner, Kenneth.
LC1099.I5958   1998
307.117—dc21   98-17268
                                                          CIP

Books published by Lawrence Erlbaum Associates are printed on acid-free paper, and their bindings are chosen for strength and durability.

Printed in the United States of America
10 9 8 7 6 5 4 3 2 1

This book is dedicated to
Gerald H. Read,
friend and Emeritus Professor of International and Comparitive Education
Kent State University
whose vision, insights, determination, and foresight
have helped so many to see from a broader vision.

Contents

ဢ ◆ ಚ

Preface

སྃ ◆ ༺

The new millennium will provide educators the world over with untold opportunities as well as obstacles in their quest to provide an education for all. Social, political, economic, and technological advances will continue to make education attainable to an ever-increasing number of students. At the same time, students served by most educational efforts will be increasingly diverse in terms of culture, race, ethnicity, and gender. Accommodating the needs of such a diverse community of learners will be no easy task, especially given the fact that teachers the world over tend to be rather homogeneous and cross-culturally inexperienced. Nevertheless, efforts to address the educational needs in many diverse societies continues to develop.

This volume, *International Perspectives on Intercultural Education*, is an attempt to expand the dialogue about multicultural or intercultural educational efforts by reviewing the various issues, policies, activities and approaches underway in many diverse nations of the world. Education researchers and practitioners from Australia, New Zealand, Malaysia, Britain, the Netherlands, Spain, Romania, Nigeria, South Africa, Ghana, the United States, Canada, and Mexico have provided a survey of the multicultural dimensions of their respective nations while analyzing the educational responses to such issues. These nations have histories rich in cultural complexity, yet they are diverse in their educational responses to these issues. There is something to be gained by studying the approaches others have taken.

This volume will be of interest and use in a variety of graduate level courses. Multicultural education courses will benefit from a global comparison of issues. International and comparative education, and teacher education in general will benefit by providing a survey of the ways in which various countries are preparing teachers to work with all children. This volume also should be of interest to educational policy analysts who will be able to compare education in a variety of contexts as they go about their business of addressing the needs of refugee, immigrant, and minority populations.

I extend my thanks to those who have provided assistance and feedback during the development of this volume. In particular, Dr. Raul Gagliardi of the International Bureau of Education in Geneva, Switzerland, offered substantial encouragement for this project from its inception and provided valuable translation of some Spanish text. Naomi Silverman, editor, guided the development of the book with sensitivity and care. I also am grateful to the reviewers who offered valuable feedback on an earlier draft of the book: Corinne Mantle-Bromley, Colorado State University; Timothy Reagan, University of Connecticut; and Richard Smith, Griffith University Gold Coast, Australia.

—*Kenneth Cushner*

Chapter 1

Intercultural Education from an International Perspective: An Introduction

ℰ ◆ ℭ

Kenneth Cushner
Kent State University

From the Americas to Australia, and throughout Europe, Africa, and Asia, nations and people are confronting increased cultural diversity in their economic, political, and social spheres. Many changes occurring within the borders of most nations force people of different backgrounds to interact in ways never imagined a generation ago. The international business community continues to expand; indigenous people claim their fair share and influence in determining the use of their nation's resources, or desire autonomy and a voice in determining the direction of their own fate; marginalized groups continue to coalesce and demand equal opportunity and greater representation; guest workers or migrant laborers continue to swell national borders, with an estimated 10 million found throughout Europe alone; and refugees continue to stream across borders to the extent that there are presently as many as 24 million people worldwide who live within the borders of another nation (Childers & Urquhart, 1994). Although so-called domestic minorities exist within all countries, immigrant minorities are on the increase in many. The former benefit by equal legal status, which is not afforded to the latter. However, nowhere is constitutional equality sufficient to counterbalance the realities many face in their schools and communities, on the job, or in society in

1

general (Khoi, 1994). The differences those outside the mainstream experience seem to be more in degree than in nature.

However, even as far back as 1966 in the United States, Coleman (1966) demonstrated that having a single approach to schooling, democratic school attendance, and so-called "compensatory" teaching were not sufficient to eliminate the inequalities found between ethnic groups (in the United States particularly between Whites and Blacks). "Such inequalities were found," as Khoi suggested (1994), "to be in response to the many mechanisms of differentiation, which may be either apparent or hidden behind supposedly technical criteria, such as the dominant language, the location and types of schools, the resources available in terms of equipment, qualified teachers, etc" (p. 79). Much seems to be lost or taken away from many through the process of education.

One response to this increased diversity witnessed across the globe has been an increase in activity related to areas commonly referred to as intercultural, multicultural, cross-cultural, or international education. Although education alone cannot change the face of many problems that exist today, it can influence the future by preparing the minds of young people to include a diversity of viewpoints, behaviors and values. Intercultural education can work on many fronts as it strives to eliminate prejudice and racism by creating an awareness of the diversity and relative nature of viewpoints and thus a rejection of absolute ethnocentrism; assists people in acquiring the skills needed to interact more effectively with people different from themselves; and demonstrates that despite the differences that seem to separate people, many similarities do, in fact, exist across groups.

Comparing various nations' approaches to multicultural education can be complicated by a number of factors (Eldering, 1996). At one level, transnational comparisons can be complicated because of the specific diversity found in different societies. Fleras and Elliott (1992) differentiated four dimensions in a society, one of which—objective reality—concerns itself with the coexistence of different groups (cultural or ethnic) within a particular nation or state. Specific groups may differ in their numbers, history, power, cultures, ethnic origins, and social status. Each multicultural society has, as Eldering (1996) pointed out, "its own genesis, and consequently its own diversity" (p. 325). Cultural and ethnic diversity can usually be attributed to slavery, immigration, or colonization. Populations in the United States, Australia, Canada, and Israel, for instance, are composed primarily of voluntary or involuntary immigrants and their descendants. Northwestern European countries, however, experienced immigration as a result of expansion after World War II as well as decolonization. Such nations as New Zealand, Australia, the United States, Mexico, and Canada have directed increasing attention to their indigenous people. Throughout Africa, people have recently found themselves within political borders that never before existed.

At another level, transnational comparisons can be complicated owing to a considerable degree of confusion regarding terminology and conceptual clarity. That is, multicultural education, in some instances, is restricted to individuals from cultural and ethnic groups outside the mainstream. In other situations, multicultural education is seen as crucial for all members of a society, and as such, is directed toward all students. The particularist approach, focusing on the perceived needs of specific ethnic or cultural groups, is most characteristic of an assimilationist ideology. It is thought that through multicultural education, those in the minority can learn the language, behavior, and thought patterns that will enable them to succeed in the mainstream. Little value is afforded the "other" culture. The universalistic approach, in contrast, is directed toward all pupils and tends to characterize a pluralistic ideology. In this context, individual and group identity and needs are recognized, valued, and allowed to flourish alongside one another.

Terminology used in any given nation with reference to various groups also differs and may reflect history as well as policy. In many European nations, such terms as *guest worker* (Gastarbeiter in Germany), *immigrants*, and *minorities* are in common use (except in Germany, which officially denies that migrants have become immigrants). The term *minority*, as used in the Netherlands, refers to immigrant groups that occupy a low socioeconomic status (SES; Ministry of Internal Affairs, 1983). The term *minority*, as used in the United States and Canada, however, has a somewhat different connotation. In these nations, the term *minority* either refers racial characteristics or emphasizes cultural "deviation" from the majority (e.g., a language minority, religious minority, etc.). Chinese, for instance, are considered minorities in the United States and Canada, but not in the Netherlands because there they do not have low SES. Terminology referring to a nation's indigenous people also may differ. In the United States, indigenous people are often referred to as *Native Americans*. In Australia they are called *Aborigines*, whereas in Canada, the preferred term is *First Nations*.

Differentiating the labels *multicultural education* and *intercultural education*, the two most commonly used terms, as well as *cross-cultural education* and *international education*, is sometimes difficult and the boundaries are often blurred. The term *multicultural education* is currently the preferred term in the literature of North America, Great Britain and Australia. History will reveal continuing efforts by the educational systems of some nations to respond to issues of race, ethnicity, and intercultural interaction. Banks and Banks (1995), two of the most prolific multicultural educators in the United States, suggested that the inspirational roots of multicultural education were launched in the 1800s by African American scholars dissatisfied with the quality of education experienced by most Blacks. Early African American scholars produced such works as *History of the Negro Race in America* (Williams, 1883), the publication of the *Journal of Negro History* (1926), and *The Mis-Education of the Negro* (Woodson, 1933), which asserted that the nation's schools and colleges were miseducating African Americans by teaching them European civilization and not the African civilizations and cultures of their own people.

The term *intercultural education*, which seems to be preferred in Europe, is used in this volume to integrate related and oftentimes overlapping and interrelated approaches. For many, *intercultural education* has a somewhat different orientation than *multicultural education*. *Multicultural*, according to Khoi (1994), refers to unrelated juxtapositions of knowledge about particular groups without any apparent interconnection between them. *Intercultural*, however, implies comparisons, exchanges, cooperation, and confrontation between groups. Problems and situations are seen as so complex that they can be dealt with only through the convergence and combination of different view points. From this perspective, intercultural education is more proactive and action oriented than multicultural education, and rather than focusing on specific problems such as learning style differences or language development, recognizes that a genuine understanding of cultural differences and similarities is necessary in order to build a foundation for working collaboratively with others. It is also recognized that a pluralistic society can be an opportunity for majority and minority groups to learn from and with one another, not a problem as it might be viewed by some.

If majority populations are to be members of an international community, which most purport to be, then they must learn how to relate effectively with other cultures. If they do not, the consequence may be similar to the horrifying events we see unfolding in Burundi and Bosnia. It is perhaps the more recent conceptions of multicultural education in the United States that reflect the implications of intercultural education. In many places and in many respects, however, the terms have been used interchangeably.

One major goal of intercultural education has been to help young people and teachers not only understand the diversity of thought, expression, belief, and practice of those who are different from themselves, but also to guide development so individuals are better skilled at living and working effectively with others. Educators today must strive to integrate fully an intercultural education and perspective while carrying on with the traditional educational needs of communities and nations. Yet these are not easy issues to adequately address. Intercultural education and training is a delicate and difficult endeavor that must be approached with the greatest of sensitivity. Bennett (1993) pointed out that intercultural interaction among human populations has typically been accompanied by violence and aggression:

> Intercultural sensitivity is not natural. It is not part of our primate past, nor has it characterized most of human history. Cross-cultural contact usually has been accompanied by bloodshed, oppression, or genocide. . . . Education and training in intercultural communication is an approach to changing our "natural" behavior. With the concepts and skills developed in this field, we ask learners to transcend traditional ethnocentrism and to explore new relationships across cultural boundaries. This attempt at change must be approached with the greatest possible care. (p. 21)

In addition to the intense reactions identified by Bennett, evidence for the unnaturalness of intercultural contact can be seen in people's everyday behaviors. Many people, including those who do not harbor intense prejudices, admit that interactions with culturally different others tend to be more anxiety provoking than interactions with very similar people. For a smaller number of people, this anxiety leads to a strong preference for interactions with similar others (a small in-group) and an active avoidance of intercultural interactions. Such people, however, will not fare well in today's world in which intercultural interactions are increasingly commonplace.

Approaches to addressing issues of multicultural or intercultural education also are quite varied. In 1933, the Service Bureau for Intercultural Education was developed in the United States, and thus was born the beginning of the intergroup education movement. Throughout the 1940s, the intergroup education movement sought to reduce racial and ethnic tensions among citizens across the United States. Among its activities, it developed and presented school assemblies and in-service programs to intensify ethnic consciousness of minority and immigrant children.

Intergroup educators introduced a plethora of pedagogical and curricular methods, particularly instructional units on minority groups and various racial, ethnic, and religious groups. The banning of books considered stereotypic and demeaning to ethnic groups was also common. The movement gave birth of many institutions and organizations devoted to intercultural pursuits. For instance, the American Field Service (known as AFS Intercultural Programs today), the world's largest student exchange organization, traces its roots to the years immediately after World War II when it was a volunteer ambulance service on the front lines.

Perhaps the most dramatic efforts to deal with diversity in American society and in its schools occurred during the 1960s and 1970s. Fueled by the general social ferment of the civil rights movement and the war in

Vietnam, numerous educational reform movements were enacted in the United States, including school desegregation, multicultural and bilingual education, mainstreaming students with special needs into regular classrooms, and gender-sensitive education. All of these programs recognized the pluralistic nature of the society in a positive rather than negative sense. Each attempted to help some educationally disadvantaged group to receive a better education within a pluralistic framework.

More recently, efforts such as those by Cushner, McClelland, and Safford (1996) and also Bennett (1995) attempt to place an integrated conception of multicultural education firmly in a global context. Most American multiculturalists, however, would agree with Banks (1993) who said, "The major goal of multicultural education is to restructure schools so that all students will acquire the knowledge, attitudes, and skills needed to function in an ethnically and racially diverse nation and world" (p. 27). School programs and practice teaching Eurocentric (or any "centric") experience, heritage, and perspective that exclude the views of others must be transformed, and young people must be helped to develop the knowledge, motivation, and skill to challenge and change systems characterized by discrimination and oppression.

A slightly different course has been taken in other countries as each have responded to their unique blend of internally and externally driven affairs. In the United Kingdom, several different approaches relating to diversity can be identified, each being more salient at one time or another, yet failing to follow some neat continuum (Figueroa, 1995). In Australia, since the White Australian policy was abolished by the Whitlam government in the 1970s, there has been a steady increase in immigrants from a multitude of nations. This has been matched by a corresponding response on the part of the educational system to address the needs of an increasingly multicultural society.

Pedagogical approaches to addressing issues of diversity, too, are quite varied. Various scholars have differentiated a number of approaches to multicultural education, among them Sleeter and Grant (1987), who differentiated five approaches found in practice: education of the culturally different, the human relations approach, single group studies, multicultural education, and education that is multicultural and social reconstructionist. These are discussed more fully in chapter 12 on the United States.

Eldering (1996) identified four approaches to multicultural education directed at two different target groups. The *disadvantage approach* assumes that students from ethnic or cultural minority groups have educational disadvantages not shared by the majority group members. This approach exclusively targets students from these groups as they are taught skills designed for success in the mainstream. The *enrichment approach* aims to help students of all groups learn more about each other's cultures. The assumptions behind this approach is that increased knowledge leads to mutual appreciation, respect, and better understanding. The *bicultural competence* approach, also for all students, attempts to make students competent in two cultures. The *collective equality approach*, the most revolutionary of all the approaches identified by Eldering (1996), focuses on the collective equality of groups rather than the equality of individuals. Such an approach, like the fifth level of Sleeter and Grant's (1987) analysis: Education that is multicultural and social reconstructionist attempts to transform the entire school system, not just some of the discreet elements such as material or curriculum.

However, not everyone is an advocate of intercultural or multicultural education. Critics of multicultural education do not come only from the far right, but as Fouts (1993) stated, "from many thoughtful individuals of all persuasions who are not satisfied with the quality of scholarship, reasoning, and evidence put forth by its proponents" (p. 358). Some opponents, particularly those in the United States, are concerned that such efforts amount to a political agenda of "separation in language and culture, a revisionist view of history as a collection of grievances to be kept alive, and a program of both historical and contemporary condemnation of American society and Western civilization" (Sowell, 1993, p. 71). Sowell continued his concerns by stating that multiculturalists' educational methods are "geared toward leading students to a set of preselected beliefs rather than toward developing their own abilities to analyze for themselves, or to provide them with adequate factual knowledge to make their own independent assessment" (p. 71). Some fear a disuniting of a nation (Schlesinger, 1992), and others see multicultural education as directly responsible for increases in ethnic and racial tensions in many U.S. urban public schools because of the emphasis on individual and group-specific concerns.

Fouts (1993) warned that the assumption that ethnic and cultural diversity provides a basis for societal enrichment, cohesiveness, and survival is not supported by historical research. However, he did suggest that "historical examples abound that show that celebrating ethnicity encourages the forces of the far right" (p. 357). He cautioned against going down a path built on a "strictly ideological and hastily accepted premise" (p. 357) rather than one established by logic, evidence, and history.

At the same time, it must be kept in mind that intercultural education is not only a western ideological approach to education, nor is it designed to impose Western liberal values on other societies. In fact, Mitchell and Salsbury's (1996) survey of multicultural efforts worldwide discovered many nations that have multicultural education programs with some sort of central direction provided from a governing body, including Columbia, the Philippines, Paraguay, and Tanzania. Their survey also found that the nations of Bahrain, Bangladesh, Cuba, Ecuador, El Salvador, Guyana, India, Kenya, Liberia, Malaysia, Mauritius, and Singapore all reported surveying textbooks for racist and sexist content.

It must be stated, however, that although toleration may in general be a good thing (ideally an outcome of good intercultural education), there may be times when certain values and practices may not be worth tolerating. One can think, for instance, of female circumcision, or apartheid beliefs and practices valued in certain societies at one time or another, but generally viewed by some on the inside and many on the outside as intolerable. This presents a complex philosophical issue open to discussion and debate among scholars, practitioners, and students of multicultural or intercultural education, which, although not generally in the scope of this book, remains one of the tensions in the field that must be kept in mind.

PURPOSE OF THIS BOOK

The focus of this book centers on the way people define the related concepts of multicultural, intercultural, cross-cultural, and international education; the specific issues they confront in their nation; and the way they actualize or make these issues practical both as individuals and in teacher education. The attempt in this volume is to ask key scholars and practitioners in their respective nations to inform us of current educational practice related to the needs of diversity. Each author was asked to respond to a similar series of guiding questions designed to allow them to present (a) a brief description of their national educational system; (b) descriptive data of demographics of their country, including various subgroups and subcultures and their experiences with the mainstream educational system; (c) a discussion of the perceived obstacles to addressing intercultural issues in schools and solutions to overcoming these obstacles; and (d) how teacher preparation institutions presently address intercultural education.

To tease you, the reader, and encourage you to apply the content presented in this volume to a possible real-world situation, you are urged to consider the following scenario. As you read each chapter and ponder the particular nuances of the individual nations, consider how you or a team of educators from that specific nation might respond to this scenario:

> Global conditions are such that there are at the present time more than 24 million people that the United Nations identifies as refugees, that is, people presently in transition from their country of origin to a potentially more hopeful situation. Your country has suddenly found itself host to a rather large number of political refugees. There is no hope that these people can return to their homeland, and your government has obligated itself to provide them with a home.

A large group of these refugees have been settling in a part of your country that traditionally has been relatively culturally and linguistically homogeneous. The refugees prefer to settle in one of two settings: in a major city where work opportunities seem plentiful, or along a major source of water where they hopefully can continue their traditional farming and fishing activities. This represents an unexpected and unplanned change for the local population. Few of the people in either of these settings have any knowledge of the refugees' language, culture, or religious beliefs.

Over the past 5 years in which this influx has been occurring, considerable tensions have arisen in the local communities, especially in the schools. Locals complain about the refugees' loud behavior, their strange language and inability or unwillingness to learn the local language, the way they raise their children, and even their health practices. Refugees in turn complain that the local communities do not open their doors to them, that they are unwilling to do business with them, and that their own young people are being forced to do things in school that go against their culture and religion. Teachers have become increasingly frustrated with their apparent inability to work well with many of the students. Tensions in the schools between young people have also increased, as the secondary schools have seen an increase in vandalism and fighting between members of the two groups.

You are on a team of education officials who have been asked to provide a plan of action to address the current situation. Using the practices and thinking that reflect the perspective of your own nation, please respond using the following questions as a guideline. How will you go about your work? What major obstacles do you anticipate? How will you go about overcoming these obstacles? What long-range actions do you propose? What major issues or concerns guide your proposal? How might teacher training be affected? How might you overcome any negative attitudes that teacher education students might have?

At the end of each chapter, you will be asked to reflect on the scenario and propose a plan of action which considers the particulars with which you have been presented.

ORGANIZATION OF THIS BOOK

The nations presented in this volume include Australia, Canada, England, Ghana, Malaysia, Mexico, the Netherlands, New Zealand, Nigeria, Romania, South Africa, Spain, and the United States, and are presented by geographic region. It is recognized that the nations represented here do not reflect a comprehensive international picture. Size restrictions for this volume just would not allow such an endeavor. The attempt, however, is to begin discussion of such issues on a global scale, and to gain a snapshot of the range and variety of complex scenarios that face many nations. Perhaps a subsequent volume will present issues experienced in such nations as India, China, Singapore, Germany, Korea, Israel, Turkey, who are facing similarly complex issues. Although the reader will find many differences in the specific issues and dilemmas facing the various nations presented, many similarities do exist in strategies and approaches that have been taken to address these issues.

Each chapter begins with a brief overview of the major issues that have come together in a particular nation around issues related to diversity. Most of this information is summarized from the recent survey conducted by Mitchell and Salsbury (1996). Each chapter ends with a few questions for the reader to consider. In addition, a World Wide Web site providing access to many of the world's newspapers is provided so readers can keep abreast of current related issues.

In chapter 2, Allan and Hill survey the manner in which the Australian educational systems have responded to the need for intercultural education. The chapter first looks at the Australian educational context, then at the demographic pattern of ethnic groups in Australia. After this, the authors explore the main thrusts of intercultural education in Australian schools and teacher education institutions—particularly Aboriginal, ethnic, and Asian studies.

In chapter 3, Bishop and Glynn review the historic pattern of cultural superiority and subordination established between European immigrants and the indigenous Maori population of New Zealand, and explore how this relationship has set the pattern for subsequent relationships with new immigrants. The authors review some of the attempts to rectify this pattern, both in schools and communities, including the introduction of philosophies and practices of multiculturalism and biculturalism. In addition, attempts at Maori autonomy, especially Maori language immersion programs, are also reviewed.

In chapter 4, Gaudart begins by exploring the national education policy in Malaysia that has continued to evolve since independence was achieved in the 1950s. The system of public and private schools that has developed is explored in terms of its ability to respond to the cultural needs of the nation and its people. In particular, the chapter explores how language and culture manifest themselves in society and its educational system, and how the current situation is not conducive to much focus on issues surrounding intercultural education.

In chapter 5, Hooghoff and Delnoy present a comprehensive look at issues of interest in the Netherlands. After a review of the educational system, demographic and linguistic data are provided that describe the political responses of the educational system to the presence of immigrants in the country. Finally, efforts at teacher training to address intercultural educational issues are presented.

In chapter 6, Figueroa focuses his discussion on England because the majority of the ethnic population in the United Kingdom can be found there, although the chapter has sufficient relevance to the rest of the

United Kingdom, in particular, Wales. The chapter explores the educational system in a broad manner, examines its general response to a changing society and political system, presents a discussion of racism in British society, and shows how teacher education in general responds to intercultural issues.

In chapter 7, Ciges and Lopez provide a survey of the Spanish educational system and its intercultural policy, paying particular attention to the interaction that occurs between the majority population and the Gypsy communities of the country. A significant amount of discussion in the chapter concerns the preparation of teachers who have had limited intercultural contact.

In chapter 8, Neumann begins his most interesting discussion by stating that "interculturally oriented education has not been under public debate in Romania. The topic is little known in the countries of central and eastern Europe and is often mistaken for education in the mother tongues of the minority communities." A window, perhaps, on what is occurring in many other nations in Eastern Europe, this chapter serves as a warning to us all.

In chapter 9, Michael and Michael present a very insightful and thoughtful analysis of historic and current influences on the potential and need for addressing intercultural education in Nigeria, and perhaps in other nations of Africa as well. Presenting a model that explores the influence of colonialization and forced integration of the many ethnic (tribal) groups into one nation-state, they argue, quite passionately, that it may be only through the efforts of intercultural education that a country like Nigeria can survive.

In chapter 10, Stonier discusses the dramatic changes currently underway throughout the society and educational system in South Africa. He begins his chapter by stating, "South Africa must exemplify an almost unique situation in terms of multiculturalism with its remarkably diverse population." The dismantling of the Apartheid system and the subsequent response of the educational system presents a most significant challenge for all of South Africa. Stonier presents a comprehensive look at current conditions and prospects for change in these most trying times.

In chapter 11, Eshun explores many of the unique cultural influences on the West African nation of Ghana. A country whose citizens speak more than 70 distinct languages, 28 of which are represented in significant numbers, provides quite a unique challenge to the educational system, both in public schools and teacher training institutions. Language policies understandably drive many of the intercultural education efforts in this country. Eshun also explores the role of religion (Christian, Muslim, and traditional), availability of textbooks, and student teaching in relation to intercultural education.

Three chapters on the Americas look in turn at the United States, Canada, and Mexico. In chapter 12, Seeberg, Swadener, Vanden-Wyngaard, and Rickel survey historic current issues in multicultural education in the United States. They introduce many concepts that seem unique to this nation, or at least at the forefront of current thinking and debate. The chapter ends with a unique look at the experiences a team of educators had collaborating on a long-term multicultural institute, which brings together university and school educators as well as parent and community teams. There is much to be learned from their analysis.

Fowler's chapter (chapter 13) on Canada, subtitled "Glimpses from the Past, Hopes for the Future", provides an overview of key historic developments that have paved the way for the multicultural society that Canada has become. Of particular concern for Canada is the degree to which issues in francophone Quebec, as well as issues related to indigenous people, can be adequately addressed and reconciled. In his summary, Fowler points out that although curricula have become less ethnocentric and more multicultural, multiculturalism still has not flourished in Canada. He also discusses possible reasons for this, many of which are shared by other authors in this volume.

In chapter 14, Huerta, Tarrow, and Gastélum present a special case of Mexico. They begin by stating that Mexico must deal with many issues significantly different from those of most other nations surveyed in this book. Mexico contends with the fourth largest population growth rate in the world, a long overlooked and disadvantaged indigenous population with its own languages, political and economic refugees from the south, and emigration from the poor rural countryside to its major cities or to its border cities and then across the porous border to its northern neighbor, the United States. This chapter includes a description of current demographic dynamics facing the country and an overview of the Mexican educational system. It surveys the indigenous population, policies dealing with immigrants from the South, and characteristics of emigration to the north, then ends with an example of a unique binational intercultural education program between the United States and Mexico designed to address the present reality faced by students who regularly move between the two nations and must contend with the unique settings of two schools. This program offers a prime example of what can occur when educators from two nations understand and accept a current situation and collaborate on its resolution.

To conclude, chapter 15 integrates much of what was presented in the preceding chapters by identifying issues that seem to be common across the various national responses to diversity as well as apparent concerns. In addition, responses by chapter authors to the common scenario presented earlier in this chapter are reviewed.

REFERENCES

Banks, J. (1993). Multicultural education: Development, dimensions, and challenges. *Phi Delta Kappan*, 75(1), 22–28.
Banks, J., & Banks, C. (1995). (Eds.). *Handbook of multicultural research*. New York: Macmillan.
Bennett, C. (1995). *Comprehensive multicultural education: Theory and practice*, (3rd ed.), Boston: Allyn & Bacon.
Bennett, M. (1993). Toward ethnorelativism: A developmental model of intercultural sensitivity. In R. M. Paige (Ed.), *Education for the intercultural experience* (pp. 21–71). Yarmouth, ME: Intercultural Press.
Childers, E., & Urquhart, B. (1994). *Renewing the United Nations system*. Geneva: United Nations.
Coleman, J. S. (1966). *Equality of educational opportunity*. Washington, DC: U.S. Department of Health, Education, and Welfare.
Cushner, K., McClelland, A., &Safford, P. (1996). *Human diversity in education: An integrative approach*. New York: McGraw–Hill.
Eldering, L. (1996). Multiculturalism and multicultural education in an international perspective. *Anthropology and education quarterly*, 27(3), 315–330.
Figueroa, P. (1995). Multicultural education in the United Kingdom: Historical development and current status. In J. Banks & C. M. Banks (Eds.), *Handbook of research on multicultural education* (pp. 778–800). New York: Macmillan.
Fleras, A., & Elliott, J. L. (1992). *Multiculturalism in Canada: The challenge of diversity*. Ontario, Canada: Nelson.
Fouts, J. T. (1993). Multicultural education and the idols of the mind: Why multicultural education is under attack. *Social Education*, 57(7), 356–358.
Journal of Negro History. Washington, DC: Washington Association for the Study of Negro Life and History.
Khoi, L. T. (1994). Intercultural education. In L. F. B. Dubbeldam, T. Ohsako, L. T. Khoi, P. Dasen, P. Furter, G. Rist, P. Batelaan, S. Churchill, K. P. Epskamp, F. M. Bustos, & G. R. Teasdale (Eds.), *International yearbook of education, volume XLIV—1994: Development, culture and education* (pp. 79–104). Paris: UNESCO.
Ministry of Internal Affairs (1983). Minderhedennota. The Hague, The Netherlands: Staatsuitgeverij.
Mitchell, B. M., & Salsbury, R. E. (1996). *Multicultural education: An international guide to research, policies, and programs*. Westport, CT: Greenwood Press.
Schlesinger, A. (1992). *The disuniting of America: Reflections on a multicultural society*. New York: Norton.
Sleeter, C., & Grant, C. (1987). An analysis of multicultural education in the United States. *Harvard Educational Review*, 57(4), 421–444.
Sowell, T. (1993). *Inside American education: The decline, the deception, the dogmas*. New York: New York Press.
Williams, G. W. (1983). *History of the Negro race in America from 1619 to 1880*. New York: G. P. Putnam's Sons.
Woodson, C. G. (1933). *The mis-education of the Negro*. Washington, DC: Associated Publishers.

Editor's Remarks

Despite its geographic isolation and recognition as an "island continent," Australia represents one of the more culturally diverse nations in the world, with a greater percentage of its citizens having been born outside its borders than any other country except Israel. The country is physically about the same size as the United States, but has a population of only one-twelfth as large. Its indigenous people or Aborigines, who have resided on the land continuously for at least 40,000 years, numbered more than 300,000 when the Europeans first arrived in 1770. The Aborigines suffered greatly after European contact so badly that by 1921 their population was less than 2% of the indigenous population at the time of British arrival.

Today, there are many indigenous microcultures in addition to the Aborigines, including Torres Strait Islanders and many Pacific Islanders. Large numbers of immigrants and refugees from around the world have settled in Australia since World War II. Melbourne, in southeastern Victoria, boasts the largest Greek community outside of Greece and the third largest Greek community in the world. More than 100 languages are spoken throughout Australia, not including the more than 150 indigenous languages.

As in the United States, education in Australia is more a function of the state than a federal concern. There is, thus, a tendency to find greater autonomy and diversity of activity in each state's pursuit of educational programming. Although a National Advisory Committee on Multicultural Education (NACME) exists to help develop policy, funding for formal multicultural education programs was terminated by the Ministry of Education by the late 1980s. Currently, teacher education does not require a course in multicultural education.

How should a nation with such a complex demographic situation approach the education of its young? How can a core of teachers from a rather homogeneous background and experience be prepared for the cultural and social complexities they surely will confront in the classroom and communities? How can the young people in this nation be most effectively prepared to interact with one another and with others on a global scale?

Chapter 2

Intercultural Education in Australia

ᔆ ◆ ᔆ

Bob Hill
Rod Allan
Charles Sturt University

This chapter examines the ways in which Australian education systems, particularly university teacher education programs, have responded to the need for intercultural education. To explore this, we look first at the Australian educational context and then at the demographic pattern of ethnic groups in Australia. The term *intercultural education* is not widely used in this country and is normally seen as a component of *multicultural education*, which, (as) viewed in the Australian context, is concerned with encouraging positive interaction between individuals from different cultures and subcultures and providing an understanding of cultural difference. Later in the chapter, we explore the main thrusts of intercultural education in Australian schools and teacher education institutions—Aboriginal studies, ethnic studies, and asian studies—and briefly discuss refugee issues.

THE NATURE OF THE
EDUCATION SYSTEM IN AUSTRALIA

Constitutionally, Australia is a federation of states (provinces). Education is the responsibility of the states. This constitutional structure has been complicated in recent decades by the increased budgetary involvement of the federal government in financing various initiatives in primary (elementary) and secondary school systems. The universities, although established under state legislation, receive most of their funding from the federal government.

State governments operate schools which are attended by 72% of all students (Burrow, 1996). The remainder attend private schools, usually run by churches, which are licensed by state governments but receive substantial federal recurrent and capital grants. School curricula are determined by state education authorities, which, until recent times, jealously guarded their curriculum autonomy. Since 1989, however, states have agreed to a process of voluntary curriculum rationalization that has involved the production of national profiles in eight different subject areas covering the compulsory years of schooling. Increasingly, although not uniformly, states' curriculum documents have become more consistent with these national profiles, with potential benefits for a number of groups including staff and students moving between states, universities recruiting nationally, publishers keen to service a national market, and state education departments anxious to achieve economies in their curriculum development.

The year 1989 saw dramatic changes in Australian tertiary education similar to those that had occurred earlier in Britain (Judge, 1991). Previously, secondary teacher education had been carried out largely in universities and primary teacher education programs in Colleges of Advanced Education (CAEs), institutions not funded for research, but established to provide innovative and cost-effective teaching and to service a narrow range of professional training. Under these reforms, there was a series of amalgamations of universities and CAEs resulting in a unified system of 36 public universities, virtually all of which provide teacher education.

Within universities, the 1990s were characterized by a considerable expansion of student numbers and a competitive pressure to be entrepreneurial and supplement the lack of commensurate government funding with income from a variety of sources, especially fee-paying students from overseas. The overwhelming majority of these students come from Southeast Asia (Alexander & Rizvi, 1993) and have been disproportionately enrolled in faculties of business and computing (Alexander, 1994). By contrast, Australian universities were prohibited from charging tuition fees to domestic students, although this will change in 1998.

AUSTRALIAN DEMOGRAPHICS AND THE EXPERIENCE OF SPECIFIC SUBGROUPS AND SUBCULTURES WITH THE MAINSTREAM EDUCATION SYSTEM

Approximately 1.7% of the Australian population are Aborigines (Madden, R., 1994). Although numerically the largest concentrations of Aborigines are in the major cities of the South, Aborigines comprise the largest proportion of the population in some geographically remote areas, especially in northern Australia. It is in these areas that European colonization has had the least destructive impact on Aboriginal languages, laws, and cultures (Hughes & Willmot, 1982).

On almost any socioeconomic indicator, the Aborigines represent the most disadvantaged sector of the Australian population. This disadvantage is a legacy of often violent dispossession of land and changing state and federal Aboriginal policies that have included segregation and, more recently, assimilation (to the extent of removing Aboriginal children from their families and placing them in nonAboriginal *White families* as a means of cultural genocide). Dramatic evidence of persistent institutional racism was revealed by the Royal Commission Into Aboriginal Deaths in Custody (1991) and in the Inquiry into Racist Violence in Australia (Human Rights and Equal Opportunity Commission, 1991). Aboriginal infant mortality rates are worse than in most third world countries, and substance abuse is endemic in a number of Aboriginal communities. Educational outcomes for Aborigines reflect long periods of neglect before the 1980s.

In 1992, the Australian High Court "Mabo" decision overturned the doctrine of "terra nullius" and recognized, for the first time in more than 200 years of imposed Australian law, that Aboriginal people had previously owned the land. This decision, although not supported by a majority of the population, symbolized a changing community acceptance of Aboriginal culture and rights and represented the beginning of a more systematic undermining of the structural underpinnings of institutional racism in Australia (Sutherland, 1994).

Racism has had other significant impacts on Australia's ethnic composition. The first act passed in Australia's federal parliament in 1901 was the Immigration Restriction Act (historically referred to as the "White Australia Policy") modeled on U.S. legislation banning Asian immigration. Throughout the earlier part of the 20th century, Australia's immigration was overwhelmingly British, to the point that in 1945, 97% of Australia's 7 million inhabitants had ancestors from the British Isles (Allan & Hill 1995).

After World War II, Australia undertook an ambitious immigration program that radically changed the demographic pattern. Within a generation, Australia was one of the most ethnically diverse nations in the world, with a higher proportion of its population born overseas than any other country except Israel (Kalantzis, Cope, Noble, & Poynting, 1990). A proportion of these immigrants were refugees. Half a million refugees have settled in Australia since World War II, making it one of the leading resettlement countries in both absolute terms and in relation to population.

In 1972, after 23 years of conservative rule, the reformist Whitlam Labor government came to power partly as a result of its recognizing the need to tailor policies to the different concerns of a pluralist Australia. The Whitlam government replaced the White Australia policy with an immigration selection points system similar to that of Canada, which was racially non-discriminatory. Asians from a large variety of countries have availed themselves of this change of policy, but three particular groups can be identified: "boat people", refugees from the warfare in Indochina in the 1980s; wealthy residents of Hong Kong who took out Australian citizenship as "insurance" against the reversion of the colony to China in 1997; and since 1980, a steady stream of illegal economic migrants from southern China. By 1996, Asian Australians comprised 5% of the Australian population. Although not usually acknowledged, Asians have adapted quickly to the Australian lifestyle. Compared with immigrants from other countries, they have been quick to learn and use English, and there is some evidence of a high rate of intermarriage with Australians of different ethnic backgrounds (Price, 1994).

This dramatic change in the ethnic composition of Australia has been remarkably harmonious. However, instances of racist abuses (Human Rights and Equal Opportunity Commission, 1991) are not denied, nor the existence on the political fringe of an anti-immigration party and attendant right-wing racist organizations. Government immigration policies have frequently preceded public opinion, although there has been bipartisan political support and retrospective endorsement by the public. There are signs that the election of a conservative government in 1996 has the potential to threaten this consensus by challenging the political correctness of previous government immigration and Aboriginal policies. Notwithstanding this recent development, Australian postwar ethnic relationships have been marked by a high degree of harmony. Many of the postwar refugees have been successful in business, academe, and politics, and their contribution has been highly valued.

In education, the election of the Whitlam Labor government in 1972 ushered in an era of great expectation for change. This accelerated the trend to greater federal involvement in ethnic affairs and also resulted in a spectacular increase in resources for education. Most importantly, it signaled a rejection of the old paradigm of assimilation that focused on "migrant education" and its replacement by the celebration of Australia's ethnic diversity. Grassby (1979), the former minister for immigration, summed up the new ethos: "We are not talking about 'migrant' children. We are talking about Australian children of many different backgrounds. Certainly it is irrelevant to talk about migrant education. What we are really talking about is education of all children to fit them for a life in a multicultural and polyethnic society" (p. 281).

The change was not instant and was often honored by rhetoric rather than reality. By the early 1980s, however, all Australian states had adopted

multicultural education policies, typified by that of the numerically largest
state, New South Wales (NSW), which enunciated its objectives in 1978
by adopting this philosophic position: "In a multicultural society each
person has a right to cultural integrity, to a positive self-image, and to an
understanding and respect for differences. Not only should each person
be exposed to positive feelings about his or her own heritage, but must
experience like feelings about the heritage of others" (NSW Department
of Education, 1978, p. 3). A ministerial policy statement was released the
following year, which formed the basis for the 1983 Multicultural Education Policy Statement and Support Documents:

> The aims of multicultural education encompass the provision of educational
> experiences which will develop in all children (a) an understanding and appre-
> ciation that Australia has been multicultural in nature throughout its history
> both before and after European colonisation; (b) an awareness of the contribu-
> tion which people of many different cultural backgrounds have made and are
> making to Australia; (c) intercultural understanding through the consideration
> of attitudes, beliefs, and values related to multiculturalism; (d) behaviour that
> fosters interethnic harmony; and, (e) an enhanced sense of personal worth
> through an acceptance and appreciation not only of their Australian national
> identity but also of their specific Australian ethnic identity in the context of a
> multicultural society. (NSW Department of Education, 1983, p. 4).

Support documents were produced in the specific areas of English as a
second language (ESL), education, community languages education, ethnic studies, intercultural education, and multicultural perspectives to the
curriculum. The last two were to be mandatory components for all
schools.

This conceptualization of multiculturalism as a component of every
child's education had radical curriculum implications. A wealth of teaching resources dealing with the lifestyles and cultures of Australian ethnic
groups were produced (National Advisory and Co-ordinating Committee
on Multicultural Education [NACCME], 1987). A plethora of literature
has also evolved demonstrating the potential for incorporating a multicultural perspective in a variety of subject areas including English, religion,
social studies, and history.

It would seem that few schools in Australia have been untouched by
multicultural perspectives. The production of classroom resources reflected education department policies. The NACCME (1987) produced a
directory of multicultural classroom resources that listed some 300 materials in English and 200 written in community languages. Cope (1987)
analyzed 650 history and social studies textbooks published since 1945
and discovered a fundamental paradigm shift from a homogeneous Australian identity oriented toward Britain to an identity celebrating ethnic

diversity. He described a trend from textbooks in 1945 that provide a narrative of progress and development in which cultural differences are described in terms of superiority and inferiority, dominance and suppression, to a new pattern in the late 1980s that depict cultures as relative, celebrate cultural difference, and challenge senses of superiority as ignorant and insensitive. Cope warned of a risk that the materials, in their patronizing niceness, may exaggerate and construct stereotypes of cultural differences, thereby providing grist for the racist mill and ignoring the potential for cultural change and convergence.

Three major criticisms have been raised concerning the emphasis on culture during this multicultural phase. Although state policies exhorted teachers to incorporate multicultural perspectives, implementation, particularly in those schools with few migrant students, was commonly tokenistic. Typical activities such as "national" days stressed the externalities of traditional culture such as food, dress, music, and dance. Bullivant (1981) argued that to equate culture with heritage was a dangerous oversimplification that ignored the adaptive and evolutionary nature of a group's culture and the extent to which cultural convergence had taken place.

Furthermore, curriculum implementation across the country was uncoordinated and unsystematic. This problem resulted in the establishment of the National Advisory and Co-Ordinating Committee on Multicultural Education in 1984 in an attempt to counter the duplication of resource development in different states and the adhoc distribution of teaching materials (Foster, 1988). The production values of many resources produced with government funding lacked professionalism, and rarely did resource development budgets provide funds for training teachers to use the resources (Cahill, 1984).

Finally, there was a developing criticism that the emphasis on culture had ignored the structural underpinnings of racism in Australian society. A growing body of critics called for a greater emphasis on affirmative action and a curriculum for working-class immigrant children aimed at achieving equal outcomes and empowering them for participation in the workforce rather than singing in their community language while they danced in the dole queue (Kalantzis, 1987).

The educational response to the changing ethnic composition in Australian schools was affected by the variety of immigrant sources and their geographic dispersal. Notwithstanding some attempts to recommend rural destinations to immigrants, and the existence of a few geographic concentrations like those of Italians in Griffith, New South Wales and Tully, Queensland (Huber 1977) and Germans in Barossa Valley, South Australia, immigrants in the 1980s and 1990s have typically settled in cities. Immigrants had a tendency to choose suburbs close to migrant reception centers or near ethnic commercial, community, or religious centers. In the main, however, the concentration of specific ethnic groups is not high, and this has implications for schools. For instance, although many state governments have a policy of promoting the teaching of community languages, few schools serve communities in which a single language other than English is spoken. The more typical pattern is for schools to service children from a wide variety of language backgrounds. One result of this is that most states have established schools of community languages operating outside school hours that enable children to study their native language. The federal government also has provided financial assistance to language schools established by ethnic organizations. By 1991, the government was funding 196,000 enrollments in programs outside school hours run by more than 500 ethnic organizations at a cost of $A6.9 million (DEET, 1991).

This diversity makes it difficult for teachers to develop a detailed knowledge of the home culture of all the children in their classes. Cahill (1984) showed that Australian teachers' knowledge about its ethnic groups was seriously deficient. Moreover, the Australian teaching corps fails to mirror Australian ethnic diversity. In Watson, Hatton, Squires, and Soliman's study (1989) of teachers entering the teaching service in NSW in 1986, only 18% of secondary and 12% (female) and 7% (male) primary beginning teachers identified themselves as other than Anglo Australian. Approximately 50,000 teachers migrated to Australia in the postwar period, but the qualifications of many from non–English-speaking backgrounds (NESBS) and third world countries were not recognized (Inglis & Philips, 1995).

The teaching profession in Australia is not unique. In 1991, Perry claimed that 640,000 immigrants who held overseas qualifications were not working in jobs that used those qualifications. For industrial reasons, teachers trained overseas found it easier to get jobs in private rather than state schools. Bridging programs enabling teachers trained overseas to gain locally recognized qualifications have been slow to materialize. Not only were there relatively few overseas-born teachers working in schools, but little research has been done to determine whether their intercultural experience has had an impact on their teaching. Most of the research (Inglis & Philips, 1995) on overseas-born teachers is carried out in a labor market rather than a curriculum paradigm.

Education for many immigrants is a means of upward social mobility, and there is evidence that greater numbers from a NESBs are represented in tertiary education than Australian-born students (Seitz, 1993). The media have given prominence to the exceptional performance in matriculation examinations of many Asian Australians (Diaz, 1992). The impressive mean performance of NESB children in the educational system, however, should not obscure the fact that there are dramatic differences within and between ethnic groups in educational outcomes. Turkish, Lebanese, and Vietnamese Australians achieve below national norms on most educational indicators. Immigrants arriving in their teens are less likely to matriculate than those who arrive at a younger age (Allan & Hill, 1995), nor do these figures acknowledge the additional obstacles that children of NESB backgrounds had to overcome to achieve these outcomes.

Aboriginal children have overwhelmingly faced an alien educational environment. NSW, Australia's most populous state, typifies the situation of Aboriginal children. Before the 1950s, Aboriginal children were variously excluded from formal schooling, required to attend segregated inferior schooling, or, in a minority of cases, permitted to attend integrated schools in which they were taught a curriculum designed to promote their assimilation and sense of cultural inferiority (Crawford et al., 1992). As late as 1972, principals in NSW schools had the power to remove Aboriginal children from their schools when any non-Aboriginal White parent objected to their presence. In 1982, responding to consistent pressure from the Aboriginal community, NSW launched its Aboriginal Education Policy, which, among other things, mandated programs to enhance the self-esteem and cultural identity of Aboriginal children and the education of all children in respect of contemporary and traditional Aboriginal society.

The incorporation of Aboriginal studies has been justified on a variety of grounds. In part, it was seen as a means of increasing intercultural understanding and sensitivity. Additionally, the recognition given to the important contribution of Aboriginal culture to Australian society was intended to reduce the alienation of Aboriginal children from their schools. It was anticipated that the new responsiveness of the curriculum would be reflected in improved educational outcomes for Aboriginal students. The extent to which these outcomes have been achieved is somewhat unclear. A review of the implementation of the NSW Aboriginal Education Policy in 1992 noted a widespread and often enthusiastic introduction of Aboriginal perspectives in a variety of subjects, especially in history and art classes of secondary schools, and in dance and social education classes of primary schools. While recognizing the pervasiveness of institutional racism in the communities served by the schools studied, the researchers noted among Aboriginal students, parents, and Aboriginal education workers a high degree of satisfaction with their schools. There was little evidence of direct racism reported by Aboriginal educators, students, or parents (Crawford et al., 1992). No attempt to explain this unexpected finding is attempted here. However, a similar finding of Aboriginal students and teachers expressing high levels of satisfaction with their schools was obtained in a national study by the Australian Bureau of Statistics (Madden, 1994). Whereas an overwhelming majority of Aboriginal parents felt welcome at their child's school, only a minority felt that they were involved in decision making there (Madden, 1994).

Nevertheless, the educational performances of Aboriginal students for a variety of reasons are substantially below state averages, and frequently below local community averages (Crawford et al., 1992). Nationally, there has been a dramatic increase in the number of Aboriginal students undertaking tertiary study, but in many cases these students have gained entry outside the normal matriculation process. Many are also undertaking "designer" courses specifically prepared for Aboriginal nonmatriculants (Madden, 1994).

OBSTACLES TO ADDRESSING INTERCULTURAL ISSUES IN AUSTRALIA

Structurally, there are few barriers to successful implementation of intercultural initiatives in Australian education. The areas of Aboriginal, Asian and ethnic studies are comparatively well resourced and complemented by significant curriculum developments. There is widespread, though by no means universal, community acceptance of multiculturalism.

In most states there are few syllabus obstacles to addressing intercultural issues. Aboriginal and ethnic studies form part of all state syllabuses and are reflected in national curriculum documents in the following areas: Studies of society and environment (Australian Education Council, 1994a, 1994b), English, and languages other than English (LOTE). Physical education, personal development, and Health also provide opportunity to study the Aboriginal and ethnic experience.

Throughout the 1990s the teaching of LOTE in primary and secondary schools has been enthusiastically promoted by both national and state governments. The federal financial promotion of LOTE continued with the change to a conservative coalition government in 1996. The motivation for this has been largely economic because the government is keen to develop skills that might increase commercial opportunities, particularly in Asia. There also have been a number of important schemes to increase teacher cultural awareness of some of Australia's regional neighbors. The Asia Education Foundation's "magnet schools" program and its Asian study tours for teachers have contributed to an increased understanding of Asian cultures among teachers and to a dynamic expansion of Asian studies, particularly in primary schools (Baumgart & Elliott, 1996). Widespread use of the Internet should support this expansion of intercultural communication in the near future.

Aboriginal studies teaching has also been extensively resourced. Aboriginal education workers have been employed in schools with a high proportion of Aboriginal students. Part of their responsibility involves assisting in teaching Aboriginal studies. Increasingly, teachers dealing with Aboriginal topics can avail themselves of assistance from professional bodies such as the Aboriginal Studies Association and research institutes such as the Institute of Aboriginal and Torres Strait Islander Studies. Many professional teacher organizations have become significantly involved in the discussion and dissemination of information relevant to intercultural education, particularly in areas of Aboriginal and Asian studies (Singh, 1991a; Williamson-Fien, 1994).

The emerging picture, then, shows curriculum niches for intercultural education, official recognition of intercultural education as a legitimate area for school study, and an increasingly adequate availability of resources and support from professional teaching organizations. Nevertheless, obstacles to promotion of intercultural education at the classroom level persist. Some of these obstacles are practical, others conceptual.

Many Australian teachers confront a crowded curriculum and increased pressure to respond to demands to meet community needs. They feel pressured to inform students about AIDS, help them develop vocationally relevant skills and attitudes, protect them from sexual abuse, and provide them with access to sophisticated technology. Although these demands are not always unreasonable or incompatible with intercultural education, some teachers feel overburdened by curriculum demands.

Another concern involves clarifying where intercultural education best fits into the curriculum. Given the crowded curriculum, teachers may abandon intercultural education to the teacher of some other subject. For example, social science teachers may feel that intercultural education is more properly contextualized in the study of LOTE. Language teachers may feel that teachers of personal development are more likely to be skilled in techniques for overcoming racism. Considerable debate occurs in professional teaching journals as to whether the learning of language is a key to intercultural understanding or whether learning a language is an inefficient use of time better spent in developing a broader cross-cultural understanding (Fitzgerald, 1994; Williamson-Fien, 1994).

Some confusion also exists as to the terminology used in relation to intercultural education. In some cases *intercultural education* is used synonymously with *multicultural education* to mean education about cultural diversity. A variation of this is its use, as in the NSW policy, as a subcategory of multicultural education concerned with understanding of different cultures and developing skills for interacting and communicating with them (NSW Department of Education, 1983, p. 4). It is in this sense that this chapter uses the term and illustrates its uses with specific examples of ethnic studies, Asian studies, and Aboriginal studies. Others would use the term to exclude studies of individual cultures and focus on what has been called *cross-cultural training* involving the development of generic skills for understanding and communicating across cultures (Cushner & Brislin, 1986; Millen, O'Grady, & Porter, 1992). *Intercultural Education* also overlaps with *antiracist education*, a term not commonly used in Australia, but one that implies a clear structural component privileging certain groups in cross-cultural communication and locates the communication in a context of global power hierarchies (Hollinsworth, 1992). Writers in this tradition reject the notion that changing racism is simply a matter of using psychologic techniques to reduce prejudice. Clearly, these terms overlap and, in practice, good classroom implementation of intercultural education will draw on common elements in the definition. Nevertheless, lack of conceptual clarity may represent a barrier to some teachers who might otherwise be motivated to implement intercultural education strategies. In part the role of university teacher education programs is providing some conceptual clarity in this area.

TEACHER EDUCATION INSTITUTIONS AND THEIR INTERCULTURAL EDUCATION ACTIVITIES

As long ago as 1980, the *Report of the National Inquiry into Teacher Education* had criticized teacher training institutions for their inability to prepare students adequately to understand and implement programs that catered to the diverse nature of Australian society (Auchmuty, 1980). Since then, student intakes in Australian universities are becoming even more culturally diverse. Three groups contribute to this diversity: Australian NESB students, Aboriginal students, and overseas (predominantly Asian) fee-paying students. As a consequence of immigration policies and the aspirations of many NESB parents, Australian NESB students are slightly overrepresented in universities, although the proportion varies in different universities and from faculty to faculty (Seitz, 1993).

There has been a dramatic increase in the number of Aboriginal students, although this has been disproportionately in courses at lower academic levels and in a narrow range of vocational areas (Madden, 1994). Assisted by federal scholarships and encouraged by special entry programs and tutorial support programs at most universities, most Aboriginal students initially were enrolled in teacher education courses. In 1994, 4,000 Aborigines were studying at universities, and 3,600 in technical and further education (Madden, 1994). The National Aboriginal Education Council set a target of training 10,000 Aboriginal teachers by 1990. Recruitment strategies, preferential employment programs, and provision of bridging courses all contributed to a dramatic increase in the number of Aboriginal teachers. One reason why the target was not achieved and why Aboriginal teachers are not represented in schools in proportion to their representation in the wider population was the tendency for Aboriginal teachers to be "poached" for employment outside the classroom.

Most Australian universities have federally funded Aboriginal centers aimed at assisting Aboriginal university students through counseling and tutoring as well as providing cultural awareness programs for non-Aboriginal staff and students of the university. Despite this, many Aboriginal students find universities culturally alienating, and attrition rates are high. Staff at the centers frequently find the conflicting expectations of their role as cultural intermediaries challenging (Hatton, 1996; Hill, 1987).

Finally, Australian universities were attended by some 40,000 fee-paying international students mainly from Southeast Asia, which attracted approximately $1.4 billion per year into the Australian economy (Alexander & Rizvi, 1993; Roy MorganResearch Center Pty, 1992).

How has this change in ethnic composition been reflected in teacher education programs? In terms of the formal teacher education programs, the inclusion of intercultural education is patchy. Hickling-Hudson and McMenamim (1993) reported on a national survey of teacher education institutions. The details of their findings should be accepted with caution. Comparison of courses is difficult; titles can be misleading; and program documentation gives few clues as to quality or teaching approach. However, their findings are likely to be accurate. They concluded that specialized multicultural courses were more likely to be offered as electives, whereas in compulsory courses, only "passing reference to cultural and linguistic diversity" (pp. 245–246) was likely to be made. Some programs did not even make passing reference to educating for cultural diversity. The authors identified a number of exemplary courses, but in general felt that multicultural references could be characterized as "tokenistic."

Aboriginal studies in teacher education programs go back some time. For example, Tatz and Chambers (1975) reported on a pioneering Aboriginal studies course at the former Armidale Teachers' College. In 1971 and 1972 they evaluated the effects of exposing all final-year students to articulate Aboriginal speakers. They found dramatic positive changes in attitudes toward Aborigines, particularly when the speakers were younger, more aggressive, and militant activists.

Two examples of more recent teacher education initiatives in the area of intercultural education come from rural universities. Singh (1991b) described Issues in Cross-Cultural Education, a course established at James Cook University (Townsville, Queensland) in the late 1980s, which included a strong focus on social justice and strategies designed to counter racism in schools. At Charles Sturt University Mitchell campus, a compulsory course, Aboriginal and Multicultural Australia, has been taught since 1981. Although the course has been modified throughout that time, the emphasis on exploring issues of social justice and sensitizing students to the experiences of minorities has been consistent.

A review of Aboriginal studies taught in preservice teacher education courses conducted in 1992 found that "very few specify Aboriginal studies as a core component of the program" (Bourke, Dow, & Lucas, 1993). One federally funded Aboriginal education package designed for teacher education preservice programs has been trial tested in more than five universities (Craven 1996). The recent national trend to extend the length of preservice primary (elementary) teacher education programs from 3 to 4 years should provide more opportunity to include greater Aboriginal studies content, but federal cuts to universities threaten opportunities to develop and evaluate such programs.

Increasingly, these sorts of courses are supported by staff at university Aboriginal education centers, which serve as a resource for Aboriginal studies initiatives throughout the universities and attempt to make the culture of the institution more inclusive (Bourke, Dow, & Lucas, 1993). For many non-Aboriginal students, the university is the first place they meet Aboriginal students on equal status terms working for common goals. Although this informal, interpersonal contact is likely to have considerable influence on intercultural understanding, no evidence exists in the literature to support this claim.

Informal contact with other students from different cultural backgrounds may also play a valuable role in intercultural sensitization (Smolicz, 1995). However, the research evidence suggests that this potential is rarely achieved, particularly in teacher education. First, few overseas fee-paying students elect to undertake teacher education, reflecting the high extrinsic value placed on university education by fee-paying students (Alexander 1994). Second, although ethnic relations in Australian universities tend to be friendly, there is often very little social interaction between Australian and Asian students (Nesdale & Todd, 1993). Where universities have introduced initiatives specifically to encourage interaction between overseas and local students, the goals have tended to be related to ensuring the successful adaptation of overseas students rather than increasing the cultural awareness of Australian students (Quintrell & Westwood, 1994). Overseas students are an underutilized resource in the intercultural education of Australian teacher education students, and programs like those introduced at the University of Kentucky to structure learning encounters between Australian and overseas students would be of great value (Hill, Thomas, & Cote, 1996; Wilson, 1993).

Despite this lack of interaction between Australian teacher education students and Asian fee-paying students, an increasingly common strategy for promoting intercultural awareness has been the development of overseas teaching practicums. In 1994, for example, 15 Australian universities offered 31 overseas group practicums. The most popular destinations were in Southeast Asia, particularly Indonesia and Thailand. Many other universities facilitated individual students, who organized their own overseas practicums and a number of overseas educational and cultural study tours. Hill, Thomas, and Cote (1995), in a follow-up study of students from two Australian universities who had undertaken overseas teaching practicums, found that the experience had exerted a very positive influence on their personal and professional growth.

The former practicum participants considered that the experience had made them more reflective and culturally sensitive; had contributed to increased confidence, tolerance, and cooperation; and had reduced their ethnocentrism. They were more interested, as a result, in Asian food, language, religion, and, to a lesser extent, Asian politics and theater. In the years between completing the practicum and participating in the survey, almost 25% of the students had revisited Asia, and 40% still communicated with people they met during the practicum. The following are typical of what respondents felt were outcomes of the practicums:

Appreciation of a different culture. Understanding that spiritual and emotional satisfaction far outweigh materialistic satisfaction that Western civilizations place so much importance on.

I am a lot more patient and try a lot harder to communicate with those struggling with English as I can only too well remember the anguish over not understanding what was going on due to the language barrier.

A very deep understanding and love of Indonesian and Asian culture. A keen awareness of the development of students understanding of Asia.

THE REFUGEE IN AUSTRALIA

Since World War II, Australia has been host to more than 500,000 refugees, and although there has not been universal acceptance for the program, generally community support has been impressive. Of 98,000 immigrants to Australia in 1995–1996, 15,000 came via the humanitarian program. From 1990 to 1995, numbers in the humanitarian program have never fallen below 11,800 in any year. In 1995–1996, the two priority groups considered were people displaced by war in the former Yugoslavia and the Gulf area of the Middle East.

Travel costs of the refugees are paid by the Australian government. Their rents on arrival are subsidized either directly by the government or indirectly by government-supported volunteer community groups under the Community Refugee Settlement Scheme. On arrival, refugees are entitled to normal social security benefits including health coverage and assistance from the Commonwealth Employment Service in locating work. In addition, refugees are offered free language tuition, translation of essential documents, use of the telephone interpreter service, and special counseling services for minors. They also have access to migrant resource centers, which provide a variety of specialist multilingual services.

The situation of illegal immigrants who claim to be refugees is more complex and controversial. These individuals are initially held in detention with minimal food and medical service. They can attend English and some vocational classes and are provided with translation and assistance in making their claim for refugee status. Successful applicants who meet the United Nations refugee criteria are offered permanent residence in Australia. Unsuccessful applicants may appeal to the Refugee Review Tribunal. Of the 2,478 "boat people" since 1989, 521 have been approved to remain in Australia. The others either are still awaiting refugee application decisions or deportation or have either returned home or traveled to third countries (Department of Immigration and Multicultural Affairs, 1996). (Readers may access the most up-to-date statistics by contacting the web site at http://16497.143.2/facts/index.htm.)

Historically, Australian schools have successfully operated as intermediaries in resettlement. The children of about half a million refugees have contributed to making Australian schools more culturally sensitive. Schools are expected to respond to an influx of refugees with the following initiatives: the introduction of the refugees' language in the school curriculum, the employment of ethnic aides from the country of origin, additional classes in English as a Second Language, the modification of social education and other curriculum areas, bilingual signs placed around the school, translation of school notices, introduction of culturally appropriate food in the school canteen, and staff development programs for teachers.

Whereas these responses would facilitate the integration of refugee children into the school, it would also be crucial to allay any concerns of "host" parents that the mainstream culture is being devalued or that academic standards are under threat. It is important that state educational bureaucracy support the schools with additional staffing and capital expenditure so the burden of fund raising by the local community is alleviated.

Cultural mediators will play a crucial role in this process. These people, based at the schools, are the lynchpin of community liaison efforts. They would participate in school planning, advise the refugee community about school expectations, communicate community concerns to the school, mediate in cultural conflicts affecting the school and community, and liaise with opinion leaders from key community organizations. Given Australia's ethnic diversity, there would be a pool of Australians who share the ethnic background of most refugee groups and who could contribute as cultural mediators.

CONCLUSION

At a national level, we have argued, somewhat complacently, that by the 1990s Australia had shaken off much of its past racist legacy and had policies in place that facilitated the access of refugees to the Australian community. We also have argued that school curricula now provide scope for intercultural education and that at least in the areas of Asian studies, Aboriginal studies, and ethnic studies, there have been substantial innovations in resource development and teaching support. A number of university teacher education programs have developed impressive programs incorporating intercultural education.

Events in 1996, however, indicated the fragility of the postwar tolerance. A newly elected independent federal member of Parliament, the populist "battler," Pauline Hanson, in her maiden speech launched a blitzkrieg against political correctness and the political bipartisan consensus on Aboriginal affairs and multiculturalism (Hanson, 1996). Her speech was followed by saturation media coverage as well as strong support on talkback radio and in letters to the editor in the press. She served as a lightning rod for those groups most disaffected by the dramatic social and economic changes that had accompanied globalization and economic rationalism. As levels of unemployment stayed close to double figures, Aborigines and Asian immigrants served as useful scapegoats.

The government's response was ambiguous. Unwilling to alienate Hanson's political constituency, the Prime Minister talked of her right to freedom of speech while the Minister of Immigration announced reductions in immigration levels. The implications of her action soon became clear as reports of anti-Asian and anti-Aboriginal violence increased. The government's business supporters became increasingly uneasy as expressions of concern by Asian trading partners to the Prime Minister's seeming vacillation became more numerous. Universities feared the repercussions in reduced numbers of Asian fee-paying students. By the time the federal Parliament passed a virtually unanimous condemnation of racism, it seemed too late to slow the momentum of the debate (Lesser, 1996).

For economic rationalists, it was becoming clear that intercultural education was not a middle-class luxury, but a contributor to a favorable trading climate. At the same time, there was a growing awareness that tolerance is easier to sustain in societies where that seemingly permit all to share equally in the benefits of economic transformation.

Schools, and in turn teacher education institutions, increasingly will be called to react rapidly to arrest the popular racism. It is unfortunate that this demand will come at a time when the newly elected federal conservative coalition government has announced severe cuts in tertiary funding causing the closure of the Faculty of Education, which had developed the national Indigenous Australian studies program for primary preservice teacher education (Craven, 1996). Nor does it seem desirable for intercultural education to be seen as something promoted when racism is on the boil and abandoned when relationships seem harmonious.

TO CONSIDER

Australia is becoming an increasingly multicultural society, and educators are beginning to recognize and respond to this diversity. Schools seem to have become quite active in preparing their young people for their place in a society that is pluralistic and culturally diverse.

1. Review current newspapers from Australia, such as The Age, which, if not available in your library, are available on the World Wide Web at www.vol.it/UK/EN/EDICOLA/quot_str.htm#menu. Search for news items that present issues related to Aboriginal land rights, the international community, interethnic conflict, and educational responses to diversity. How do current issues related to diversity relate to what you have just read? What is the current state of affairs regarding such people as Pauline Hanson and her supporters? What struggles continue around indigenous issues?

2. What can your nation and schools learn from the experiences of Australia?

3. How can young people in Australia be most effectively prepared to interact with others on a global scale? What resources seem to be available in Australia to assist young people in developing a global or intercultural perspective?

4. Australia frequently receives immigrants and refugees from many nations of Southeast Asia. Given what you have just read, how would you respond to the scenario presented in chapter 1. What steps should schools take in responding to the needs of newly arrived immigrant groups?

REFERENCES

Alexander, D. (1994, April). Culturally constructed educational marketing. *The Social Educator, 12*(1), 34–42.

Alexander, D., & Rizvi, F. (1993). Education, markets, and the contradictions of Asia– Australian relations, *The Australian Universities' Review, 36*(2), 16–20.

Allan, R., & Hill, B. (1995). Multicultural education in Australia: Historical development and current status. In J. A. Banks & C. M. Banks (Eds.), *Handbook of Research On Multicultural Education*. New York: Macmillan.

Auchmuty, J. J.(1980). *Report of the national inquiry into teacher education*. Canberra: Australian Government Publishing Service.

Australian Education Council. (1994a). *Studies of society and environment: A curriculum profile for Australian schools*. Melbourne: Curriculum Corporation.

Australian Education Council. (1994b). *A statement on studies of society and environment for Australian schools*. Melbourne: Curriculum Corporation.

Baumgart, N., & Elliott, A. (1996). *Promoting the study of Asia across the curriculum: An evaluation of the first three years of the Asia Education Foundation*. Faculty of Education, University of Western Sydney, Nepean, New South Wales.

Bourke, E., Dow, R., & Lucas, B. (1993). *Teacher education preservice: Preparing teachers to work with Aboriginal and Torres Strait Islander students*. Adelaide: Aboriginal Research Institute, University of South Australia.

Bullivant, B. M. (1981). *Race, ethnicity and curriculum*. South Melbourne: Macmillan.

Burrow, S. (1996, Spring). To all Australian educators. *Australian Educator*, 11.

Cahill, D. B. (1984). *Review of the commonwealth multicultural education program*. Melbourne: Commonwealth Schools Commission, Phillip Institute of Technology.

Cope, B. (1987). *Racism, popular culture and Australian identity in transition: A case study of change in school textbooks since 1945*. (Occasional paper No 14.) Wollongong: University of Wollongong. Centre of Multicultural Studies.

Council for Aboriginal Reconciliation. (1993). *Addressing the key issues for reconciliation*. Canberra: Australian Government Publishing Service.

Craven, R. (1996). *Teaching the teachers: Indigenous Australian studies for primary preservice teacher education*. New South Wales: School of Teacher Education, University of New South Wales, Sydney.

Crawford, L., Crawford, L., Hill, B., Bates, T., Meyenn, B., Paskes, J., McKennen, D., & Edwards, M. (1992). *The first of its kind*. New South Wales: NSW Aboriginal Education Policy Implementation Evaluation. NSW Department of School Education and Charles Sturt University.

Cushner, K., & Brislin, R. (1986, November–December). Bridging gaps: Cross-cultural training in teacher education. *Journal of Teacher Education*, 51–54.

Department of Employment, Education and Training. (1991), *Australia's language: The Australian language and literacy policy*. Canberra: Australian Government Publishing Service.

Department of Immigration and Multicultural Affairs. (21 June, 1996). Fact Sheets (online) Retrieved via Netscape http://16497.143.2/facts/index.htm.

Diaz, T. (1992, January 14). Coincidentally, they are also clever. *Sydney Morning Herald*, p. 3.

Fitzgerald, S. (1994, April). The study of Asian societies in schools. *The Social Educator, 12*(1), 55–61.

Foster, L. E. (1988). *Diversity and multicultural education: A sociological perspective*. North Sydney: Allen & Unwin.

Grassby , A. J. (1979). It's time for migrant education to go. In P. R. de Lacey & M. E. Poole (Eds.), *Mosaic or Melting Pot?: Cultural Evolution in Australia* (pp. 278–282). Sydney: Harcourt Brace Jovanovich.

Hanson, E. (1996). *Maiden speech*. Retrieved via Netscape http://demos.anu.edu.au:7007/cgi-bin/pastimepub/article.pl?dir=years/1996/sep/10/hansard/reps&art=39.

Hatton, E. (1996, April). Dealing with diversity: The failure of teacher education. *Discourse, 17*(1), 25–42.

Hickling-Hudson, A., & McMeniman, M. (1993). Curricular responses to multiculturalism: An overview of teacher education courses in Australia. *Teacher and Teacher Education, 9*(3), 243–252.

Hill, B., Thomas, N., & Cote, J. (1995, November). *A preliminary report on the audit of overseas practicums.* Paper presented to the Australian Association for Research in Education, annual conference, Newcastle.

Hill, B., Thomas, N., & Cote, J. (1996). *Into Asia: Australian teaching practicums in Asia.* Melbourne: Asia Education Foundation.

Hill, R. J. (1987). *A case study of the Mitchell CAE enclave program for Aboriginal students.* Unpublished MED (Honors) thesis, University of New England, Armidale.

Hollinsworth, D. (1992). Cultural awareness training, racism awareness training, or anti racism?: Strategies for combatting institutional racism. *Journal of Intercultural Studies, 13*(2), 37–50.

Huber, R. (1977). *From pasta to pavlova.* Brisbane: Queensland University Press.

Hughes, P., & Willmot, E. (1982). A thousand Aboriginal teachers by 1990. In J. Sherwood (Ed.), *Aboriginal education: Issues and innovations.* Perth: Creative Research.

Human Rights and Equal Opportunity Commission. (1991). *Report of the national inquiry into racist violence in Australia.* Canberra: AGPS.

Inglis, C., & Philps, R. (1995). *Teachers in the sun: The impact of immigrant teachers on the labour force.* Canberra: Bureau of Immigration Multicultural and Population Research, AGPS.

Judge, H. (1991). Schools of education and teacher education. *Oxford Studies in Comparative Education, 1*(1), 37–55.

Kalantzis, M. (1987). Racism and pedagogy. *Teaching History, 20*(4), 45–48.

Kalantzis, M., Cope, B., Noble, G., & Poynting, S. (1990). *Cultures of schooling: Pedagogies for cultural difference and social access.* Basingstoke: Falmer Press.

Lesser, D. (1996, November 30). Pauline Hanson's bitter harvest. *Good Weekend,* pp. 18–28.

Madden, R. (1994). *National Aboriginal and Torres Strait Islander survey: Detailed Findings* (Catalogue No. 4190.0). Canberra: Australian Bureau of Statistics.

Millen, M., O'Grady, A., & Porter, J. (1992). Communicating in a multicultural workforce: Pragmatics and a problem-centred approach to cross-cultural training. *Prospect, 7*(2), 46–56

National Advisory and Co-ordinating Committee on Multicultural Education. (1987). *Resources materials directory.* Canberra: AGPS.

Nesdale, D., & Todd, P. (1993). Internationalising Australian universities: The intercultural contact issue. *Journal of Tertiary Education Administration, 15*(2), 189–202.

New South Wales Department of Education. (1978). *Multicultural education: A consultitative document.* Sydney: Government Printer.

New South Wales Department of Education. (1983). *Intercultural education. A support document to the Multicultural Education Policy 1983.* Sydney: Multicultural Education Centre.

New South Wales Department of School Education. (1992). *Multicultural education plan, 1993–1997.* Sydney: Government Printer.

Price, C. (1994). Ethnic intermixture in Australia. *People and Place, 2*(4), 8–11.

Quintrell, N., & Westwood, M. (1994). The influence of a peer-pairing program on international students' first year experience and use of students services. *Higher Education Research and Development, 13*(1), 49–57.

Royal Commission into Aboriginal Deaths in Custody. (1991). *National Report,* Vol. 1. Canberra: AGPS.

Roy Morgan Research Centre Pty. (1992) *Survey of international students studying in Australia.* Canberra: DEETYA.

Seitz, D. (1993). The political dimension of intercultural research: The Australian experience. *Quality and Quantity, 27,* 411–420.

Singh, M. (1991a). Geography's contribution to multicultural education. *Geographical Education, 6*(3), 9–14.

Singh, M. G. (1991b). Issues in cross-cultural education: Inverting the education studies. *Curriculum in Teaching Education, 4*(1), 161–167.

Smolicz, J. J. (1995). The emergence of Australia as a multicultural nation: An international perspective. *Journal of Intercultural Studies, 16*(1&2), 3–24.

Sutherland, J. (Ed.). *Improving relationships,* (Key Issue paper No.2). Canberra: Council for Aboriginal Reconciliation, Canberra: Australian Government Publishing Service.

Tatz, C., & Chambers, B. (1975). Cultural accommodation: The Armidale experiment. In D. Edgar (Ed.), *Sociology of Australian education*. Sydney: McGraw-Hill.

Watson, A., Hatton, N., Squires, D., & Soliman, I. (1989). *The staffing of schools and the quality of education* (unpublished report). New South Wales: University of New South Wales. Sydney.

Williamson-Fien, J. (1994, April). The study of Asian societies in schools: Questioning the assumptions. *The Social Educator, 12*(1), 62–69.

Wilson, A. (1993, Winter). Conversation partners: Helping students gain a global perspective through cross-cultural experiences. *Theory Into Practice, 32*(1), 21–26.

Editor's Remarks

Aotearoa/New Zealand, first settled by Polynesians around 800 AD, is a nation today comprised of slightly more than 4 million people. Although first European contact occurred in 1642, the first real significant influx of Europeans took place in 1769 when Captain James Cook reached the land. From 1769 until 1840, when Europeanization was occurring, the culture and civilization was more Maori than it was British. The Treaty of Waitangi, signed between the European settlers and the Maori in 1840, set the stage for the sharing of power and decision making throughout the country. More than most countries in the world where Europeans came into extended contact with indigenous people, the Europeans and Maori in New Zealand have strived to maintain a pluralistic society. The Maori have maintained their own identity far better than most indigenous groups in other parts of the world although it is by no means perfect. As this chapter shows, although a sense of collaboration exists in New Zealand as nowhere else on the planet, the potential desired through the Treaty of Waitangi has yet to be realized. In addition to issues surrounding indigenous rights and education, New Zealand, particularly North Island, has experienced an influx of immigrants and refugees from throughout the Asian and Pacific region, which acts to further strain an educational system that struggles with understanding the role and responsibility of educating children from outside the mainstream.

How should a nation which, more than many in the world has at its roots a treaty directing equity in all that society has to offer, direct its educational system more adequately to address the needs of its immigrant, refugee, and indigenous populations while preparing all for an interdependent, global society? How can a teaching force from a predominantly homogeneous background and experience become more culturally connected in New Zealand?

Chapter 3

Achieving Cultural Integrity in Education in Aotearoa/New Zealand

଼ଠ ♦ ଓଷ

Russell Bishop
Ted Glynn
University of Otago

THE CONTEXT OF NEW ZEALAND

The historical pattern of cultural superiority and subordination established between the European migrants and the indigenous peoples of New Zealand has set the pattern for subsequent relationships with new migrants. Some attempts have been made to rectify this pattern by introducing the philosophies and practices of multiculturalism and biculturalism. However, such policies largely have not been successful. These policies have ignored the importance of the need to address the relationship between the dominant Pakeha (people of European origin) and the indigenous population because the aspirations of the indigenous people are subsumed within the majority culture's designs for the future of New Zealand. Unless this relationship can be changed, the dominant–subordinate pattern of intercultural relationships will remain.

Development of the Pattern
of Intercultural Relationships

Two peoples created the nation of New Zealand when, in 1840, lieutenant-Governor Hobson and the chiefs of New Zealand signed the Treaty of Waitangi on behalf of the British Crown, the Maori people, and their descendants. Maori people have long seen the Treaty as a charter for power sharing in the decision making processes of this country, for Maori determination of their own destiny as the indigenous people of New Zealand, and as the guide to future development of New Zealand. Posttreaty government policy in New Zealand has moved from one at first opposed totally to these aspirations to one only recently attempting to come to terms with Maori and non-Maori aspirations for equity and social justice through self-determination.

Despite the promises of the Treaty of Waitangi, the history of Maori and Pakeha relationships in New Zealand since the signing of the Treaty has not been one of partnership, of two peoples developing a nation, but one of political, social, and economic domination by the Pakeha majority, and marginalization of the Maori people through armed struggle, biased legislation, and educational initiatives and policies that promoted Pakeha knowledge codes at the expense of the Maori (Bishop, 1991; Simon, 1990; Walker, 1990; Ward, 1974). Despite the created myth that the New Zealanders are "one people" with equal opportunities (Hohepa, 1975; Simon, 1990; Walker, 1990), results of Pakeha domination are evident today in the lack of equitable participation by Maori people in all positive and beneficial aspects of life in New Zealand, and by their overrepresentation in the negative aspects (Pomare, 1987; Simon, 1990).

In education, for example, the central government's sequential policies of assimilation, integration, multiculturalism, and biculturalism (Irwin, 1989; Jones, McCulloch, Marshall, Smith, & Tuhiwai-Smith, 1990) along with programs such as Taha Maori (Holmes, Bishop, & Glynn, 1992; Smith, 1990), while ostensibly showing concern for the welfare of the Maori people, effectively maintains pressure on Maori people to subjugate their destiny to the needs of the nation state, the goals of which remain largely determined by the Pakeha majority.

In short, the development of New Zealand since the signing of the Treaty of Waitangi in 1840, despite continual armed and passive resistance by the Maori people, has been one in which the Pakeha majority has benefited enormously and in which the Maori have been politically marginalized, culturally and racially attacked, and economically impoverished within their own country.[1] These claims hold as true for education as for all areas of economic and social policy.

The implications of this historical pattern for peoples of other cultures who migrate to New Zealand is profound. The dominance of monoculturalism and monolingualism is so pervasive in New Zealand that the majority culture appears to be unable to accept cultural diversity as a positive feature that new immigrants bring to the nation state. As a result, new migrants (as opposed to those who arrived here in the 19th century) are seen by the majority Pakeha culture as having deficiencies that need remedial action. Furthermore, since the reforms promoted by the Education Act of 1989, the new market-driven approach to education means that Asian students for example are being seen as economic commodities who bring money to educational institutions. Little is heard of pedagogic assets and opportunities for cultural diversity in the classroom.

Dominant–subordinate intercultural relationships have a profound effect on language maintenance with consequent impact on cultural retention and identity. A 1995 study by the Maori Language Commission on the current use of Maori language by Maori 16 years of age and older showed the effects of the dominant–subordinate relationship pattern on language retention and maintenance. The study showed that the majority (60%) of the adult Maori population speak some Maori, although the range of language ability varies considerably. Of those who speak some Maori, only 6% were in the high/very-high fluency category, with a further 8% identified at the medium-high level. This indicates a drop in the number of fluent adult Maori speakers since the last Maori language survey in the mid-1970s. At that time, 18% of the total Maori population were estimated to be fluent speakers of Maori.

Furthermore, the survey results suggest that fluency among adult speakers of Maori remains greatest in the older age groups with consequent implications as aging proceeds. It is estimated that 44% of speakers

---

[1]Research has contributed to and continues to contribute to the persistent attacks on Maori cultural integrity, and as a result has promoted Maori political and economic marginalization and the subsequent impoverishment of Maori people in Aotearoa/New Zealand today. Despite Maori people being one of the most researched people in the world, in the domain of knowledge definition there is a great deal of evidence that much research into Maori people's lives and experiences, conducted by educational and other researchers, has been parasitic, that is of benefit to the researchers more than to those who have been the objects of study. It has been the researchers, rather than the people being researched, who have determined the research agendas, controlled the research processes, and reported the research outcomes in terms defined to suit their worldviews. Consequently this has contributed to the marginalization and impoverishment of the Maori people. In short, this process of research has maintained the power to define what constitutes research and the criteria for evaluation and presentation of research finding in the hands of those people doing the observing, gathering, and processing of data as well as the construction of meaning from/about the research experiences.

in the high/very high fluency category are age 60 years and older, whereas a mere 3% are between 16 and 24 years of age. In addition, levels of fluency are higher in rural areas than in urban areas. Regional differences also exist. A higher proportion of the total number of adult Maori speakers in Waikato/Bay of Plenty/Gisborne (8%) are of high/very-high fluency. This is the region served by the university with the greatest focus on delivering tertiary education through the medium of the Maori language. In Northland/Auckland the equivalent proportion is 5%, and in the remainder of New Zealand it is 6%. The situations in which Maori is most used are the marae (meeting place; 37%), school (34%), and church (27%) (Education Gazette, Feb, 1996).

These statistics clearly demonstrate how the majority culture has treated the indigenous population in New Zealand. Because the pattern of dominant–subordinate relationships is pervasive, it is suggested that this is the likely model for relationships with new immigrants that may produce similar outcomes.

ASSIMILATION AS POLICY

Article two of the Treaty of Waitangi guaranteed the Maori people chieftainly control (tino Rangatiratanga, that is, self-determination) over all that they treasured (taonga katoa), particularly the power to define what constitutes a treasure and the power to protect, promote, prefer, and proscribe treasures (Jackson, 1993). Despite this guarantee, Pakeha political control over decision-making processes in education within the context of an assimilationist agenda has marginalized the Maori language, cultural aspirations, and Maori-preferred knowledge-gathering and information-processing methods and contexts. These things are all treasures (taonga) as defined by the Maori themselves.

The education system developed in New Zealand after colonization attempted to replace a preexisting and complex system,[2] and subsequently attempted to deny or belittle its existence. Furthermore, the introduced

---

[2]As King (1978), Metge (1983), and Salmond (1975) reported, these learning processes continue today in the Maori world, exemplified in the oral art forms of whaikorero (oratory), karanga (ceremonial call) and pakiwaitara (storytelling). The records of the hearings of the current Waitangi Tribunal are today an accessible Maori. Learning processes emphasize the importance of many Maori concepts and their contextual relationships. These include whakapapa and the nature of humans in relation to creation stories, the birth of Te Ao Marama (the world of light that was revealed when Tane separated his parents, Rangi, the Sky Father, and Papa, the Earth Mother), the search for the kits of knowledge and the subsequent messages contained in these kits for humankind, an awareness of the importance of Mauri-Mana-Tapu-Noa, and the complementarity of these concepts (Irwin, 1984; King, 1978; Marsden, 1975; Metge, 1976, 1984; Pere, 1982, 1988; Rangihau, 1975; Walker, 1978).

system considered the Maori language and culture a prime obstacle to the educational progress of Maori children and instigated practices to eradicate them. Colonization within education has been further promoted by the belief that the Maori do not have a full literature, rather only arts and crafts, and that they therefore are a simple culture not worthy of serious concern within the mainstream school curriculum. In the wider context today, this assimilationist agenda remains pervasive, and when applied to relationships with other cultural groups, this agenda denies that ethnic minorities bring anything of intrinsic or educational value to the nation state beyond superficial celebrations of feasts and holy days.

The outcome of the dominance of non-Maori knowledge codes coupled with the economic and political marginalization of the Maori has meant that there is currently a crisis in Maori education: underrepresentation of Maori in the "success" indices and overoccupation of the "failure" indices (Davies & Nicholl, 1993; Jones, et al., 1990). The crisis is well summarized by the Waitangi tribunal in its conclusion:

> The education system in New Zealand is operating unsuccessfully because too many Maori children are not reaching an acceptable level of education. For some reason they do not or cannot take full advantage of it. Their language is not protected and their scholastic achievements fall far short of what they should be. The promises of the Treaty of Waitangi of equality of education as in all other human rights are undeniable. Judged by the system's own standards, Maori children are not being successfully taught, and for that reason alone, quite apart from the duty to protect the Maori language, the education system is being operated in breach of the Treaty. (Hirsch, 1990, p. 24)

Impact of Research

Research into Maori people's lives and activities has promoted the assimilationist agenda through a process of reification, that is, the removal of cultural elements from their sense-making context. This not only has had belittling effects, but also has helped to destroy the historical memory for Maori people. Giroux and Friere in Livingstone (1987) concluded thus:

> Forgetting instances of human suffering and the dynamics of human struggle not only rendered existing forms of domination "natural" and "acceptable," but also made it more difficult for those who were victimized by such oppression to develop an ontological basis for challenging the ideological and political conditions that produced such suffering. (p. xv)

Such circumstances led many Maori people to forget the contemporaneous elements that contributed to making total sense of their lives and their history. Furthermore, myths created as part of the dominant discourse are taken up by many Maori as truths, this creating many social, psychologic, and human development problems for Maori people.

This process over time is very powerful. For example, non-Maori and Maori educators commonly, suggest that Maori children "do well with their hands," preferring not to deal with abstract concepts. This is a myth created in the 19th century that can be directly sourced in the rationalization for the limited curriculum created for Maori children in the "native schools" (Simon, 1990). This myth is exploded when Maori children learn effectively in Maori cultural contexts within the contemporary Maori educational system, for example, in Kaupapa Maori education institutions or through immersion in hui (gatherings) at marae. In these contexts, teaching is constantly conducted within and through abstract concepts, metaphors, allusions, and imagery.

The large body of knowledge created about Maori, essentially by non-Maori for non-Maori purposes over generations, has become very powerful and oppressive. This created knowledge permeates the domain of everyday life through school texts, popular literature, and mass media, which engage in their own particular and peculiar selection processes of storytelling and sensationalism. The remnants of the 19th-century evolutionary theories of monogenetic and polygenetic sources of racial differentiation (Belich, 1987; Bishop, 1991; Simon, 1990), together with deficit or cultural deprivation theories common in the 20th century, have created a legacy of cumulative discourse about racism that over time has become a self-fulfilling prophecy for many Maori and non-Maori peoples alike and affects relationships between all cultural groups in New Zealand today.

The Native Schools

The adaptability and flexibility of Maori culture was suppressed during the late 19th and early 20th centuries when education for Maori children was subsumed within the needs of the new nation state, which were defined by the settler-controlled General Assembly. The Education Act of 1867 developed the first part of what was to become a two-tier education system. The part developed for Maori children was controlled by the central government's Department of Education, which oversaw the development of native schools in rural Maori communities. In 1877, the second-tier provincial board controlling education for the children of the settlers was introduced. Due to the dominance of the settlers in all aspects of New Zealand life, this second tier eventually became the mainstream educational provider for all New Zealanders. However, the native schools were very influential among the mainly rural Maori people, especially until World War II.

In contrast to the full national curriculum taught in the board schools, the native schools operated a limited public school curriculum, emphasizing health and hygiene and manual dexterity, all of which were taught in the English language. Teachers were to use Maori only as a means of introducing English. Furthermore, by the turn of the century, Maori language had been banned from the school grounds (Edwards, 1990), a prohibition often enforced by corporal punishment. This practice was to continue into the 1950s. In 1930, for example, a survey of Maori children attending native schools estimated that 96.6% spoke Maori at home. By 1960 this percentage had dropped to only 26%.

These native schools served to limit the ability of Maori people to compete with the rapidly expanding commercial farming sector, the beneficiaries of which dominated the politics of the country (Simon, 1990; Simpson, 1984) by emphasizing training for manual work. Maori were considered to be unsuitable for "mental work." The native schools promoted this goal by limiting the curriculum that was taught, subsequently suppressing Maori language and culture, then limiting the avenues of higher education for Maori children. Such policies effectively marginalized the mainly rural Maori population from equal participation in the economic and political mainstream.

The war years, 1939 to 1945, and the following years were to affect Maori people profoundly. Many Maori families lost young men during World War II. Maori people entered the postwar reconstruction period bereft of many who would have been leaders and participants in the new world opening up as a result of the postwar prosperity. After World War II, Maori people moved to the cities in one of the most rapid urbanizations undergone by any people in the world. Coupled with the decimation of young Maori men during the war, the migration triggered a breakdown of tribal and extended family units as young people moved to the cities, leaving behind older family and tribal sources of language, customs, and culture. The effects of the earlier education policies on language retention along with the rapid urbanization of Maori people was profound. Although the Maori language had been excluded from schools for nearly a century, rural Maori communities had maintained the discourse of Maori. Urbanization into a totally unsympathetic environment provided such a "body blow" to the Maori language that in 1979 its death was predicted. (Benton, 1979).

INTEGRATION AS POLICY: EFFECTS OF URBANIZATION

During the period of mass urbanization after World War II, Maori children entered mainstream schools organized within the developing New Zealand traditions of free, secular, and compulsory education. However, these altruistic values also embraced numerous covert values, attitudes, and assumptions that further promoted success for the children of the dominant group. These included values (Metge, 1976) such as individual competition, individual achievement, and self-discipline, in which abstract analysis and compartmentalized thinking emphasized the removal of spirituality from culture. The educational system promoted achievement based on mastery of abstract concepts, from written texts that were alien to New Zealand, in the context of self-development and individual betterment. Such values stood in sharp contrast to the experiences of many Maori children who had been socialized into family, community and peer groups that valued both group competition, and cooperation, that was dominated by both group achievement and peer solidarity, and that emphasized complementarity of abstract and concrete thought, physical and social achievements, and religion and culture. Such socialization emphasized the interdependence of the group and the individual.

Such conflicts created cultural and psychologic tensions for children, tensions that were further exacerbated by the manner in which the values of the dominant group were expressed in school organization, the selection and training of teachers, the behavior of teachers, the choice of subjects, the curriculum within the subjects,[3] the relative emphasis and resourcing allocated to particular areas of interest, and the stated and unstated agendas of priorities and goals (Metge, 1990). Because the schools were organized monoculturally, Maori students often found that their cultural knowledge was unaccepted, their intentions and motivations misinterpreted, and their language and names mispronounced. This amounted to a systematic assault on their identity as Maori people. Their resulting confusion was often manifested as frustration, inadequacy, and failure, which in turn was confusing to well-meaning but poorly trained teachers.

However, it was not until 1960 that statistics and data identifying Maori disadvantage on a number of indices, including education, were published (Hunn, 1960). As a result of this new analysis by a committee organized by and for the majority culture, a new solution to the challenge of cultural diversity was suggested. According to this new solution called "integration," instead of the minority culture and language being destroyed, the minority groups were to be integrated with the culture of the dominant group. In effect, the best of both cultures would be integrated into one

---

[3]One example of the effect of outsider selection of curriculum material on the identity of indigenous peoples is seen in the way in which Maori culture was studied in the schools of this period. Maori culture was presented in the curriculum as it was supposed to have been in Pre-European times. Contemporary Maori culture was ignored.

culture. Those elements of Maori culture that had "stood the test of time" would become part of a New Zealand culture while the Maori maintained their own identity. This approach never questioned administrative and control structures being dominated by one culture nor the reasons why ethnic minorities were invisible in decision-making processes. It also did not encourage the maintenance of ethnic minority languages and cultures.

In effect, the new policy was no real improvement for the Maori over the earlier notion of assimilation because as Hunn (1960) suggested, compared with living a "backward life in primitive conditions," Maori people would be much better off conforming to the Pakeha way of life. Hunn equated this way of life with modernity and progress. No reference was made to the cause of Maori impoverishment other than indications that it was the result of rural or desultory living. In effect, the proposed solution was a further denial of Maori culture and language as a means of addressing life's problems. Such an approach reinforced the notion that living as Maori remained a problem, a deficiency.

Empirical researchers sought to explain how such situations occurred. Much educational research was inspired by the currently fashionable approach in the United States that focused on "cultural deficiencies." Research conducted in the early 1960s by Lovegrove (1966) was of this type. He undertook a comprehensive study designed to investigate whether or not there were significant differences between Maori and European school children on tests of scholastic achievement and certain selected determiners (i.e., intelligence, home background, attitude toward school, speed of performance, and listening comprehension). He sought also to assess the relative importance of these variables in determining the scholastic achievement of Maori and European children.

As a result of his study, Lovegrove (1966) claimed that Maori and European children from almost comparable home backgrounds performed similarly on tests of scholastic achievement. From this he concluded that "it should be remembered that reasons for Maori retardation (in the education system) are more probably attributable to the generally deprived nature of the Maori home conditions than to inherent intellectual inferiority" (p. 31). In other words, the Maori child was able to compete with the European child, "providing home conditions have some degree of similarity" (p. 33).

As a result, Lovegrove (1966) suggested that there might be cultural "retardants" creating the disparity. He identified in particular that the reality of the Maori rural home was perhaps different from the type of upbringing a child needs to ensure progress at school. However, he further suggested that because intellectual differences (as measured by intelligence tests) existed between the races, even if Maori homes were able to provide enough support for the child in the primary years, it would appear that the "environments they [Maori parents] provide are not conducive to the development of the complex intellectual processes assessed by tests of intelligence" (p. 34). For example, Lovegrove observed that the Maori child's home compared with the home of a European child is less visually and verbally complex as well as less consciously organized to provide a variety of experiences, which are essential to broaden children's intellectual understanding.

Maori children were therefore "suffering a pathology" that manifested itself in inadequate language and intellectual development. Such pathologies were thought to be the result of a deficient cultural background. The solutions projected for Maori children's underachievement were catch-up programs, additional remedial assistance, and the like. In other words, an attempt would be made to accelerate and emphasize the implementation of the previous policy of assimilation (now termed *integration* by Hunn, 1960).

Attempts to critique the foundations of such ideas were made by other researchers (Harker & George, 1980; see Watson, 1967, 1972, cited in Metge, 1990), but the ideas of Maori culture being deficient remained so entrenched in the common knowledge of the dominant culture that these ideas of deficiency continued to be dominant in education department publications, school organization, and teachers' attitudes and behaviors for many decades (Metge, 1990; Simon, 1984).

The idea that Maori home conditions constituted the prime contributor to academic underachievement was a major step forward in scholastic reasoning about Maori children. Before this, it was thought that Maori people were intellectually (genetically) inferior, a belief rooted in the social Darwinism and polygenesist racism of the 19th century (Belich, 1987; Bishop, 1991; Simon, 1990). Research such as that by Lovegrove in the 1960s at least gave hope that something could be done for the children, in the way of compensatory programs similar to the Headstart programs developed in The United States. Nevertheless, this focus on cultural differences (rather than racial inferiority) itself engendered some depressing conclusions about the state of Maori education more than a decade later.

Harker (1979) recognized that cultural differences and different value systems between those who developed the educational institution and cultural minorities will have an impact on the educational achievement of minority culture children. He suggested that such realizations will create pressure either to "attempt to restructure the value system of Maori children in order to bring it into line with the requirements for success in the school environment," or to "make adjustment to the school environment [such as curriculum reform] in order to provide greater continuity with the Maori value system" (p. 49), or some combination of these.

However, Harker concluded that the former solution had been tried without success for over a century, and the second was hopeless because no matter what changes were made to the criteria for success at school, "those groups with high cultural motivation to succeed will adapt and continue to succeed under the new criteria. . . . Hence achievement differences cannot be ameliorated by changes to the educational system" (p. 49).

This may sound depressing, but what is more depressing is Harker's conclusion that the problem may not be one of searching for ways of catering to ethnic diversity, but rather one of questioning the wisdom of insisting on equalizing performance for all ethnic groups. Harker's (1979) conclusion is grim; "If New Zealanders are genuine about their society as a multicultural one, in which all cultures are accorded equal status, *then perhaps we have to learn to live with some measure of achievement differences between ethnic groups*" (p. 50; italics added).

MULTICULTURALISM AND BICULTURALISM

Gradually during the 1970s and the 1980s ideas of multiculturalism as a means of addressing and catering to ethnic diversity replaced integration as the dominant educational policy foundation. Notions of multiculturalism were expressed in school curricula, (e.g., social studies), in which notions of exploring cultural diversity, celebrating differences, and promoting cultural identification were advocated. Furthermore, these programs sought to involve the cultural and language practices of all ethnic groups represented in schools, and in so doing enhance the self-esteem and cultural identity of all students.

Despite these good intentions, these pedagogic values and practices, while embracing a range of different ethnic groups internationally, were not readily applied to Maori students or their language and culture. Contemporary Maori culture remained invisible in the majority of mainstream classrooms. Furthermore, when other cultures were studied, the majority culture remained the major referent in mainstream schools. Children were encouraged to compare those other cultures with their own, a strategy that is developmentally sound in that children began by understanding their own culture first, then learned to define their own culture through a process of comparison with a different culture. However, because monocultural Pakeha teachers continued to dominate the education system, and because these teachers, being part of the dominant majority, did not perceive that they themselves had a culture and promoted the nonculture phenomenon, children of different cultures were forced in their learning to see others through the eyes of the majority culture. In effect, it was actually the culture of the teacher that became the yardstick for comparison (see Alton-Lee, Nuthall, & Patrick, 1987). As a result, children of that culture continued to take for granted that theirs was the main reference point, a process that reinforced the ever-present and persistent notions of cultural superiority and reinforced for Maori children that in these classrooms their culture was treated as an "other."

Gradually, during this period, the Department of Education began responding to pressure from Maori people (Awatere, 1981) and started to promote a philosophy of biculturalism as a preferred approach to understanding multiculturalism (Irwin, 1989). It was suggested that the majority culture needed to address the Maori–Pakeha relationship first before a multicultural approach could be developed in New Zealand. Such arguments were based on the need to recognize the Treaty of Waitangi as the founding document of New Zealand. Maori people were seeking visibility in their own country and inclusion in the mainstream education system on equal terms. The Maori argued that the relationship between Maori and Pakeha must be addressed in such a way as to remove the dominant–submissive pattern and to develop the partnership pattern envisaged in the Treaty of Waitangi. Relationships with other peoples could then be developed from this bicultural basis.

One practical implementation of the biculturalism policy has been the development of Taha Maori (literally the Maori side) program in schools. This program was an initiative of the former Department of Education in the early 1980s in response to the growing call among Maori and non-Maori educators for some recognition of the place of Maori as tangata whenua (indigenous people) in Aotearoa (the Maori name for New Zealand). To clarify this voice in education, former race relations conciliator, Walter Hirsch, in 1989, interviewed a number of Maori and non-Maori educators about the achievement of Maori children in schools. One of the subjects covered in these interviews was taha Maori, defined as "Maori perspectives being developed in all aspects of school organization and curriculum" (Hirsch, 1990, p. 37). In his report to the Ministry of Education in 1990, Hirsch stated that the people he spoke to during the preparation of the report had at least two expectations of taha Maori.

The first expectation was that taha Maori programs would have the potential for validating Maori culture and language in the minds of Pakeha New Zealanders. In a research study of the impact of taha Maori in the schools of Southern New Zealand, Holmes, Bishop, and Glynn (1992) identified that this potential is being realized. The study indicated that a generally positive attitude now exists among the communities sampled toward the validity of Maori culture and language. Maori initiatives such as kohanga reo, kura kaupapa Maori, bilingual units, enrichment studies, and immersion classes are receiving positive support also from an increasing number of Pakeha New Zealanders. Such an outcome is important, because, as Ritchie (1991) pointed out, there is a tremendous need in New Zealand for "attitude modification techniques" to reduce Pakeha prejudice. The provision of simple factual information about Maori educational aspirations and initiatives may be all that is required to begin this process of attitude change. Taha Maori programs in southern schools are helping to meet this need.

The second expectation that Hirsch (1990) identified was that "taha Maori [would have] the potential to help Maori students feel a greater sense of identity and self-worth on the one hand and may enhance their educational achievements as well" (p. 38). The results of the study by Holmes, Bishop, and Glynn (1992) suggest that goal is being met only to a very limited degree because the curriculum remains geared to the needs and aspirations of majority culture members. Furthermore, data showed clearly that there is widespread lack of understanding by schools and their boards of trustees about which Maori perspectives should be developed in all aspects of school organization and curriculum. This lack of understanding is seen in the almost exclusively monocultural school "mission statements." Only one in the study explicitly acknowledged the need for a Maori perspective.

Taha Maori sought to add a Maori perspective to a curriculum, the central core of which was decided by the majority culture, rather than include Maori worldviews as any substantial component in the curriculum-planning process. Maori people are seen as resources to be drawn upon, rather than partners to be included in the process of education. This research identified (within southern New Zealand at least) numerous examples of Maori resources being used to implement mainstream curriculum initiatives without any recognition to the financial, cultural, and spiritual costs involved. The intention may have been benign, but the effects have been the belittlement of the partnership principles embodied in the Treaty.

It is significant that at the same time as mainstream educators were attempting to introduce a Maori perspective into the (structurally unaltered) curriculum, Maori people were developing and privately funding preschool "language nests" for the preservation of the Maori language. In effect, even if taha Maori was originally intended to address issues of Maori achievement in schools, it is most unlikely that it could address the underlying issue of retrieving a colonized language and culture because taha Maori (as an implementation of biculturalism) was designed to meet the aspirations of the Pakeha majority and not those of the Maori people.

In effect, attempts to promote biculturalism within the educational mainstream has meant that the focus of change has been on the Pakeha society. This focus on teaching Pakeha people about Maori culture has often consumed resources at the expense of Maori language and cultural aspirations. Such a situation is exacerbated by existence of little change in the monocultural status and approach of those in control of teacher education. Preservice teacher training programs still attempt to teach all trainees a smattering of Maori language (days of the week, colors, simple greetings, etc.) rather than meet the aspirations of Maori people for in-depth training in the use of Maori as the medium of instruction. The vast majority of teachers in the schools are still monocultural Pakeha, which means that changing the mainstream education system to meet the aspirations of Maori as well as Pakeha people is an enormous task.

The clear message from these studies into attempts by the mainstream to address cultural diversity is that when mainstream educators and politicians attempt to see the ethnic diversity as a challenge they must respond to alone on their own terms, they inevitably fail to address the aspirations and needs of the other parties. The next section details how Maori initiatives have begun to address Maori aspirations and how mainstream policymakers in response are understanding how a pattern of partnership can be fostered within the country.

KAUPAPA MAORI:
MAORI EDUCATIONAL INITIATIVES

During the period when attempts to address the challenge of ethnic diversity continued to be defined by members of the majority culture, Maori critique of these mainstream initiatives saw the development of a proactive, Maori political discourse termed Kaupapa (agenda) Maori[4] (Awatere, 1981; Irwin, 1989; Smith, 1990, 1992a, 1992b; Smith, 1991; Walker 1990). Kaupapa Maori emerged from within the wider ethnic revitalization movement (Banks 1988) that grew in New Zealand after the rapid Maori urbanization of the post-World War II period. This movement blossomed in the 1970s and 1980s with the intensification of a political consciousness among Maori communities (Awatere, 1981; Walker, 1990).

---

[4] Smith (1992b) described Kaupapa Maori as "the philosophy and practice of 'being and acting Maori'" (p. 1). It assumes the taken for granted social, political, historical, intellectual, and cultural legitimacy of Maori people in that it is a position in which "Maori language, culture, knowledge, and values are accepted in their own right" (p. 13). Furthermore, Kaupapa Maori presupposes positions committed to a critical analysis of the existing unequal power relationships within our society. These include rejection of hegemonic belittling, "Maori can't cope" stances, simplification and commodification of Maori intellectual property, and the development of a social pathology analysis of Maori underachievement (Bishop, 1995) together with a commitment to the power of conscientization and politicization through struggle for wider community and social freedoms (Smith, 1992a)

More recently, in the late 1980s and the early 1990s, this consciousness has figured in the revitalization of Maori cultural aspirations, preferences, and practices as a philosophical and productive educational stance and resistance to the hegemony [5] of the dominant discourse.

Kaupapa Maori responded to the dual challenge of imminent language death and consequent cultural demise, together with the failed succession of government policy initiatives such as assimilation, integration, multiculturalism and biculturalism to sustain Maori cultural and language aspirations (Jones et al., 1990). Maori educator Graham Smith (1992b) explained that this development occurred among Maori groups across all educational sectors, such as Te Kohanga Reo, Kura Kaupapa Maori, and Waananga Maori and included other groups such as the NZ Maori Council, The Maori Congress, Maori health and welfare bodies, and Iwi authorities. For Maori, the specific intention was to achieve "increased autonomy over their own lives and cultural welfare" (Smith, 1992b, p. 12). In education, this call for autonomy was in response to the lack of programs and processes within existing educational institutions that were designed to "reinforce, support or proactively coopt Maori cultural aspirations in ways which are desired by Maori themselves" (p. 12). Smith further suggested that the wish for autonomy also challenged the "increasing abdication by the State of its 1840 contractual obligation to protect Maori cultural interests" (p. 10).

Maori demands for autonomy in this context is generally articulated as tino Rangatiratanga (literally "chiefly control", metaphorically "Maori self-determination"). This call is often misunderstood by non-Maori people. It is not a call for separatism, nor is it a call for non-Maori people to stand back and leave Maori alone, in effect to relinquish all responsibility. It is a call for all those involved in education in New Zealand to reposition themselves in relation to these emerging aspirations of Maori people for an autonomous voice (Bishop, 1994, 1996).

The early post-Treaty education system that developed in New Zealand, the mission schools (Bishop, 1991), the native schools (Simon 1990), and the present mainstream schools (Irwin, 1992) have all been unable to "successfully validate matauranga [knowledge] Maori, leaving it marginalized and in a precarious state" (p. 10). Furthermore, whereas mainstream schooling still does not serve Maori people well (Davies & Nicholl, 1993), the Maori schooling initiatives of Te Kohanga reo (Maori medium pre-

---

[5] The concept of hegemony is used here in the sense defined by Foucault (Smart, 1986), who suggested that hegemony is an insidious process gained most effectively through "practices, techniques, and methods which infiltrate minds and bodies, cultural practices which cultivate behaviors and beliefs, tastes, desires and needs as seemingly naturally occurring qualities and properties embodied in the psychic and physical reality of the human subject" (p. 159).

schools), Kura Kaupapa Maori (Maori medium primary schools), Whare Kura (Maori medium secondary schools), and Whare Waananga (Maori tertiary institutions), "which have developed from within Maori communities to intervene in Maori language, cultural, educational, social and economic crises . . . , *are successful in the eyes of the Maori people*" (Smith, 1992b, p. 1, italics added).

Te Kohanga Reo

Ironically, the first major Maori educational initiative, Te Kohanga Reo (Maori medium preschools), resulted from pressures outside of the education sector. It was during a review of the department of Maori Affairs in 1977, in response to the concern that the Department was "culturally removed from Maori people" (Irwin, 1990, p. 113), that a working party was sent throughout the country speaking and listening to local Maori communities. They received an unequivocal message. Maori people wanted an education that "maintained their own lifestyles, language and culture whilst also enhancing life chances, access to power, and equality of opportunity" (p. 111).

A series of hui held in the early 1980s followed soon after, and these meetings focused on the concern about language loss and urged the establishment of "language nests", places where the language could be nurtured. There was much scepticism voiced in the wider community about the potential of such initiatives and much discussion of Maori problems as seen by outsiders, such as Maori having an impoverished community base, limited traditional cultural resources, few capital resources, and alienation from the traditional cultural base. Nevertheless, outsiders were not aware of the power to be released when these new educational initiatives tapped into the cultural aspirations of Maori people to revitalize the language and culture. The success of the language nests (TKR) has been phenomenal.

Since the opening of the first center in 1982, there has been rapid growth. By 1987 there were 513 centers operating. By 1993 the number had grown to 809, surpassing both kindergartens (582) and play centers (577; Bishop, Boulton, & Martin, 1994). In 1982, only 30% of Maori children age 2 to 4 years, compared with 41% of non-Maori children, participated in early childhood contexts. By 1991, the Maori participation rate had risen to 53% largely as a result of kohanga reo fostering increased Maori participation in early childhood education (Davies & Nicholl, 1993). By 1993, 14,027 Maori children (96.6% of students) were enrolled at kohanga reo that had proliferated around the country, representing 49.2% of Maori children in early childhood education. However, despite this growth, the participation rate for non-Maori children in early childhood education has increased at a faster rate than for Maori children. In 1985, Maori children made up 22% of all children in early childhood education. In 1992, this percentage, despite a large numeric increase, had fallen to 17%, a further indicator of the continued socioeconomic impoverishment of Maori families,

That the language nests do foster the language is confirmed in research reported in Hohepa, Smith, and McNaughton, (1992). Early research in 1968 by Dame Marie Clay (cited in Hohepa et al., 1992) had identified that a sample of 77 urban Maori children were unable to understand or follow instructions in Maori. In contrast, the Samoan children she studied were found to be predominantly bilingual, understanding both Samoan and English.

In 1989, Clay's assessment tool was used by Smith et al. (1989, cited in Hohepa et al., 1992) to examine the language competencies of a Maori group of children ages 5 to7 years in a Maori immersion school (kura kaupapa Maori). These children were graduates of Te Kohanga Reo, and they were found to have bilingual competencies similar to those of the bilingual Samoan children in Clay's original study. Furthermore, these are children whose parents are not necessarily strong in Maori language and culture. Indeed, these were the children of the generation studied by Clay in 1968.

The kaupapa (philosophy/agenda) of Kohanga Reo is that (a) children will learn the Maori language and culture including spiritual values through immersion; (b) language and cultural learning will be fostered for all members of Te Kohanga Reo whanau (this includes adults as well as children); (c) members of TKR whanau will learn a range of other skills such as administration and financial control; (d) collective responsibility will be fostered; (e) all involved will feel the sense of belonging and acceptance; and (f) the content, context and control of learning will be Maori (Irwin, 1990, p. 117).

The involvement of whanau (extended family principle: literally all ages being represented) has meant that Maori parents have been able to exert a significant degree of local control over the education of their children despite changes in government. The whanau approach is characterized by a collective decision-making approach, and each whanau has its own autonomy within the wider philosophy of the movement (Irwin, 1990, p. 118). Hence, control over what children should learn, how they should learn it, and who should be involved in the learning are in the hands of the controlling whanau.

Some outcomes of TKR are that young children leave TKR-speaking Maori feeling positive about their language and culture. The language and cultural practices of native speakers have also been affirmed. Parents have been stimulated to learn Maori. There has been a socioeconomic intervention through activation of whanau, and participation by parents in the education of their children has been stimulated. TKR has arrested the fragmentation of the traditional language and cultural base.

"By far the most significant message to come out of kohanga reo is that Maori are able to run big enterprises just as well as anyone else and that they can do this in a mix of languages and cultures and amid much criticism and scepticism" (Brell, 1995, p. 11). This has occurred despite the fact that funding for TKR came entirely from the community until 1990, when the national TKR trust was able to gain state funding. The government review of TKR concludes that "TKR is a vigorous, lively movement, has arrested the fragmentation of the traditional cultural base, has revitalized the use of marae, and is helping preserve the Maori language. All this had come about through the autonomy of the Kohanga Reo within the kaupapa" (Irwin, 1990, p. 119). In other words, Maori people control the decision making over how, when, where, and why for the education of their children.

Such a dramatic turnabout has important implications for language acquisition and classroom processes. Kaupapa Maori educational initiatives are based on the notion that language is the key to the culture, and that language and culture together are keys to sociopolitical interventions. In other words "acquiring linguistic knowledge and acquiring sociocultural knowledge are interdependent" (Hohepa et al, 1992, p. 334). Such sociocultural approaches to language acquisition stand in contrast to previous dominant assimilationist ideologies in that children are socialized through learning, and language learning is organized by sociocultural processes. In this way, language learners are active, not passive. Drawing on Leontiev's theory of activity, Hohepa et al. (1992) suggested that it is "through participation in structured social activities that language learners acquire linguistics and sociocultural knowledge. These social actions are, in turn, socioculturally and linguistically structural and organized" (p. 334). Furthermore, as sociocultural and linguistics knowledge structures activity, so does activity create and recreate knowledge in both domains.

The research undertaken by Hohepa et al (1992) suggested that TKR acts as an enculturating context by providing a culturally structured environment within which children develop. Language development plays a vital role in this process. In their study, "culturally preferred contexts and beliefs as well as activities were found to provide contexts or to act as setting events for specific language mechanisms such as language routines and language focusing strategies in this kohanga reo. Furthermore, these resulting language mechanisms in turn set up contexts for the passing on or teaching ways of thinking and acting which are culturally valued" (Hohepa et al., 1992, p. 343).

As a further outcome of the study, routines after repetition of language with immediate social reinforcement were capable of being modified in order for roles to shift and language flexibility to progress. The language focusing strategies identified in the study can be linked to Maori preferred pedagogies; looking, listening, and imitating, that is modeling (Metge, 1983). Metge (1983) observed that traditionally Maori place great emphasis on memorization and rote learning and teaching by demonstration so that people are able to participate appropriately in Maori sociocultural contexts in which oral participation and presentation are crucial.

EDUCATIONAL RESTRUCTURING:
MAORI AUTONOMY

The success of Te Kohanga Reo, the development of the first Maori immersion primary schools, and a growing voice for self-determination in educational matters by Maori people coincided with New Zealand's fourth Labor government's (1984–1990) radical restructuring of school administration according to recommendations made by the Taskforce to Review Educational Administration (Picot, 1988). The main thrust of the restructuring was for policymaking to remain the domain of a new Ministry of Education, whereas responsibility for many administrative decisions was to in the hands of locally constituted boards of trustees.

Under the new provisions, all schools were to ensure that their "policies and practices seek to achieve equitable educational outcomes for both sexes; for rural and urban students; for students from all religions, ethnic, cultural, social, family, and class backgrounds; and for all students irrespective of their ability or disability" (New Zealand Ministry of Education, 1988, p. 8). Each board of trustees was required to accept "an obligation to develop policies and practices which value our dual cultural heritage" (New Zealand Ministry of Education, 1988, p. 6).

However, many Maori parent groups remained unconvinced that such reforms were likely to meet their cultural aspirations. They preferred for their children to continue with the Maori medium education that had been started in the kohanga reo. Initially, the government was reluctant to allow the development of new Maori medium primary schools within the new provisions for state schools. That is to have their own autonomy while following very serious representation by Maori leaders and educationalists, Kura Kaupapa Maori were incorporated into the reform (The Education Act, 1989) legislation as a fully recognized and state funded schooling alternative within the New Zealand state education system (Graham Smith, personal communication, 1994).

Subsequently, the Ministry of Education has undergone considerable policy shifts in response to the growth of Kaupapa Maori educational initiatives. Learning the Maori language as a subject in its own right was a traditional approach fostered by the Ministry and the previous Department of Education, but now in the mid-1990s, policy direction is toward "making the language the center of the learning process within whole educational institutions and their communities. Kura kaupapa Maori, Maori immersion education, and using Maori as a medium for implementing new curricula are the key components of developing te reo (Maori language) in Aotearoa" (Ministry of Education, 1995, p. 12).

The Ministry of Education is committed to supporting the establishment and administration of kura kaupapa Maori, to providing suitable accommodation, and to identifying resources needed. The first kura was established at Hoane Waititi marae in 1984, and 12 others were established by 1989, mostly without state support. However, provisions have been made for the establishment and state funding of kura on the same basis as that for other state funded schools. A total of 38 kura had been approved by June 30, 1995, and approval has been given for 15 new kura kaupapa Maori to be established over the next 3 years.

In contrast to the 1960s, the current focus of Ministry policy is much closer to the Maori's aspirations for education. Instead of blaming the children and their homes and condemning Maori language as an impediment to development, current policies focus on te reo Maori (Maori language) as an essential cornerstone of Maori development. Policy is underwritten by the need to address Maori achievement rates, which in mainstream educational contexts still fall behind those of non-Maori. Perhaps the most dramatic shift in policy has been from a paternalistic approach to one that argues for "increasing the opportunities for Maori to take more responsibility for the control of Education" (Brell, 1995, p. 7).

It is now seen by the Ministry of Education that "Maori language, Maori education, and Maori development are inextricably linked. Maori see education as a key component of a wider strategy for greater self-determination" (Brell, 1995, p. 7). One outcome of this approach has been the 1992 decision by the Ministry of Education to introduce a Maori medium curriculum that would have outcomes identical to those of the mainstream curriculum but would follow different pedagogies, knowledge, and information systems to achieve those outcomes. Within this curriculum, structures and procedures have been developed to give the Maori control over decision-making protocols on language use and pedagogical developments as they relate to the Maori language. In this way the policymakers are attempting to facilitate Maori parents in having a greater say and more responsibility in the education of their children. This is seen as a key to improving Maori achievement in education.

This model of self-determination has become a burning issue for an increasingly large proportion of the Maori population. They see language as absolutely essential to their essence, their being, and their identity as Maori. The Maori people want to maintain their integrity, which comprises te reo (language) tikanga Maori (Maori customs) and a matauranga (knowledge) base, the foundation from which Maori people are able to express themselves and participate in the world.

There remains, however, a serious constraint on the provision of Maori medium education, and that is the availability of teachers fluent in te reo Maori. Spolsky (1987) estimated "a need for at least 1,000 qualified Maori bilingual teachers over the next decade" (p. 21). He suggested a number of ways to address this problem: training fluent Maori speakers as qualified teachers, developing Maori fluency in qualified teachers, and training Maori bilingual teachers (Waite, 1992). However, despite the obvious need, teacher training institutions have been slow to respond. Pem Bird, head of Maori studies at the Auckland College of Education maintained that the revitalization of the Maori language remains in jeopardy because of the continued shortage of Maori teachers. He along with Waite and others called for a national languages policy, and more particularly, a national strategic plan that would unite all providers of teacher education in a common purpose, "producing teachers with the ability to deliver education in the Maori language, within a Maori context and derived from a Maori language base, in satisfactorily large numbers to ensure that all parents who choose to have their children educated through Maori can, in fact, realistically exercise that option" (Pem Bird, personal communication, 1996).

Past education policies removed Maori as a community language from the homes of most Maori families. Now schools are seen as the catalyst for revitalization, and as identified in a study of language transference from te Kohanga reo to the home (Tangaere, 1992), often leading to revitalization of the language in the home as well. However, despite recent policy shifts, the residual effects of 150 years of marginalization and monolingualism are profound.

IMPLICATIONS FOR THE DEVELOPMENT
OF NEW POLICIES

Language Implications

A major outcome of the political and economic colonization of New Zealand by English-speaking Europeans is that contrary to practice in many other parts of the world, the level of bilingualism in the total New

Zealand population is extremely low. When bilingualism occurs, it is found mainly in minority language groups, among Maori speakers, and in minority ethnic communities including new settler language speakers. Bilingualism is rare among the majority of the population, which consists primarily of New Zealanders (82%) of European descent. No language other than English features in the top 10 most popular subjects at secondary school (Waite, 1992, p. 19).

The monolingualism that has marked education and New Zealand society for some decades has an inertial effect on student desires to undertake study of a language, especially at senior levels. Evidence of this effect is that the limited number of students learning te reo Maori are in the senior secondary schools (15% of Maori who learn Maori language in schools). This limits the pool of students able to take up tertiary study in the language and thus to undertake training in Maori educational contexts.

The low incidence of bilingualism among first-language speakers of English is derived from historical ideas of cultural superiority. Although such ideologies nowadays are being widely challenged, monolingualism is still being fostered by the somewhat erroneous impression that English is the international language. As a result, it is felt that New Zealanders on the whole have little need to learn other languages for other than purely utilitarian (economic and trade) reasons. Hence, much is made over the benefits for trade and tourism of learning the languages of, for example, trading partners such as the Japanese, the Koreans, and the Malaysians. Increasingly, within the New Zealand business community, bilingualism is seen as a benefit for the entrepreneur desirous of entering the largely competitive international marketplace by ensuring that market research, contracting, and personal contacts can be made on the client's terms. This is seen as an essential ingredient in promoting and developing economic and trade relationships. Similarly, on the rapidly diversifying domestic scene, bilingualism with English alongside economic and trade languages increasingly is a skill sought after in teaching, tourism, journalism, interpreting, translation, and social work.

However, although monolingualism and monoculturalism remain dominant, opportunities for promoting bilingualism are denied people unable to maintain their own language or unable to acquire an adequate knowledge of English. It is sharply ironic in New Zealand today that there is an increasing demand for bilingual Maori–English speakers in education (Education Gazette, 1966), but that this demand cannot yet be fully met by adult Maori people because of their loss of language and culture created by the past emphasis in the education system on monolingualism.

Policymakers in New Zealand have been from the majority monolingual culture, and thus are essentially unaware of the aspirations of Maori people for the revitalization of their language as an integral element of the culture and cannot appreciate the extent to which the language and culture have been eroded by the education system. Maori people, however, have recently developed their own educational initiatives and are focusing educational practice on their language as a means of transmitting their culture through the curriculum. They have contested and won a share of state education funding to support these initiatives. This model is one that policymakers for new settler migrants could well emulate. Unless they do, community languages used in New Zealand will continue to decline.

Despite attempts to develop language maintenance programs for languages other than English, such provision has to contend with the continued dominance of English as a medium of instruction, a dominance reinforced by primary school level preservice teacher training that does not make available training in language teaching.

The continuing dominance of monolingualism is seen in the newly drafted National Curriculum of New Zealand (Ministry of Education, 1991). This document specifies the seven "essential learning areas"—mathematics, science and environment, technology, social sciences, the arts, physical and personal development, and language.

The learning area of "language" includes English (which is a required study) and may optionally include Maori, community languages, and international languages. That is, for first language speakers of English, the learning of another language is not proposed as a required part of the common curriculum. As a result, the pervasiveness of monolingualism is unlikely to change in the foreseeable future.

Community Languages

Monolingualism has had a similar impact on other community languages in New Zealand. In a recent meta-analysis of three studies evaluating community language loss in Wellington (the capital city of New Zealand), Janet Holmes (1990) observed that the "language shift to English occurs over at most four generations, and is sometimes completed in as few as two. The rate of shift appears to be greater for some than others, but the fact of shift and the direction of the shift seem inevitable" (p. 19).

Holmes' (1990) meta-study covered three community language groups, the Chinese, Greeks, and Tongans. The Chinese community first came to New Zealand in significant numbers in the 1880s. There are a number of fourth-generation Chinese New Zealanders living in Wellington today. In contrast, the Greek community in Wellington was established in the 1920s and the majority of the Greek community are therefore second- and third-generation Greek New Zealanders. The Wellington Tongan community is the most recent, dating largely from the 1960s, a time when many

Pacific Island peoples (such as Samoans, Nuieans, Cook Islanders, and Tokelauans) moved to New Zealand during the post-World War II economic boom in search of employment and better education for their children. Most adults of these Pacific Island communities are first generation New Zealanders. These three communities were used to trace language shift in an immigrant population over four generations.

Community languages do not disappear easily. What tends to happen is that the language slowly retreats from more public settings to more private ones, as the number of proficient speakers diminishes. The current pattern of language use among the three communities illustrates this clearly. In the Tongan community, people in the community still safely assume that a person who is Tongan will speak Tongan. By keeping close contact with one another at home, socially, and even at work, Tongans are able to use their language often. In the Greek community, despite a relatively close residential and occupational proximity, the youth find it easier to speak English, yet will speak Greek to older people of the community, irrespective of the location.

This situation also exists in the Cantonese Chinese community. Chinese is generally spoken to and by older Chinese, but significantly this is mainly in Chinese domains with a marked decline of proficiency among the younger generations. The number of places—home, church, community social events, work, and school—where the community language can be heard steadily contracts over the generations. The private language patterns (of thought, counting, praying, dreaming), also show a similar pattern of erosion. English has replaced Cantonese for young Chinese, and is steadily replacing Greek for young Greeks.

Some factors that speed up language shifts include intermarriage, especially if the noncommunity member is the mother. School attendance by children and men working in non-community language contexts also hasten the language shift. Women tend to retain their use of the community language longer than do their husbands and children. Teenagers also are a clear indicator of shifting preferences in language use.

In all three studies examined by Holmes (1990), the children's attendance at school was the single most important means for the English language to invade the home. "It is at this point that parents find it hardest to continue to use the community language to children who reply in English" (p. 25).

English as a Second Language Provisions

A recent Organizations for Economic and Development (OECD) survey of reading literacy indicated that although New Zealand was among the highest scoring countries in reading achievement, it had the largest average difference between language majority and language minority students (Wagemaker, 1993, in McPherson, 1994).

English as a second or other language (ESL) funding falls short of what is required. This is occurring as the number of children from non-English speaking backgrounds (NESB) entering schools is growing rapidly, now totaling approximately 46,000 NESB students in New Zealand, of whom 61% need ESL support (Ministry of Education 1993 figures). Funding for ESOL is targeted at only 13,000 children throughout the school system which leaves approximately 20,000 students identified as being in need of additional support, but for whom no extra resources are available. The majority of these children are in the primary school. This situation is exacerbated by inadequate preservice primary teacher training in this area and the prevalent notion that young children will learn complex language use in context.

Overseas researchers (Baker, 1993, cited in McPherson, 1994) suggested that this assumption is incorrect. Of equal importance is the suggestion by Cummins (1988) and Baker, (1993, cited in McPherson, 1994) that unless children learn the majority language within a context that incorporates and values their home language and culture in the curriculum, they are likely to be disabled by an education that effectively limits their potential to develop fully either their home language or the introduced language. Early total immersion in English of minority language speaking children "may have deleterious effects on their general language development, if no support is given to their first language development" (Waite, 1992, p.18). The problems of limited educational support to first language are denial of identity, denial of cultural self determination, denial of opportunities for future education and employment in that area, and speakers receiving an extensive formal education in their own language who recognize and use more words in that language than speakers who do not. This means that languages not used across the curriculum in formal education over an extended period do not necessarily achieve high levels of vocabulary extension (Waite, 1992).

Whatever the case, it is clear that learning needs to be built on children's ability in their home language. Such suggestions help us understand more fully the reasons for Maori (and other Polynesian) children's low achievement in mainstream classrooms. Their home language is denigrated and denied them, and they enter an English language context without the necessary base to develop the more complete usages of language. The frustration of the older generation is heard when they recall that leaders of a previous generation were fluent in both languages and able to participate in both. Their frustration is that younger Maori are unable to participate fluently in either language.

The concentration of NESB students in South Auckland, a low socio-economic area, further exacerbates problems of resourcing and teacher stress. Provision of support is made even more complex because not all NESB students are from similar backgrounds. Indeed there are at least three major categories, each with its own subcategories.

New Settlers.   The fastest growing section of this group comprises Chinese speaking families who have moved to New Zealand as business migrants, for example from Hong Kong and Taiwan. In 1991, 13% of NESB students were in this category compared with 7.5% from the refugee/reunification of families scheme. However, this latter group requires special care and attention owing to the fact that many (for example from Cambodia) have never participated in formal schooling (Cochrane Lee & Lee, 1993, cited in McPherson, 1994).

New Zealand-Born Citizens.   This group includes those children who are graduates of kohanga reo and Pacific Island language nests. The manifest inability of mainstream schools to cater to the needs of these children created the impetus to initiate Maori medium primary education. However, for some foreseeable time not all parents of kohanga graduates will be able to support their children or indeed want their children to enter the kura kaupapa Maori contexts. This challenge needs to be addressed in a systematic manner rather than the ad hoc fashion of current practice. The movement of Kohanga graduates into primary schools is currently creating a demand for Maori medium education in the primary sector and is beginning to have an impact on the secondary sector as well with consequent implications for teacher education. Currently, there is only one college of education (State Teacher Training Institution) conducting training programs for Maori immersion teaching and one for bilingual programs.

The Ministry of Education is attempting to respond by making support for Maori medium education a priority and targeting funding at programs most likely to produce fluent Maori speakers (Ministry of Education, 1995). Such approaches are based on the New Zealand experience of kohanga reo and overseas research (Waite, 1992) indicating that full medium immersion programs in the minority language are the most effective means of educating children to be fluent bilinguals.

To support those programs most likely to achieve the aim of revitalizing the language, Ministry of Education policy initiatives were aimed at supporting those mainstream schools offering immersion or near immersion programs. As of July 1993, 13% of schools (358 of 2,772) offered some form of Maori medium education described as follows with the percentage of schools using each (Ministry of Education, 1994).

- Maintenance programs (4.98%), which Maori is the medium of instruction and the context of interaction between 81% and 100% of the time
- Development programs (3.07%), in which Maori is used between 51% and 80% of the time as a temporary expedient
- Emerging programs (2.74%), in which Maori is used between 31% and 50% of the time and English is the main language of communication and instruction
- Minimum programs (2.13%) offered less than 31% of the time
- No immersion program (87.09%)

Fee-Paying Students from Other Countries.   The third largest category is fee-paying students from other countries. Numerous secondary schools are recruiting students directly from overseas in an attempt to subsidize reductions in government funding. There is a growing concern that some schools may be regarding these students in commodity rather than human terms. In 1992, 2,259 fee-paying students attended schools in New Zealand, 1,269 of them from Asian countries (Ministry of Education, 1993).

Adults.   Adult settlers from non-English speaking heritages also face many problems when arriving in a monolingual context characterized by a dominant–subordinate relationship between English speakers and the language and culture of others. Community language maintenance for the first generation adult group is not such a problem as it is for the children. However, opportunities for adults to learn English are often limited. For example, Pongudom (1995) reported that the adults of the Cambodian community in Dunedin had difficulty attending educational institutions to learn English because of their need to work to support their large families. Opportunities to learn English at their places of employment were also limited because the low-skilled jobs they could get provided few opportunities for learning to speak English. The types of jobs they held did not allow them to speak to others. In fact, such interchange was discouraged in some settings as not being essential to the job. Such situations further exacerbate potentially low levels of English, which also limits access to information and services, thus hampering participation in activities of the wider society (Dawkins, 1991, cited in Waite, 1992).

When the opportunities of parents to learn English are much fewer than those of their children, parents are less able to participate in their children's formal learning contexts. Their ability to function as role models, facilitators of learning, enhancers of educational achievement, and advocates for their communities is severely restricted. There is also a danger that their parenting role itself will be disrupted when their children acquire English at the expense of their home language (Wong-Fillmore, 1991).

Because the ideology of monolinguism predominates for the non-English speaking minorities, learning to speak English in New Zealand is essential to enabling equitable access to education, the labor force, and social services. However, learning English at the expense of maintaining the home language places many refugees at a disadvantage in attempting to participate equitably in the employment and education sector. Pongudom (1995), writing about the Cambodian community in Dunedin, suggested that education and consequent employment is not simply a function of being assimilated into the majority culture. Rather, it appears that those refugees who are most successful become fluent in English while maintaining a strong sense of cultural identity.

If enforced assimilation and cultural denial, as happened to Maori people, also happens to recent settlers, it seems clear that they will be less likely to maintain a strong sense of identity, with consequences in terms of self-confidence and self-esteem.

The Need for a Languages Policy

The need to establish a coherent and comprehensive New Zealand language policy has been highlighted for the last 20 years. Although there is currently no such policy available, a major report, *Aoteareo*: Speaking for Ourselves was produced by the Ministry of Education in 1992 (Waite, 1992). This report acknowledged the need for all New Zealanders to have a sound knowledge of standard New Zealand English, but strongly advocated the benefits of bilingualism. An attempt was made in the report to balance social justice issues with the government's trade- and economic-based desires and visions as outlined in the draft document, Education for the 21st Century (Ministry of Education, 1993). The Waite (1992) report proposed six ranked priorities for public policy: revitalization of the Maori language, second-chance adult literacy, children's ESL and first-language maintenance, adult ESL, national capabilities in international languages, and provision of services in languages other than English (McPherson 1994, pp. 18–22). The need for such a policy has never been more pressing, but processes of dominance and subordination must not drive its development. Partnership as promised in the Treaty of Waitangi is a more preferable and enduring course.

TO CONSIDER

Debate and activity surrounding multicultural or intercultural education in New Zealand continues to grow, particularly in areas related to Maori culture and language. Although never a matter of agreement by all, in New Zealand there appears to be a greater understanding of the need for intercultural understanding than in most nations of the world. Language revitalization programs, the increasing use of the Maori language generally in society, and the apparent openness with which educators debate issues all point to at least a tolerance toward integration that may not exist to the same degree in other parts of the world.

1. *Review current newspapers from New Zealand available on the Worldwide Web at www.vol.it/UK/EN/EDICOLA/quot_str.htm#menu. Search for news items that present issues related to Maori rights, immigrant issues, and New Zealand's role in the international community. How do these current issues relate to what you have just read in the chapter? What struggles continue around Maori affairs?*

2. *What can your nation and schools learn from the experience of New Zealand?*

3. *How can young people in New Zealand be most effectively prepared to interact with others on a global scale? What resources within New Zealand appear available to assist young people in developing a global or intercultural perspective?*

4. *New Zealand, like Australia, frequently receives immigrants and refugees from many Asian and Pacific Island nations. Given what you have just read, how would you respond to the scenario presented in chapter 1. What steps should schools take in responding to the needs of newly arrived immigrant groups?*

REFERENCES

Alton-Lee, A., Nuthall, G., & Patrick, J. (1987). *Take your brown hand off my book: Racism, in the classroom* (Set 1, Item 8). New Zealand Council for Educational Research: Wellington New Zealand.

Awatere, D. (1981). *Maori sovereignty.* Auckland: Broadsheet.

Banks, J. (1988). *Multi-ethnic education: Theory and practice.* Boston: Allyn & Bacon.

Belich, J. (1987). *The New Zealand wars and the Victorian interpretation of racial conflict.* Auckland: Penguin Books.

Benton, R. (1979). *Who speaks Maori in New Zealand.* Wellington: New Zealand Council for Educational Research.

Bishop, R. (1991). *He whakawhanaungatanga tikanga rua: Establishing links: A bicultural experience.* Unpublished masters' thesis, Department of Education, University of Otago. Dunedin, New Zealand.

Bishop, R. (1994). Initiating empowering research. *New Zealand Journal of Educational Studies,* 29(1), 1–14.

Bishop, R. (1996). *Collaborative research stories: Whakawhanaungatanga.* Palmerston North: Dunmore Press.

Bishop, D., Boulton, A., & Martin, S. (1994). *Education trends report* (Vol. 6[1]) Wellington: Ministry of Education.

Brell, R. (1995). *Managing education realities in Asia and the Pacific.* Seapreams 14th Regional Symposium December 4–8, 1995, University of Auckland. Auckland, New Zealand.

Davies, L., & Nicholl, K. (1993). *Te Maori i roto i nga mahi whakaakoranga: Maori in education.* Wellington: Ministry of Education.

Edwards, M. (1990). *Mihipeka: Early years.* Auckland: Penguin.

Glynn, T. (1985). Contexts for independent learning. *Educational Psychology,* 5(1), 5–15.

Glynn, T., Fairweather, R., & Donald, S. (1992). Involving parents in improving children's learning at school: Policy issues for behavioural research. *Behaviour Change* (Special issue on behavioural family intervention), 9(3) 178–185.

Harker, R. (1979). *Research on the education of Maori children: The state of the art.* Paper presented to the first National Conference of the New Zealand Association for Research in Education. Victoria University, Wellington.

Harker, R., & George, R. (1980). *Conclusions and consequences: Some aspects of M.N. Lovegrove's study of Maori and European educational achievement reconsidered.* Paper presented to Priorities in Multi-Cultural Education conference, Department of Education, Wellington.

Hirsch, W. (1990). *A report on issues and factors relating to Maori achievement in the education system.* Auckland: Ministry of Education.

Hohepa, M., Smith, G. H., Smith, L. T., & McNaughton, S. (1992). *Te kohanga reo hei tikanga ako i te reo Maori: Te kohanga reo as a context for language learning* (Educational Psychology, Vol. 12, numbers 3 & 4, pp. 333–346). Auckland.

Hohepa, P. (1975). The one people myth. In M. King (Ed.), *Te Ao Hurihuri: The world moves on* (pp. 98–111). Auckland: Hicks Smith.

Holmes, J. (1990). Community languages: Researchers as catalysts. *New Settlers and Multicultural Education Issues,* 7(3), 19–26.

Holmes, H., Bishop, R., & Glynn, T. (1992). *Tu mai kia tu ake: Impact of taha maori in Otago and southland schools* (Te Ropu Rangahau Tikanga Rua Monograph No. 4). Department of Education, University of Otago.

Hunn, J. K. (1960). *Report on the department of Maori affairs.* Wellington: Government Print.

Irwin, J. (1984). *An introduction to Maori religion.* Bedford Park: Australian Association for the Study of Religions.

Irwin, K. (1989). Multicultural education: The New Zealand response, 1974–84. *New Zealand Educational Journal of Education,* 24(1), 3–18.

Irwin, K. (1990). *The Politics of kohanga reo.* In S. Middleton, J. Codd and A. Jones. (Eds.), New Zealand educational policy today: Critical perspectives. Wellington: Allen & Unwin/Port Nicholson Press.

Irwin, K. (1992). *Maori research methods and processes: An exploration and discussion.* Paper presented to the joint New Zealand Association for Research in Education/Australian Association for Research in Education Conference. Geelong, Australia.

Jackson, M. (1993). *The Treaty of Waitangi.* Seminar presented to Community and Family Studies Department, University of Otago.

Jones, A., McCulloch, G., Marshall, J., Smith, G. H., & Tuhiwai-Smith, L. (1990). *Myths and realities: Schooling in New Zealand.* Palmerston North: Dunmore.

King, M. (1978). Some Maori attacks to documents. In M. King (Ed.), *Tihei Mauriora: Aspects of Maoritanga* (pp. 9–18). Auckland: Longman Paul.

Livingstone, D. W. (1987). *Cultural pedagogy and cultural power.* Massachusetts: Bergin & Garvay.

Lovegrove, M. N. (1966). The scholastic achievement of European and Maori children. *New Zealand Journal of Educational Studies,* 1(1) 16–39.

Maori Language in Education (1996, February). *Education Gazette,* 75(2) pp. 1–2. Wellington: Ministry of Education.

Marsden, M. (1975). God, man and the universe: A Maori view. In M. King (Ed.), *Te Ao Hurihuri: The world moves on.* (pp. 143–164) Auckland: Longman Paul.

McPherson, J. (1994). Key issues in language education in Aotearoa/New Zealand. In J. McPherson, *Making changes: Action research for developing Maori language policies in mainstream schools* (pp. 5–20). Chapter 1. Wellington: NZCER.

Metge, J. (1976). *The Maoris of New Zealand: Rautahi.* London: Routledge & Kegan Paul.

Metge, J. (1983). *Learning and teaching: He tikanga Maori.* Wellington: Department of Education.

Metge, J. (1990). *Te Kohao o te ngira: Culture and learning.* Wellington: Learning Media, Ministry of Education.

Ministry of Education. (1988). *Tomorrow's Schools: The reform of educational administration in New Zealand.* Wellington: Government Printer.

Ministry of Education. (1991). *The national curriculum of New Zealand: A discussion document.* Wellington: Learning Media.

Ministry of Education. (1993). *Education for the 21st Century: A discussion document.* Wellington: Ministry of Education.

Ministry of Education. (1994). *Trends Report,* 6(1), October 1994.

Ministry of Education. (1995). *Nga Haeata Matauranga: Annual Report 1993/94 and Strategic Direction 1994/95.* Wellington: Ministry of Education.

New Zealand Official Yearbook. (1995). Wellington: Statistics in New Zealand.

Pere, R. (1982). *Ako: Concepts and learning in the Maori tradition.* Hamilton: Department of Sociology, University of Waikato.

Pere, R. (1988). Te wheke: Whaia te maramatanga me te aroha. In S. Middleton (Ed.), *Women and girls in education.* (pp. 6–19). Wellington: Allen & Unwin.

Picot, B. (1988). *Administering for excellence: Effective administration in education: Report of the taskforce to review education administration.* Wellington: The Taskforce.

Pomare, E. (1987). *Hauora: Maori standards of health.* Wellington: Department of Health.

Pongudom, W. (1995). *Acculturation at a cost: Language and educational difficulties experienced by Cambodian refugees in Dunedin.* Unpublished doctoral thesis. University of Otago.

Rangihau, J. (1975). Being Maori. In M. King (Ed.), *Te ao hurihuri, the world moves on: Aspects of Maoritanga* (pp. 165–175). Auckland: Hicks Smith.

Ritchie, J. (1991). *Becoming bicultural.* Wellington: Hui Publications.

Salmond, A. (1975). *Hui: A study of Maori ceremonial greetings.* Auckland: Reed & Methuen.

Simon, J. (1984). "Good intentions, but . . . " *National Education* 66(4), 61–65.

Simon, J. A. (1990). *The role of schooling in Maori-Pakeha relations.* Unpublished doctoral. thesis. Auckland University.

Simpson, T. (1984). *A vision betrayed: The decline of democracy in New Zealand.* Auckland: Hodder & Stoughton.

Smart, B. (1986). The politics of truth and the problems of hegemony. In D. C. Hoy, (Ed.), *Foucault: A critical reader* (pp. 157–173). Oxford: Basil Blackwell.

Smith, G. H. (1990). Taha Maori: Pakeha capture. In J. Codd, R. Harker, & R. Nash (Eds.), *Political issues in New Zealand education* (pp. 183–197). Palmerston North: Dunmore.

Smith, G. H. (1992a). *Research issues related to Maori education* (The Issue of Research and Maori Monograph No. 9). Department of Education, University of Auckland.

Smith, G. H. (1992b). *Tane-nui-a-rangi's legacy . . . propping up the sky: Kaupapa Maori as resistance and intervention.* A paper presented at the New Zealand Association for Research in Education/Australia Association for Research in Education joint conference. Deakin University, Australia.

Smith, L. T. (1991). Te rapuna i te ao marama: Maori perspectives on research in education. In J. R. Morss, & T. J. Linzey (Eds.), *The politics of human learning: Human development and educational research* (pp. 46–55). Dunedin: University of Otago Press.

Spolsky, B. (1987). *Report of Maori–English bilingual education.* Department of Education, Wellington.

Tangaere, J. (1992). *Language transference from Te Kohanga Reo to home: The roles of the child and family.* Unpublished master's thesis, University of Auckland.

The Education Act 1989 in Statutes of New Zealand. Wellington, New Zealand Government
    Printer.
Waite, J. (1992). Aoteareo: Speaking for ourselves. Wellington: Ministry of Education, Learning
    Media, Wellington.
Walker, R. (1978). The relevance of Maori myth and tradition. In M. King (Ed.), Tihe Mauriora:
    Aspects of Maoritanga . . . (pp. 19–33). Auckland: Methuen.
Walker, R. (1990). Ka whawhai tonu matou: Struggle without end. Auckland: Penguin.
Ward, A. (1974). A show of justice. Auckland: Auckland University Press/Oxford University Press.
Wong Fillmore, Lilly. (1991). When learning a second language means losing the first. Early
    Childhood Research Quarterly 6, 323–346.

Editor's Remarks

Malaysia is comprised of the Malay Peninsula and the coastal portion of Borneo, which are separated by roughly 400 miles of the South China Sea. Because of its geographic location, the Malay Peninsula has long been a trade route between East and West, and between China and India. As a result, many complex problems related to ethnic pluralism and interaction have evolved over the past 1,500 years, and have had a powerful impact on the region. During the period of British colonization, the educational emphasis was on reading and writing the English language. After World War II, considerable attempts were made to reunite the country by unifying its three main ethnic groups: the Malays, Chinese, and Indians. When Malaysia finally became in independent nation, the Malays were behind the Chinese and Indians in educational attainment, especially in the areas of science, business, and technology. Similarly, Malaysians have struggled hard to bring educational parity between the rural and urban areas of the country.

As Professor Gaudart explains, there is no multicultural education policy in Malaysia today. How can a nation such as Malaysia with its culturally diverse population and history of cultural interchange and colonization approach the education of its young in today's highly interdependent world? How can a nation, which has for so long looked inwardly and struggled to develop and maintain a national identity, develop a core of teachers and professionals who understand and accept the cultural and social complexities that confront nations and people today?

Chapter 4

Interculturalism in Education: A Malaysian Perspective

৪০ ◆ ৫৪

Hyacinth Gaudart
Universiti Malaya

The Malaysian education system is based on a national education policy that evolved from the education policies of the 1950s when Malaysia made its first moves toward independence. The education policy, refined in 1979, attempts to create a united and disciplined society that fulfills the requirements needed by the workforce of a country striving toward development. In many ways it has sought to combat the British colonial heritage, which had robbed the people of their pride and failed to foster unity or any sense of a national identity. Harmony has been the major aim for this young country with its diverse population.

The education policy recommends certain strategies for the fulfillment of its aims, and the Ministry of Education strives toward ensuring that these strategies are upheld. The strategies as planned, and as listed by the Prime Ministers Department of the Government of Malaysia on the Internet (Jabatan Perdana Menteri, 1996) are as follows:

- To establish the national language, Malay, as the major medium of instruction in schools.
- To have a nationally planned curriculum for the entire country, with an orientation towards the Malaysianization of all types of schools.

- To encourage a common system of national examinations for all.
- To improve the administration of education in Malaysia.
- To improve the standard of education in Malaysia.
- To provide opportunities for education for at least 9 years.
- To democratize education by providing equal educational opportunities for all, paying special attention to sectors of the population who were disadvantaged, including those in rural areas.
- To provide primary education, following the New Curriculum for Primary Schools (KBSR) with its emphasis on reading, writing, and arithmetic, and to continue that education into the secondary school and the Unified Curriculum for Secondary Schools (KBSM). The major aim of the new curricula would be to educate individuals toward a balance in their thinking and feeling, with a morally and ethically sound approach to life.
- To expand the number of vocational and technical schools.
- To expand, improve, and provide greater opportunities for university level education, mainly in the applied sciences and arts.
- To improve the spirituality, morals, and discipline of young Malaysians through education.
- To make the teaching of the national language and English compulsory in all schools and, at the same time, to provide opportunities for other languages, like Chinese and Tamil, to be studied.
- To encourage participation in cocurricular activities that would lead to greater discipline— activities like the military cadet corps, police cadet corps, scouting, "puteri Islam," and so on.

Malaysia has a centralized system of education under the umbrella of the Ministry of Education. It is organized "at four hierarchical levels, namely national, state, district/division/residency and school" (MIMOS, 1996:file:///A|/edu2.html). There are 20 divisions in the Ministry of Education; 12 professional divisions and 8 administrative Divisions (MIMOS, 1996: file:///A|/edu2.html).

However, even though the Malaysian national education system is a centralized one and the curriculum a national one, a number of alternative education systems also have been allowed to function side by side with the government-financed public school system. In addition to the many different public schools, there are also private schools of varying types. These various types of schools give rise to differences in interculturalism and are therefore worth discussing. To obtain a full picture of education in Malaysia, it is necessary to understand something about the alternate schools and their contribution to society. The following section begins by describing the systems of non-mainstream education in Malaysia, then focuses on education in public schools.

NON MAINSTREAM SCHOOLS

Schools in the private sector may be divided into four major types: Mandarin-medium secondary schools, Islamic-based schools, middle- and upper-middle-class primary schools, secondary schools, preschools, foreign schools, and special schools, especially those for the mentally challenged.

Mandarin Medium Secondary Schools

All Mandarin medium primary schools are public schools, so only Mandarin medium secondary schools are private schools. Many have existed from the British colonial era and boast beautiful old buildings combined with more modern additions. The schools themselves are very large, as are most classes. In the southern state of Johor, for example, one Mandarin medium secondary school boasts an enrollment of approximately 10,000 students. Classes of over 40 and often 50 students do exist. Although other schools may not be that large, they are often larger than public secondary schools.

Islamic-Based Schools

Although some Islamic-based schools are directly under the jurisdiction of the Ministry of Education, others are administered by different organizations. These Islamic-based schools are often small and not widespread. Islamic schools can be divided into two types: (a) those whose students follow at least 6 years of education (primary plus secondary school), and sometimes 11 years of education, and (b) those that open their doors to students who attend after regular school hours to study Islamic knowledge. Neither type of school is currently regulated by the schools' division of the Ministry of Education. They are governed by state-based Islamic bodies or are privately owned and operated. While these schools sometimes seek the assistance of the Islamic Division of the Ministry of Education, there is no obligation to do so.

Some of the type b schools not only cater to children and adolescents, but also open their doors to adults who would like to have time for reflection, or who want to learn more about Islam. Some of the schools are therefore residential in the sense that accommodation is provided for students to live with the teacher in his hut or in huts built specifically to accommodate students. The accommodation is usually free or may have a minimal charge. In turn, students help in the running of the commune by cleaning, cooking, planting vegetables, and so forth.

Private Middle-Class Schools

These schools are of the type that most Western-educated persons would recognize, private schools in which students pay fairly high fees for the privilege of being in relatively small classes and having greater personal attention given to them. They have been set up only in major cities, mainly Kuala Lumpur, Petaling Jaya, Kuching, and Pulau Pinang (Penang), and may be primary, secondary, or both. Whereas most of the schools officially follow the national curriculum and teach all subjects, except languages, in Malay, there are also schools that unofficially follow a bilingual education curriculum so that students study half a day in Malay and half a day in English.

At the time of this writing, preschools in Malaysia are private enterprises and not overseen or regulated by the Ministry of Education, except when a person seeks permission to start a preschool. Plans are underway, however, to change this situation and allow for greater supervision and accountability from the preschools. There are also plans to set up government-funded and government-operated preschools to serve the needs of rural children and those from the lower income groups in urban areas.

A variety of preschools exist, the more prominent ones promising to educate children according to Montessori methods. There are also Christian- and Islamic-run preschools with an obvious focus on religious ideals, and some preschools run by Chinese organizations with Mandarin as the medium of instruction.

Foreign nationals have also been allowed to set up schools that cater to the needs of their nationals and other foreigners in Malaysia who are interested in obtaining a particular type of education for their children. The largest number of such schools are probably the British-based schools, following a British-style system of education and preparing students ultimately to face the British examinations. Other schools are run by Americans (the International School) and the Japanese who also have their own school in Petaling Jaya.

Special Schools

The final type of non-mainstream schools cater to students with special needs. These schools are funded and run by organizations such as mental health organizations, which in turn depend on public donations to keep their schools in operation. These are the types of schools to be found outside the universally recognized Malaysian public school system. No attempt has been made to analyze them in detail because it is believed that this brief description is sufficient to present a picture of the varied alternatives to public education that exist in Malaysia. Some of the non-mainstream types of schools play a large role in the attitudes toward interculturalism in Malaysia and are discussed again in a later section.

PUBLIC SCHOOLS

The Malaysian education system comprises 6 years of primary and 5 years of secondary education, with, for the time being, an additional 2 years of postsecondary, preuniversity education (although this practice is currently under debate and may soon change). University education traditionally consisted of 4 years for a first degree, but has recently been changed to 3 years for most degrees. All degree-granting institutions, until very recently, have been public institutions. Recent policy has permitted the establishment of universities by the private sector, although they remain under the surveillance and control of the Higher Education Division of the Ministry of Education. In the K–12 system, or perhaps one should say the 1–13 national system of education, we find that the mainstream public schools may be divided into three types: primary, secondary, and postsecondary.

Primary Schools

Children enter into the first year of the primary school at the age of 6 or older and are assigned to a school, usually according to their residential address. It would be relevant when considering interculturalism in Malaysia to point out that in the primary schools, a number of languages are available as the medium of instruction, the three main languages being Malay, Mandarin, and Tamil. Parents choose the language medium of instruction in which they want their children to begin their education, always choosing to send their children to a school in which the language of instruction reflects their ethnicity. There are Malay children in Mandarin-medium schools, for example. Malay and English are compulsory languages taught in all schools.

Secondary Schools

In public secondary schools, the sole medium of instruction is Malay. Primary students from the other language media schools, on finishing their primary school education, move into special classes in the secondary schools wherein they are taught intensive Malay to prepare them for the change of the medium of instruction to Malay. Students also study English intensively at this level. There is provision, however, for students from non-Malay medium schools who have sufficient ability in Malay to skip the Malay language class and thus move faster through the school system. Many Chinese students, however, prefer to carry on in private Chinese schools in which the medium of instruction remains Mandarin.

Students who remain in public schools may apply for a place in residential schools or remain in day schools. Residential schools have been established in all of the Malaysian states and cater to the brighter students who may be disadvantaged by remaining in their usual environment, typically a rural area, in which facilities may be limited. In these schools, students concentrate mainly on science-based subjects, but are also encouraged to learn a third language other than Malay and English. The more popular languages demanded are Arabic, French, and Japanese (Gaudart, 1992).

The first residential school was established in colonial times to train the young sons of the social elite for positions of importance in society. That residential school, the Malay College Kuala Kangsar, still has the distinction of graduating future leaders of Malaysian society.

Students also may be admitted to technical and vocational schools. The technical schools are usually residential schools in which students are introduced to the principles of various types of engineering. In vocational schools, students learn a variety of skills from masonry to auto mechanics.

Postsecondary/Preuniversity

After the final year of the secondary school, students are placed in postsecondary classes, known as Sixth Form classes, in which they prepare to take the Sijil Tinggi Pelajaran Malaysia, an examination to establish who qualifies to enter local universities. There appears to be a plan at present to discard these classes in favor of matriculation classes.

THE EDUCATION SYSTEM AS A WHOLE

In keeping with the national education policy, the Malaysian education system is centralized, and the curriculum is a national one planned for the entire country. As an extension of this curriculum, and also in keeping with the national policy, there are national examinations at primary and secondary school levels. The aims of these examinations differ from level to level.

The national primary school examinations are mainly diagnostic, not just evaluating students but teachers and the schools as well. Children who do well in these examinations are allowed to skip a grade and go to a higher level. Those who do not do well are not penalized, but simply proceed to the next level. Some people would like to see this changed and a system of retention introduced, but this is currently not the practice.

The lower secondary school examinations sort students into science, arts, technical, and vocational branches. In Malaysia, this is referred to as "streaming." Students in all streams take some similar subjects and some different subjects for their final year (year 11) examinations. Those who do well and plan to study at a local university then apply to be selected for Form Six (or preuniversity classes). However, private schools, especially schools in which the medium of instruction is Mandarin, have designed their own curricula. These schools also have their own examinations (the Chinese Senior Middle Three examinations), which are recognized not only in Taiwan, but also by some institutions in Canada, Australia, and Britain. Students do take the Malaysian national examinations, but are not totally dependent on the results, knowing that they have recourse to the Chinese school examinations, American SATs, and so on.

Other private schools follow the planned syllabus, but develop what they consider a curriculum more appropriate to their own schools. Such flexibility is also spreading among the public schools in which the principals are being encouraged to take over as curriculum leaders, and teachers have been encouraged to develop materials and programs that would better meet the needs of their students.

THE APPROACH TO TEACHING CULTURE AND LANGUAGE

At the time of this writing, the Malaysian educational policy does not explicitly target interculturalism or multiculturalism. What it does do is emphasize striving for an understanding of different cultures. An examination of the social studies curriculum, even at the elementary level, reveals introductions to various world religions and philosophies. Children are also introduced to the history and geography of the world at an early age so that by the end of their lower secondary education, they have already been exposed to much of world history and geography.

However, efforts to introduce the young to the rest of the world are not restricted to the social studies syllabus. Other syllabuses also attempt to acquaint students with issues outside Malaysia. One example is the syllabus for English as a Second Language (ESL) (although English is more a foreign language than a second language in the American sense of ESL). In the secondary school English language syllabus, different themes encourage students to explore fellow Malaysians' way of life as well as people in other countries. When placing emphasis on the Malaysian way of life, themes in the syllabus encourage projects and research on the customs of different ethnic groups such as weddings and festivals. Students are encouraged to interact and learn from one another, thus expanding their worldview of various cultural events. Where the outside world is concerned, students are introduced to the way of life in other countries, starting with the Southeast Asian (ASEAN) countries, then moving out to the rest of the world. Materials for learning English are drawn from sources outside Malaysia and range from literature to tourist brochures. English language reading tests in schools include work written in varieties of English other than the native strains (e.g., writings of Chinua Achebe) and also writings of non-native speakers of English. Roald Dahl, for example, remains on the reading list of the lower secondary curriculum.

This content-based approach to learning and teaching about a foreign language allows the transfer of knowledge of other cultures to the young Malaysian. The education system also encourages students to learn other languages. Malay and English are compulsory languages for all students to learn. Besides these two languages, a variety of other languages are also offered, and most children become trilingual. The Education Act provides that if 15 or more parents demand instruction in a particular language, that language should be taught. The constraint to this is that there may not be teachers available to teach the requested languages. An example is Creole Portuguese, the mother tongue of a number of children in the state of Melaka (or Malacca). Because the Creole has not been sufficiently analyzed linguistically for the analysis to be handled pedagogically, the language cannot be taught. When possible, however, languages in demand have been offered as subjects in the school system.

DEMOGRAPHICS

Malaysia is a multilingual, multicultural nation in Southeast Asia, with a 1996 population of about 18 million people. Its territory is divided by the South China Sea so that on one side of the Sea is Peninsular Malaysia with a population of about 14.6 million people. It is attached by a narrow isthmus in the north leading to Thailand. To the south is the small island of Singapore, and to the west, Sumatra and Java, the large islands of Indonesia. To the east of Peninsular Malaysia in the South China Sea is the island of Borneo. On that large island lie the states of Sarawak and Sabah with a population of about 3.3 million people. The Philippines lies to the east of the states of Sarawak and Sabah, and Kalimantan, an Indonesian territory, lies to the south. Sarawak also surrounds the tiny, oil-rich country of Brunei.

HISTORY

In the early 15th century, the Malaysian kingdom of Melaka was a powerful force in Southeast Asia. It had a well-protected harbor and was a prominent port of call for Asian and Middle-Eastern merchants and travelers. It was on the trading route between China and India, about half-way between the two vast empires. Another attractive feature, strange as it may seem, was that Melaka was also on the path of two monsoon winds that alternated in direction at different times of the year. This allowed ships to sail in the direction of their trading partners. Melaka was therefore a natural port of call, a resting place, and an intercultural market place (Ibrahim, 1979; Loh, 1976; Purcell, 1948; Stevenson, 1975). The Malaysian kingdom of Melaka was also a place where Chinese (now known as "Babas and Nyonyas") made their homes, intermarrying with local Malay girls, developing a dialect of Malay, and creating a Malay–Chinese culture, which remains unique to this day (Purcell, 1948). Indians, referred to locally as "Chitties" (Gaudart, 1992) too made their homes here, also intermarrying, integrating, and speaking their own dialect of Malay. Later, with the coming of the Portuguese and the Dutch, Melaka became even more cosmopolitan, a place where Asian and Western norms and values mixed and matched. Malaysians, whether by design or force of circumstances, learned very quickly how to deal with different cultures and their ways of thinking.

In the 19th century, the British spread their control over the Malaysian states and, with colonization, floods of immigrant workers were brought in, changing the ethnic mixture of the country in a short space of time. Schools were built with various hidden agendas, not least among them being the supply of labor for various levels and types of colonial enterprise (Furnival, 1948; Sidney, 1927).

English medium schools were built, which taught from British-based textbooks, and Malaysians were encouraged to adopt the worldview of their colonial masters, thus coming middle persons between the British colonial government and the general populace, the first officeworkers and bureaucrats (Gaudart, 1992). There were also Chinese and Tamil medium schools. But because the British had no clear education policy (Kok, 1978), the schools reflected the cultures of China and India, becoming rather ethnocentric (Koh, 1967). Changes in the curriculum in China, for example, was immediately reflected in the curriculum of Chinese schools in Malaysia (Beebout, 1972).

There were also schools taught in the Malay language that had an even more restricted curriculum because the British feared that the Malay child would know more than his parents and feel superior to his or her father and the traditional way of life (Ibrahim, 1979). Basket weaving and net making, rather than literacy skills, were the main foci of the curriculum in these schools.

Combined with a policy of divide-and-rule, at independence (Peninsular Malaysia in 1957 and the whole of Malaysia in 1963) Malaysia found herself with a divided society in which different cultures represented quite different lives. In the 1960s, for example, it was fairly common to stereotype persons by their ethnicity, which easily placed them in particular occupations and/or locations: Indians were in the plantations and also worked the railroad; Indian Muslims were cloth merchants; Chinese were in business; Malays were typically farmers, except on the East coast of Peninsular Malaysia where they were fishermen; one particular group of Indians, known locally as "Chettiars" or "Chetty" were money-lenders, as were Punjabis (Sikhs) who also were watchmen at jewelry stores and banks; the natives of Sarawak and Sabah (e.g., Ibans and Kadazans), lived in the jungle; the Chinese lived mainly in the towns, and so on. Each culture and subculture had its own worldview and found it difficult to understand or tolerate others. In that sort of diverse, stratified, and uncompromising society, the early Malaysian leaders sought to find answers to the nation's problems. They decided that the answers would lie in education. The result was the education policy discussed in the first section.

MALAYSIAN SUBCULTURES

Before looking at interculturalism in Malaysia it is necessary to keep in mind that Malaysians, although living in a small country, are not uniformly alike and thus hold different worldviews according to their own subcultures. Interculturalism for each of these groups may not mean quite the same thing as it would to another subculture. Let us therefore consider the various subcultures.

If Malaysian society were subdivided into subcultures, the first division in the minds of most people would be ethnicity. There are supposedly three major ethnic groups in Malaysia: the Malays, Chinese, and Indians. This is, however, an oversimplification of the real situation as we see in the section on the Klang Valley, which describes a small specific area around the capital city. Aside from the three major groups, there are also other minority groups comprising, among others, Filipinos, Eurasians, Thais, and Caucasians. Although small in number, their cultures have a significant influence on the major cultures.

The second division that exists is a division between rural and urban dwellers. In a broad general view of the situation, it can be observed that whereas many urbanites have access to information and contacts outside

Malaysia, those in rural areas are more restricted in what is available. Inevitably, therefore, their worldviews differ.

It would be very simple if there was only a rural–urban difference. However, such is not the case. Within the urban or rural division, there are also differences according to the region from which the person comes. A person who has lived his entire life in the urban center of Kuala Lumpur, for example, may have a different worldview from someone who has lived all his life in the urban area of Kota Baru in the northern state of Kelantan on the border with Thailand, or Sandakan in the state of Sabah.

In the attempt to identify the wider cultural areas, the urban areas should be divided further into: Sabah, Sarawak, the urban areas of the east coast of Peninsular Malaysia, the west coast of Peninsular Malaysia, and the Klang Valley. The rural areas could be subdivided into the cultural areas of Sabah, Sarawak, the east coast of Peninsular Malaysia, the south and central rural areas of the west coast of Peninsular Malaysia, and the northern rural areas of the west coast of Peninsular Malaysia. Such divisions are broad, and within each geographic area are various subcultures. Such an example is one urban division, the Klang Valley.

The Klang Valley

The Klang Valley is probably the most highly industrialized, commercialized, and thus urbanized center in Malaysia. Kuala Lumpur, the Malaysian capital city, is found in the Klang Valley. Within its urban structure, however, we find subcultures that break down according to various categories.

Nationality. Subcultures in this category arise because of the large numbers of non-Malaysians in the Klang Valley. Within each nationality group there are further subcultures. Each of these foreign subcultures come into contact with different local subcultures, perhaps because of religion, occupation, or education. Each has an influence on the others.

Ethnicity. Officially, there are three main ethnic groups in Malaysia and a number of minority groups. It is too simplistic, however, to classify each ethnic group as belonging to a similar subculture. For example, the Indians draw their roots from different areas of the Indian subcontinent and categorically point out their differences. Many Sri Lankans do not want to be considered "Indians." Many Punjabis feel the same way. Bengalis have their own times of the year for celebrations, and those dates may be different from those observed by the Hindu Tamils, and so on.

Each of these groups thus forms its own subculture, and depending on other factors such as religion and education, may be further subdivided.

Religion.   Although religion may appear to be one apparent criterion for identifying subcultures, we must be aware that there are subgroups within each religion, perhaps belonging to different branches and representing considerable differences in what they may believe.

The two major religions in the valley are Islam and Christianity. Islam may be the national religion of Malaysia, but not all Muslims have a similar worldview, nor indeed a similar view of what Islam is and what it stands for. In the Klang Valley, therefore, we have splinter Muslim groups, which form subcultures unique to themselves. Until recently, some lived in communes segregated from the rest of Malaysian society, but with apparent links to similar groups in other Muslim countries. Recent government action has forced these groups to be less overt in their way of living, but they remain obvious, especially by the way they dress.

It is the same with Christians. They belong to different Christian movements, which may or may not share similar worldviews. Some are passionately evangelical; others are not. Some believe that social reform should be the main agenda; others prefer religious reform, or feel that religion should be private rather than manifested publicly, and so on.

Education.   Although education is a means of intercultural understanding, it is also a source for the creation of subcultures. There are five language media of instruction in Malaysian elementary schools, which are supported entirely by public funds. There are three main media, Malay, Mandarin, and Tamil, and two minor ones, Telegu and Punjabi. In private education there are also bilingual Malay–English schools, which may also teach a third language. In addition, the private Mandarin medium secondary schools have their own systems of examination.

The different language media of instruction give rise to different subcultures, and in each language media there may be further splits due to other social variables. Consider the Mandarin medium schools for example. Although the medium of instruction is Mandarin, children come to school with various dialectal mother tongues. Although a minority of Indians and Malays do attend these schools, the students are mainly Chinese. However, within the Chinese society are *clans* with their own organizations, support groups, and club houses.

At the secondary level, too, some of the students from Chinese medium primary (elementary) schools move into Malay medium secondary schools and are forced to interact with students of diverse cultural backgrounds. But other students continue in private Chinese medium secondary schools in which they continue to interact with only those from the Chinese subculture.

Differences are therefore inevitable. Views of what interculturalism is, or should be, also differ. One subculture might aim toward Malaysianization of society first, equating that ideal with nationalism. From their point of view, it is imperative to understand what being Malaysian is before understanding the rest of the world. Another subculture may aim toward understanding the West first and would view life from Western-type philosophies. Yet a third subculture might set as its priority each understanding his or her ethnicity first.

Members of each subculture would want to have an interpretation of the world and international events through the philosophies of their ethnic philosophers or leaders, even if these leaders lived in different countries, and at a different periods of time. Such differences among subcultures are exciting if they are considered as differences, not points of dissension. But they definitely create a variety of worldviews.

Socioeconomics. The socioeconomic positions and occupations of the parents also determine differences in the worldviews of their offspring. Children who have traveled to other countries with their parents, lived abroad, and interacted with those of different cultures from an early age, for example, are bound to hold worldviews different from those who have never left the Klang Valley and who have never interacted with any non-Malaysians. Also, most middle-class children in the Klang Valley have access to technology such as television and the Internet, which those from poorer homes do not have. The access to technology will contribute a great deal to the way the future generation will view others.

These various subcultures are not discrete divisions. However, they overlap in some areas and are separate in others. As a result, even more subcultures are formed. Religion, for example, cuts across ethnicity in many ways. Consider the ethnic Malay group, Bumiputera, the largest ethnic group in Malaysia. From the religious perspective, it can be observed that whereas all Peninsular Malaysian Malays are Muslims, Bumiputera groups in Sabah and Sarawak (sometimes subdivided as Pribumi) may be Muslim, Christian, worshipers of traditional gods, and so on. The same is true of the aboriginal tribes of Peninsular Malaysia, some of whom live in the Klang Valley. On the other hand, there are Malaysians who, although ethnically different, may share lifestyles that make them share worldviews. Middle-class Malays, Indians, and Chinese, for example, who have attended similar types of schools and have lived abroad, may share more with each other than with another Malay, Indian, or Chinese of the same religion but with a different geographic, social, and educational background.

HOW TEACHER PREPARATION INSTITUTIONS ADDRESS INTERCULTURAL EDUCATION

Discussion of ethnic issues has been considered a source of possible strife in Malaysia. This was borne out in the May 13th riots of 1969, a period of strife that Malaysians, understandably, would rather not see repeated. This avoidance of discussing ethnic-based issues, however, has resulted in an evasion of any direct attempt to place such a sensitive issue in any curriculum, whether the curriculum be for the school or for teacher education. In some of the universities, however, the teacher education program does include multicultural education, but because of time constraints, very little time can be given to it.

Instead the issues are dealt with in an indirect way. Intermingling among student teachers from various interracial groups in the teacher colleges is encouraged, for example, as it is also encouraged in teacher preparation programs in the universities. Students work together on various projects and so learn to interact better with those of other ethnic groups. Schools themselves, especially Malay medium schools, are ethnically mixed as are the staff rooms (or teachers' rooms) in the schools. There remain no plans, however, for any concerted effort to make multicultural or intercultural education a major part of the teacher education curriculum nor the education of young people.

CONCLUSIONS

Where intercultural learning is concerned, there are advantages to being a small country determined to succeed in the face of the larger and more powerful nations. Malaysia is one such country. Through necessity, Malaysians have been forced to observe and learn about other cultures and also to tolerate even what may seem strange to some Malaysians.

However, this willingness to learn about other cultures can certainly be encouraged further. Hoopes (1979) said that intercultural learning is not the gathering of information about other cultural groups. He believed that what it really means is "learning another culture so as to be able to experience what it is like to be part of it and to view the world from its point of view; learning it so as to be able to function effectively and comfortably within it" (p. 17). If we accept Hoopes' stand on what intercultural learning is really about, then Malaysia, like most other countries, still has a long way to go.

One of the problems facing education in Malaysia at the present time is that students learn about other world cultures but it is doubtful how much empathy or even sensitivity to those cultures is created. Although students learn about the cultures within Malaysia, many have little contact with foreign peoples and therefore have little knowledge or understanding of other cultures. This is especially true of the cultures of Africa, the Pacific, and South America. Not having intercultural education well articulated in the curriculum is thus a disadvantage.

The advantage of the present situation, however, is that sensitivity to other cultures can be integrated into the curriculum more fully than if it were a particular subject in the curriculum, a likely fate once the policy spells out that intercultural education should be part of the curriculum. Malaysians have seen previous examples of such a development, as for example with moral education and living skills. The problem with having such subjects taught as formal subjects is that some students disregard the message conveyed, viewing it as part of the propaganda being generated. This prevents full assimilation of the values being communicated.

Furthermore, it will be impossible at the present time to implement any sort of concentrated effort in intercultural education, with language and personnel being important considerations. This is so despite the fact that better teaching in intercultural communication, so essential to intercultural education, is sorely needed. There are just not enough teachers able to carry out the tasks adequately. For example, Malaysia uses English as one of its major languages for international communication. But there are barely sufficient general-purpose English language teachers in the schools today.

The necessary alternative would be the private sector taking more responsibility for intercultural education. This would not be inappropriate because intercultural education is intimately linked with international interaction and diplomacy at different levels. But there too, the same problems are present. There are just not enough sufficiently trained personnel to teach intercultural communication or intercultural education. At a more basic level, there are just not enough teachers in general to meet the needs of the current population. Despite large classes averaging 40 in a class, Malaysia is currently short 18,000 teachers across many subject areas (Wong, 1996).

What can be taught, therefore, is an awareness of differences, with learners taking responsibility for their own learning and teaching. This means a change in teaching and learning styles, a change that already has been articulated.

But then, where will learners get the information for teaching themselves to be interculturally aware? One way is through visiting other countries. The idea of traveling internationally is a concept that many Malaysians accept. They hope to enjoy at least one such trip in their lifetime. In other words, most Malaysians like the idea of seeing new lands and meeting different people, but few can afford to do so. For the young, it remains a dream they hope to realize at some distant point in the future.

At the same time, for those whose parents can afford the expense, there is the attraction of tertiary education in another country. Many young Malaysians study abroad, either supported by their parents or government scholarships, choosing to study in such countries as United States, Britain, Australia, New Zealand, Canada, Egypt (and other countries in the Middle East), Taiwan, India, Hong Kong, and Japan. Students also attend universities in Indonesia, the Philippines, Germany, and France.

More Malaysian students will have the opportunity to study abroad for a few weeks now that transfer of credit courses from foreign universities to local universities has been officially sanctioned. The University of Malaya currently allows its students to take courses in foreign universities and transfer the credits to the University of Malaya. The first group of students to do so has been from the Faculty of Education. An arrangement for the transfer of credits from the University of Hawaii began in 1994. However, although those making the exchange have been loud in its praise, appreciating how much they have learned from the visit, not many students can afford the stay of 6 weeks for the first summer session.

Another possibility for intercultural exchange has been opened up through an idea introduced by the prime ministers of Malaysia and New Zealand. They have suggested a work exchange program so that each year a certain number of students from Malaysia could work for a few weeks in New Zealand during their long vacation while the same number of students from New Zealand work in Malaysia during their summer vacation. If this is realized, it will mean a great step forward in encouraging intercultural learning. Students who have been unable to experience life in another culture because of insufficient funds will now be able to support themselves while they are in another country. They probably would still need to raise their own airfares, but the total expenses involved in the experience will be considerably reduced.

Finally, for those who cannot afford to live abroad, the only alternative source of experience appear to be television and literature. However, most of the time this is a method of hit or miss. Teachers who are unacquainted with West African lifestyles, for example, are very likely to misinterpret portions of Achebe's work, and so misguide their students. American television, including MTV, which is so popular among the youth, is often erroneously taken to represent the complete picture of American culture. But even though the media has its limitations, it is still better than ignoring other cultures completely.

The need for intercultural education exists. Implementing a plan of action to carry it out requires a concerted effort. However, although intercultural education could be seen as a massive task highly unlikely to be accomplished in a lifetime, it is necessary for a start to be made. That starting point should be at the teacher education level where, at present, no hint of the necessity of intercultural education is acknowledged. Thus dichotomies exist. Whereas students in residential schools learn at least three languages, teachers are allowed to ignore differences and similarities in the international community. We therefore need to start with the teachers so that the problems required to experience intercultural living are treated with the sensitivity they deserve in the classrooms of the future.

TO CONSIDER

At the present time, Malaysia does not have a well spelled out educational policy nor formal program designed to address multicultural or intercultural education. Rather, such efforts are said to be integrated into the school curriculum in such areas as social studies and moral education. Neither do any special efforts exist at the moment to address such concerns in teacher education programs.

1. Review current newspapers from Malaysia available on the Worldwide Web at www.vol.it/UK/EN/EDICOLA/quot_str.htm#menu. Search for news items that present issues related to the international community, interethnic conflict, immigrant rights and issues, and educational responses to diversity. How do current issues concerning diversity relate to what you have just read?

2. Given the current state of affairs, what would you propose that policymakers and educational professionals should do? On what would you base your argument?

3. What strengths currently exist in the country, in the people, and in the history, which might serve as a source to begin change efforts?

4. What problems would you predict for a nation such as Malaysia if current policy and practice remains in force?

5. Malaysia has seen its share of refugees over the years. Given what you have just read, how would you respond to the scenario presented in chapter 1. What steps should schools take in responding to the needs of newlyarrived immigrant groups?

REFERENCES

Beebout, H. S. (1972). *The production surface for academic achievement: An economic study of Malaysian secondary schools.* Unpublished doctoral dissertation, University of Wisconsin, Madison.

Furnival, J. S. (1948). *Colonial policy and practice.* London: Cambridge University Press.

Gaudart, H. (1992). *Bilingual education in Malaysia..* Townsville, Australia: James Cook University of North Queensland.

Hoopes, D. S. (1979). Intercultural communication concepts and the psychology of intercultural experience. In M. D. Pusch (Ed.), *Multicultural education: A cross-cultural training approach.* Yarmouth, Maine: Intercultural Press.

Ibrahim, S. (1979). *The impact of national medium schools on attitudes related to national integration in peninsular Malaysia.* Unpublished doctoral dissertation, University of Wisconsin, Madison.

Jabatan, P. M. (1996). Internet publication from the Prime Minister's Office [On-line]. Malaysia: Available: http://smpke.jpm.my:1025/gn-data/dasar/dasa24

Koh E. K. (1967). *Education for unity in Malaya.* Chicago: National Sunday School Association, Commission on Research in Christian Education.

Kok L. F. (1978). *Colonial office policy towards education in Malaya 1920–1940.* Unpublished master's thesis, University of Malaya, Kuala Lumpur, Malaysia.

Loh, P. (1976). *Seeds of separation: British politics and education policy in the federated Malay states 1870–1950.* London: Oxford University Press.

Purcell, V. (1948). *The Chinese in Malaysia.* London: Oxford University Press.

Sidney, R. J. H. (1927). *In British Malaya today.* London: Hutchinson.

Stevenson, R. (1975). *Cultivators and administrators.* Kuala Lumpur: Oxford University Press.

Wong S. (1996, May 7). A special focus on the 7th Malaysia plan. *The Star.*

Editor's Remarks

In 1983, the Dutch government officially stated that the Netherlands is a multicultural society, and that most migrants from the former colonies (including the Moluccans, Surinam, and the Dutch Antilles) and the Mediterranean region (Turkey and Morocco in particular) had become immigrants. Today, these immigrants, which make up approximately 6% of the total population of 14 million, are living mostly in cities with populations greater than 100,000.

The ideological discourse concerning immigrants centers around two basic values that permeate Dutch society: equality of opportunity and equivalence of cultures (inclusive of religion). It appears that Islam is fast becoming institutionalized with one fourth of the Muslim children studying Qur'an lessons at the more than 375 mosques.

Under the 1985 Primary Education Act schools must prepare children for life in a multicultural society. After much discussion and debate, the Dutch government has opted for a minorities policy that aims at integration of ethnic minorities as well as the preservation of their cultural identity. There are now policies aimed at eliminating educational arrears, especially among young children of Moroccan and Turkish origin. In addition, a cultural policy composed of monocultural courses (of the country of origin) for minority students and intercultural education for all has been established. Unfortunately, no financial assistance has been made available to institutionalize such practice.

How should a nation with as complex a demographic situation as the Netherlands approach the education of its young? How can a core of teachers from a rather homogeneous background and experience be prepared for the cultural and social complexities they are certain to confront in the classroom and communities? How can the young people in this nation be most effectively prepared to interact with one another?

Chapter 5

Intercultural Education: Approaches in the Netherlands

℘ ◆ ℘

Hans Hooghoff
Resy Delnoy
National Institute for Curriculum Development

It is probably with justification that the Netherlands is regarded as a "rather active nation" when it comes to intercultural education, as Kenneth Cushner wrote in a letter to the authors. However, it is worth considering that there is virtually and inevitably a gulf between theory and practice. This discussion attempts a fairly critical look at both policy and practice in order to sketch a realistic picture.

The chapter begins with a description of the educational system in the Netherlands, including a few developments that have led to the establishment of the current system. The chapter then presents demographic and linguistic data, describes political responses on the part of the educational system to the presence of immigrants in particular, considers the impact of these in educational practice, and describes efforts in teacher training, in particular those that relate to intercultural education.

BRIEF DESCRIPTION OF THE DUTCH EDUCATIONAL SYSTEM

The emphasis in this chapter is on primary education and the foundation course (roughly the first 3 years of secondary education) because these are the types of education normally followed by students as long as they are receiving compulsory education. Other educational aspects are mentioned

92

merely insofar as they are important in the context of the subject of this discussion, namely intercultural education.

The State and Education

The Constitution of 1798 was the origin of education as a field of interest for the national government. The first Agent for National Education was appointed in that year. The underlying theme was that whoever has charge of the children holds the future in their hands. At that time education was essentially what individual teachers imparted to their students, but the various church communities also wanted to exert their influence. The concession the government made to the church groups in the 20th century to maintain the principle of separation of church and state is known as compartmentalization. This is the historical Dutch response to the different natures of specific groups as these differences manifest themselves. The concession also implies the division between state and privately run education as it still exists today. The state is not concerned with religion; in other words, it is secular.

The changes that took place in education in the 1960s were the direct precursors of the current system. Economic growth, the rapid rise in living standards, and an increase in the number of students in those years led to various changes. The state became increasingly involved in the way education was organized, partly from the standpoint that education is extremely important for the quality of a democratic society and also as a motivating force for economic development. One idea here was that there was a great deal of hidden talent among students from lower socioeconomic environments, that this talent could be identified and developed by education, and that students who came from a disadvantaged background could become more involved in the democratic society.

Since the 1970s, an educational priority policy has been followed to tackle arrears in education caused by social inequality. This policy can be summarized as promotion of equal opportunities. In this context consideration should be given, in particular, to the unequal picture that emerges with respect to participation in education and the educational results achieved when students are viewed from the perspective of different social categories, namely social environment, ethnicity, and gender. (Ethnicity is often described as reference to group membership on the basis of common memories, a shared culture and often a common language and religion.)

The underlying concept is that such inequalities can, in principle, be redressed or at least steered in the right direction. After all, it is improbable that the allocation of categories runs parallel to individual differences in talent. Cohort research shows that over 70 years, the relation between the educational level achieved by adults and their environment of origin has become more distant (Storimans, 1993). This supports the policy that equality of opportunities is served by further growth in participation in education.

A distinctive feature of the current educational system is that it combines a centralized education policy with decentralized administration and management of schools. The brief of the Minister of Education and Science is to control education by means of legislation and regulation, having due regard for the provisions of the Constitution. The main tasks of central government relate to its responsibilities for structuring and funding, for the provision of state education, and for inspection, examinations, and student grants and loans. The government also bears legal responsibility for the promotion of innovation in education.

The administration and management of schools is organized at the local level. The municipal authorities are the competent authorities for state schools. The competent authorities for privately run schools are foundations or associations. There is little difference between the powers of the governing bodies of state and those of privately run schools. A distinguishing feature is that the governing body of a state school may not refuse admittance to students on the grounds of their ethical beliefs, whereas the governing bodies of privately run schools do not have to meet this criterion. The number of competent authorities for schools in the Netherlands is approximately 6,300. Almost 70% of students attend privately run schools.

The Constitution guarantees freedom of education and religion. There is separation between church and state and there is no state religion. Freedom of education is guaranteed under Article 23, which relates to: (a) the freedom of groups to found schools and provide education in accordance with their religious or other—ethical or educational—convictions, (b) the financial equality of education in both state and privately run schools, and (c) the responsibility of the local authority to guarantee adequate provision of state schools.

According to the Constitution, state education must honor the religion or philosophy of all students. It is the task of the state school to expose ethno- and cultocentrism. A privately run school is allowed to propound a vision that differs from the task of state education. Because equivalent demands have to be laid down for education in both state and privately run schools, the regulations for both types of schools must produce an adequate effect, taking the "direction" into account (Storimans, 1993). The qualitative standards set by the Ministry of Education apply to education in both state and privately run schools. They determine the subjects to be studied, the numbers of lessons to be provided, attainment targets and examination syllabuses, and national examinations.

The 1969 Compulsory Education Act states that every child must receive full-time education from the first school day in the month after his or her fifth birthday until the end of the school year in which the student attains the age of 16 or has completed at least 12 full years of schooling. At least part-time education is compulsory until the age of 18. In practice, nearly all children attend school from the age of 4 years. In 1989 expenditure on education accounted for 7 % of the gross national product and amounted to 2,000 Dutch Guilders per head of population.

Types of Schooling

The education system is comprised of the following: (a) primary education for children between the ages of 4 and 12 years; (b) privately run primary and secondary education for students of all ages from 3 to 20 years who have special educational needs; (c) secondary education for students who have completed primary education, available in the forms of lower general secondary education (MAVO) for students ages 12 to 16 years; (d) higher general secondary education (HAVO) for students ages 12 to 17 years; (e) preuniversity education (VWO) for students ages 12 to 18 years; (f) prevocational education (VBO) for students ages 12 to 16 years; (g) intermediate vocational education (MBO) for students ages 16 to approximately 19; (h) adult general secondary education (VAVO); and (i) higher education, which is subdivided into higher vocational education (HBO) for students ages of 18 to 22 years, university education at the undergraduate level (WO) for students ages of 18 to 22 years, the open university for students ages 18 and older, and part-time vocational courses and adult education.

Primary Education

In 1989 almost 1.5 million children were receiving primary education in more than 8,000 schools: 35% were state schools and 65% privately run schools. Primary education is free, although some schools do demand a parental contribution. In 1989 about 29% of children receiving primary education were attending Protestant schools, and about 33% were attending Roman Catholic schools. A few Jewish, Islamic, and Hindu schools exist. These groups, as Catholics and Protestants did in the past, make use of the possibilities offered by the system. There are also privately run nondenominational schools, usually operating on specific educational principles, such as those of Montessori, Petersen, and Steiner.

More immigrant students attend state schools than privately run schools, although the proportion of immigrant students attending Protestant and Catholic schools is substantial, irrespective of the ethnic origin of the students concerned. Nonreligious privately run schools with a strong pedagogic profile, such as Montessori schools, are far less attractive to immigrant communities (Fase, 1994).

In primary schools, the official school year runs from August 1 to July 31. There is a 6-week summer holiday. The minimum number of school days per year is 200. Children in the first four forms attend school for 22.5 hours a week, whereas older students attend for 25 hours a week.

Primary teachers are qualified to teach all subjects to all age groups. In addition, a school may have a few specialist teachers, for example for physical education, music, Turkish, or Frisian. The student–teacher ratio is about 1 to 22. More than 60% of teachers are women.

In principle, primary schools provide 8 consecutive years of schooling. Schools are free to decide on their own internal organization. A common arrangement is eight forms, each with children of the same age. Primary education helps to lay the foundation for children to go on to secondary education. The objectives of primary education, as laid down in the Primary Education Act, are to promote the emotional, intellectual, and creative development of the child and to further the acquisition of essential knowledge as well as social, cultural, and physical skills. The aim is for a steady, uninterrupted process of development. Concerning this aspect, it is important that under the 1985 Act there is a legal requirement for teaching to take due account of the fact that students are growing up in a multicultural society. Since 1990, schools have been required to include what is known as a broader care section in the school plan of action. That is, the school must define, among other things, what facilities are available for students who have learning and development difficulties.

Schools are free to draw up their own teaching curriculum, although this must always include the following subjects, if possible in an integrated form: sensory and physical education; Dutch; mathematics; English; various factual subjects, including geography, history and science (biology), sociology (including civics) and religious movements; creative activities, including the use of language, drawing, music, handicrafts, play, and movement; and self-reliance (i.e., social and life skills, including road safety; and health instruction). Schools in the province of Friesland are also required to teach Frisian and may conduct some lessons in that language. Students with a non-Dutch background may also receive some lessons in their own mother tongue.

Teaching Staff in Primary Education.   The average age of teachers has shown a gradual rise to 39 in recent years. More than 95% of teachers completed their training before 1985, that is, before the introduction of the reforms affecting primary schools. The majority of teachers have many years of experience and have been working in their current school for some considerable time. There are few teachers of non-Dutch nationality working in primary education.

Secondary Education

Secondary education is schooling provided for students, generally at the age of 12 years, who have completed state or privately run primary education. Almost 12% of students in their first year of secondary education have one parent born outside the Netherlands. Several secondary schools offering different types of education may be combined in a single school. Since the academic year 1993–1994, all preuniversity education (VWO), higher general secondary education (HAVO), lower general secondary education (MAVO) and prevocational education (VBO) courses have all started with a foundation course. In principle, the foundation course is a 3-year course providing a broad general education in which no strict distinction is made between general and technical subjects. Schools can spread the foundation course over a period of at least 2 years and no more than 4 years.

As in primary education, every secondary school produces its own school plan of action, giving an overview of the school organization and course content and a schedule of lessons. Subjects are taught by teachers qualified to teach one or more subjects. For the first 3 years of VWO, HAVO, MAVO and VBO courses, all students must follow a compulsory core curriculum of 15 subjects (the allotted time is 3,000 hours). The remaining 20% of the time available (840 hours) is devoted to additional subjects chosen by the school.

Although not obligatory, the recommended subject breakdown over the 3-year period is as follows:

Dutch, 400 hours
English, 280 hours
second foreign language (French, German), 240 hours
mathematics, 400 hours
biology, 120 hours
physics and chemistry, 200 hours
computer and information technology literacy, 20 hours
history and civics, 200 hours
geography, 140 hours
economics, 80 hours
technology, 180 hours

social and life skills, 100 hours
visual arts, music, dance and drama (at least two of these), 280 hours
physical education, 360 hours

The remaining 20% of the time can be used for subjects such as Latin, religious instruction, teaching in the student's mother tongue, prevocational subjects, subjects from the core curriculum, individual tuition, or study and career guidance.

During the foundation course, students receive a minimum of 1,000 50-minute teaching periods in the subjects of the core curriculum in each academic year. The relation between the foundation course and VWO, HAVO, MAVO, and VBO is defined in the school's plan of action. At the end of the second year of the foundation course, students are given a recommendation on what further course of study they should follow by the competent authority.

The school-leaving examinations for VWO, HAVO, and MAVO are made up of national examinations and examinations set by the school. The examinations set by the school are held in all subjects during the final year of the course and are marked internally. The national examination for each subject is the same for all students attending a given type of school, and all candidates sit for the examination at the same time. A student's final grade is the arithmetic mean of the grade achieved in the internal examination and the grade achieved in the national examination. Marks are awarded on a scale ranging from 1 (very poor) to 10 (excellent).

Education is free for all students up to the age of 16 years. However, there are costs to be met in the purchase of books and teaching materials. Students 16 years and older have to pay annual tuition fees, the level of which is set each year. In 1990–1991, 683,662 students were receiving secondary general education in a total of 1,242 schools. They were taught by a total of 37,143 teachers, of whom 25,961 were men and 11,182 women. There were 232,823 students (140,777 boys and 92,046 girls) who followed VBO courses taught by a total of 15,975 teachers, of whom 11,648 were men and 4,327 women.

DEMOGRAPHIC DATA

The Netherlands has a population of about 15.5 million living in an area of 41,864 km^2. The population density is highest in the west of the country. About 90% of the population is indigenous if nonindigenous is defined as one or both parents having been born abroad. In the Dutch context, certain groups of immigrants are often referred to in terms of cultural minorities. This term corresponds to the terms ethnic, religious or linguistic minorities, used in the international context (Storimans, 1993).

The breakdown of the population according to religion gives the following picture: In 1991, Roman Catholics made up the largest group (34%), followed by members of the Dutch Reformed Church (17%) and the Reformed Church (8 %). Moslems account for 3.7 % of the population, and Hindus 0.5%. About 37 % of the population practice no religion. Recent decades have seen a society based on denominations become the most secular country in Europe.

Demography offers no easy means of defining and registering nonindigenous groups. Large groups of the population, such as those originating in Surinam, the Antilles/Aruba, and the Moluccas, were not born in the Netherlands but do have Dutch nationality. It is not easy to obtain an accurate picture as to how the ratio of indigenous to nonindigenous population relates to the ratio of inhabitants holding passports of the country of residence to inhabitants holding passports of their country of origin, because naturalization procedures can be started after 5 years of residence. Anyone who remains legally in the Netherlands for more than 5 years can obtain a residence permit, which is valid for an unrestricted period but expires in the event that the holder moves abroad. As for the four largest minority groups, about three quarters of the Turkish and Moroccan heads of households hold such a residence permit.

If the regulations are left out of consideration, it is even more difficult to decide how many generations it takes for members of a minority group of foreign origin to become part of the indigenous population. Government policy does not regard inhabitants belonging to the third generation of nonindigenous immigrants as part of a group having nonindigenous origin.

Although there has always been immigration, over the past 30 years the number of immigrants has become appreciably greater than the number of emigrants. It therefore follows that the Netherlands has de facto become a country of permanent immigration. This fact is acknowledged by the government and the majority of political parties, but it is also admitted that there is still a lack of suitable, well considered, and coherent political measures (Kroon & Ton, 1992).

The fact that the Netherlands was a colonial power for a long time has contributed to the levels of immigration. More than half of the ethnic minority groups originate from the former colonies of Surinam, the Netherlands Antilles, and what is now Indonesia. The latter group includes the subgroup of those born in the Moluccas. Immigration from the Indonesian archipelago took place mainly in the 1940s and 1950s. Immigrants from Surinam and the Caribbean islands emigrated to the Netherlands mainly in the past 30 years.

The next largest group of immigrants is made up of those known as guest workers and their families. The members of this group come from the countries around the Mediterranean and arrived mainly during the past 30 years. Although guest working has existed since the mid-1950s, it was not until the end of the 1960s and the early 1970s that the families started to be reunited. Approximately half of this group is made up of Turks. Moroccans form the next largest group.

Asylum seekers make up a third group of immigrants. The number of refugees and, more particularly, the number of children of refugees is not known (Tesser, 1993). However, compared with the total migrant population, their numbers are very small. Since 1945, approximately 40,000 refugees have been granted asylum, the largest groups being Czechs (in 1948 and 1968), Hungarians (1956), Eritreans/Ethiopians (since 1970), and Vietnamese (since 1976) (Kabden, Meijer, & Veen, 1991). Various small groups also have been admitted, such as Turkish Christians, Ugandans, and Kurds. In recent years refugees have been arriving from a large number of countries and include Iranians, Tamils, Syrians, Ghanaians, Somalis, and Pakistanis. Between 1980 and 1989 approximately 50,000 people applied for asylum of whom about 7,000 were granted refugee status.

The fourth group of immigrants is made up of those who for the most part originate from Western industrialized nations. The number of illegal immigrants is estimated to be 100,000.

On the basis of sociocultural criteria, immigrants can be subdivided into two large subgroups (Kroon & Vallen, 1992). The first includes immigrants and their children born in the Western industrialized nations or other comparable countries. Their sociocultural background does not differ from that of the indigenous population, or does so only to a slight extent. This group (e. g., Germans, French, Belgian, British and Americans) generally finds few problems with regard to participation in society. The second subgroup includes immigrants and their children whose sociocultural background differs substantially from that of the indigenous population (e.g., Turks, Moroccans, Surinamese, Chinese, and Moluccans). This group makes up the majority of the immigrant population. The majority of these immigrants generally encounter considerable problems in the various social domains, including education.

The immigrant population is not uniformly distributed over the country. A very large proportion of the immigrant population lives in the four large cities of Amsterdam, Rotterdam, The Hague, and Utrecht. More than half of the Surinamese community, for example, lives in these areas. Of all immigrant children, more than half attend schools in the 17 Dutch towns having a population of 100,000 or more. High concentrations of students from a single immigrant community are rare. More than three fourths of all schools have only a few or no nonindigenous students. In addition, there are a number of schools that cater exclusively to nonindigenous students (Islamic and Hindu schools and schools with a high concentration of nonindigenous students). Schools in the major cities have high percentages of nonindigenous students.

Languages

The national language is Dutch, which is a Germanic language. This is the official language and also the language used in schools. In the province of Friesland, Frisian is spoken by approximately 400,000 people and is the official language of the provincial and local councils. In Friesland, lessons are given in both Dutch and Frisian. Schools are legally obliged to teach Frisian, but there are no regulations concerning the scope and content of the teaching.

Dutch is the standard language in education. However, Frisian or any other local dialect in common use may be chosen as the language of instruction. For reception of students having a non-Dutch cultural background and for their integration into the educational system, the student's mother tongue also may be used as the preferred language for instruction.

Although the available data on countries of origin and numbers of nonindigenous inhabitants are fairly accurate, the information available with regard to the languages spoken by these people is quite poor. The number of languages in use has grown and continues to grow, and it is difficult for teachers and schools to respond in an adequate manner. One problem is that it is often unclear what languages are involved and the significance of these to those who speak them. Given the diversity of the immigrant population outlined earlier, it can be said that the diversity in languages is enormous.

POLITICAL RESPONSES TO THE PRESENCE OF IMMIGRANTS IN EDUCATION

In this section, the policy that developed over the years is discussed, beginning with the relation between policy and research. The next section begins with the general policy for tackling the problems of those who have fallen behind, because this policy is coupled in a later stage with the policy for tackling the educational disadvantages of nonindigenous students. Immigrants frequently find that they have fallen behind for various reasons. Topics relating specifically to minorities are then discussed, including teaching in the student's mother tongue and culture (Onderwijs in Eigen Taal, en Cultuur [OETCC]) and teaching in Dutch as a second language (Onderwijs in Nederlands als tweedetaal [NT2]). Topics that affect minorities and relate to the entire population then follow, including intercultural education (intercultureel onderwijs [ICO]) and measures to tackle discrimination and racism. In the discussion of these four topics, the educational system in practice and current proposals for change also are considered in addition to policy.

Policy and Research

In the Netherlands the term "minority research" is used in reference to research relating to immigrants. There has been substantial growth in minority research in recent decades. In contrast to the practice elsewhere, where attention is also paid to more general processes, research in the Netherlands usually is restricted to matters concerning immigrants. The focus is mainly on the problems of ethnic minorities, such as integration and education of minorities. Theoretical studies are fairly rare, which may explain why Dutch research plays a modest role when considered on the international scale. The bulk of the research is focused on policy, much of which is commissioned by the government. Because the government sees research mainly as an instrument, it is interested almost exclusively in policy-oriented research into acute social problems.

Tackling the Problems of Those Who Have Fallen Behind

Provision of equal opportunities for a successful school career and exploitation of all available talents are two factors that have led to the development of a policy for tackling and, as far as possible, eliminating the problems of those who have fallen behind in education, especially the children of unskilled workers. In the 1974 Policy Plan for the education of groups that have fallen behind, only a few nonindigenous children were designated as a target group. It was recognized that there were parallels between the children of foreign employees and Dutch children of unskilled workers, but at that time it was still assumed that immigrant children would return with their parents to their country of origin.

By the time the Policy Plan was published in 1974, the first oil crisis had already taken place. The economy was stagnating, and a restrictive policy was in force on the admittance of foreigners. Since that time, migrants have been admitted on humanitarian grounds because of international obligations in the European Union (EU) context or because of national interest. Admittance on humanitarian grounds covers highly divergent categories: reuniting of families, establishment of families, the admittance of asylum seekers, the reception of displaced persons, and the granting of asylum. Admittance for the purposes of reuniting and establishing families is based on international law. Admittance of asylum seekers is decided in each individual case. Admittance on the grounds of national interest relates almost exclusively to the migration of labor. In the case of non-EU residents, admissions on these grounds is, in principle, permitted only when there are no opportunities within the EU nations for meeting labor shortfalls.

Until the early 1980s, there was a separate educational policy laid down in the Policy Plan for Cultural Minorities in Education for minority students. The Plan names four points addressed by the policy with respect to minorities in education: tackling the wide-ranging educational disadvantages of students from the minorities, initiating measures for the initial assimilation of students coming into the Dutch system from elsewhere, teaching student's in their mother tongue and culture, and providing intercultural education.

Since 1980 a policy has been developed to tackle the educational disadvantages of cultural minorities. This policy relates not only to the children of foreign employees, but also to children whose country of origin is the Moluccas, Surinam, the Netherlands, the Antilles, or Aruba. The premise here was that the majority of families from minority groups in the Netherlands would remain in the country. The policy on minorities was developed and implemented during this time.

Since 1983 the policy has been directed toward ethnic groups that are socially disadvantaged and for whose presence the government has accepted a certain degree of responsibility. The reasons for this vary. Some groups (refugees) have come to the Netherlands at the invitation of the government. Other groups have a colonial past that plays a role, and in the case of many immigrants who have come to take up work, the government bears a special responsibility as a consequence of recruiting agreements with the countries of origin. The policy on minorities also covers travelers and gypsies. The reason for the inclusion of these categories is historical and dates from the time when the concept of nonconformity was important (Lucassen & Köbben, 1992). The largest target groups under the policy on minorities are the Surinamese, Turks, Moroccans, and those from the Antilles/Aruba.

In defining its policy, the government places the emphasis on socioeconomic disadvantages. As a consequence, the insight into the ethnic–cultural differences, which are important for many minority groups, fades into the background and is often equated with disadvantage. As a result, certain ethnic groups are left out of consideration. European Union nationals are excluded from any specific policy, as are third-generation nonindigenous inhabitants. The government puts forward this policy as a way of implementing of Article 27 of the International Convention on civil and political rights (Storimans, 1993).

In the 1970s and 1980s the socioeconomic position of minorities, which for the majority of the groups was already not advantageous, deteriorated further. At the same time, there was a substantial increase in the numbers belonging to minority groups (Tesser, 1993). To cope with the aforementioned problems, the emphasis of the policy on minorities was shifted further toward the integration of the minorities into society. Education and labor were the most important points of attack.

However, toward the end of the 1980s it became apparent that, despite all the initiatives, there had been hardly any improvement in the social position of ethnic minorities, which still exhibited high unemployment, disappointing educational results, and a lack of participation in society. The policy regulations for indigenous and nonindigenous disadvantaged groups were then combined in the Educational Priority Policy. Under this policy there were fewer special regulations for ethnic minorities, and greater emphasis was placed on regulations for students coming from a low socioeconomic background. Integration of the educational policy for minorities with the stimulation policy led to OETCC and ICO also being incorporated into the priority policy. This led to a coupling of policy relating to cultural differences with policy relating to disadvantaged groups, which many felt to be undesirable. After all, the OETCC, and certainly the ICO, had objectives which had nothing to do with improving the position of those at a disadvantage (Tesser, 1993).

Even though there is still a long way to go, the educational standards achieved by the younger generation of minority groups are showing an upward trend. However, Moroccan and Turkish students in particular achieve significantly and substantially lower scores in the standard language and math tests at the end of primary schooling than do other groups (Fase, 1994). Nonindigenous students tend to do well in foreign languages in secondary education. When selecting the subjects for their final examinations, they choose, on the average, more foreign languages than do their indigenous classmates. Also on the average, they achieve somewhat better grades in French and German.

There also has been progress in the numbers of students from minority groups following higher forms of secondary education and higher vocational education. However, nonindigenous students are still clearly behind compared with indigenous students. Of the indigenous population, those from the Antilles and Surinam are coming closest to the educational standards.

More nonindigenous than indigenous students are leaving school with no qualifications.. For instance, in 1993–1994 30% of students with parents born in the Antilles, Surinam, the Moluccas, Morocco, or Turkey dropped out of school. The corresponding percentage for students with Dutch parents or parents of other ethnic groups is 17%. The figure for students with parents born in "another country" is somewhere in between. In general, nonindigenous students are three to four times more likely to drop out of education than students whose parents were born in the Netherlands (Bosma, 1994).

The position of ethnic groups in education is still weak. This can be explained by the relatively short time that many students have lived in the Netherlands, inadequate knowledge of Dutch, and the low educational standards and behavior of their parents. The measures taken by the government to promote improvement in education for ethnic groups include improvements in the general educational policy, supplemented when necessary by specific measures and the social renovation policy. One specific measure is teaching the student's in their mother tongue (and culture).

Teaching in the Student's Mother Tongue and Culture (OETCC)

To understand OETCC, it seems worthwhile here to focus attention on a striking characteristic of the Dutch OETCC, the fact that this policy has undergone various fundamental changes in course. The functions of the OETCC have been redefined several times. For quite some time the government adopted an ad hoc approach in response to the arrival and presence of immigrants. The fact that the policy has hardly any basis in empirical research also plays a role. Although a relatively large amount of research has been carried out with respect to OETCC, there has been little research to establish the effects of the various measures and virtually no research into the validity of the basic premises. The vast majority of the research carried out has been aimed at application, addressing the demand for specification of OETCC (Lucassen & Kobben, 1992).

The legal system has provided opportunities for specific teaching in ethnic minority languages during normal school hours in primary schools since the mid 1970s. It was decided that this teaching should focus on, inter alia, access to cultural heritage. With a pluralistic vision in view, this teaching offers nonindigenous groups the opportunity of maintaining and developing their own language and culture. The important feature here is the right to education in the official standard language of the country of origin (with the exception of the Moluccans and Turkish Armenians, who have the right to education in the language spoken at home).

This right to education in the official standard language of the country of origin is enjoyed by those groups that fall under the official policy on minorities and whose official mother tongue is not Dutch. This means, for example, that Chinese are excluded (on the basis of their socioeconomic status), as are the children of Surinam and Antilles nationals (on the basis of language). The policy on minorities relates to the following groups: groups and individuals living in caravans, members of ethnic minority groups legally residing in the Netherlands insofar as these groups are Moluccans, inhabitants whose mother country is Surinam or the Netherlands Antilles, foreign workers and their families from the region around the Mediterranean, gypsies, and refugees.

The government has based its selection of the groups that come under consideration for OETCC partly on the European Community guideline of July 25, 1977. The latter relates to the education of immigrant workers' children and to children whose parents originate from countries having a recruitment agreement with the Netherlands (Storimans, 1993). On financial grounds, the OETCC had to be restricted to large groups of students. The selection also was based on consultations with education experts and claims put forward by ethnic minority groups and their spokesmen. Consequently, the inner logic determining what groups are in or out is far from obvious (Fase, 1994).

Until 1980, the OETCC policy encouraged people to return to their mother country. After that date, more psychologic functions have been assigned to OETCC, and this area has acquired a supporting function for intercultural education. The function therefore is shifting in the direction of support for learning Dutch and other skills. The cultural component is being switched to intercultural education.

The regulations of OETCC regarding secondary education compare with those for primary education, although the number of minority languages available is still restricted to Turkish and Arabic as optional subjects. As yet, these languages can be chosen only by Turkish and Moroccan students. Arguments are being put forward to make these subjects available to all students, partly to improve the standing of the subjects.

Education in the Students's Mother Tongue and Culture in Practice. Teaching in the student's mother tongue is, first of all, the responsibility of schools and their governing bodies, which decide whether to provide such lessons as well as the time allotted, the methods used, and the pedagogic orientation. Little research data is available on OETCC in practice. Most of the data relate to the largest language groups: the Turks and the Moroccans. In the 1990–1991 school year, more than 66,000 primary schoolchildren received teaching in their mother tongue and culture in a total of 1,200 schools. The language groups concerned included (in descending order): Turkish, 32,297; Moroccan, 28,266;

Moluccan, 1,656; Cape Verdian, 1,128; Spanish, 965; Portuguese, 615; Serbs/Croats, 554; Italian, 274; Greek, 241; and Tunisian, 209.

A full 85% of this teaching takes place during school hours. Outside of school this type of teaching is given only to students who come from the former Yugoslavia, Greece, Portugal, Italy Spain, and those belonging to the smaller language groups.

OETCC lessons predominantly consist of language learning and activities relating to the culture and society of the country of origin, with religion playing only a minor role. In the lower school, the focus in language teaching is on learning new vocabulary and concepts. In the upper school, formal aspects such as spelling and grammar play an important role. Speaking and listening is practiced in reading lessons. The lessons on the student's own culture place considerable emphasis on the geography and history of the country of origin. These lessons usually summarize the education given in the country of origin.

A large proportion of these lessons are given by teachers who have obtained their teaching qualifications in the country of origin. They often do not have the expertise to give these lessons in a way that supports the learning of Dutch. Many OETCC teachers work at several schools.

Partly because the policy in the majority of cases prescribes that the standard language of the country of origin must be the language taught, and because for many children this is not the language spoken at home, teaching in the students' mother tongue is not proving very beneficial. In the case of Moroccans, Kurds, Moluccans, and Cape Verdians, among others, the language spoken at home differs from the national language. A further important factor in determining the returns from OETCC is the difference in the degrees of proficiency reached by students in their own language. There is a relationship between these differences and the length of time the child has been in the Netherlands and whether the student is a first-, second-, or third-generation immigrant. Even in the case of groups for which the language taught in the OETCC lessons is the same as that spoken at home, OETCC teachers are confronted with students who speak Dutch at home and for whom their mother tongue is a foreign language.

Proposals for Change. A few proposals for change, put forward on the basis of the data on OETCC teaching in practice, are under discussion. Three changes are proposed: (a) The OETCC must be awarded independent status because of the fundamental right of nonindigenous groups to development of their own cultural identity. To this end, teaching must pay attention to the student's own language and cultural elements, such as the geography and history of the countries of origin. (b) The OETCC must be organized entirely outside school hours. The argument in favor of this is that under current practice, when OETCC is given in school hours, nonindigenous students usually miss a significant proportion (about 10%) of the normal curriculum. (c) The OETCC must be based on demand and, in principle, must be available to all nonindigenous groups. This implies that more groups than hitherto will have a right to this form of education.

Dutch as a Second Language

In contrast to ICO and OETCC, educational policy with regard to NT2 (Dutch as a second language) is less well defined—there is no legislation. Since the 1970s, the policy has provided for the establishment of so-called link classes: Children are given intensive NT2 language lessons in the centrally organized classes, then are integrated into the normal education system. Although the government made funds available, it was not involved in the organization or curriculum for this type of teaching. This led to a wide diversity in teaching practice because the schools were responsible for teacher qualifications, course content, course material, and the transfer of students into the normal education system (Fase, 1994).

Since 1981, the education policy has underlined the importance of NT2 for children from minority groups. Since 1988 a memorandum has been in effect that incorporates measures for improving the quality of NT2. Schools have three options for obtaining additional teacher hours or financial support for NT2. The majority of schools opt for the regulation under which the teacher–student ratio per class is reduced, which often means that no explicit NT2 teaching is given.

Dutch as a Second Language in Practice.   In practice, a differentiation is made between NT2 lessons given to students entering the primary school system at the compulsory age for starting school and those given to immigrant students entering the school at a later stage. The measures for those entering school at a later stage have led to the establishment of various methods for the reception of these children: integrated, central, and combined reception.

In the case of *integrated* reception, the students enter an ordinary primary school in the same class as other students and merely receive additional lessons in Dutch as a second language. *Central* reception is used in special reception schools that cater solely to older children entering the Dutch educational system. In the case of *combined* reception, the children of immigrant parents entering the Dutch system spend half their time in a special reception school and the remainder in an ordinary primary school. In practice, students in the central and the combined reception schools are given appreciably more hours of language teaching than those in the integrated reception system. In the case of central reception, problems arise on transfer to the ordinary primary school. As a result, language development stagnates, and the benefit of the reception year can be lost (Tesser, 1993).

In general, children of immigrant parents starting school at the normal starting age are given few NT2 lessons because many schools hold the view that children born in the Netherlands have no need for special lessons as they already have some knowledge of Dutch. As a consequence, quite a few immigrant children have to learn Dutch as a second language at the same time they must be learning other subjects in that language, while receiving very little extra help. The NT2 course material for those starting to learn Dutch is better developed than that for students at a more advanced stage.

Since the end of the 1980s, when a survey revealed the existence of four significant bottlenecks, more attention has been paid to the quality of NT2 teaching. The first bottleneck was that teachers have inadequate knowledge and are insufficiently qualified in NT2 teaching and acquisition. The second bottleneck was that there were insufficient teaching aids of adequate quality for NT2. A third bottleneck was the lack of solutions to specific problems that immigrant children entering school both at the normal starting age and later have with Dutch. As far as the fourth bottleneck is concerned—the lack of coordination and direction of developments in NT2 at the national level—a scientific project group has recently been set up in an attempt to find a solution.

Proposals for Change. The task of the aforementioned project group is central monitoring and coordination of the content of national and local initiatives regarding NT2. The project group is further required to stimulate support for new initiatives and experiments regarding both content and funding. This group has annual funds of 5 to 10 million Guilders available. Schools can submit project proposals to this group, either individually or together with others. Among other things, the project group has taken the initiative to improve teaching in such a way that both Dutch nationals with poor language skills and immigrants for whom Dutch is a second language are both able to benefit. New training programs have been developed for the acquisition of Dutch as a second language and for the initial reception of new arrivals, and these were introduced in the 1992–1993 school year. These programs are intended for teachers in primary and secondary schools, and for those following the various teacher training courses. One problem facing the implementation of modernization proposals on a broader scale is that teachers follow further education courses only on a voluntary basis. There is not a great deal of interest in further education courses in NT2.

Intercultural Education (ICO)

Stimulated by an influential committee, the aim since 1979 has been to devise policies for intercultural education that have specific meaning not only for immigrant students or students from ethnic minorities, but also for the dominant groups in the school system. There has always been a strong emphasis on mutual understanding, or "acculturation", as it has been defined in official documents. Beyond this, further objectives for intercultural education also have been introduced, especially since 1987. The change accents possible cognitive benefits (knowledge and understanding of ethnic diversity) as well as various social and moral benefits (the fight against ethnic prejudice, discrimination, and racism). Initially, ICO was regarded as a topic that could be dealt with in the context of certain other subjects, such as geography and history. Later, the belief was that ICO not only is an education principle for all areas of learning and education, but that it also has consequences for relations with parents as well as the composition of the teaching staff and of the various representative bodies in the school.

In recent years many initiatives have been taken on behalf of and in schools to promote ICO. But despite the numerous efforts on the part of teaching staff and others, ICO still occupies a less important place in educational practice than many would desire. There are various reasons for this. Monoethnic schools can easily neglect multicultural teaching, whereas multiethnic schools can hardly escape it. The diversity of response in terms of subject areas, teaching methods, and teacher qualifications is enormous. In addition, when ICO was introduced, little attention was paid to the implementation of the new measures. The policy was vague, and this stood in the way of introduction, certainly as far as new and identity-sensitive tasks were concerned. Furthermore, the influx of nonindigenous students since 1978 has meant that schools have been faced with massive problems that demand an adequate response.

Although there is a substantial degree of consensus regarding the need to pay attention in primary schools to the fact that Dutch society is multicultural and multiethnic, schools are still experiencing substantial problems in putting this into practice. In the classroom, ICO is often reactive teaching, in which teachers react to interethnic or intercultural situations. However, the majority of teachers lack specific training to cope with such situations. Among other things, the lack of teacher training in ICO and the fairly slow circulation of course material cause educational practice to lag behind the ideas on good ICO. Because the majority of teachers in the profession at present were trained in a single culture and a single language, they have been able to develop little sensitivity for what is different. As a result, little attention is paid to heterogeneity in the classroom, or this is regarded as a phenomenon that is not important as far as teaching is concerned (Delnoy, 1995).

Teaching in the Netherlands is still highly text-oriented compared with that in other countries. For students who do not have a good grasp of Dutch—and these are frequently the multilingual students—this often leads to difficulties because inadequate understanding of a text can lead to mistakes or incomplete understanding of concepts. In addition, many teachers hold the opinion that children born in the Netherlands and able to cope with everyday Dutch will also be able to grasp the cognitively more difficult school language. As a result, some problems remain undiscovered and unsolved. Furthermore, Dutch is mainly taught as the mother tongue, virtually without any regard to the linguistic background of the student population. This implies, inter alia, that when dealing with questions of grammar and spelling teachers often appeal to the linguistic intuition of the students. The fact that there can be great differences in the linguistic intuitions of the children, depending on their linguistic backgrounds, is not always sufficiently recognized.

However, the presence of multilingual children in the educational system also has led to changes that can be understood under the term "intercultural education". Teachers have made changes in the way they teach in order to improve the results achieved by multilingual children. For instance, they have adopted a more classical approach, giving an oral explanation of difficult written texts. They assign more exercises and pay greater attention to the meanings of words. Furthermore, the acquisition and application of learning strategies have become an aspect of education. It is considered that once students are aware of learning strategies, they are able to work independently. This creates time for the teacher to help individual students who are not able to cope with the material on their own.

The development of ICO in secondary education is, in general, lagging behind that in primary education. Here, too, it is difficult to translate the objectives into course content. For example, an analytic study investigated the content for general education in the first stage of secondary education (Schreuder, 1995). It was though that general education would provide "shared culture", a term that has two meanings. In both meanings the element of communality and generality comes to the fore, either as the result of general education or as its content. The current communality of the subjects in the foundation course is not its starting point but its end objective. Dutch language and history should be the subjects that provide a shared cultural basis for all students. However, this basis at present consists mainly of typically Dutch and European cultural elements. The conclusion is that assimilation is apparently one of the unexpressed (social) objectives of the foundation course (Schreuder, 1995).

Proposals for Change. A fairly influential committee has urged that ICO be implemented in such a way that it becomes possible for all schools to achieve the legal target in the short term. In pursuing this goal, account must be taken of two developments taking place.

The first development is the increasingly multicultural nature of society as a consequence of nonindigenous families arriving. The nonindigenous groups represent a range of cultures and subcultures. The second development relates to the increasing participation of the Netherlands in international contexts, in particular, the European context. Numerous changes result from the increased blurring of national borders. According to the committee, education must prepare students for this new situation. The committee, consequently, has laid down two minimum requirements for the new ICO. The first requires that teaching provide basic material on the ethnocultural diversity of Dutch society and the growing collaboration within Europe. This knowledge must contribute to the development of European awareness and respect for other cultures. Internationalization thus offers new opportunities for bringing multicultural society up to date, especially for schools that have only a few or no nonindigenous students.

The second requirement is that an antidiscrimination policy be followed. To this end teaching materials must be screened for prejudice and discrimination and for intercultural content. A further factor here is that schools must follow guidelines relating to the occurrence of discrimination and methods for tackling it. A further topic in the discussion on desirable ICO is education promoted via international law and directed toward and explicitly concerned with human rights.

Tackling Discrimination and Racism

Tackling discrimination and racism has a longer tradition outside than inside the educational system. Various organizations provide information and disseminate material in this regard. The Anne Frank Foundation in Amsterdam, which regularly organizes exhibitions and conducts the aforementioned activities, is internationally renowned.

In recent years so-called discrimination report points or bureaus have been set up. These usually are independent foundations or associations to which people can turn with complaints about discrimination. The bureaus deal with the complaints by mediation or sometimes by taking legal action. In some cases, the bureaus also can refer people to another institution. Apart from dealing with complaints, which is their primary task, the bureaus also conduct public information activities, advise on policy, and carry out small-scale research concerning discrimination complaints. A number of organizations also have a documentation department. In 1993 there were 44 report points.

Various government agencies are involved in tackling discrimination and racism. Since 1990, the Ministry of Justice has had a coordinator who is responsible for monitoring and stimulating the antidiscrimination policy of both this department and that of the Public Prosecutor. An antiracism program aimed specifically at schoolchildren and organizations working for young people began in 1993. The initiative was taken by the ministries responsible for education and culture.

Tackling Discrimination and Racism in Education. As yet, little research has investigated interethnic and intercultural classroom situations and conflicts and the way in which teachers handle and should handle these. However, primary schools report that hardly any racist incidents occur. When these do arise, the teachers are expected to take direct corrective action, and the majority do so. Racist incidents in secondary education would appear to be more numerous and also more serious. However, there is no accurate data, and there are no indications that teachers adopt a negative attitude toward students from ethnic–cultural groups. It is a fact, however, that the majority of teachers are not trained in dealing with interethnic situations and conflicts.

The majority of schools still have no rules of conduct for students, teachers, and parents with regard to discriminating behavior. One complaint is that nonindigenous parents are insufficiently involved in education. Moreover, nonindigenous groups are hardly represented as school principals, group teachers, members of or the school council, parents' council or board of governors. Conferences and other meetings on the prevention and tackling of discrimination and racism are organized for schools and others involved in education.

TEACHER TRAINING

In the Dutch education system, teacher training courses leading to qualifications for teaching in the various types of schools fall under the higher education system composed of higher vocational education (HBO), university education (WO), and higher open distance learning. In 1993 there were 83 HBO colleges, about 70% of them privately run. In 1990 there were 28,205 students attending full-time or part-time teacher training courses: 13,772 students training as primary teachers, of whom 2,506 were men, 14,433, training to be secondary teachers, of whom 6,383 were men.

There are three types of teaching qualification. Primary school teachers are required to have successfully completed a training course for primary teachers. This course takes 4 years to complete, and successful students obtain a qualification that entitles them to teach all subjects and all age groups in primary schools. Grade 2 teachers are qualified to teach students in the first 3 years of VWO and HAVO courses as well as all classes in MAVO and VBO schools. Grade 2 teachers also are qualified to teach the foundation course. Teacher training courses require 4 years of study (or 5 years for technical subjects) and lead to a qualification for teaching one subject. Grade 1 teachers, in contrast, have a university degree entitling them to teach students of all ages in the secondary education system. Courses take 4 years to complete and lead to a qualification for teaching one subject.

In general, teacher training courses are rarely held in high public esteem. However, stringent requirements are imposed on the training, and these change relatively fast because of social changes. Education is expected to meet high expectations because it is seen as contributing to (preventative) solutions for a number of social evils such as drug abuse, environmental pollution, discrimination, and unsafe behavior. Like other institutions, training colleges are faced with financial concerns linked to economic conditions.

As far as ICO is concerned, a formal start to development of teacher training courses for primary education was made in 1985. At that time ICO was obligatory for teaching in primary schools. In the early period, ICO usually was no more than a factor considered as an option. Since 1985 an opportunity has been given every year for a limited group of teachers to take part in a further training course on intercultural education, for which the government provided the impetus. In the beginning fairly little interest was shown in this course. Data from the 1991–1992 school year show that the majority of teacher training colleges for primary education did take some account of ICO, but that this subject was not integrated into the curriculum.

In the current situation, increasing attention to ICO is apparent. In the teacher training colleges for primary education, ICO appears to be an obligatory subject. Because no recent data were available on intercultural education in teacher training courses for secondary education, a short written questionnaire on this subject was sent out for the purposes of this chapter. Teacher training colleges for primary education were also asked to provide written answers to a few questions. The data that follows are based on information obtained from 12 (of the total of 55) teacher training colleges for primary education and 7 training colleges for the first stage of secondary education. Slightly more than 50% of the institutes approached responded at the beginning of the summer holiday. All of the responding colleges do pay attention to ICO. In the case of one college, this is not an obligatory subject.

Teacher training colleges for primary education devote a minimum of 28 and a maximum of 280 periods in the 4-year course to ICO. These figures relate to ICO as an obligatory course for all students; some colleges also offer ICO courses as options. In some cases ICO is integrated into the program, so the number of periods was not quoted. The wide spread in the number of periods has no direct significance for the year of the training course in which the students follow the ICO course. Some institutes offer ICO in every year of the course, whereas others restrict this to 2 or 3 years of the course, usually the later years.

The ICO courses are offered by training colleges under various names, the most common being ICO, Dutch as a second language, and cultural streams. Other terms used are counteraction of ethnocentrism and racism, education topics, and study weeks.

The questionnaire also asked the training colleges to indicate how they define ICO. The definitions provided by the colleges were brief in most cases, but ranged over a wide spectrum. Because these definitions portray the type of education offered by the training colleges, they are summarized per college in the following discussion.

One college has not yet specified a definition; another refers to the definition used in a specific program; and yet a third adopts precisely the same definition as that used by the government. Two colleges place the emphasis on the attitude of the teachers they are training. One of these also mentions the aspects of equal opportunities and tackling the problem of students who have fallen behind as definition components of ICO. A further college states that the students must gain insight into the reasons why students are lagging behind and explains that mutual understanding and equal opportunities form part of their ICO definition. Still another college mentions three aspects they consider important for ICO: making students aware of the need for ICO, acquisition of ICO skills, and knowledge of ICO history. One of the remaining colleges handles ICO in the context of putting the superiority of certain cultures into perspective. The last college gives priority to learning about the cultures that exist in the Netherlands as well as the prevention of discrimination. The definition provided by one college is the most comprehensive: having knowledge and insight about cultures, backgrounds, standards, and values; equipping students for a society of people with different cultural backgrounds; and tackling prejudice and racism.

The ICO picture as outlined by the training colleges for teachers in secondary education shows some correspondence with that given by the training colleges for primary education. In six of the seven colleges, the program includes an ICO component that transcends all subjects and is

obligatory for all students. These colleges also include obligatory intercultural components in every subject for which teachers are trained. The scope
varies from 40 to 160 periods. One college offers ICO as an option only.

Like the definitions given by the training colleges for primary education, the definitions provided by the teacher training colleges for secondary education are brief. One college uses the definition of ICO as given
by the Ministry. A second college sees the obligation to provide multicultural education as something that follows in the college's tradition of
emancipation. A third college defines ICO as consideration of the extent
to which views and opinions are rooted in culture. A fourth college deals
with the principles of Dutch and other cultures: standards and values along
with cultural–social developments. A fifth college describes ICO as education aiming for equality in a society of different ethnic groups and
cultures in one country. A sixth college bases its ICO training on preparation for an intercultural society and the development of specific knowledge for this. The final college phrases its definition as follows: to do
justice to different cultural identities, pluriformity; respect for and acceptance of the values of others.

In recent years a series of publications on the theory and practice of
ICO have been published, with government support, for teacher training.
Various projects related to teacher training also have been carried out
(Hendriks, Jos, & Tjitter, 1992).

In teacher training for NT2, there have also been significant developments.
Whereas until just a few years ago there were still complaints that expertise
in the area of second language teaching was thin on the grounds that there
were no obligatory application or further training courses, various initiatives have blossomed in recent years (Appel, 1991). Training has been
organized for teachers who work in the reception of students entering
primary education part way through the course, and there are pretraining
courses for tutors in teacher training, so that the latter are equipped to
provide supplementary training. Intensive supplementary training courses
for teams of teachers in primary schools are also available in various towns.
It is now possible to specialize in NT2 or cultural minorities.

There are still hardly any nonindigenous group teachers in primary
education. A major reason for this is that few of the nonindigenous
population follow a teacher training course. The vast majority of nonindigenous teachers in primary education teach OETC.

CONCLUSION

In the preceding text, an effort was made to outline a picture of the many
developments that have taken place in practice and educational policy

within a fairly short period of time. First of all, the arrival of highly diverse groups of immigrants presented schools with major challenges in the first instance. Taking students who speak no Dutch at all or not enough Dutch to follow the lessons in a class forces teachers to change their teaching practices.

The early days of worker immigration turned teachers into pioneers because at that time there was still no body of experience they could use to their advantage. We take this opportunity to praise all those teachers who, often in very difficult circumstances, tried to change their teaching to improve the results achieved by all the children in their classes. The fact that not all initiatives led to the desired result does not make the efforts any less praiseworthy.

Now teaching material that meets the requirements regarding intercultural content is available, and more knowledge and experience has been built up with regard to good intercultural education. But a great deal of effort and creativity still is demanded on the part of teachers because the problems have not yet been solved. Fascinating experiments are being carried out in many schools, and although these usually do not make the front page, they are of great importance for the children. However, a lot of effort is yet needed before education can be described as intercultural to a large degree.

A core task for policymakers should be to intensify the intercultural nature of educational practice. The policy modifications that have been implemented to date must be seen as the willingness to change course in the face of results that are less than successful. However, it is desirable that policy changes in the future be based to a greater extent than in the past on the results of research to develop the education system and examine the results of measures implemented.

The fact that an ICO project group is operating at the national level offers good prospects for stimulating ICO development in schools.

TO CONSIDER

The Netherlands is becoming an increasingly multicultural society. The government, in 1983, recognized this, and educators are beginning to recognize and respond to this diversity. Schools are seemingly becoming more active in preparing their young people for their place in a society that is pluralistic and culturally diverse. Compared with many countries of the world, the Netherlands may be among the leaders in determining standards concerning intercultural education. But the policy there lies largely in the integration of immigrants alongside the preservation of their original cultures, and this ultimately must be remembered. At the same time, the gap between official policy and practice remains great, and support to realize these efforts must be forthcoming.

1. Review current newspapers from the Netherlands, available on the Worldwide Web at www.vol.it/UK/EN/EDICOLA/quot_str.htm#menu. Search for news items that present issues related to the international community, interethnic conflict, immigrant rights and issues, and educational responses to diversity. How do current issues related to diversity relate to what you have just read?

2. What can your nation and schools learn from the experiences of the Netherlands?

3. How can young people in the Netherlands be most effectively prepared to interact with others on a global scale? What resources seem to be available within the nation to assist young people in developing a global or intercultural perspective?

4. The Netherlands frequently receives immigrants and refugees from many regions of the world. Given what you have just read, how would you respond to the scenario presented in chapter 1. What steps should schools take in responding to the needs of newly arrived immigrant groups?

REFERENCES

Appel, R. (1991). Nederlands als tweede taal in het onderwijs: Stand van zaken en perspectieven [Dutch as a second language in the education system: Current status and prospects]. *Spiegel* 9(2), 9–24.

Bosma, H. (1994). Allochtonen in het voortgezet onderwijs (Nonindigenous students in secondary education; cohort 1989). In *Kwartaalschrift Onderwijsstatistieken,* 1994 Commissie Evaluatie Basisonderwijs [Primary Education Evaluation Committee]. *Onderwijs gericht op een multiculturele samenleving* [Education aimed at a multicultural society]. The Hague: Sdu.

Delnoy, R. (1995). *"Dat zou je intercultureel kunnen noemen?" Taalonderwijs in verandering* ["That's what you could call intercultural?" Language teaching in a state of flux]. Enschede: SLO.

Fase, W. (1994). *Ethnic divisions in Western European education.* Münster/New York: Waxmann.

Hendriks, F., Jos, H. & Tjitte, W. (1992). *Intercultureel onderwijs: Basisboek voor leraren* [Intercultural education: A primer for teachers]. Leeuwarden: ECN/NHL.

Kabdan, R., Meijer, P. G., & Veen, A. (1991). *Onderwijs aan vluchtelingen; Een onderzoek naar groepen vluchtelingen in het Nederlandse onderwijs* [Teaching refugees. A study of refugee groups in the Dutch education system]. Amsterdam: SCO.

Kroon, S., & Ton, V. (1992). *Mehrsprachigkeit; Bildungspolitik und interkultureller Unterricht in den Niederlanden* [The multilingual factor: Educational policy and intercultural teaching in The Netherlands]. Revised version of a lecture and workshop given at the Volkshochschule Brigittenau in Vienna on November 29, 1992.

Lucassen, L., & André, J. F., Köbben, J. (1992). *Het partiële gelijk: Controverses over het onderwijs in de eigen taal en cultuur en de rol daarbij van beleid en wetenschap, 1951– 1991* [Partly right: Controversies relating to teaching in the student's mother tongue and culture and the role played by policy and science, 1951–1991]. Amsterdam: Swets & Zeitlinger.

Schreuder, P. (1995). *Algemene vorming in een multiculturele samenleving* [General education in a multicultural society]. Utrecht: University of Utrecht.

Storimans, Th. (1993). *Het recht op anders zijn: In het bijzonder met betrekking tot minderheden in het basisonderwijs* [The right to be different: With particular reference to minorities in primary education] Doctoral dissertation. Nijmegen: Katholieke Universitat.

Tesser, P. T. M. (1993). *Rapportage Minderheden 1993* [Minorities Report 1993]. The Hague: Dutch Social and Cultural Planning Office.

Editor's Remarks

England has a long history of public education, which places it among educational leadership around the world. Many critics, however, have accused the English system of being dualistic, that is, providing differently for the rich and poor. However, attempts have been made in the post-war period to provide an equitable education for all. This includes addressing issues related to cultural diversity in a nation that in recent years has become increasingly pluralistic. A major consequence of a history of colonization by England has been that its doors were open during the post-war period to immigrants from such diverse nations as Pakistan, India, Sri Lanka, Cyprus, and several nations of Africa and the Caribbean. In addition, people from Vietnam, Italy, Ukraine, and Ireland, among others, add to the cultural milieu.

Some have suggested that a real impetus for discussion of multicultural education in Britain was with the Swann Report of 1985. This report, as expanded on in this chapter, proposed that the nation's teachers should demonstrate an appreciation of diversity of culture, religion, and linguistic backgrounds. Subsequently the Education Reform Act 1988 led to a stress on the notion of entitlement for all students.

How should a nation such as England address its current ethnic and "racial" diversity? How can teachers begin to transcend what many perceive as a highly Eurocentric orientation and approach to education that resists change? How can young English students best be prepared for an increasingly intercultural and international future?

Chapter 6

Intercultural Education in Britain

୫ଠ ◆ ଓଃ

Peter Figueroa
University of Southampton

Most of the minority ethnic population in the United Kingdom (UK), (i.e., England, Wales, Scotland and Northern Ireland), is found in England. Hence, this chapter will focus mainly on the situation in England, although the basic issues will also be relevant to the rest of the United Kingdom, and in particular to Wales. The education systems in Scotland and Northern Ireland are different from those in England and Wales, which essentially share a common system.

The term "*intercultural education*" is much less common in Britain than "*multicultural education*." More importantly, there is no general agreement about terminology. The author tends to use "*multicultural*" and '*intercultural*' interchangeably. Used descriptively, multicultural or intercultural refers to the presence of and greater or lesser interaction and interrelation between more than one cultural tradition or style in a society or social arena. However, the phrase multicultural education or intercultural education, indicates a set of educational ideals, referring to the educational goals and implications of promoting constructive, creative, mutually respectful interrelationships between different cultural traditions or styles. *Antiracist education* refers to the educational goals and implications of combating racism in all its forms, and of promoting equity, social justice, solidarity, and social well-being for all. The author often uses "*multicultural antiracist education*," or "*intercultural and antiracist edu-*

cation," to indicate that intercultural, antiracist, and social equity goals are all essential to education. (Figueroa, 1991; Leicester, 1986).

THE EDUCATION SYSTEM

The Education Reform Act 1988 and subsequent legislation and developments have substantially altered the state-controlled education system of England and Wales. Until that date, this education system had been regulated by the Education Act 1944, which was a devolved system with central government in the guise of the Ministry of Education, subsequently the Department of Education and Science, playing a minimal role. Education was the responsibility of local education authorities (LEAs), although schools had a great deal of autonomy. The system was marked by diversity, even fragmentation, but there was the possibility of responding to local needs.

That has all changed. The Education Reform Act 1988 centralized control, giving extensive powers to the responsible minister, the Secretary of State for Education and Science, subsequently the Secretary of State for Education and now the Secretary of State for Education and Employment. Central to this was the introduction of a largely prescriptive subject-based national curriculum specifying attainment targets, with assessment required at the end of four key stages: at ages 7, 11, 14, and 16. Compulsory schooling ends at 16, and the main school-leaving examination, the General Certificate of Secondary Education (GCSE), is taken at that point. However, a large proportion of students continue in full-time education to about the age of 18, many of these taking the so-called A level examinations normally required for university entrance.

The Education Reform Act 1988 has dramatically reduced the power and role of LEAs. At the same time, individual schools, and in particular their governing bodies, have been given budgetary responsibility and control of their affairs under a regime of central control and tight accountability. This is referred to as the local management of schools (LMS). The governing bodies of the schools are made up of unpaid amateurs, but they include the Head and are intended to represent the teachers, parents, the local community, and the world of business. Central control is enforced, among other things, by the required publication of test and school-leaving examination results, and by a rolling program of inspections, centrally controlled.

The basic pattern for provision of compulsory education in the state system, although variations exist, consists of primary school (ages 5 to 11 years) or infant school (ages 5 to 7 years) plus junior school (ages 7 to 11 years) followed by secondary school (ages 11 to 16 years). At the secondary level schools may be comprehensive, grammar or, less frequently, secondary modern. Since 1988 there also have been grant-maintained schools, which come under direct central control. These are essentially schools that have been encouraged to opt out of the LEA system altogether. A small number of city colleges, likewise under central control, have also been established.

In addition to this state education system and to a partial state nursery school system, there is also a substantial private, or independent, education sector, which has long catered to those who have the means to pay for this education. This sector is not bound by the Education Reform Act 1988. However, independent schools do often take on board many of the requirements of the national curriculum.

BRITISH SOCIETY, POLICIES, AND PRACTICE

Britain is a multicultural society, with a history marked by many waves of immigrants. The presence of Black people in Britain has a very long history (Fryer, 1984). However, it was the expansion of Europe from the beginning of the modern era some 500 years ago that led to a significant growth in the African and Indian heritage populations in Britain and other parts of Europe. The European transatlantic slave trade and the development of the British Empire, in particular the colonies in the Americas and the Raj, were the key factors, with Black people being brought to Britain through these connections from the 16th century on (Fryer 1984; Little 1948). In 1768 Granville Sharp, the abolitionist, "put the number of black servants in London at 20,000, out of a total London population of 676,250" (Gerzina, 1995, p. 5). By the 19th century a substantial Black population "permeated most ranks of society, through the length and breadth" of Britain (Walvin, 1973, p. 72).

World War I saw people from around the British Empire (including the Caribbean, Africa, and India) rally to the cause. Many of these entered the war industry or the armed forces in Britain. The same pattern was perhaps even more striking during the World War II. However, the Royal Commission on Population (1949) regarded the prospect of increased immigration as undesirable because "the sources . . . of suitable immigrants are meager and the capacity of a fully established society like ours to absorb immigrants of alien race and religion is limited" (p. 1225).

Nevertheless, after World War II, amid decolonization, political and social turmoil, and poverty and unemployment in many places, and with the rebuilding of Britain and the rest of Europe, massive migratory movements took place in many directions around the world, with people seeking better lives as workers or as refugees. Large numbers, especially from the Republic of Ireland, the Indian subcontinent, and the Caribbean entered Britain. Indeed, Britain mounted recruitment campaigns in India and the Caribbean. Nevertheless, it is the peoples from these latter two areas that have been seen as particularly problematic, and who, along with other non-White people are often referred to as ethnic minorities in Britain.

The most comprehensive, up-to-date information on the size and distribution of this population is based on the 1991 census. This census introduced an ethnic question in addition to a previously existing birth-place question. However, because a single category for the White popu-lation was used, it is not possible to identify the White population descended from recent immigrants, although it is possible to identify the minority ethnic population, whether immigrant or not. This suggests that the problem identified by the policymakers is less to do with cultural difference or recent immigrant background, and more to do with "race" or non-White ethnicity.

Out of a total population of some 54,860,000 in Great Britain (GB) (England, Scotland, and Wales), this non-White minority ethnic popula-tion represented only about 5.5%, totaling some 3,006,500 (Owen, 1992). The proportion in England was about 6.3% (i.e., some 2,906,500 out of approximately 47,026,500) compared with 1.4% in Wales and 1.3% in Scotland (Owen, 1992). In 1995, about half of the minority ethnic population in Britain were immigrants, but this was the case for only one in eight of those under the age of 16 (Office for National Statistics, 1996; figures for spring 1995).

However, although these minority ethnic groups live in all parts of Britain, they are unevenly distributed, and are to be found primarily in the conurbations. In fact, 56% of the minority ethnic population of Great Britain lives in the Southeast of England, and more specifically, 45% lives in Greater London. Ethnic minorities represent 20% of the Greater London population, over one-fourth of the Inner London population, 30% of the Inner London borough of Lambeth, and a full 45% of the Outer London borough of Brent. They represent 15% of the population of the West Midlands Metropolitan County, 16% of the city of Bradford, and 22% of the city of Birmingham (Owen, 1992).

Furthermore, compared with the White population, a larger proportion of the minority ethnic population are of school age, the ethnic minorities constituting 9.3% of the population younger than 16 in Great Britain (Office for National Statistics, 1996). In state schools in Birmingham, 39% of the population are from minority ethnic groups (Birmingham City Council Education Department, undated, c. 1997).

The minority ethnic population in Britain is extremely diverse, with origins in many countries including India, Pakistan, Bangladesh, Sri Lanka, several Caribbean nation states, and several African countries. Those from Africa include East African Asians from Kenya, Uganda, and Malawi. Each group has a strong sense of a distinctive ethnic identity (Department of Education and Science, [DES], 1985).

The Inner London Education Authority found in 1989 that among its 280,000 or more students, 184 different languages other than English were spoken in the home (Inner London Education Authority [ILEA] Research and Statistics, 1989). In England as a whole, there are some 12 languages other than English, each with at least 100,000 speakers. These include Chinese, Arabic, Panjabi, Urdu, Italian, and Spanish. Although there are no reliable statistics, there are also many Creole speakers.

Despite the great diversity, the minority ethnic groups do have some things in common (Eggleston, 1986). For example, they share an aspiration to be "fully accepted as equal members" of British society (DES, 1985, p. 760). Above all, they tend to share inequality, disadvantage, and the experience of racism.

The unequal social location of minority ethnic groups within the society can be seen on a whole range of social indicators including unemployment, housing, and education (Brown, 1984; Figueroa, 1991; Gillborn & Gipps, 1996; Jones, 1993; Owen, 1993, 1996; Modood et al., 1997).

The unemployment rates in 1991 are shown in Table 6.1 (Owen, 1993):

TABLE 6.1

Unemployment Rates by Ethnic Groups, Great Britain, 1991:
All Working Ages and Ages 16 to 24

	All Ages		Ages 16–24	
	Women	Men	Women	Men
	(%)	(%)	(%)	(%)
Bangladeshi	34.5	30.9	36.2	20.5
Black African	24.7	28.9	35.9	41.6
Pakistani	29.6	28.5	35.3	36.1
Black other	18.3	25.5	25.5	35.2
Black Caribbean	13.5	23.8	24.1	37.6
Indian	12.7	13.4	18.8	23.4
Chinese	8.3	10.5	14.2	15.4
White	6.3	10.7	11.4	17.4
Minority ethnic overall	15.6	20.3	24.9	30.9
Entire population	6.8	11.2	12.1	18.1

Source: 1991 Census Local Base Statistics (Economic and Social Research Council purchase); Crown Copyright; Adapted from Owen (1993), Tables 6 & 7.

In 1991 only 1.8% of White people lived in households with more than one person per room, whereas the proportion for minority ethnic households overall was 13.1%. Breaking this down, it was 15.1% for Black Africans, 29.7% for Pakistanis, and 47.1% for Bangladeshis (Owen, 1996).

In the field of education, minority ethnic groups tend to experience many disadvantages, although here too there are many differences between and within groups. For instance, there has been overrepresentation among students in schools for the educationally subnormal and among those excluded from school, in both cases especially for Caribbean boys, (Coard, 1971; Gillborn & Gipps, 1996; Tomlinson, 1982).

On educational achievement, the picture is complex, and there are problems with much of the available data (Figueroa, 1991; Gillborn & Gipps, 1996). Nevertheless, educational achievement correlates not only with social class and gender, but also with ethnicity (Gillborn & Gipps, 1996). Indian students, who of all the main minority ethnic students are the most likely to come from a nonmanual background, often achieve better GCSE results than their White peers, but this is not universally true. On the average the Pakistani students do not have as good academic achievement as their White counterparts. The Bangladeshi, who are more likely than all the other main minority ethnic students to have a manual background, used to have very poor GCSE results, but their achievement, in the London borough of Tower Hamlets at least, has improved significantly in the 1990s. It is especially Caribbean students, and in particular the boys, whose results are among the worst on the average (Figueroa, 1991; Gillborn & Gipps, 1996).

There is a good deal of evidence to suggest that racism in the wider society and within the education system may largely help to account for the social and educational inequality of many within the minority ethnic population. (Brittan, 1976; Brown, 1984; Brown & Gay, 1985; Daniel, 1968; European Parliament Committee of Inquiry into Racism and Xenophobia, 1990; Figueroa, 1991; Gillborn & Gipps, 1996; Kelly & Cohn, 1988; Modood et al., 1997; Smith, 1977).

It is important to stress here that racism takes many different forms, and does not refer only to an expressly articulated doctrine or theory, to virulent hatred, to formal disabilities imposed on individuals or groups because of their "race", or to vicious attacks on individuals or groups in the name of "race". In addition to all of these, racism also operates in more subtle and unintentional ways, and often even when there are express intentions of ensuring equal opportunities (Figueroa, 1991; Gillborn & Gipps, 1996). There are individual, interpersonal, institutional, cultural, and structural aspects of racism, some of which are more hidden or deeply embedded than others (Brandt, 1986; Figueroa, 1991).

In the years after World War I, there had been a series of serious race riots in which White people attacked Black people and their property (Fryer, 1984; Little, 1948; Walvin, 1973). Again, after World War II there were many similar incidents beginning in 1948 (Fryer, 1984; Walvin, 1973). The worst such riots took place in Notting Hill, London, in 1958. Slogans used included: "Down with Niggers," and "We'll kill the Blacks" (Fryer, 1984; Walvin, 1973).

These events had a great impact. There was a strong reaction of those who wanted Black immigration to be stopped and Black people "repatriated." But those who stood for fairness, equality, an end to discrimination, and more constructive relationships between all groups in society also reacted strongly. Self-organization among Black people, too, increased (Rose et al, 1969).

However, immigration controls seemed to be the first consequence of these events and of the burgeoning pressure groups opposed to Black immigration (Rose *et al,* 1969). Thus, the first postwar law to control Black immigration, the Commonwealth Immigrants Act 1962, was passed by a Conservative government. It was only the first of several acts (for instance, the Commonwealth Immigrants Act 1968, the Immigration Act 1971, the British Nationality Act 1981, the Immigration Act 1998, and the Asylum and Immigration Act 1996) which, along with various administrative arrangements, including changes to immigration rules from the 1960s to the present, progressively stopped Black immigration and removed existing rights from Black groups (Figueroa, 1995). The passing in record time of the racist Commonwealth Immigrants Act 1968 to keep out Kenyan Asians who were British citizens with British passports severely shook the immigrant communities (Rose et al., 1969, p. 619), and led to protests by Black people.

In 1963 White parents of children at two primary schools in West London organized a protest against the presence of "immigrant" children (mainly Indians and Pakistanis) in these schools (Rose et al., 1969). As a result, the Minister of Education, Sir Edward Boyle, stated in Parliament that, the "de facto segregation between immigrant . . . and native schools" must be opposed, and he adumbrated a policy of dispersing minority ethnic students (House of Commons, 1963–1964, column 439).

Immediately after this Parliamentary debate, the first official education publication relating to the presence of immigrants in Britain, *English for Immigrants,* was published (Ministry of Education, 1963). It took an assimilationist approach, and highlighted immigrants as problems and the problems of immigrants (Ministry of Education, 1963). The policy of "dispersal" was set out officially in Circular 7/65 by the Department of Education and Science (DES), the successor to the Ministry of Education (DES, 1965), and in a White Paper shortly afterward (Prime Minister,

1964–1965). These again stressed the problems supposedly created by the presence of immigrants.

In recent years there has been a substantial increase in reported racially motivated attacks (Racial Violence, 1993; and Racist Attacks and Harassment, 1993). A Home Office (1981) report showed that Asians were 50 times more likely than White people to suffer racial victimization, and African Caribbeans 36 times more likely. In 1992 "at least eight people died as a result of racist attacks" (Racist Attacks and Harassment: The Epidemic of the 90s?", 1993).

A recent survey found that 90% of White people in Britain think that people in the country are prejudiced against minority ethnic groups (Institute for Public Policy Research, 1997). A similar proportion of African-Caribbean, Asian, and Jewish people held the same view. In another survey, almost 30% of 16-to-24 year olds disagreed that all "races" are equal, and almost 30% admitted to having committed an act of racism (Britain's intolerant youth, 1997).

Several studies have shown the existence of racism in schools, and in particular that widespread racist name calling and bullying take place (Figueroa & Swart, 1986; Gillborn, 1990; Macdonald, Bhavnani, Khan, & John, 1989; Mirza, 1992; Nehaul, 1996; Sewell, 1997; Wright, 1986, 1992). The excessive levels of African Caribbean underperformance and exclusion raise questions about stereotyping and about the working of the system. There is evidence that teachers interact with minority ethnic students, and not least with African Caribbean students, in terms of stereotypes and myths: termed racist frames of reference by the author (Figueroa, 1991; Gillborn & Gipps, 1996; Sewell, 1997).

There also have been incidents of extreme racist violence in schools or in situations affecting young people. One of the most publicized cases was the 1986 stabbing to death of a South Asian boy in a school (Macdonald et al., 1989). Gillborn and Gipps (1996) listed several incidents of violent racist attacks on children and young people that took place in 13 different months between 1991 and 1994. These resulted in the deaths of one South Asian youth, two Black youths, and two White youths.

However, alongside racism, British society is also marked by antiracist forces and democratic traditions, institutions, and ideals. Among the positive developments over the years have been the passing of increasingly better laws against "racial" discrimination in 1965, 1968, and 1976. Also, a Committee of Inquiry into the education of minority ethnic children was set up in 1979, which produced its final report in 1985 (DES, 1985). Many LEAs and some schools and institutions of teacher education produced multicultural or even antiracist policies about the same time (Figueroa, 1995). Some LEAs have also adopted policies and procedures for dealing with racist harassment in schools (e.g., Hampshire County Council Education Department, 1991). Also, many members of the minority ethnic communities and their White sympathizers have worked constructively and persistently for a better deal.

The Race Relations Act 1976 outlawed both direct and indirect discrimination based on "race", color, nationality, citizenship, or ethnic or national origins in a very wide range of spheres, including education. This act also set up the Commission for Racial Equality (CRE) to oversee the implementation of the law, to coordinate the policy on "race" relations, and to promote harmonious community relations. Despite limitations, especially the weaknesses of the implementation provisions, which have to some extent been subsequently strengthened, this act remains a bulwark.

The Committee of Inquiry into the Education of Children from Ethnic Minority Groups came about largely because the Caribbean community in the 1960s and 1970s, in addition to setting up supplementary schools and calling for such action as the teaching of Black Studies, strongly expressed their concern about the situation of their children in the education system (DES, 1985).

An interim report of this Committee of Inquiry, The Rampton Report (DES, 1981), highlighted so-called "West Indian underachievement," and emphasized the factor of racism, although it stressed that there was "no single cause" (DES, 1981, p. 72). The highlighting of racism caused a furor, and a new chair, Lord Swann, was appointed.

The main message of the final report, the Swann Report (DES, 1985), may be summarized as follows. The response of the education system to immigration and ethnic minorities in the post-war period had moved broadly from assimilationism, through integrationism, to multiculturalism (DES, 1985, pp. 191–199). However, none of these approaches had successfully met the needs of the ethnic minorities, nor had these minorities been absorbed into the society. The multicultural approach was confused and had impinged only on schools in multiethnic areas. Britain today, however, is a plural, multiethnic society requiring a pluralist approach that enables minority and majority ethnic groups "to participate fully in shaping the society . . . within a framework of commonly accepted values, practices and procedures," while maintaining "their distinct ethnic identities" (DES, 1985, p. 5). The watchword should be "diversity within unity" (DES, 1985, pp. 7–8). However, "the major obstacle" (DES, 1985, p. 8) was racism, both "individual attitudes and behaviour" and the "more pervasive 'climate' of racism" (DES, 1985, p. 36), including "institutional policies and practices" (DES, 1985, p. 8). Multicultural education, relevant to all children, should help them to respect cultural diversity and to be free of "inaccurate myths and stereotypes about other ethnic groups" (DES, 1985, p. 321). Education "must reflect the diversity of British society and indeed of the contemporary world" (DES, 1985, p. 318). It must promote the values of equality and justice, provide "true equality of opportunity" for all and combat racism, removing practices and procedures that are discriminatory directly or indirectly, and intentionally or unintentionally (DES, 1985, p. 325). Education must cater to all individual educational needs, including "any particular educational needs" of minority ethnic students (DES, 1985, p. 317). Pastoral needs must also receive attention to avoid, for example, conflict between the requirements of students' "fundamental religious beliefs and the provisions of the school" (DES, 1985, p. 326). Finally, the Swann Report makes the following three points. First, these goals can be achieved only if the curriculum and indeed the whole work of the school are permeated by the "multicultural perspective" (DES, 1985, p. 323). Second, both initial and in-service teacher education (INSET) must likewise be permeated (DES, 1985). Third, the education and teacher education systems should do much more to rectify the underrepresentation and unequal position of ethnic minorities in the teaching profession.

Although the Swann Report occasioned much debate, and although many LEAs formulated policies and established some INSET courses in response, the Central Government did not act on many of its recommendations (Swann, 1993). It was also overtaken within 3 years by the Education Reform Act 1988.

This Act does offer some opportunities to promote multiculturalism and equity. It states that the curriculum should be "balanced and broadly based," should promote "the spiritual, moral, cultural, mental, and physical development of students at the school and of society," and should prepare "students for the opportunities, responsibilities, and experiences of adult life" (GB, 1988: Part I, Section 1), which, of course, is life in a plural society and a plural world. The National Curriculum, which the Act introduced, the requirement that all students should do GCSE English, mathematics, and science, and the related notion of entitlement which has been developed, make it probably more difficult for minority ethnic students to be channeled away from academic endeavors. Similarly, the centrality given to testing and assessment seems to promise fairer assessment.

The Act also requires that all the principal religions in Britain should be addressed in Religious Education, although it does insist that priority should be given to Christianity. Moreover, the Act underlines the rights and role of all parents. Furthermore, the National Curriculum Council (NCC), set up by the 1988 Act, identified, in its guidance to schools, a multicultural cross-curricular "dimension," and included some relevant issues in its proposed cross-curricular "theme" of citizenship. The NCC also established a special Multicultural Task Group (Figueroa, 1995; NCC, 1990a, 1990b: Tomlinson, 1993).

However, the Education Reform Act 1988 also in crucial ways represents a threat to multicultural, antiracist, and equal opportunities education. It did not highlight such issues, and actually represented a step backwards from previous relevant developments, and in particular from the Swann Report, which it ignored. It was inspired by the two main tendencies, neoliberal and neoconservative, within the New Right ideology, which was dominant under unbroken Conservative rule between 1979 and 1997 (Whitty, 1990).

The neoliberals stress a free market and individual (consumer) choice, and conceive of education mainly as an instrument of economic well-being. But minority ethnic groups tend to have relatively little power in the marketplace. Indeed, the stress on the market and accountability probably tends to make schools more wary of accepting or retaining at least some groups of minority ethnic students, that is, those who may be seen as likely directly or indirectly to reduce the school's standing on various performance indicators such as attendance and results on Standard Assessment Tasks (SATs), GCSEs, and A-level examinations. In fact, in recent years exclusions from both primary and secondary schools have risen significantly. There is evidence to suggest that it tripled over a 3-year period during the early 1990s (Gillborn & Gipps, 1996). Black Caribbean, Black African, and Black Other students are the most likely to be excluded, with Black Caribbeans, especially the boys, being hit the hardest. The rate of exclusion for Black Caribbean students in 1993–1994 was almost six times that for White students (Gillborn & Gipps, 1996).

The neoconservatives stress traditional values, a narrowly conceived national identity, and a (largely monocultural) canonical academic curriculum. Thus the centralized subject-based national curriculum affords little recognition to multicultural education, and even less to antiracist education. What recognition these have been given has been as "cross-curricular dimensions."

In the first place, however, multicultural and antiracist issues cannot be adequately dealt with primarily as "dimensions" because there are important bodies of knowledge as well as skills, attitudes, and values that need exploring and developing in their own right and in a focused way. Secondly, as most of the available energy, resources, and time have gone into realizing the subject-based national curriculum, cross-curricular aspects, in particular multicultural and especially antiracist education, have been largely neglected among the massive changes and pressures flooding from the Education Reform Act (e.g., Bagley, 1992). Moreover, publication of the report produced by the special Multicultural Task Group was actually withheld, although this report was by no means very radical (Figueroa, 1995; Tomlinson, 1993).

Finally, the Education Reform Act not only weakened LEAs, but also abolished the Inner London Education Authority (ILEA). However, because multicultural education initiatives often had been taken at the LEA level, and in particular by the ILEA, they now often came under threat.

TEACHER EDUCATION AND INTERCULTURAL ISSUES

Like other sectors of the education system in England and Wales, teacher education has in recent years been the object of right-wing-inspired central government control and reform (Judd & Crequer, 1993). Also, like these other sectors, and indeed even more than in schools, teacher education has on the whole paid inadequate attention to multicultural and especially antiracist education (Adelman, 1993; DES, 1979; DES, 1985; Siraj-Blatchford, 1993).

There are currently two main routes of initial teacher education: the consecutive and the concurrent. With the more popular consecutive model, the student initially obtains a first degree, then does a 36-week secondary, or 38-week primary, professional teacher education course leading toward the Postgraduate Certificate in Education (PGCE). With the concurrent model, the student usually follows a 3- or 4-year Bachelor of Education (BEd) program, which combines first-degree work with professional teacher education. The PGCE and the BEd have validity throughout England and Wales.

Recent centralizing tendencies go back to the 1980s. The Council for the Accreditation of Teacher Education (CATE) was set up in 1984, reconstituted in 1990, and more sharply centralized in 1992 when the role of the previously important local CATE committees was eliminated. Criteria and the procedures for securing approval of initial teacher education courses were set out by the Department of Education and Science in 1984 and 1989 (DES Circular 3/84 and 24/89) and reformed by its successor, the Department for Education (DFE) in 1992 (DFE Circular 9/92).

The 1992 accreditation criteria were formulated in terms of teaching competencies, focused largely on subject teaching. These reforms essentially reduce and constrain the control of higher education institutions (HEIs), stress practice over theory, and take a technicist rather than a professional or broad educational approach. The use of the expression initial teacher training (ITT) rather than initial teacher education (ITE) is symptomatic.

The Education (Schools) Act 1992 provided for the Secretary of State to assign functions to Her Majesty's Chief Inspector of Schools (HMCI) in relation to the training of teachers. The Secretary of State reinforced these functions in 1996. Furthermore, the Education Act 1994 requires the newly instituted Teacher Training Agency (TTA) to allocate funds and student numbers to ITT providers only if satisfied on a range of inspection evidence and quality assessments, in particular from the Office for Standards in Education (OFSTED), itself established in 1992, and from the HMCI.

In 1996 OFSTED and TTA produced, for immediate use in accreditation, a *Framework for the Assessment of Quality and Standards in Initial Teacher Training.* This *Framework*, like the 1992 criteria from which it derives, is mainly orientated toward subject knowledge and technical and managerial criteria. It makes no direct reference to broader social, cultural, or other contextual aspects, and little direct reference to student teachers' critical self-knowledge or personal development, teacher–student interaction, or student motivation. Furthermore, in 1997 the TTA developed "new ITT requirements . . . and . . . new QTS [qualified teacher status] standards to replace the competencies in Circulars 9/92 and 14/93" (OFSTED & TTA, 1996: 8; TTA, 1997). These were likewise mainly focused on subject knowledge, technical competence and classroom management. The TTA is also moving toward a national curriculum for teacher training.

Limited data suggest that student teachers, and no doubt teacher educators, are often inadequately aware of the multicultural and antiracist education issues, and often tend to be ill-informed and to share the stereotypes and myths of the wider society (Cohen, 1989; DES, 1985; Figueroa, 1989, 1991; Higher Education Funding Council for England [HEFCE], 1995; and Siraj-Blatchford, 1993). Besides, minority ethnic groups are underrepresented among student teachers, and even more among teacher educators (DES 1985; HEFCE, 1995). Worse still, there is some evidence that minority ethnic student teachers frequently experience racism, especially during their school placements (HEFCE, 1995; Siraj-Blatchford, 1993).

In fact, student teachers following the consecutive route will obtain their first degree on a regular undergraduate program with usually no orientation toward the multicultural society or education. Furthermore, recent legislation has specified that at least two thirds of the time on the secondary (and about half on the primary) PGCE course must be spent in schools gaining practical experience. Hence the time available in the teacher education institution, usually a University Department of Education or an institution of higher education affiliated with a University, is severely limited to some 12 weeks in the call of the secondary PGCE, while the equivalent time for the primary PGCE is about 20 weeks. Much of this limited time is concerned with teaching methodology and related issues focused on the student's chosen subjects. Intercultural and related issues constitute only one set within a large range of professional issues that the PGCE course needs to address in the little remaining time.

Time constraints are also great in the BEd program, because the program must accommodate first-degree work, a substantial program of practical experience, teaching methodology, and related issues, as well as the large range of professional issues, including intercultural and antiracist issues. Furthermore, in both models, the substantial time spent by student teachers in schools may offer little preparation in intercultural or antiracist education because many schools have little awareness or understanding of such issues. They are also frequently likely to have few, if any, minority ethnic students or staff.

In the 1980s, DES, CATE, and the Council for National Academic Awards (CNAA), which at the time was the national accrediting body for non-university degrees and teacher education courses, did begin to recognize the need for multicultural teacher education. The DES in its 1984 criteria for initial teacher education referred specifically to the "diversity of . . . ethnic and cultural origins," and also required that student teachers should learn how "to guard against preconceptions based on the race or sex of students" (DES, 1984, paragraph 11). The CNAA (1984) required teacher education courses "to include antiracist and multicultural content" (Adelman, 1993, p. 101).

However, the CNAA directives were watered down in 1986 to a requirement that teacher education should be provided "without racial discrimination" (Adelman, 1993, p. 101). After the passing of the Education Reform Act 1988, the DES (1989) requirements were formulated in terms of student teachers learning how to build in the "cross-curricular dimensions" in their teaching (Siraj-Blatchford, 1993). Subsequently, the successor to the DES, the DFE (later again reorganized into the Department for Education and Employment; DFEE), and CATE became primarily concerned with the delivery of the subject-based national curriculum. The closest the DFE came in its 1992 criteria to denoting intercultural issues was in its requirement that the foundation should be laid for the newly qualified teachers to be capable of developing "an awareness of individual differences, including social . . . and cultural differences" (DFE, 1992, paragraph 2.6.4).

Likewise, the only specific references in the *Framework for the Assessment of Quality and Standards in Initial Teacher Training* that could be considered as explicitly relevant to multiculturalism are those to student teachers' need for planning "opportunities to promote students' spiritual, moral, social, and cultural development," and to the training necessary for preparing students to do this (OFSTED & TTA, 1996, pp. 14, 18). In a recent comprehensive consultation document on *Standards for the Award of Qualified Teacher Status*, the only references directly relevant to multicultural antiracist education seem to be the requirements for student teachers to "plan opportunities to contribute to students . . . cultural development"; to set "high expectations for all students notwithstanding individual differences, including gender, and cultural and linguistic backgrounds"; and to "have a working knowledge and understanding of . . . antidiscrimination legislation" (TTA, 1997, pp. 7, 8, 11).

THE OUTLOOK

The post war period in Britain has seen substantial immigration into Britain, especially in the 1950s and 1960s. The reactions within the education system and in the wider society have varied across a wide range from rejection, through assimilationism, integrationism and multiculturalism to antiracism. After advances, especially in the late 1970s and the 1980s, there were retreats from multicultural and antiracist education, especially as teachers grapples with the massive and rapid right-wing-inspired changes flowing above all from the Education Reform Act 1988 and subsequent policy developments. However, the long ascendency of right-wing ideology seems to be coming to an end. New Labour won a landslide electoral victory in 1997. The rhetoric of the New Labour Government has been somewhat more promising; but any specific policy or especially practical focus on multicultural antiracist education is still awaited.

What, then, is the outlook? The New Labour Government has expressed a strong commitment to education, and has started to introduce some initiatives relevant to multicultural antiracist education. Its first White Paper, *Excellence in Schools* (DFEE 1997), indicates that its 'top priority' is 'raising standards' (p. 24), and speaks of 'the Government's core commitment to equality of opportunity and high standards for all' (p. 3). The employment minister in the New Labour Government, Andrew Smith (1998:3), has also asserted their commitment through the Advisory Group on Raising Ethnic Minority Pupil Achievement, which the previous Government set up in the Department for Education and Employment shortly before the end of their term of office, to promoting methods 'effective in raising minority pupils' achievement', to consulting on the monitoring of performance and the addressing of underperformance, and to giving 'guidance on . . . tackling racial harassment and stereotyping . . . and reducing exclusion'.

Other initiatives include: the setting up of a Social Exclusion Unit in the Cabinet Office (Social exclusion unit launched, 1997/1998); the inclusion of measures to tackle racial violence in the Crime and Disorder Bill (Bid to tackle racial violence, 1997/1998); and the incorporation of the European Convention on Human Rights (Protecting human rights, 1997) into British law.

However, in addition to a commitment to education, and to generalized policies on equal opportunities, human rights and the improvement of educational standards, what is needed from Central Government are policies, schemes, funding and above all practical actions targeted on the needs of minority ethnic students and on multicultural antiracist education for all. Similarly, LEAs, to which the present Government is restoring some of their recently lost powers, need to reassert their commitment and to bring forward practical programs in these twin areas.

In the meantime, how can committed teachers, educationalists, education officers, members of the minority ethnic communities and other interested parties, help to promote multicultural antiracist education and to ensure social justice and constructive social relations between the different groups?

What are some of the key principles to guide the development of awareness of, and understanding about, multicultural antiracist issues, and the development of appropriate educational policies and practices? The literature (e.g., Figueroa 1991; Hampshire County Council Education Department 1987; Massey 1991; Roberts and Massey 1993) suggests that key principles would include the following:

- All of the interested parties need to be involved, and to enter into dialogue with each other, if anything of lasting value is to be achieved;
- The rights of all, and therefore the mutual obligations of all, must be recognized;
- Each person's unique individuality must be recognized, as also their inextricable interdependence with others;
- Truth must be respected, but so must the fallibility and corrigibility of knowledge;
- The centrality of values, but also their fallibility and corrigibility, must be recognized;
- People, groups and cultures must be accepted and respected in their difference, and the value of cultural diversity recognized;
- A questioning stance must be taken towards all cultures (including one's own), acknowledging that all cultures have strong and weak points and include unexamined, taken-for-granted assumptions;
- Similarities between individuals and across groups and cultures must be recognized and built on;

- Basic values of equality, justice, liberty, solidarity, openness, pluralism and antiracism must be critically examined and critically assumed as fundamental goals;
- There must be a vision, a positive vision; goals must be clarified; targets must be defined; structures, strategies and programs must be devised;
- Monitoring, review and revision must take place regularly.

More specifically, in all aspects of the school, its life, and work, the following must be systematically and consistently addressed: racism in all its forms; cultural diversity and intercultural relations; the realization in everyday practice of equity, liberty and solidarity, and the positive promotion of these values. Also, the personal and social needs and problems of the individuals and groups, of minorities and majorities, of the victims of harassment and of the perpetrators must be addressed.

Many people might need convincing. Arguments that could be used to persuade reluctant, hostile, dubious or indifferent parents, students or teachers include the following types:

- legal (requirements of the Race Relations Act 1976);
- human rights and justice;
- moral (doing onto others as one would have done onto oneself; not causing hurt, distress, disadvantage);
- empathy;
- economic (otherwise a waste of human resources and talent);
- social (otherwise a time-bomb threatens society; benefiting from the cultural riches; the quality of life for all).

Any action plan would need to address: goals, policy formulation, strategies, style and approach, structures, information gathering and analysis, specific programs, monitoring, review and rolling modifications (Hampshire County Council Education Department 1987; Massey 1991; Roberts and Massey 1993). It is not possible to focus on and develop all of these aspects here. Besides, it is important that, within the overall framework, each institution develops appropriate arrangements, procedures and programs to deal with its specific situation and needs. However, it is desirable to focus on some specific points.

What is intended by structures here is the idea that, in addition for instance to developing a whole-school policy and programs, the school needs formally to assign to a person or committee the task of ensuring that the policy is implemented, the programs run effectively and the policy, strategies and programs are kept under review. Such a person or committee needs to have status and authority within the school, and the backing of the Head. Although it is essential to have some such explicit structure, it is also crucial that the entire school community, including parents, should be widely consulted and as fully informed and involved as practicable (Roberts and Massey 1993).

Information gathering and analysis would include: pinpointing existing school practice that is of direct relevance and value to the present concerns; identifying the needs and resources (some of which might not be immediately obvious or appreciated) among the students and staff; and ascertaining the relevant issues in the wider community, the views and needs of all sectors, and the key factors.

The specific programs would need to address each aspect of the particular educational institution, and would themselves need to specify such matters as: aims, objectives, targets, means and methods, and arrangements for evaluation and modifications. Significant aspects that these specific programs would need to address would include: institutional structures and organization; managerial styles; institutional ethos or philosophy; staffing; staff development; curricular contents; teaching styles and methods; teaching-learning resources; assessment of students; allocation of students to classes or other learning groupings; pastoral concerns; the physical plant and environment. There are also the all-pervading issues of identity development and of language that indicate the importance of the development of mother tongue or community language, as well as of high levels of proficiency in English. Again, it is not possible to elaborate on all of these points here, but some particular aspects can be highlighted.

As far as staffing is concerned, it is important that the minority ethnic communities are properly represented on the teaching staff as soon as possible. This would help to send positive messages of equity of esteem for the various communities and cultures both to members of the minority communities, and to the wider community. Such teachers could also act as role models, providing desirable motivation and support to students from similar backgrounds as themselves. Besides, they could provide valuable input from particular perspectives to the thinking and arrangements within the school.

As far as curricular contents are concerned there should be a specific place on the timetable when the relevant issues related to cultural diversity, inequality and racism can be explicitly addressed. In addition to this the curricular implications for each of the other subjects on the timetable should be addressed.

Pastoral concerns would include matters such as those relating to: personal and social development; specific personal and religious or other non-curricular cultural requirements or needs; comportment; disciplinary arrangements and procedures; and the relevant organizational structures and arrangements. There should be a specific policy and appropriate procedures in place for dealing with racist or ethnicist harassment or bullying, and related problems. (See, e.g., Hampshire County council Education Department 1991). This should form an integral part of the established disciplinary arrangements of the school, and would address such matters as racist namecalling, teasing, jokes, innuendo, graffiti and verbal or physical attacks. There should be an established procedure for dealing with such incidents: recording them, counseling the victim, disciplining and educating the perpetrator, and discussing the related issues as appropriate in class, in assembly and in the relevant planning fora.

Attention must also be given to the physical plant and general environment of the school. One needs to avoid the situation in which everything around the school transmits monocultural messages. Instead, the cultural diversity of the society and intercultural and antiracist messages must be made evident around the school.

Finally, for the schools to have deep and lasting success in their efforts they need to act in consort with other institutions, and, as already indicated, Central Government needs to give clear lead and to establish the necessary framework and infrastructure, while LEAs should develop and make pubic appropriate policies, and, among other things, should support relevant INSET programs. Local teacher education institutions should also, in ways similar to schools, develop policies and pursue practical plans of action. They should also seek to establish INSET programs for school teachers, as well as staff development for their own staff. Furthermore, schools and institutions of teacher education must also collaborate with other agencies which seek to combat racism and to promote justice, equity, multiculturalism and social well-being, such as: the CRE, the Runnymede Trust, the Antiracist Teacher Education Network (ARTEN) and the National Antiracist Movement in Education (NAME).

CONCLUSION

This chapter started with an overview of the education system in England and Wales. It then provided a review of cultural diversity in Britain, especially in the post-war period, and of inequality and racism as these have affected the minority ethnic groups there. It discussed the main relevant problems, policies and practice that developed in that period, giving particular attention to education and teacher education issues. It ended by setting out the main principles and strategic and practical considerations involved in devising a plan of action for dealing with the relevant educational issues in a plural society which is also at least to some extent marked by racism. Present-day plural Britain is rich in potentialities and creative energy, as well as fraught with likely tensions. The issues are complex, many faceted and difficult, so that there is no simple or once-and-for-all blue-print for dealing with them and no quick or simple answers. Opportunities must be created for the interested parties to come together constructively, for the tensions to be addressed and controlled, and for the potentialities and creative energy to be released and positively harnessed.

TO CONSIDER

England, more than many countries, has been addressing issues related to diversity for some three decades. Although problems are far from having been eliminated, many professionals are now sensitive to the issues.

1. *Review current newspapers from England (and from throughout Britain) which, if not available in your library, can be found on the World Wide Web at www.vol.it/UK/EN/EDICOLA/quot_str.htm#menu., or listen to broadcasts of the BBC. Search for items that present issues related to ethnic groups' rights and issues, interethnic conflict, and educational responses to diversity. How do current issues of diversity relate to what you have just read? What struggles of people continue to exist?*

2. *What can your nation and schools learn from the experience of England?*

3. *How can young people in Britain be most effectively prepared to interact with others on a global scale? What resources seem to be available in England to assist young people in developing a global, intercultural or antiracist perspective?*

4. *Britain frequently receives immigrants and refugees from many different nations. Given what you have just read, how would you respond to the scenario presented in chapter 1. What steps should schools take to respond to the needs of newly arriving immigrant groups?*

REFERENCES

Adelman, C. (1993). Access to teacher training and employment. In G. K. Verma (Ed.), *Inequality and teacher education: An international perspective* (pp. 100–107). London: Falmer Press.

Asylum and Immigration Act. (1996). London: Her Majesty's Stationery Office.

Bagley, C. A. (1992). *Back to the future, Section 11 of the Local Government Act 1966: LEAs and multicultural/antiracist education.* Slough, Berkshire: National Foundation for Educational Research in England and Wales.

Birmingham City Council Education Department. (undated, c. 1997) *Success for everyone.* Mimeograph distributed at the conference on Raising Achievement: Combatting Racial Inequality at the Institute of Education, February 25, 1997, University of London.

Brandt, G. L. (1986). *The realization of anti-racist teaching.* London: Falmer.

Brandt, G. L. (1986). *The realization of anti-racist teaching.* London: Falmer.

Britain's intolerant youth. (1997, February). *The Runnymede Bulletin,* No. 300, p. 8.

British Nationality Act. (1981). London: Her Majesty's Stationery Office.

Brittan, E. (1976). Multicultural education 2: Teacher opinion on aspects of school life, Part 2: Students and teachers. *Educational Research, 18*(3), 182–191.

Brown. C. (1984). *Black and White Britain: The third PSI survey.* London: Heinemann Educational Books.

Brown, C., & Gay, P. (1985). *Racial discrimination: Seventeen years after the act.* London: Policy Studies Institute.

Coard, B. (1971). *How the West Indian child is made educationally subnormal in the British school system.* London: New Beacon Books.

Cohen, L. (1989) Ignorance, not hostility: Student teachers' perceptions of ethnic minorities in Britain. In G. K. Verma (Ed.), *Education for all: A landmark in pluralism.* London: Falmer.

Commonwealth Immigrants Act. (1962, c. 21). London: Her Majesty's Stationery Office

Commonwealth Immigrants Act. (1968, c. 9). London: Her Majesty's Stationery Office.

Council for National Academic Awards. (1984). *Notes on multicultural education and the professional preparation and in-service development of teachers.* London: Author.

Daniel, W. W. (1968). *Racial discrimination in England.* Harmondsworth: Penguin.

Department for Education. (1992). *Initial teacher training: Secondary phase* (Circular No. 9/92). London: Her Majesty's Stationery Office.

Department of Education and Science. (1965). *The education of immigrants* (Circular 7/65). London: Author.

Department of Education and Science. (1979). *Developments in the BEd degree course.* London: Her Majesty's Stationery Office.

Department of Education and Science. (1981). *West Indian children in our schools* (Rampton Report, cmnd. 8273). London: Her Majesty's Stationery Office.

Department of Education and Science. (1984). *Initial teacher training: Approval of courses* (Circular No. 3/84). London: Her Majesty's Stationery Office.

Department of Education and Science. (1985). *Education for all* (Swann Report, cmnd. 9453). London: Her Majesty's Stationery Office.

Department of Education and Science. (1989). *Initial teacher training: Approval of courses* (Circular No. 24/89). London: Her Majesty's Stationery Office.

Education Reform Act. (1988, England and Wales, c. 40). London: Her Majesty's Stationery Office.

Eggleston, J. (1986). Multicultural society: The qualitative aspects. *Research Papers in Education,* 1(3), 217–236.

European Parliament Committee of Inquiry into Racism and Xenophobia. (1990). *Report* (document A3-195/90, rapporteur: Glyn Ford). Strasbourg: European Parliament.

Figueroa, P. (1989). Student-teachers images of ethnic minorities: A British case study. In S. Tomlinson & A. Yogev (Eds.), *Affirmative action and positive policies in the education of ethnic minorities: International perspectives on education and society* (Vol. 1, pp. 213–231). Greenwich, CT: JAI.

Figueroa, P. (1991). *Education and the social construction of "Race."* London: Routledge.

Figueroa, P. (1995). Multicultural education in the United Kingdom: Historical development and current status. In J. A. Banks & C. A. M. Banks (Eds.), *Handbook of research on multicultural education* (pp. 778–800). New York: Macmillan.

Figueroa, P., & Swart, L. T. (1986). Teachers' and students' racist and ethnocentric frames of reference: A case study. *New Community, XIII* (Spring/Summer): 40–51.

Fryer, P. (1984). *Staying power: The history of Black people in Britain.* London: Pluto.

Gerzina, G. (1995). *Black England: Life before emancipation.* London: John Murray.

Gillborn, D. (1990). *"Race", ethnicity and education: Teaching and learning in multi-ethnic schools,* London: Unwin-Hyman/Routledge.

Gillborn, D., & Gipps, C. (1996). *Recent research on the achievements of ethnic minority students* (OFSTED Reviews of Research). London: Her Majesty's Stationery Office.

Hampshire County Council Education Department. (1987). *Education for a multicultural society* (prepared by Alec Fyfe, County General Advisor for Multicultural Education). Winchester: Author.

Hampshire County Council Education Department. (1991). *Combating racial harassment: County guidelines for schools, colleges, and other educational establishments.* Winchester: Author.

Higher Education Funding Council for England. (1995). *Special initiative to encourage widening participation of students from ethnic minorities in teacher training.* Bristol: HEFCE.

Home Office. (1981). *Racial attacks* (Report of a Home Office Study). London: Her Majesty's Stationery Office.

House of Commons. (1963–1964). *Parliamentary debates* (Hansard, 1963, November 27, 5th series, Vol. 685, Cols. 433–444). London: Her Majesty's Stationery Office.

Immigration Act. (1971, c. 77). London: Her Majesty's Stationery Office.

Inner London Education Authority Research and Statistics. (1989). *Language census* (Report RS 1361/89 written by J. Sinnott). London: ILEA.

Institute for Public Policy Research (1997). *Racial attitudes survey.* London: Institute for Public Policy Research.

Jones, T. (1993). *Britain's ethnic minorities: An analysis of the labour force survey.* London: Policy Studies Institute.

Judd, J., & Crequer, N. (1993). The right tightens its grip on education. In C. Chitty & B. Simon (Eds.), *Education answers back: Critical responses to government policy* (pp. 120– 125). London: Lawrence & Wishart.

Kelly, E., & Cohn, T. (1988). *Racism in schools: New research evidence.* Stoke-on-Trent: Trentham.

Leicester, M. (1986). Multicultural curriculum or antiracist education: Denying the gulf. *Multicultural Teaching, 4*(2), 4–7.

Little, K. (1948). *Negroes in Britain: A study of racial relations in English society.* London: Routledge & Kegan Paul.

Macdonald, I., Bhavnani, R., Khan, L., & John, G. (1989). *Murder in the playground: The Burnage report* (The Report of the Macdonald Inquiry into Racism and Racial Violence in Manchester Schools). London: Longsight.

Massey, I. (1991). *More than skin deep: Developing anti-racist multicultural education in schools.* London: Hodder & Stoughton.

Ministry of Education. (1963). *English for immigrants* (Pamphlet No. 43). London: Her Majesty's Stationery Office.

Mirza, H. S. (1992). *Young, female and Black.* London: Routledge.

Modood, T., Berthoud, R., Lakey, J., Nazroo, J., Smith, P., Virdee, S., and Beishon, S. (1997) *Ethnic minorities in Britain: Diversity and disadvantage* (the fourth national survey of ethnic minorities). London: Policy Studies Institute.

National Curriculum Council. (1990a). *Curriculum guidance three: The whole curriculum.* York: Author.

National Curriculum Council. (1990b). *Curriculum guidance eight: Education for citizenship.* York: Author.

Nehaul, K. (1996). *The schooling of children of Caribbean heritage.* Stoke-on- Trent: Trentham.

Office for National Statistics. (1996). *Social focus on ethnic minorities.* London: Her Majesty's Stationery Office.

Office for Standards in Education and Teacher Training Agency. (1996). *Framework for the assessment of quality and standards in initial teacher training 1996–1997.* London: OFSTED.

Owen, D. (1992). *Ethnic minorities in Great Britain: Settlement patterns* (1991 Census Statistical Paper No. 1). Coventry: National Ethnic Minority Data Archive, Centre for Research in Ethnic Relations, University of Warwick.

Owen, D. (1993). *Ethnic minorities in Great Britain: Economic characteristics* (1991 Census Statistical Paper No. 3). Coventry: National Ethnic Minority Data Archive, Centre for Research in Ethnic Relations, University of Warwick.

Owen, D. (1996). *Towards 2001: Ethnic minorities and the census.* Coventry: National Ethnic Minority Data Archive, Centre for Research in Ethnic Relations, University of Warwick.

Prime Minister. (1964–1965). *Immigration from the Commonwealth* (White Paper, 1965 August, vol. Xxviii, cmnd. 2739). London: Her Majesty's Stationery Office.

Race Relations Act (1976, c. 74). London: Her Majesty's Stationery Office

Racial violence. (1993, September). *The Runnymede Bulletin,* No. 268, p. 4.

Racist attacks and harassment: The epidemic of the 90's? (1993, July). *Black to Black*, p. 1.

Roberts, A., & Massey, I. (1993). Managing change in schools. In A. Fyfe & P. Figueroa (Eds.), *Education for cultural diversity: The challenge for a new era* (pp. 301–317). London: Routledge.

Rose, E. J. B., Deakin, N., Abrams, M., Jackson, V., Peston, M., Vanags, A. H., Cohen, B., Gaitskell, J., & Ward, P. (1969). *Colour and citizenship: A report on British race relations.* London: Oxford University Press.

Royal Commission on Population. (1949). *Report* (cmnd. 7695). London: His Majesty's Stationery Office.

Sewell, T. (1997). *Black masculinities and schooling: How Black boys survive modern schooling.* Stoke-on-Trent: Trentham.

Siraj-Blatchford, I. (1993). Social justice and teacher education in the UK. In G. K. Verma (Ed.), *Inequality and teacher education: An international perspective* (pp. 89–99). London: Falmer.

Smith, D. J. (1977). *Racial disadvantage in Britain* (The PEP Report). Harmondsworth: Penguin.

Swann, Lord (1993). *Education for all*: A personal view. In A. Fyfe & P. Figueroa (Eds.), *Education for cultural diversity: The challenge for a new era* (pp. 1–8). London: Routledge.

Teacher Training Agency. (1997). *Standards for the award of qualified teacher status.* London: TTA.

Tomlinson, S. (1982). *A sociology of special education.* London: Routledge & Kegan Paul.

Tomlinson, S. (1993). The multicultural task group: The group that never was. In A. S. King & M. J. Reiss (Eds.), *The multicultural dimension of the national curriculum* (pp. 21–29). London: Falmer.

Walvin, J. (1973). *Black and White: The Negro in English society, 1555–1945.* London: Allen Lane.

Whitty, G. (1990). The New Right and the national curriculum: State control or market forces? In B. Moon (Ed.), *New curriculum—National curriculum* (pp. 15–22). London: Hodder & Stoughton.

Wright, C. (1986). School processes: An ethnographic study. In J. Eggleston, D. Dunn, & M. Anjali, with C. Wright (Eds.), *Education for some: The educational and vocational experiences of 15–18-year-old members of minority ethnic groups* (pp. 127–179). Stoke-on-Trent: Trentham.

Wright, C. (1992). *Race relations in the primary school.* London: David Fulton.

Editor's Remarks

Spain has a history that reflects significant intercultural interaction and occasional tension. Historically, the Iberian Peninsula has been one of the most culturally diverse parts of Europe. From the earliest years, the Mediterranean, or Iberian portions of Spain have been in opposition with the central and northern Celtic regions. In the late 1400s, when religious unity was thought to be necessary for political unity, in other parts of Europe, Spain was leading the way in religious conformity, demanding that its non-Christian microcultures (including Jews and Muslims) convert to Christianity or be exiled. At the same time, colonization and great exploration was underway, with some of the world's best-known explorers coming from Spain, among them Christopher Columbus, Vasco Nunez de Balboa, Ferdinand Magellan, and Hernando Cortes.

Today, the country is composed of a variety of people, including indigenous microcultures of Castillians, Catalans, and Basques; immigrants such as Asians and Africans; groups such as the Gypsies; and religious groups of all kinds. Although the official language of the country is Spanish, each state has the right to choose the instructional language of its choice. Compounding this scenario are the many isolated villages and towns struggling to appreciate the pluralistic nature of the nation.

Much of today's emphasis on multicultural education in Spain can be traced to the words of Jose Maria Maravall Herrero, who was Minister of Education and Science during most of the 1980s. Through writings, Herrero suggested that the educational system must contribute to the integration of society, foster equality of opportunity, promote the cohesion of the nation, and socialize citizens to hold democratic values.

How should a nation with such a complex and diverse history direct its educational system to more adequately address the needs of its multicultural population while preparing young people for an increasingly interdependent future?

Chapter 7

The Challenge of Intercultural Education in Spain

ℬ ◆ ℭ

Auxiliadora Sales Ciges
Rafaela Garcia Lopez
University Jaume

THE SPANISH EDUCATION SYSTEM
AND ITS INTERCULTURAL POLICY

To understand the multicultural reality in Spain and how the education system confronts this phenomenon, it is necessary to know, on one hand, how the Spanish state structure is organized, and on the other hand, the several levels of multiculturalism. Regarding the first issue, since the Constitution of 1978, the Spanish state has been organized into municipalities, counties, and autonomous communities. Seventeen autonomous communities exist now and six of them have full responsibility in education: Catalonia, Basque Country, Galicia, Andaluci, Canary Islands, and Valencia. However, the state has reserved the following responsibilities for itself: (a) the general arrangement of the education system; (b) the general curriculum of teaching; (c) the establishment of a core curriculum and the regulation of other conditions to obtain, issue, and approve academic degrees and professional qualifications in all Spanish territory; and (d) High Inspection.

All the autonomous governments in Spain establish laws and dispositions to regulate the education system in their territories and especially to look after the culture and language of their nationality or region. This is related to the second issue: multiculturalism. Spain is a pluricultural and plurilingual country. In addition to having diverse local cultures with their differing languages, which have lived together in the Spanish territory for several centuries now, one ethnic group has traditionally been excluded: the Gypsies. Also to be taken into account is the remarkable increase in the past few years of the immigrant population—foreigners who increase the cultural and ethnic diversity that neither the social system nor the education system in the society is prepared to accommodate. Finally, to make this situation more complex, Spaniards are learning to be members of the European Union (EU).

For the preceding reasons, the multicultural reality in Spain can be analyzed on four levels, which show different problems that require different solutions. The levels can be defined as local cultures officially accepted, with a certain degree of political, economical, and educational autonomy; Gypsy culture, without recognition or participation in the various organs of government; cultures of immigrant people, most of them from Northern Africa, Portugal, Central Africa, Latin America and, in a smaller number, from Eastern Europe; and European culture, that implies acquiring a wider vision of Spain's integration in Europe and thus a wider intercultural sensitivity for all its citizens.

The Spanish multicultural reality demonstrates a complexity and richness and leads us to the conclusion that intercultural education concerns immigrants, nationalists, and ethnic minority groups because it is a social and educational matter addressed to all the citizens, whatever their culture, social class, sex, religion, or race. Precisely because Spain is so diverse and pluralistic, intercultural education is and must be an issue that involves all ethnic groups, especially in these increasingly global times. At the same time, Spain's problems are internationalized and the decisions of the governments cannot be taken in an isolated way. This means that when diversity is recognized and valued, intercultural education becomes essential in a democratic society. Only then does this awareness make equality from plurality possible, because homogeneity of values and interests does not exist even in a monocultural society. But on account of the political, economic, and cultural models that reign in current capitalist societies, serious conflicts are generated among the cultural groups that share the social space, and the positive development of this pluralism is no longer possible. Those conflicts are revealed in the attitudes that Spaniards have toward immigrants and social and ethnic minorities, which makes pluralism not only necessary, but urgent in shaping the values and attitudes within the intercultural model. These attitudes are expressed not only in a verbal way, but also very often in violent actions against minority groups. Such actions are the result of the increasing racist and xenophobic attitudes used to justify the conception of the cultural and social minorities as scapegoats of the structural economic and political problems.

HOW DOES THE SPANISH EDUCATION SYSTEM COPE WITH THE CHALLENGE OF INTERCULTURAL EDUCATION?

According to sociological studies, the complete and proper integration in the education system of all the cultural groups living together in Spain, especially Gypsies, is still a challenge, despite notable efforts made in the past years. The Law of General Arrangement of the Educational System, (LOGSE, 1990), will govern the coming years' attempts to adapt Spanish schools to the new context, including the state of autonomies, technological and cultural changes, and the European labor market. The permanent adoption of the educational system to the social demands and educational needs of the different groups is a fundamental goal. But to achieve this objective, it is necessary to conduct research analyzing the specific problems that present themselves to educators concerning immigrants and, in particular, the Gypsy minority. In addition, the priorities that should be made in educational policy, to aid the development of the immigrants' own cultural identity and their active and full citizenship in the Spanish society, must be considered.

The objectives foreseen by LOGSE clearly show that the educational objectives in Spain, as in many other European countries, approximate an intercultural perspective. However, the incorporation of these objectives into the educational policy has been much more overdue than in other European nations, basically because Spaniards used to emigrate to Germany, France, other European countries, and Latin America to improve their economic conditions and to escape the civil war. Thus, emigrants from other countries did not choose Spain primarily because the Spanish economic, political, and social conditions were not adapted to their interests. This situation began to change in the mid-1970s.

Since the Council of Europe Foundation in 1949, two topics have been given priority: civic education and international and intercultural relationships. But it was not until the early 1980s when the First Conference on Intercultural Curriculum took place in Holland (1982) and the Second Conference held in London (1984) proposed the study of the current process for international and intercultural understanding that the analysis on the classroom reality in Europe finally took place.

In spite of the considerable increase in cultural and ethnic groups since the 1960s and 1970s in the principal countries of France, Germany,

England, and the European capital cities of Paris, London, and so forth, educational institutions had a late reaction. In many cases, this cultural pluralism was met with reticence and hostility by certain social sectors and educational policymakers. As was said before, Spanish educational law (LOGSE) incorporates an intercultural approach, at least in its basic principles. The main objectives of this law, according to its preliminary title, are (a) the complete personality development of the students; (b) respect for fundamental rights and liberties, and tolerance for the democratic principles; (c) acquisition of intellectual and technical work habits as well as scientific, humanistic, historic and aesthetic knowledge; (d) qualification for professional activities; (e) respect toward the linguistic and cultural pluralism in Spain; (f) preparation to participate actively in the social and cultural life; and, (g) education for peace, cooperation, and solidarity among peoples.

It is evident that four goals out of the seven make direct or indirect reference to cultural diversity. In harmony with the guideline from the Council of European Ministers, a series of principles and objectives have been proposed that should precede the action of public powers in the educational field and that rebound directly for the integration of students from other cultures in the Spanish society. These include the development of students who respect individual liberty; exercise tolerance and solidarity; acquire democratic habits and mutual respect; fight against inequality and discrimination for reasons of birth, race, sex, religion, or opinion; and work for peace, cooperation, and respect for diversity. The problem now is to operationalize these objectives from teacher training to school organization, the curriculum, the textbooks, and teaching materials.

The reform of the Spanish education system undertaken in 1990 comprises general system teaching and special system teaching. The first includes kindergarten (not compulsory, from 0 to 6 years of age); primary school (compulsory, from 6 to 12 years of age); secondary school, which contains compulsory secondary education (from 12 to 16 years of age), high school (from 16 to 18 years of age), and the vocational training of middle and high level (the technical alternative to high school); and university studies. The special system teaching includes artistic and languages teaching (although the several communities with educational responsibilities incorporate some others unique to their individual regions).

It is the central government that provides a common general curriculum for the general teaching schedule in order to guarantee the minimal content of teaching throughout the Spanish territory. The Curricular Design Development is based on two documents concerning schools: The Educational Project of Center (PEC) and The Curricular Project of Center (PCC). The Educational Project of Center states the educational goals of every school. The school community establishes the framework of all its strategies as the guide and the way they should follow to reach those educational goals. The Curricular Project of Center is elaborated by teachers. It implies the making of decisions concerning the elements that define the curriculum: what, how, and when to teach and evaluate. Teachers have to make decisions about the objectives and content, their distribution and timing in relation to the educational levels; the methodology that should be used; the school space and time organization; the materials used; and the evaluation criteria.

The Classroom Program is the third level of curriculum concern: Every teacher should prepare a group of Didactic Units in chronological order for every academic discipline and educational level. At this level it is necessary to include values in harmony with the PEC, the PCC, and the students' experiences, beliefs, and their context. In fact, the development of the LOGSE in the Curricular Designs of the Ministry of Education and Science includes the areas of natural, social, and cultural environment; artistic education; Spanish and foreign languages; sensitivity toward solidarity and the elimination of discriminatory attitudes; the knowledge of cultural and artistic manifestations of different human groups; an emphasis on bilingualism to facilitate intercultural understanding, in those communities that have their own language; and positive attitudes toward other languages. As for compulsory secondary education, in the areas of language and literature, foreign languages, and the social sciences (geog - raphy and history), positive attitudes toward cultural diversity, democratic coexistence, and critical attitudes opposing prejudices and stereotypes of all types are more clearly promoted. All these minimum curricular contents defined by educational policy would allow the introduction of intercultural education in the whole curriculum at all levels from kindergarten to secondary school. In spite of deficiencies in the implementation of the LOGSE, there is a need to reflect multicultural phenomena in all the expressions and perspectives of the school curriculum. It is fundamental to plan social educational actions especially aimed to reach students from cultural minority groups, who usually belong to underprivileged sectors of society. For this reason, attention to the educational needs of Gypsy and immigrant students is carried out by the frame of the Compensatory Education Programs.

CULTURAL AND ETHNIC DIVERSITY IN SPAIN: PROSPECTS OF INTEGRATION IN SCHOOL AND SOCIETY

The goals and objectives assumed by the Spanish education system reform show the intent of responding to the demands of a multilingual and multicultural society. Without considering this analysis as an exhaustive typology of educational contexts related to ethnic and cultural diversity, this section once again employs the three levels of multiculturality set out in the previous section.

In the first place, there exist "historic nationalities," with marked and differentiated linguistic and cultural characteristics within the Spanish state. In Spain there is one official language for the entire Castelian state, but because Spain is a state of Autonomies, those that possess their own language are officially considered bilingual territories. In Galicia, Galician and Castilian are both spoken; in the Basque Country, Euskera is spoken; and in Catalonia, Valencia, and Baleares Islands, Catalan is the common language.

These languages, which have been repressed and disparaged in several historic periods during the last centuries, are being restored by nationalists opposed to the hegemony of the Castilian cultural model. The process of linguistic normalization through the education system and its public institutions represents an effort to respect and develop the many cultures of the region. These, however, sometimes collide with the cultural groups that, in the face of this apparent bilingualism and "biculturality," feel their political interests threatened. In spite of the latent and evident conflicts with regard to the linguistic problem and cultural loyalties, people from other parts of Spain, immigrants from all around the world, and a great number of Gypsies have also settled down in these Autonomies, which favor cultural diversity even more.

The main problem of integration in school is related to language learning. The legitimate right to a full expression and the cultivation of minority languages, which were politically repressed for a long time, results today in a positive discrimination in favor of these languages, thus creating conflict with the Castilian speakers who feel disadvantaged in the face of the bilingual population.

In the second place, it must not be forgotten that Spain is no longer a country of emigration but is now a country of immigration. This new situation demands a better understanding as well as a search for organizational and methodologic strategies to attend to these new needs. In recent years, after Italy, Spain has turned into a country of immigrants comprised of members from the EU and other industrialized countries; immigrants from Asia who come as tourists and ask for asylum; and finally, those from sub-Sarahan Africa. Moroccan immigration is a particular development in Spain, its evolution having had two phases: immigration until 1970 toward Ceuta and Melilla, both on the African continent, and then after 1970, immigration toward the Iberian Peninsula. The massive immigration from Latin America is more recent. Spain is yet one of the European countries with fewer immigrants (1.8% to 2% of the total population in

1993) than countries such as Belgium (10%), France (8.2%) or Germany (7.2%) traditionally, that have received immigrants from other European countries, but it is also true that the number of immigrants settling in Spain make the cultural composition more and more complex and multicolored.

In 1955, 66,000 foreigners resided in Spain, but in 1994 there were more than 400,000 resident foreigners. Not all this incipient immigrant population enters the country enjoying the same prestige and rights. Surveys on attitudes toward foreigners and the violent expressions of racism and xenophobia of certain groups such as neonazis, and against Moroccan, sub-Sarahan Africans, and Latin Americans not only happens in Spain, but also in other European countries known as "developed countries", such as France, Germany, Austria, Belgium, and Italy.

There has thus been an increase in the number of children coming from many different countries who now are attending public school programs. Foreign immigrants can be divided into three groups or categories: (a) highly qualified foreigners coming from other industrialized countries and countries that do not belong to the EU and (presenting few, if any, integration problems and generally well regarded and accepted by the Spanish population); (b) slightly qualified immigrants that hold illegal status and are not very well regarded and considered in Spanish society; and (c) illegal immigrants who are isolated and excluded, and do not possess social security or other social services (such immigrants do not have access to the educational or professional system, and thus experience loss of self-esteem which draws them further away from the society in which they live).

The Ministry of Education provides the same rights and conditions to all students in the country, regardless of their country of origin or legal status. What is more, since the Resolution of May, 1995, it is not compulsory to present a resident's credential document for admission to the public schools.

As previously stated, immigration in Spain is only now becoming a problem. On the one hand, immigrants are hired as cheap labor by employers. On the other hand, they are considered a threat by local workers. Statements are often heard blaming the immigrants for all of Spain's social problems including drugs, unemployment, criminal activity, and so forth. In addition, immigrants' issues result in some cultural, linguistic, racial, and prejudicial negative attitudes and conflicts the schools, thus encouraging some parents to take their children to monocultural schools. A surprisingly wide range of society considers immigrant families a threat to their security and welfare because these families monopolize state services.

Finally, we must bear in mind the intolerance and aggressiveness against immigrants and their goods. Racism is on the rise in some parts of Europe. In France, for example, racist statements have been made routinely by some political parties. In Germany, many cases of racist aggressions against refugees and their homes have been seen. In Spain, although the problem is not as bad, aggression against Gypsies, Africans, Arabs, the homeless, and homosexuals have been carried out by skin-head gangs. It is ironic that Spain does not consider itself a racist country, even when its history textbooks talk about the expulsion of Jews and Arabs, and the conquest of America (Catholic kings period). Obviously, it is racist behavior to talk about the Gypsies in textbooks without reference to their culture and history.

The educational answer together with the economic and sociocultural one should guide the way in which students are taught to be respectful and understanding, emphasizing the following aspects: (a) the actual cultural pluralism and existence of different ways of understanding society, religion, and habits of Spain; (b) the living conditions in different countries and the reasons why people may feel the need to emigrate because of economics, politics, wars, and so forth; (c) the most important landmarks in racism's history and racist ideas, observed from a thorough study of this problem in the EU, Germany, South Africa, and the like, as well as more recent Spanish history (the expulsion of Jews and Arabs, the conquest of America, the Gypsy problem); (d) the contribution of science concerning discrimination and racism including biology, genetics, and psychology; (e) respect for human rights, for the movement, and for the history of the pursuit of liberty and equality of human kind; and, (f) acknowledgment and respect toward others regardless of their race, sex, origin, or religion (Etxeberria, 1992).

The Gypsy Population in Spain

The Gypsies constitute a nonterritorial cultural group whose claims to become Spanish citizens are based on the acknowledgment of their difference and their right to have equal say in social and political decisions. Nevertheless, because of their nomadic tradition, they do not claim a territory nor independent institutions, something that is more common among the various nationalistic movements emerging from the modern state.

Concerning intercultural education, coexistence with the Gypsies is the most significant problem faced by Spanish society. The Gypsies arrived in Spain in the 15th century. At the beginning, they were well accepted. They were free to live within Spanish territory and interacted well with peasants and villagers. Their craftsmanship and the ease with which they entertained were highly valued among the Spanish people.

The hegemony of Christianity ended the peaceful coexistence between cultures and religions (Jews, Christians, and Arabs), and a period of fanaticism and repression soon followed with no place for tolerance. In the name of faith, the Catholic kings (1479–1515), together with the Church, determined the basis of Spanish ideology: a unique sole political power, one religion, one language, one culture, and therefore one way of being and feeling. In this scenario, the Gypsies were seen as dangerous and difficult to tame and control. It was here that the political repression against the Gypsies began—and it continues today.

The highest percentage of the present-day Gypsy population in Spain resides in Andalucia. The Gypsies have their own set of rules and norms, which regulate their coexistence and are the basis for their collective identity as well as a guarantee for their survival and permanence as a people. These rules and norms constitute an authentic, albeit unwritten, legislative body, which receives total commitment, support, and acceptance on the part of the Gypsy population. The Gypsies are a people who, in spite of having no territory or fatherland, maintain an agraphic culture handed down from generation to generation. From the Gypsies' point of view, their culture, like that of anyone else, consists of their language, laws, and compendium of traditions, customs, rites, and artistic expressions.

A large number of cliches and falsehoods have created a "black legend" surrounding the Gypsies. This legend has been fed by prejudices such as those that render the word "Gypsy" as synonymous with thief, lazy, or conflictive. Since the 1978 Constitution, efforts have been made to standardize the presence of the Gypsy minority within the greater Spanish community. For the Gypsies themselves, this standardization entails finding a way to maintain their differentiated identity while making it compatible with a recognition of their condition as Spanish citizens. It seems, however, that after almost 20 years of democracy, expectations of the Gypsies have not been fulfilled. At an educational level, there is an insistence for the need to integrate the younger members of the Gypsies into labor-insertion programmes and plans, but company managers do not employ them due to generalized prejudices. Moreover, because of failure and absenteeism of Gypsies at school, there is a tendency to put the blame on their family environment, thus exonerating the teachers and schools.

No census has been made of the Gypsy population because the general population census does not include ethnic data. The Gypsy population in Spain is the highest among the 15 countries making up the European Union. According to a survey carried out in 1985 by the Home Office Ministry of Administrative Assistance and Population, the Gypsy population in Spain was estimated to be more than half a million people. With their high level of growth estimated at 5.2% per year, the number of

Gypsies in Spain today has reached approximately 800,000. According to the Report on the Study and Situation of the Educational System carried out by the Ministry of Education and Culture, the schooling of the Gypsy population is tending toward standardization regarding the school enrollment rate as well as the age at which children are being incorporated into schools. However, in general terms, the incorporation of Gypsy children into the schools is still an unsteady and irregular process due to high rates of absenteeism and an early school-leaving age. The majority of Gypsies are included in compensatory projects because of their socioeconomic status. These actions have been geared toward improving their scholastic and social integration, increasing their expectations of scholastic and social promotion, decreasing factors responsible for their cultural uprooting, foreseeing segregation problems, and preventing them from becoming the object of segregatory attitudes.

The key problems of schooling Gypsy children are many, and represent a very real clash of cultures. Together with the conditions and requirements before their admittance to schools, major problems are both objective and subjective in nature. Conditions of a subjective nature include the rejection and refusal from parents and teachers alike regarding the admittance of Gypsy children within the school, and a lack of interest and desire on the part of Gypsy parents for their children to attend "payo" schools (the term used by Gypsies in referring to anyone not of their culture or group). Conditions of an objective nature include the linguistic barrier, social handicaps, inferiority of financial resources, and lack of adequate nourishment, hygiene, health, and medical care.

In 1992, The General Secretary for the Association of Gypsies assessed the educational situation of Gypsy children from various aspects. Their conclusions are summed up as follows:

1. Despite an increasing standardization regarding the admittance of the Gypsy population to schools in recent years, 20% of the children still do not receive schooling until they are of a later age, and a further 21% do not receive any schooling at all due to parental decision.
2. Absence of Gypsy children from class for more than 3 months during one school year is 43%.
3. Only 54% of Gypsy children receive schooling in primary schools.
4. The failure to acquire a steady rhythm of study, routine, and norms at school continues to be one of the fundamental problems of Gypsy children. On a day-to-day basis, 60% do not attend school.
5. Only 6% of Gypsy children have a socioeconomic status equal or superior to the average of their classmates.
6. The academic performance of Gypsy children is considerably below average, and 25% have serious difficulties at school.

7. More than 50% of Gypsy families do not seem to be particularly motivated toward schooling, or at least do not have high expectations from such. Only 48% of families want their children to remain in school and complete compulsory secondary education.
8. Among the teachers 43% do not consider it necessary to introduce or include historical or cultural features and aspects of this ethnic group in the educational process.

Although the Spanish population consists of different historical and social phenomena, the same basic question remains: How can different groups who are or feel themselves to be culturally different in a society that although democratic, is not egalitarian, best learn to function effectively in a pluralistic society. It was precisely this idea that brought about multicultural thinking in other countries.

THE INTRODUCTION OF INTERCULTURAL EDUCATION IN SPANISH SCHOOLS

In their 1992–1993 report, the Center for Investigation into Social Reality found that Gypsies were the least esteemed of all social groups, and as such were more susceptible to discrimination. With regard to people's level of tolerance, the most targeted group was drug addicts, followed by Gypsies, then prostitutes. In eighth place were Moroccans, followed by Black Africans, then South Americans.

These results are highly significant if we contrast them with the surveys carried out by Francisco Andres Orizo (1983, 1991) regarding the values of Spanish people. In 1982 the percentage of those who assessed the Gypsies as "undesirable neighbors" was considerably less. Included within the "people of other races" section, they appeared in 7th place after alcoholics, exconvicts, political extremists, the emotionally unstable, and members of sects. Immigrant workers and foreigners were 11th in the list. Likewise, in 1990, homosexuals and people with AIDS were considered to be more undesirable neighbors than Muslims (in 9th place), other races (in 10th position) and immigrants (11th).

The profile of people who manifest racist or xenophobic attitudes toward Arabs, Gypsies, and Africans is, generally speaking, that of a person with right-wing political tendencies, age 50 years older, of low social status, who has never been abroad. No matter how the situation is viewed, minority cultural groups are regarded as a nuisance and a threat to neighborly coexistence by many in the Spanish population. Gypsies, Africans, and Magrebies continue to occupy the first three places on the list of those people with whom parents would forbid or disapprove of their daughter having an emotional or affective relationship.

Those interviewed perceive a higher discrimination on the part of their families, friends, and Spanish people in general toward Gypsies than toward immigrants. However, 44% believed that the presence of immigrants from less-developed countries produced a higher level of delinquency, and 55% think it created a rise in unemployment among the Spanish people. It is interesting to note that these attitudes and opinions continue to be maintained, although very few of those interviewed have actually had any formal contact or relationship with Magrebies, Africans, South Americans, or Gypsies. Even among those who have maintained a conversation with somebody from one of these racial groups, 65% consider that there was no change whatever in their opinion. This clearly indicates prejudices and stereotypes that can be formed due to a lack of knowledge and understanding, yet continue to exist and even be strengthened despite direct contact with the stereotyped groups or individuals. This occurs because the relation has been preconditioned by previously formed ideas and concepts regarding these groups.

These attitudes are reproduced in schoolchildren and teachers (Calvo, 1990) who manifest a strong rejection toward Gypsies, Magrebies, and African Negroes, blaming them for the exclusion and isolation they suffer, and in the more extreme cases demanding their expulsion from Spain or even their extermination, even though they all are apparently aware of the universalist discourse of equality and the importance placed on pluralism and difference. Likewise, in school textbooks and other teaching material, racism and xenophobia are reflected by the exclusion of certain cultural groups from the curriculum and the stereotyping of other cultural models, together with a denial of the existence of racism in Spain. However, it is in the school itself that these attitudes must be changed, that there exists an ethic and democratic need to educate citizens for a plural and diverse world from the perspectives of a tolerant coexistence, teacher training, and reform in curricular contents.

Moreover, racist and xenophobic attitudes should not be dealt with at school only. There is a need for intercultural social policies that propose, plan, and create awareness campaigns for Spanish people regarding migratory phenomena, in an attempt to discover and understand the causes that have motivated others to abandon their country of origin as well as the living conditions of the immigrants in the country that has received them. Until now, this task has been developed and put into practice by the Ministry of Social Affairs through publicity campaigns against cultural and social discrimination in a variety of social areas: labor, community, education, and so forth. The social repercussions so far have been positive, although greater planning is required within intercultural programs of a much more widespread nature so as to prevent their becoming mere isolated and anecdotal actions.

Confrontation Between Gypsy and "Payo" Cultures. All reports put together by Gypsy associations suggest that the central problem for the Gypsy population lies in the majority group's inability to admit and recognize the Gypsies' right to be different. Traditional Gypsy education is by oral tradition, which of course makes sense within an agraphic culture. For this reason, when a Gypsy realizes that development and progress within a majority society implies at least being able to read and write, he accepts the existence of schools to this end but no further, and attempts to limit the years of schooling so that the child will not become impregnated with those values that the majority society attempts to instil through schooling.

Gypsy schooling, in fact, generally begins late and is of a very short duration because their concept of infancy and childhood tends to be quite different. In Gypsy tradition, 12-year-olds are already considered fit for adult life in general, and as such the idea of remaining at school beyond those years has little relevance. Furthermore, their sense of protection toward children is in conflict with the care, attention, and discipline offered by an institution that is not of their own family. The organization, timetables, values, hierarchies, physical structure, and transmitting agents of schooling are contradictory to the values that Gypsy children feel within themselves and their environment. As such, feelings of displacement, assault, or aggression within a scholastic atmosphere are evident, and rules and learning styles are unfamiliar to many.

Furthermore, because school does not prepare people for life in the Gypsy world and culture, and therefore does not enable them to develop and carry out those jobs and professions in which Gypsy adults are habitually involved, it is considered necessary for the children to leave school in order to learn how to live in their own world. In addition, admitting Gypsy children to school is often a very difficult and complicated process because of the complex enrollment procedures and administrative requirements for their integration into educational centers. This situation requires greater flexibility and democratization of the existing school structure and organization, so that the culture, administration, and contents of schooling reflect the diversity of the nations' population. If this were done, schooling would be more motivating for Gypsy children; they would develop a satisfactory and dynamic cultural identity; and they would more likely integrate with the greater society. Likewise, it is necessary to encourage families to become more involved in the education of their children and encourage them to commit themselves to decision making within the school according to the democratic participation established by law, thus enabling them to make their voice heard as a collective member of the educational community.

Teachers' Attitudes in the Face of Cultural Diversity

A 1995 investigation carried out in the community of Valencia concerning primary and secondary school teachers' attitudes toward intercultural education and cultural diversity (Sales, 1997) revealed a sample of the opinions and predispositions of teachers regarding the introduction of an intercultural perspective in teaching. Teachers considered intercultural education necessary in schools and teacher training in order to provide equal opportunities and attitudes of respect toward people of different cultures. However, teachers displayed very little of these intercultural attitudes themselves. Many believe that intercultural education is a question for minority cultures only and does not affect pupils in the majority culture, nor involve transformations within the school, and as such should be handled by specialists and experts who are not directly connected with the school, or by teachers who are themselves from other cultures.

Teachers' attitudes toward cultural diversity are far more negative than those they express toward intercultural education. Their expectations regarding pupils from cultural minorities are negative, and they blame these pupils for lowering the quality of learning in the classroom and for creating problems of a disciplinary nature, especially in the case of Gypsy children. Likewise, teachers display very little intercultural sympathy and sensitivity in their work. They tend to reject other cultural values and refuse to question their own values. Teachers tend to maintain negative stereotypic ideas concerning minority cultures and would prefer to live in a social context wherein interpersonal relationships are confined to people from their own culture and country.

This brief description of the attitudes of teachers working in multicultural contexts reveals the difficulties and problems that exist in the incorporation of new cultural content within the school together with the educators' resistance in the face of intercultural perspectives rather than their acceptance of a vision geared more toward assimilation and compensation.

Lack of Teachers' Knowledge and Training. Teacher training is one basic pillar of educational reform and change. Some of the obstacles that intercultural education faces in schools include teachers' attitudes, aptitudes, and lack of experience. On one hand, teachers tend to exhibit strong racial and cultural prejudices, particularly because they are accustomed to working with relatively homogeneous students and traditional, ethnocentric methods. On the other hand, university programs have not prepared teachers to teach in diverse contexts. There are no compulsory courses dealing with intercultural education in the college curriculum for teacher education students. Optional courses for future teachers and educators on this topic can be found only in a few universities. This means that only motivated students interested in cultural diversity will attend those courses, whereas those that show more racist attitudes and disregard for others will not choose these courses. Once the teacher is actually working in a school, the only opportunity he or she has to get some training is through the teachers' centers. These centers arrange monographic courses on important current issues to update teachers in strategies, theories, methods, resources, and possible innovations to be applied in their classrooms.

The authors of this chapter have developed an educational model with a sound theoretical base and flexible structure, which can be adapted to specific school contexts. The focus of the course is on educational strategies and resources from an intercultural perspective, aiming to change the attitudes of preservice teachers and their students toward cultural diversity. We offer a pedagogic assessment for all primary and secondary teachers in the Valencian community who are interested in intercultural attitudes and provide them with the possibility of designing intercultural programs in their own schools. The basic aims of the course are the following: (a) to know and analyze the evolution of different intercultural education models and their goals; (b) to explain the importance and need to teach these attitudes in general education, and especially in intercultural education; (c) to change attitudes by knowing and applying educational techniques such as strategies for active participation, cooperation in the classroom, and persuasive communication; and (d) to offer pedagogic assessment for the development of intercultural programs in schools.

Our methodology has focused on three main strategies: (a) the theory of concepts, models and educational techniques using teaching materials such as books, photos, songs, and audiovisual materials; (b) small work groups to elaborate activities and design programs; and, (c) debates on intercultural concepts, work groups, and any questions that participants may consider interesting to share and contrast with others in order to develop their own programs.

These three methodologic strategies are similar to the methodologic approach we propose for school programs, and their fundamental objective is to link theory and practice, adapting our intercultural model to every teachers's own style and their school context. We also try to promote experiences, exchange, and dialogue among teachers, so that with pedagogical help, they will have the chance to revise their educational practice. At the same time, teachers can participate in innovative program design and development from an intercultural point of view and take advantage or their community resources, getting parents and cultural associations involved in these activities. From this approach, the course has continuity because we work with the teachers, helping them in an on-going evaluation of the entire process (qualitative and quantitative feedback). With all this, teachers feel responsible for the development and permanent training to improve the programs.

Support from Educational Administration and Educational Institutions. In research designed to gain an understanding of the multicultural reality of Castellon county schools, Sales (1997) found that the main complaint of school staff was the lack of institutional support and coordination with social workers, involving problems such as school absenteeism of students belonging to minorities and their improper use of economic assistance. School staff also complained that administrators seem to use schools as a collection of odds and ends, and also as a place where somebody has to solve those problems that other social institutions do not know how or do not want to solve. From this point of view, intercultural education becomes a fashionable, trendy subject, and therefore, useless. Some of these criticisms insinuate that the schools have tried to consider intercultural education as a possibility, but they have given up because of the lack of political and social support. Obviously, this last opinion comes from a disappointed and sceptical group of teachers who do not believe in these educational innovations that, according to them rarely are realized.

A survey of 134 Valencian schools, found that many schools made great statements about intercultural principles but did not put them to practice. In the very few cases of intercultural principles put into action, the activities were only extracurricular or addressed specific individual problems "to solve adaptation or integration problems" related to foreigners and immigrants.

In many cases, intercultural education was considered the responsibility of external institutions and special staff—counselors, psychologists, family associations, and the like, but not the responsibility of the more global influences of school organization, curriculum, methodology, and teacher training. Furthermore, our own research demonstrated that throughout the last 10 years of intercultural program development, many programs were full of good intentions but never came to practice, nor were they evaluated in a proper way. Therefore, their results could not be circulated, and criteria for the improvement could not be provided.

Lack of Intercultural Interest Due to the Number of Diverse Students in Schools. Our own research also showed that some schools with students from diverse backgrounds do not include diversity management in their educational project of center (PEC), nor do they carry out intercultural activities because they consider the number of these students to be too small. Some other schools do not carry out activities to promote positive attitudes toward diversity precisely because they treat all their students as equals. The activities usually developed in schools are isolated and folkloric, with most of them simply geared toward adapting minority students to the traditional curriculum. Despite the fact that some schools include values of respect and tolerance toward cultural diversity in their educational project, they do not actually develop them in specific activities. Therefore, it is believed by many that if there are no integrational problems (read assimilation) or if there are no minorities, it is not necessary to undertake special actions. Intercultural education is related only to the problems that Gypsies and immigrants provoke.

To overcome this narrow perception, once again, solid teacher training is essential in order to prepare teachers to work in diverse contexts, diversifying those cultural models transmitted at school, or at least reviewing the dominant model as the only one and incorporating strategies of cooperative learning that break away from traditional methodology. This is a way of preventing racist attitudes and behaviors in teachers and students, and especially of disassociating the concept of interculturalism from compensation or deficit.

Absence of Intercultural Research. In Spain there are no reliable demographic data or sociologic and pedagogic research on minority children's integration in the school context. Without this research, it is very difficult to plan pedagogic actions that are not too general and thus are able to deal with real problems. Educational policy must take into account and expedite the research on intercultural education, so it can respond to the socioeducational issues posed by cultural diversity. Especially from university and nongovernmental organizations, such a response would allow us to anticipate and prevent conflicts and similar situations in the future, because a progressive increase of the immigrant population is foreseen.

TEACHER TRAINING AND PROFESSIONAL DEVELOPMENT THROUGH INTERCULTURAL CURRICULUM DESIGN AND EVALUATION

Although the preamble of the LOGSE is full of concepts such as equality, pluralism, tolerance, liberty, consensus, progress, and social participation, the daily reality of schools is very far removed from these ideals. The reform and its new discourse has been elaborated without previous social debate. Therefore schools are still in a state of confusion, trying to come to terms with administrative demands and working without any counseling. This situation has converted a democratic and decentralized discourse into a neoliberal discourse of "every man for himself."

Meanwhile, textbook editors continue to make money by benefiting from the lack of curricular definition and the teachers' confusion, and even end up defining the curriculum itself by influencing and determining content organization, classroom activities, and even assessment criteria. Most of these are full of stereotypes, prejudices, and cultural exclusions that reveal the economic interests behind their content and slowly soak into school culture without too much resistance. It would seem obvious that the private economic interests of any publisher cannot solve or put the finishing touches to curricular designs in schools because they leave teachers isolated and with goals and interests that are not democratic or educational (Apple, 1996).

Professional development involved in curricular design means an open, critical, and creative curricular model whose final definition is the responsibility of teachers and the school community, based on the debate and elaboration of their educational project, favoring in this way a better understanding and knowledge of the complex teaching–learning process from a global conception of education as a whole. Intercultural programs should be included in daily school practice and curriculum so that educators may think about and develop their own creativity and professional ethics. They should explicitly clarify which educational models guide them, which values and attitudes they want to teach, and how they shape the general objectives and methodology that they are to develop in activities within the classroom and throughout the course. In multicultural tradition, the transition from assimilation to pluralism made educators think about including in the curriculum not only different cultural traditions, but also questions about a school structure that could be both racially and culturally isolating. This was a movement from pluralism to antiracism. This new curricular model takes into account the function of school materials, the hidden curriculum, educational policies, and students' and teachers' awareness of their own racist attitudes. That is to say, the new curricular model is created not only for minority group children, but also for all students and all schools as "an educational frame of mind that would impregnate the whole of school life" (Leicester, 1988, p. 97).

Intercultural curricular organization leads once again to the central question: How do we change a school culture to provide equal opportunities for all group members, and how do we respect diversity within a democratic framework of decisions, dialogue, and communication among diverse social collectives? This implies the inclusion of all those voices that are absent from school contexts: the feminine world, the rural world, infant culture, homosexuals, the working class, the handicapped, pensioners, and ethnic and cultural minorities. The cultures of these groups have been systematically excluded, trivialized, distorted, or stereotyped.

In any case, when teachers in particular and the school community in general design a curriculum, they should express their implicit theories, their decisions, and their professional capacities through a selection of those activities and contents that best fit in with their educational project. In many cases, the critical analysis of didactic material is a spectacular and innovative advance for those schools that do not have a sufficient budget to use new technologies or didactic materials. However, they do use journals, magazines, movies, songs, exhibitions, television and radio programs, students' mail exchange, field work, or visitors' participation as educational resources. In this way, they recover languages and learning channels that are different from those traditionally used in schools and that reflect diverse learning and communication styles that favor equal opportunities for all groups.

The design and creation of activities force teachers to make their pedagogic style explicit and to become aware of their own attitudes, values, and expectations regarding their students' achievement linking contents, methodology, materials, and goals. In fact, school tasks are not only an instrument for connecting curriculum and teaching style, but they also create certain socialization conditions. Teachers plan tasks and strategically place them within school time, in order to state particular climates, relationships, values, and attitudes that attempt to strengthen a certain way of organizing students' behavior. When a teacher includes a task in his classroom, he or she is not only showing the proper academic knowledge the student should learn, but also the attitudes and behaviors that students are expected to adopt. All of this learning is not only intellectual but also emotional, social, and moral, and is standardized in an implicit (hidden curriculum) or explicit way in school tasks. If school staff manage their practice from an intercultural model, they must display the underlying values and attitudes inherent in their tasks as well as their evaluative criteria, that is to say, throughout the whole teaching–learning process.

One of the first things a student learns on coming into the educational system is to answer to the demands of others, to be constantly evaluated by everybody; to adapt his or her expectations to the school evaluation criteria, and to feel failure or success according to external judgments. This learning is part of the hidden curriculum in classroom life, as Jackson (1991) described so well. It is also part of the student socialization process in school.

Intercultural curricula should promote a self-evaluation process, which means that students learn to adapt the direction of their efforts to the achievement of their objectives, analyzing their own learning process or the reasons behind their failure and discovering new perspectives. This evaluative approach is close to the critical definition of an intercultural school based on a reflection of individual and collective educational activity in order to understand the educational process. The school community articulates its democratic participation through dialogue as the only means of eliminating resistance without denying conflict, using it as a tool for change and for the exchange of perspectives and negotiations of controversial interests. In this way, the process of evaluation is understood as a collective commitment to review educational practice, sharing some values and attitudes that become a reference to educational action and the evaluation itself of students' improvement.

This curricular conception and its evaluation means that teachers should not shield themselves behind the current invasion of cultural relativism in order to give up their role as educators of attitudes and values in a democratic and pluralistic school. This ethical commitment requires a pedagogic training that turns teachers into theoretical–practical professionals who elaborate and re-elaborate their own theories from a development of their professional activity within a social and cultural context from which they work as social agents for collective transformation (Martinez, 1995).

Teacher training is a fundamental task of school reform within an intercultural educational policy (Fermoso, 1989; Sleeter, 1992). Teachers should not be blamed for the school's resistance to new educational models that break the hegemony of dominant paradigms, because their own socialization as professionals is imbued with ethnocentric values whose questioning supposes a "de-enculturation" that is not always institutionally promoted. On the one hand, macropolitical changes aimed at reforming education for a democratic and intercultural society should be based on a micropolitical debate in schools. On the other hand, such changes should rest on the training of those teachers who are going to implement the curricular, organizational, and ideological reform that intercultural schools require. A lack of such debate together with a lack of support from educational administration regarding a real transformation of school structure and culture makes teachers, saturated with work and confused by psychologic technical terms, lose faith and reaffirm their old attitudes and values. Thus, potential change foreseen at a macropolitical level can be diluted between school passivity and routines.

Therefore, it is indispensable to have initial and permanent training in intercultural education, not only for technical qualifications, but also for theoretical and practical reflection of teachers about their educational work (Cuevas & Tarrow, 1989). To reach this objective, an interesting idea is the development of teacher centers as places for discussion and debate toward social, political, and moral commitment, within what Giroux and McLaren (1990) called "a language of possibility." In these centers, teachers from different schools, contexts, educational levels, and areas of knowledge could organize their own improvements, exchange innovative experiences, and be aware of their own educational perspectives through debates, in order to do research together on pedagogic tasks linking theory and practice. This is one way to save teachers from "discapacitation" and individualistic isolation, making them feel themselves to be active agents within the practical decision-taking process, the elaboration of theoretical thought and the awareness of collective power. The need and effort to create these centers as networks for exchange and cooperation between teachers is not a strategy only in Spain, but one that is also promoted by European educational institutions due to the interdependence of educational policies among countries in a multicultural and multilingual Europe (Kodron, 1993).

Strategies for Teacher Training

One of the basic elements of any eduational program is the staff that implements it. For this reason, all intercultural education programs include teacher training in some form or other, albeit considering teachers responsible for program design and development or among the educational agents involved in the program. In a direct or indirect way, all the programs undertake the training of teachers and other social agents who are going to develop intercultural programs. Some of the strategies used in the national and international programs that we have analyzed (Sales, 1997) are as follows: training teachers to work in culturally and linguistically diverse contexts, usually university courses for future bilingual programs teachers, and theoretical courses on intercultural education; specific workshops on a particular cultural group in order to know their traits as well as their cognitive and socialization styles; courses arranged by teacher centers to develop intercultural programs in school as an essential element of educational project philosophy for the whole school community; training within those multicultural schools that require special information from teacher centers on interdisciplinary group materials and strategies for every school and preparing teachers to manage diversity and conflicts; work groups set up in teacher education centers and teacher centers to elaborate new didactic materials for multicultural classrooms; educational authorities handing out orientation guides and materials to schools and teachers who are interested in using cultural diversity in their classrooms; theoretical conferences on intercultural education objectives and how to apply basic principles to each context; strategies and educational techniques provided for teachers already working in diverse contexts; an exchange of ideas and experiences among professionals in the field of education in order to discover, understand, and discuss the solutions and actions used in different environments; teacher exchanges (European projects for teacher mobility) that inform about other educational contexts; and, training of monitors, trainers, and counselors, participating as educational agents in the programs to support the tasks of teachers in schools.

TO CONSIDER

1. *Review current English language versions of newspapers from Spain available on the Worldwide Web at www.vol.it/UK/EN/EDI-COLA/quot_str.htm#menu, searching for items that present items related to Gypsies, immigrant issues, and the continuing struggles of the Basque and other communities. How do these current issues relate to what you have just read?*

2. *Are there Gypsies living in your country? Are they, for the most part, a silent or invisible minority? Currently more than 1 million Gypsies live in the United States. Find out about educational efforts, such as the one in Tacoma, Washington, which address the needs of this growing community.*

3. *What can your nation and schools learn from the experiences of Spain?*

4. *How can young people in Spain be most effectively prepared to interact with others on a global scale? What resources in Spain appear to be available for assisting young people in developing a global perspective?*

5. *Spain has had its share of immigrants throughout its history. Given what you have just read, how would you respond to the scenario presented in chapter 1. What steps should schools take in responding to the needs of newly arrived immigrant groups?*

REFERENCES

Andres, O. F. (1983). *Espana, entre la apatia y el cambio social. Na encuesta sobre el sistema europeo de valores: El caso espanol.* Madrid: MAFRE.
Andres, O. F. (1991). *Los nuevos valores de los espanoles.* Madrid: S.M.
Apple, M. W. (1996). *El conocimiento oficial: La educacion democratica en una era conservadora.* Barcelona: Paidos.
Calvo, B. T. (1990). *Espana racista? Voces payas sobre los gitanos.* Barcelona: Anthropos.
CIRES. (1992–1993). La realidad social en Espana. Madrid: Fundacion BBV.

Cuevas. M. J., & Tarrow, N. (1989). Propuesta para incluir educacion multicultural en la formacion del profesorado de E.G.B. *Revista interuniversitaria de formacion del profesorado*, 6, pp. 401–408.

Etxeberria, F. (1992). Educacion intercultural: Racismo y europeismo. *Educacion multicultural e intercultural*. Granada: Impredisur.

Fermoso, E. P. (1989). Politica curricular en una sociedad multicultural. *Revista de ciencias de la educacion*, *139*, 287–299.

Giroux, H., & McLaren, P. (1990). La educacion del profesorado como espacio contrapublico: Apuntes para una redefinicion. In Popkewitz, T. (Ed.), *Formacion del profesorado: Tradicion, teoria, practica* (pp. 244–271). Valancia: Servei de Publicacions de la Universitat de Valencia.

Jackson, P. W. (1991). *La vida en las aulas*. Madrid: Morata.

Kodron, Ch. (1993). European dimension, multiculturalism and teacher training: An experience in a network of training institutions. *European Journal of Teacher Education*, *16*(1), 69–77.

Leicester, M. (1988). Educacio Moral en una societat multicultural. *Symposium internacional de filosofia de la educacion*, *1* (pp. 91–125), Universidad Autonoma de Barcelona, 91–125.

LOGSE. Ley de Ordenacion General del Sistema Educativo (1990). Madrid: Ministerio de Educacion y Ciencia.

Martinez, B. J. (1995). El profesorado en el tercer milenio. *Cuadernos de pedagogia*, *240*, 23–28.

Sales, C. A. (1997). *Educacion Intercultural y Formacion de Actitudes. Propuesta de programas pedagogicos para desarrollar actitudes interculturales en Educacion Primaria y Secundaria*. (Unpublished) Tesis Doctoral, Servei de Publicacions de la Universidad de Valencia.

Sleeter, C. E. (1992). Restructuring schools for multicultural education. *Journal of teacher education*, *43*(2), 141–148.

Editor's Remarks

Romania's history includes the existence of numerous independent cultures based on many distinct languages. Today, Romania is a country with a population of about 22 million people, the majority (20 million) being Romanian. Roughly 2 million people represent such diverse groups as Hungarians, Roma (Gypsies), Jews, Turks, Greeks, Germans, Italians, and many nations from the former Soviet republics. Although at least 18 minority cultures can be found in Romania today, this demographic reality is often ignored. The tendency today is to assimilate minorities into the majority culture, with the result, for instance, of a high dropout rate for students of Hungarian origin.

Intercultural or multicultural education has not been a hotly debated topic of discussion among most of the public, nor in the professional community of Romania. Even with the sudden and recent political changes thrust on Romania, and in spite of its rich cultural mosaic, there still remains a long tradition of fear of interculturality. Principles of democracy, while stated on paper, seldom are put to practice. The current working of many government documents leaves much to individual interpretation, and thus there is a tendency to retain a monocultural identity and tradition.

Chapter 8

Intercultural Pedagogy as an Alternative to a Monoculturally Oriented Education: The Case of Romania

᎙ ◆ ᎐

Victor Neumann
Romania

Interculturally oriented education has not been under public debate in Romania. The topic is not well known in the countries of Central and Eastern Europe and is often mistaken for education in the mother tongues of the minority communities. There are a number of reasons why this form of pedagogy lags behind, the major reason being the lack of competencies in this field. Political trends, conservative as a rule, did not encourage development of an open pedagogy sensitive to transnational communication. Now at its beginnings, the civil society has only sporadically intervened in this process, not having the expected impact on the representative personalities of culture, let alone on the politicians in power.

The extremely varied cultural heritage in different regions of Romania might well be valued in fundamental human sciences research, then in intercultural education. The linguistic and religious communities within Central and Eastern Europe reflect convergence on all fields. The civilization of each country cannot be fully made to stand out without knowledge of the mutual transfer of ideas, customs, traditions, creations, expressions, and different forms of thinking and existence. Without such an effort at restoration, major moments in the history of political thought and in actual political life cannot be understood, nor can the deeper meanings of the written culture be decoded.

The habitat of the people in this region of Europe, including Romania, as a consequence of a history in which interference prevailed, has many features in common. Interculturality is the very consequence of the overlappings. A fear of interculturality has been introduced through the "romantic autopoetic philosophy," whose trend has been dominated by the *Volksgeist* concept. This explains why the totalitarian regimes of the 20th century benefited from the political thinking of the nation–states in the 19th century.

A BRIEF DESCRIPTION OF THE
ROMANIAN EDUCATIONAL SYSTEM

The law of education adopted by the Romanian Parliament in 1995 mentions that the state should promote the principles of a democratic education and that its organization and content cannot be structured according to exclusivist and discriminatory political, ideological, religious, and ethnic criteria. The right to a differentiated education is incorporated in the concept of educational pluralism (Education Law 84, 1995). The national education system is comprised of: kindergarten; compulsory education, including primary and secondary school; postsecondary education, including high-school, vocational school, and apprentice schools; higher education, inclusive of university, post-high school, and foremen school; postgraduate education; and doctorate programs.

The process of education is subordinated to the Ministry of Education and has the following structure: Department of Financial Control; Department of International Relations; Department for High Education and Scientific Research in Higher Education; Department of Human and Financial Resources; Department for Material Resources; Department for European Integration; Department for Primary and Secondary Education; Department for School and Extracurriculum Activities; Department for Education, Strategy, and Development; Department for Education of National Minorities; Department for Education of Romanians Living Abroad; Department for Coordination of the Reform Project for Primary and Secondary Education; Department for Coordination of the Reform of the Higher Education; Department for Curricula and Teachers' Training; SOCRATES National Agency; and the LEONARDO National Agency (Euridyce Unit Romania, 1996).

According to the Education Law 84/1995, the Ministry of Education has the following responsibilities: "to coordinate and control the national educational system; to organize the school network; to establish the number of students per school by consulting with the schools, the local authorities, and other interested local parties; to approve the educational plans, curricula, and textbooks for primary and secondary education; to organize national contests for the development of textbooks and to finance their publishing; to elaborate the methodology for the university entrance examination; to coordinate the scientific research in the education system; to approve the establishment of secondary schools, vocational training schools, colleges, and faculties; to approve the organization and functioning regulations for the subordinated units; to elaborate, approve, and distribute education materials; to coordinate the activity of the subordinate university libraries; to supervise the training and specialization of teachers; to appoint, transfer, and keep the records of the personnel in public schools; to assess the national education system; to elaborate and implement the long- and short-term strategies for the education reform; to elaborate the specific norms for the school constructions and facilities; to establish the procedure of recognition for the studies and diplomas; to establish the structure of every year of study, final exams, entrance examinations, and school holidays for primary and secondary education; to develop and control the assessment system for students, teachers, and professors; to distribute to each of its subordinate units the due share of budget and to ensure the units comply with the established financial norms; to develop, diagnose, and assess studies for the reconstructing and modernization of the educational system; to develop specific programs for students with special emotional, physical, and psychological needs; to manage (counseling and control) auxiliary staff; to cooperate on protocol with the Romanian Diaspora states to promote education in Romanian; and the control of financing performance" (Education Law 84/1995).

The following conclusions can be drawn: the Ministry of Education assumes the responsibility to guide, control, elaborate, and establish the assessment criteria for the professional merits and the promotion of teachers and professors; to establish the curricula for the primary, secondary, high, and vocational schools; and to establish the remuneration for the teachers, professors, and auxiliary staff.

The initiatives of the universities and educational research institutes are also subordinated to the Ministry of Education. Autonomy of the public universities are merely on paper because many of the senate's proposals must be approved through ministerial order. Accredited private education institutions are also under professional control of assessment commissions constituted at the level of the Ministry of Education. The possibility of real competition is controversial in this case too. Quite often, such methods encourage obscure procedures for accreditation of the private education institutions.

In addition, most of the grants abroad depend on the Ministry's approval and control, this authority being justified by the law to manage all international contacts. The central position of the Ministry—the fact that it comes from the political parties in power—makes it easier for such parties to interfere in the direction of education. This aspect is important, considering the political background in which doctrines are not very well outlined. The possibility of making decisions in a one-sided way without compulsory consultation of the subordinated institutions—an aspect resulting from the perpetuation on the pyramidal organization—essentially prevents the solution to many of public education's problems. The impossibility of autonomous coordination of educational activities by the universities and by the County General Inspectorates obstructs not only the chance for self-administration, but also the chance of a region training its own pedagogues, teachers, and professors according to its intellectual needs, interests, and financial possibilities. The same centralism inherited from the previous totalitarian regimes, perpetuated through the articles of Education Law 84/1995, facilitates the intervention of the state's office holders in the administration of local institutions. The professional relationships among researchers, the teaching staff, and Romanian and foreign institutions also are coordinated by the Ministry of Education.

The local school network institutions of primary and secondary education are managed by School Inspectorates led by a general inspector. The School Inspectorate, established in each county, is comprised of a managing board composed of the general inspector (president); the deputy general inspectors; the subject inspectors; the director of the teachers resource center; the chief accountant and the legal adviser of the Inspectorate; and an advisory council, composed of education institution directors, prestigious teachers and professors, parents, and representatives of the local authorities, the religious communities and of the local companies. The general inspector, his or her deputies, and the head of the teachers resource center are appointed by the Minister of Education.

The main responsibilities of the County General Inspectorate include the following: to recommend a local school network to the Ministry of Education; to create, with the approval of the Ministry of Education, public education institutions, including kindergartens, primary schools, lower secondary schools, and institutions of vocational and apprenticeship training; to ensure the appropriate personnel for the education institutions; to organize the specialization courses for the teachers and professors; to organize the scientific research; to coordinate the organization entrance examinations, graduation examinations, and school contests; to control the education process in the subordinated institutions; and to coordinate the activity of the teacher resource center and the school libraries.

As can be seen, the general inspector of the County General Inspectorate is also president of the Council of Administration (managing board) of the institution. This essentially means that all decisions are made by one person benefiting by real dictatorial powers in the absence of control by a board. To be general inspector and the president of the Council of Administration at the same time means that democratic consultation is on paper only. The same is the case with the school principals, who are simultaneously the president of the school board and the president of the managing board (Council of Administration). The institutions of primary and secondary education are directed by principals. According to the law, the principals are assisted in their governing activity by the school board and the managing board. The principal and the assistant principals are appointed by the general inspector. This is one of the totalitarian ways to impose decisions in the education system of Romania in the years of transition toward democracy.

According to Article 6 of the Constitution (passed in 1992) the state recognizes and warrants to persons belonging to ethnic minorities the right to preserve, develop, and express their ethnic, cultural, linguistic, and religious identity. In addition the measures of protection taken by the government in order to preserve, develop, and express the minorities' identity must be in accordance with the principles of equality and nondiscrimination regarding other Romanian citizens. The Law of Education says that Romanian citizens have equal rights and free access to all levels and forms of education regardless of his or her social and material condition, sex, race, nationality, political, or religious affiliation.

Much of the wording and content of this law allows for contradictory interpretations regarding the aforementioned issues. For example, stipulations that can be interpreted as being restrictive such as: "during the secondary and the high school period, the *History of the Romanians* and the *Geography of Romania* is taught in Romanian," or "the main sub-jects—within the public education (vocational, apprentice, economic, administrative, agrarian, forest, agro-alpine schools), as well as within the post high school education—are taught in Romanian, providing, as well as possible, the assimilation of the speciality terminology in the mother tongue" (Education Law 84/1995). The fact has not been overlooked by the representatives of the Hungarian (Magyar) minority of Romania, who even in the project phase of the law launched an alert on the legislator's intent to introduce "subsidiary legal stipulations," thus restricting the text of the Constitution (Bugajski, 1995–1996; Romanian Magyor's Democratical Union [RMDU], 1994).

Using the phrase "the history of Romanians" as the title of a subject taught in high school and university brought, and still brings about, ideological disputes because it perpetuates 19th-century clichés and reflects contradictory viewpoints between the majority and minority populations. If we examine the general dispositions of the law, we can conclude that one of the declared objectives is to promote the attachment towards the homeland, toward the historical past and the traditions of the Romanian people (Education Law 84/1995), which reflects a monocultural viewpoint that guided the legislation of many East and Central European states during their formative period or during their time of dictatorship.

Regarding such concerns as multiple identities, pluriligual phenomenon, different regional cultures produced by the 18 minority communities of Romania, multiple denominations and the relationship between them, and the study of the intercultural phenomena, the law does not provide proper stipulations that are self-understood in a democratic country. From the aforementioned law there does not result any systematic concern to preserve the richness of diverse traditions that might facilitate quicker access to a plural culture for the Romanian citizens. On the contrary, what results is an exaggerated concern to assimilate the majority's ethnic traditions, and to appropriate the history and geography in accordance with the monoculturally oriented ideologies that prevailed during all Romanian political regimes of the 20th century, beginning in 1918. Including general principles— formally adapted to democratic speech—the Education Law does not cover the demands of modern pedagogy. It lacks stipulations for the study of alternatives that might benefit the entire population, which means nothing else but the diminution of Romania's chance of real adjustment to its inner multiculturalism, to the cultural diversity of Europe, and to a democratic mentality in which the role of the citizen comes first.

DEMOGRAPHICS OF ROMANIA, INCLUDING VARIOUS SUBGROUPS AND SUBCULTURES AND THEIR EXPERIENCES WITH THE MAINSTREAM EDUCATIONAL SYSTEM

Romania has an area of 238,391 square kilometers and a population of more than 22 million inhabitants composed of many different linguistic and religious communities. The majority group is represented by the Romanians (about 20 million inhabitants). The minorities include Hungarian (Magyar), Roma, German, Serbian, Ukrainian, Slovak, Czech,

Croatian, Turkish, Jew, Lipovenian-Russian, Bulgarian, Polish, Armenian, Greek, and Italian people. The most numerous minority is the Hungarian (Magyar) population of 1.62 million inhabitants (1992 census). The number of the Roma (Gypsy) population is quite uncertain, but was thought by the 1992 census to be about 400,000 inhabitants, although other statistics show a number ranging from 1.8 to 2.5 million people. Other minorities are quite insignificant in number: 70,000 Germans, 50,000 Ukrainians, 40,000 Turks, 22,000 Serbians, 9,400 Jews, 9,200 Slovaks, and 7,000 Croatians. Two communities that played a major role in Romania's history have decreased considerably; the German and the Jewish inhabitants who numbered 550,000 and 420,000 inhabitants, respectively, just after World War II. Both communities left Romania during the communist dictatorship for political and economic reasons.

The experience of the various groups that compose contemporary Romania's population shows, for the most part, a long period of living together, even since the Middle Ages. Multiculturalism has been favored here by the geographic diversity of the regions as well as by their administrative and political affiliation with the empires that existed in the central, eastern and southeastern part of Europe, including the Hapsburg, the Turkish, and the Tsarist Empires. For example, the counties of Transylvania, Banat, Maramures, and Partium were in the Hungarian Kingdom during the Middle Ages (from the 11th to the 16th centuries). During the period from 1542 to 1699, Transylvania was the only region in Central and Eastern Europe that benefited by the status of autonomous principality with its commitment to pay a yearly tribute to the Turkish Empire. The Hungarian Kingdom had been conquered by the Turks at Mohács in 1526, so the Hungarian political class was restricted to the East (in Transylvania). The period as a principality was a flourishing one economically and culturally under the influence of the Renaissance and the Reform. The Royal House was under the rule of the Calvinist Hungarian aristocracy.

Banat was an Ottoman province from 1552 to 1716 under the name of Sanjak of Timisoara (a subdivision of a Turkish province) and was included in the Pashalik of Buda. Then, for a period of two centuries all the mentioned regions were included in the Habsburg Empire that became, after 1867, the Austro-Hungarian Empire. Bessarabia was part of the Tsarist Empire, and Wallachia, Moldavia, and Dobrudgea had been under the influence of the Ottoman Empire or subject to its direct rule for five centuries. Bukovine, another border region of Romania (part of it is included, nowadays, in the north-eastern part of Romania, and another part in the Ukraine) has itself a meandering history. It has been the meeting point of the Polish, Russian, Austrian, and Romanian political and economic interests for five centuries. Hence it has inherited a patrimony of great diversity.

In general, the empires facilitated the life together of many linguistic and religious communities within the same region. At other times, they played the role of arbitrator between two or more groups with divergent viewpoints as of their origin, historical right, religion, and administration. The communitary pluralism was born in direct relation to the policy of the mentioned empires, kingdoms, or principalities. It is obvious that this pluralism has generated an emulation in all fields of activity: organizational, financial, commercial, scientific and artistic. The plural history from the 16th to the 19th centuries created the premises of modernization in the regions. The autonomy of the towns and villages of Transylvania called for good communication and understanding. The legislative authorities had representatives of all human groups belonging and living in each region. The Transylvanian nobility had not been divided according to linguistic criteria.

The common cultural phenomena were registered for the first time in the documents of the Transylvanian Diet in Turda, 1557, which stipulated that "everyone lives after the law he or she chooses." In 1568 the Diet proclaimed the complete freedom of faith, thus generating a form of tolerance among the four recognized denominations in Transylvania at that time: Unitarian, Calvinist, Catholic, and Evangelic. The Greek–Catholic Church of Romania, settled in 1701 with the intention to convert the mass of Orthodox adherents reveals, in its turn, the possibility of coexistence of Orthodoxism and Catholicism, and not the falling out between them that their hierarchs often announced. The Greek–Catholic religion had been recognized by the Pope, being among the denominations accepted by the Habsburg authorities, later by the Austro-Hungarian rulers, and after the unification of Transylvania with Romania, by the Romanian officials.

The author proposes two essential aspects for consideration: first, the existence of many independent cultures based on different languages, and second, the mixture that generated a civilization with multiple origins. In this latter sense, the spiritual Romanian-Hungarian convergences (generating similar mental reflexes) are the consequence of the two living together over a long period of time beginning in the centuries of the Middle Ages. The same holds true for the Romanian-German, Romanian-Turkish, and Romanian-Jewish coexistence. All of these set a specific imprint on the contemporary Romanian civilization.

One of the greatest deficiencies of the Romanian education system is that it did not question the equality of chances. Even though almost all official documents stipulate that minorities have the right to instruction in their mother tongue, the County School Inspectorates do not always take into account the demographic reality. That is, when those institutions establish their education plans, they deprive the students belonging to minority communities of their right to learn in their mother tongue, ignoring the necessity to set up schools with teaching in languages other than that of the majority's. There are cases when the Inspectorates do not respect the students' right to continue their instruction in their mother tongue at the vocational schools or other apprentice schools. This is the reason for the low percentage of Hungarian students in high schools compared with the percentage of the Hungarian (Magyar) inhabitants in those regions. The situation can be understood through statistics on the changes in the ethnic composition of students in higher education at Babes-Bolyai University of Cluj from the year 1958 to 1993. Whereas the number of students who study in Romanian increased from 2,917 (in 1958) to 10,102 (in 1993), the number of students who study in Hungarian increased only from 1,266 to 1,917 in the same period. During the same time, a decrease can be noticed in the number of German students, from 102 to 9. This data demonstrates, on the one hand, the carelessness of the schools with regard to preserving plurilingual education, and on the other, the intention of assimilation more evident during Ceausescu's nationalist– communist dictatorship.

The problem of integration in schools of children belonging to the Roma minority has not been completely neglected, but it has not been very successful either. Today, many facts and explanations are put forward to explain the problem of integration in schools and society of this group, including the lack of specialists in this field, and therefore the lack of strategy concerning how best to work with these children, the nonobservance of the school curricula, and ignorance concerning the means of communication specific to the Roma minority. To all these can be added the fact that in some cases skin color results in marginalization of the group, and in other cases the group marginalizes itself.

The integration of the Roma communities continues to be a problem in many of the East and Central European countries. This presents not only a social question, but a cultural one as well, a question that institutions should consider when they begin to focus on the civic education of the whole population. The education program of the majority population must be seriously adjusted in order to eliminate racist ideologies and practices that happened in certain cases, voluntary or involuntary, on account of the trainers' and political and sociocultural authorities' behavior. The new Minister of Education said that education in Romania, on the whole, suffers from its administrative system, especially from its excessive centralism ("22" Magazine, 1997). Such a statement of fact is motivated by the weak organization of the civil society.

Perceived Obstacles and Solutions
to Addressing Intercultural Issues in Schools

Studies concerning intercultural phenomena have been completely neglected in Romania. Inheriting the mental reflexes promoted by the extreme right and extreme left totalitarian regimes, Romania has remained behind in promoting interculturally oriented topics. For a better understanding I (the author) am going to refer to some dysfunction created out of schools. By this I mean the perpetuation of thinking based on traditions that ignore or are ignorant of the ways that others think and act in the contemporary world. Aspects of this come from a certain education practiced in the family, particularly in close societies.

For example, a visible obstacle to promoting interculturalism is represented by the collectivist habitat. Such an orientation may bring about a closing of the mind, suspicion, fear of the unknown, and the tendency to assimilate into the crowd. The idea of sacrifice is promoted only in the name of the collective good. Individualism, on the contrary, is often mistaken for selfishness.

This kind of behavior has its origins in the medieval rural community, very well preserved until nowadays. A society structured on village ideals and life forms rejects the urban behavior rules. The transition from village to city requires crossing from one set of rules to another, an aspect completely ignored by Ceausescu's dictatorship, which initiated the forced industrialization and the great migration of the village people to the factories from the urban milieus. If we cross-examine the way in which the couples who settled in towns in the last decades educate their children, we can learn how the chain of dependencies, taken from the rural milieu, is multiplied (voluntarily or involuntarily).

The collective way of life is conveyed from one generation to another, which means that even today the successor or mature adult refuses to assume individual responsibilities. His or her complexes of superiority and inferiority, very often due to the violent breaking off of family relationships, shows the persistence of a collective mentality reticent to innovation and to the lifestyle changes. Among the examples that show the cultural maladjustment to the urban milieu are the discriminatory attitude against the old, the sick, the disabled, homosexuals, and women, attitudes that stay at the origin of resentments against other linguistic and confessional communities (Hungarian, Roma, Jewish). As a consequence, such a background reveals some of the main elements that contribute to obstruction of an interculturally oriented education, and that hinder understanding the role of pluralist thinking.

In its turn, the official education system is only partial and lately adapted to the European rules. The fact that the Parliament allots a very small budget from the state budget to education means that this field is being neglected by many important social segments. The emphasis put on the training of so-called elite students (as the leaders of the Ministry of Education in the Vacaroiu cabinet declared) shows how a stale way of thinking about education has been inculcated from the top, perpetuating the totalitarian thinking of Ceausescu's regime.

Even though some of the researchers called attention to the discrepancies between the theory that rules Romanian education and the theory that stays at the basis of Western education, the Romanian bureaucrats of the ministry have never noticed that the role of modern education is to prepare a well-trained professional middle class. The lack of a few well-argued theoretical reference points of an educational policy, and the serene acceptance of a system long ago obsolete shows why nowadays the reform in this field is on the same phase as in 1990. The superficial way in which topics such as interethnic and intercultural relationships are approached has visible consequences in the development of the civil society and in the establishment of a natural communication between two or more human communities. Consider the example offered by the Babes-Bolyai University of Cluj, which in March 1997 continued to oppose solving the Hungarian (Magyar) community's request concerning the establishment of an independent higher institution teaching in the second language of the region.

In summary, the perceived obstacles to addressing intercultural education are determined by the attempt to preserve the 19th-century political ideology (promoted by the states of Central and Eastern Europe after 1848), which says that the "nation" concept is overlapping with the "ethnic" one; the lack of a culture and belief concerned with the rights and the obligations of the citizens; the preservation of behavior and thinking characteristic of closed, totalitarian societies; an ignorance about minority languages and cultures; the minor role and place of individual initiative; the persistence of the centralized political and administrative system; the perpetuation of the myth of democracy during the interwars of Romania; the use of textbooks containing stereotypes that sustain the nationalist-oriented education; the mutual permission or maintenance of the suspicion and inequality of opportunities for members of the minority communities; the propagation through the media of confusion regarding the Holocaust and World War II; and the influence of the mass media in creating and perpetuating myths.

Solutions proposed for overcoming those obstacles include introducing compulsory plurilingual education for all children in regions with mixed population; elaborating history, literature, geography, and ethnography textbooks, which contain information about the culture, the traditions, the language, and the religion of the minority communities living in Romania, as well as data about the convergences between these cultures and the majority one; introducing laws against any type of discrimination toward minorities; granting equal opportunities in professional competition to all citizens of the country irrespective of nationality, sex, religion, or race; promoting interculturally oriented advanced studies within the department of social sciences in universities; decentralizing the education system and granting legal opportunities to local organization and administration of the education in minority languages; granting the material and professional support to apply inerculturally oriented education in all teacher training colleges; introducing the new core curriculum concerning the study of history in secondary and high schools, a curriculum that would stress the convergent dimension of civilization and the molding of open thinking responsive to alternatives, giving up the excerpts based on stereotypes that feed chauvinistic, antisemitic, and racist political speeches; using the common cultural heritage in the benefit of the country's culture and civilization; delivering civic education courses at the primary and secondary educational levels; disseminating local examples of interculturality in schools, lycées, colleges, universities, cultural institutions, and media; promoting the principles of an antiracist education in schools; granting the trainers' professional and civic competencies in the field of interculturally oriented education; and stimulating nongovernmental organizations to set up and promote civic education with an intercultural perspective for history, tradition, and religious thinking of the minorities, as well as for the study of intercultural phenomena.

TEACHER TRAINING COLLEGES
AND INTERCULTURAL EDUCATION

The educational institutions of Romania are not sufficiently open to information coming from sources other than those of the higher hierarchy. Some of the researchers state that it has gotten so far as to sacralize the formal rule and hierarchical subordination (Oprescu, 1997).

The result after analyzing the way the Romanian educational system works is that the initiative of the teacher, and the student, or the school, is completely discarded. What is the reason for such an attitude? The educational services offered by schools, colleges, lycées, and universities have the possibility of imposing an ideologic trend and defying the interests of the local communities. They do not reflect the multiple cultures, languages, and denominations belonging to various regions of the country. On the contrary, they show the state's control over the education system and the subordination of every teacher, teacher trainer, student, school, lycée (high school, college), and university. Thus, promoting monoculturality became the main ideologic support of the education institutions. The lack of cultural diversity made an important and large segment of the collectivity reject the changes, blinded it to any type of pluralism, and opposed the tendencies of opening toward other forms of cultural expression.

Along with the education institutions that bear the working peculiarities of the totalitarian regimes, the ideologic orientation of the most popular means of mass media, namely television, helped to produce the great void in education of cultural and political diversity. Through television, propaganda of all the ideas and activities having as a main support the "ethnocultural" concept and not that of the "civil society" are perpetuated. The preference to politicize the television programs' function of the governing party (or coalition of parties) guaranteed that the most important public TV channel would be completely deprived of a coherent theory of programs. This is one of the factors causing clumsy, or, at any rate, nonprofitable education.

The teacher trainer colleges are part of the education system. They respond—perhaps more than other educational institutions,—to the same state control. Their activities are among the most standardized. Namely, they obsequiously obey bureaucratic forms established by the ministry.

Interculturally oriented education is not addressed in teacher training colleges, and their curricula does not indicate the need to teach two or more cultures or the convergence between them. The literature, history, tradition, and denomination of minorities also are not taught. The minority languages, seen only as a means of intercommunity communication, have been and are completely ignored. Teaching of Romania's history and literature has often resulted in poor understanding of the cultural interferences and their concrete results. The main goal, declared or not, of the ministerial curriculum is to indoctrinate the students with the same monocultural ideology (often carrying the signs of xenophobic stereotypes).

The result is a very low level form of education that does not require explanations or questions, let alone the formation of thinking adapted to a plurality of cultures. The initiatives in the sense of curricula renewal are rejected or neglected by the politicians, whose backgrounds do not permit them to join theories, doctrines, and methodologies that are not part of the standard thinking. The competence of the teachers and teacher trainers is low, hence their lack of creativeness and open dialogue with students. The free exchange of ideas is discouraged. Instead, rigid quarterly and weekly planning by the hierarchical fixed teaching norm and by the differentiation between teachers with leadership positions is encouraged. This phenomenon brings about the perpetuation of the education system through control.

Additionally, there exists the isolation of science from reality, a very common practice in the teacher training colleges. All these elements are not innocent delays, as might be believed at first sight. Rather, they show how the ethnic centralist state can survive at the height of globalization era. The teacher training colleges are tributary to the aforementioned framework. With their role of preparing teachers, these schools are more seriously involved in a rather narrow cognitive domain. Once they submit to totalitarian rules, it is obvious that they contribute to the preservation of one-sided information and thus train pseudocompetent persons in the field of education, culture, and civic action. Subsequently, the issue of competitiveness in the Romanian education institutions left to the narrow-minded bureaucrats, whose school milieus engender a lack of appeal for high-IQ students. There are many cases in which this is the reason for the lack of professionals at the university chairs.

It has to be emphasized that in certain social milieus the need to change both the education system and its legislative framework is felt. Students and their parents often remark on the enormous discrepancy between the endless theory they must cram into their minds at school and the practical problems they face in everyday life that require another type of thinking. An interculturally oriented pedagogy represents a credible alternative to the monocuturally oriented one prevalent today at each educational level in Romania. It is obvious that through this alternative there might be many useful solutions that could make Romanian and Western programs compatible. Such projects might stimulate competition, competence, and a sense of unification through the dissemination of the complementary doctrines. Intercultural pedagogies, perhaps more than the others, have as their goal the possibility to change a country's population to integrate into political, economical, and administrative supranational structures that will prevail into the next millennium.

TO CONSIDER

On a worldwide scale, Romania has remained behind in promoting intercultural or multicultural education. A number of ideas have been proposed to facilitate intercultural understanding among students in Romania, including compulsory language training for all, the inclusion of minority group studies in the curriculum, laws forbidding discrimination against minorities, encouragement for social scientists to make intercultural issues

*an integral part of their domain; development of a new core curriculum in
history that emphasizes Romania's rich cultural heritage; and formation
of a curriculum that emphasizes multiple perspectives and experiences.*

1. *Review current newspapers or news reports from Romania. Search for
news items that present issues related to the international community, interethnic conflict, and educational responses to diversity. How do current issues
related to diversity relate to what you have just read? What struggles continue
around interethnic issues?*

2. *What can your nation and schools learn from the experiences of
Romania?*

3. *How can young people in Romania be most effectively prepared to
interact with others on a global scale? What resources seem to be available
within Romania to assist young people in developing a global or intercultural perspective?*

4. *Romania occasionally receives immigrants from other nations. Given
what you have just read, how would you respond to the scenario presented in
chapter 1. What steps should schools take in responding to the needs of newly
arrived immigrant groups?*

REFERENCES

Bugajski, J. (1995–1996). The many faces of nationalism. In *Uncaptive minds* (Vol. 8, Nos. 3–4, p. 24). Washington: Institute for Democracy in Eastern Europe.

Education Law 84/1995. (1995). Romania's Gazette, year VII, number 167, 31st of July 1995, Title I: "General Provisions", Article 5, Paragraph 2, and Article 12, Paragraph 2.

Euridyce Unit Romania. (1996, October). Central authorities. In *The structure of education and initial training system in Romania* (pp. 3–4). Bucharest: Ministry of National Education.

Oprescu, D. (1997). Politica si educatie [Politics and Education, nn.]. *Sfera Politicii no.45*, pp. 2–3.

Romanian Magyar's Democratical Union (RMDU). (1994). *Documentele UDMR, 2*, Cluj, pp. 18–23.

"22" Magazine. (1997, February 29). An interview with Virgil Petrescu, the Minister of Education. *"22" Magazine, no.8*, pp. 8–9.

Editor's Remarks

Nigeria is, in many ways, typical of many nations on the African continent. It was colonized by the British and gained its independence in 1960. Nigeria's geographic boundaries were externally determined, and its European-based economic and political systems were imposed over its indigenous systems. There have been constant struggles from within as numerous ethnic groups battle against one another for control of institutions and activities that were never previously given much attention. Ethnic groups, which before colonization were separated by natural boundaries (mountains and rivers) and centuries of development and evolution, were suddenly thrust together by the colonial powers. Without a history of intercultural interaction or education, these ethnic groups were suddenly interacting in one another's life and space, therefore tensions and apprehensions mounted.

The authors of this chapter stress the necessity to understand the complexity of the current situation, and to identify the links between politics, education, and ethnicity. They go further by challenging the reader to propose ways in which curriculum development and educational activity can be separated from developments in the United Kingdom and increasingly the United States, and to show how intercultural education can be, perhaps, the most critical impetus for change.

Chapter 9

Multiculturalism in the Context of Africa: The Case of Nigeria

ಹಿ ♦ ೮ಽ

Steve O. Michael
Yetunde A. Michael
Kent State University

True multiculturalists are, in essence, avowed globalists. Globalism, in this context, is a philosophy that embraces the search for understanding cultures of the world and how nations wrestle with cultural issues. Although globalists recognize differences in the socioeconomic– political environment of each nation, they strive to understand how educational policymakers, educators, and political leaders from different nations attempt to resolve their cultural issues. This understanding is important as we compare and contrast cultural issues, educational policies, and social strategies across the nations of the world.

Therefore, a global multiculturalist is interested in Australian educational and social policies toward their Aborigines, Canadian responses to their cultural problems, or multicultural issues in Africa. A focus on Africa is of particular interest because of its unique historical, sociological, economic, and political background. Africa is a continent that has witnessed countless external invasions and colonial administrations. The fragmentation of the continent into countries was done primarily without the consent of the indigenes, the neoeconomic and political systems were imposed at the expense of the indigenous economic and political systems, and in spite of its natural resources, the continent is ravaged with abject poverty at a magnitude that is unparalleled anywhere in the world.

Given this context, what kind of cultural issues are problematic in African countries? What approaches have been tried, and what results have been realized? How are nations that have experienced hegemonic domination, brutal subjugation, and inhumane slavery dealing with issues of minorities? These questions and several others form the central focus of this chapter. However, in answering these questions, Nigeria as a nation will form the basis of analysis and discussion. In concluding this chapter, the issue of new immigrants to Nigeria will be examined. Indeed, one may argue that there are no two nations in Africa exactly alike. But this is true of any two nations in the world. Nigeria is unique not only because of the sheer magnitude of its population and ethnic compositions, but also because of its wealth and strategic position within the continent.

However, in spite of its unique background, Nigeria is a typical nation among many African countries. Like many African countries, Nigeria was colonized and had to struggle to regain its independence. Its geographic boundaries were externally determined, and the economic and political systems were imposed over its indigenous systems. It is a nation that constantly experiences inner tumult as different ethnic groups battle against each other. Nigeria has fought and survived a civil war, and the possibility of another one looms on its horizon. Indeed, when viewed in the light of other African nations, Nigeria reflects, perhaps on a larger scale, social and cultural problems characteristic of Africa.

The Problem of Definition

Pluralism, cross-culturalism, interculturalism, multiculturalism, and diversity are a few of the concepts common in the literature. Although some authors have tried to differentiate between and among these concepts, attempts to provide concise definitions for each have been problematic. Therefore, for the purpose of this chapter, all these concepts are used synonymously.

Multiculturalism assumes a different meaning within the context of Africa. This is so because the line that separates cultures is frustratingly blurred in Africa. Two distinct ethnic groups may share very close and similar cultures yet be at war with each other over a seemingly frivolous factor that keeps them apart. Two ethnic groups with the same culture may find variation in accent enough reason for erecting barriers between themselves.

The term *ethnic group* is hereby used instead of *tribal group,* which traditionally has defined the language and cultural groups in Africa. The contemporary usage of the term *tribe* has pejorative connotation. Hence, the preference for the term ethnic group. It should be pointed out though that many African writers themselves use the term tribal group to describe their people. However, because the pejorative connotation is essentially a Western phenomenon, ethnic groups are substituted for tribal groups in this text.

Historical Background

The present problems of a nation cannot be understood without attention to its history. Therefore, our discussion of multicultural education in Nigeria starts with a reflection over the country's historical background, which is divided into three periods for the purpose of clarity.

Precolonial Africa. Precolonial Africa was characterized by ethnic groups living in isolation and fortified by mountains, thick forests, or large rivers. Divided by geographic barriers, pockets of Africans metamorphosed into distinct ethnic groups with different languages, as well as varied cultural and religious practices, even when living only a few miles apart.

Without means of communication, many of these ethnic groups developed their own myths and suspicions about other ethnic groups. Relationships among these groups were highly volatile and hostile, and interethnic wars became the only contacts that many of these groups had with each other.

The situation just described was more indicative of southern Nigeria than the northern part. Ethnic isolation was greater in the south because of the geographic or natural barriers than in the north where the mild subsaharan desert made the nothern villages and towns relatively accessible. Before the colonial incursion, the Usman Dan Fodio's jihad of the 16th century had already conquered several villages and towns in the North and had established the Islamic rule over this territory.

Consequently, the Hausa-Fulani ethnic group located in the extreme north of the country (Fig. 9.0) was the first group to embrace Islam and thus became the ruling class of the North. The northern empire was under the rulership of the Sultan of Sokoto, who presided over other *Emirs* (rulers of villages and towns in the Muslim-dominated area). The goal of Ultiman Dan Fodio's jihad was forcefully to convert Africans who lived from Egypt down to the Atlantic Ocean in West Africa. The jihad fell short of its goal because of the thick forest that prevented easy penetration from the middle belt of the country down to the Atlantic Ocean. This accounts for the reason why Nigeria is populated predominantly by Muslims in the North and Christians in the South.

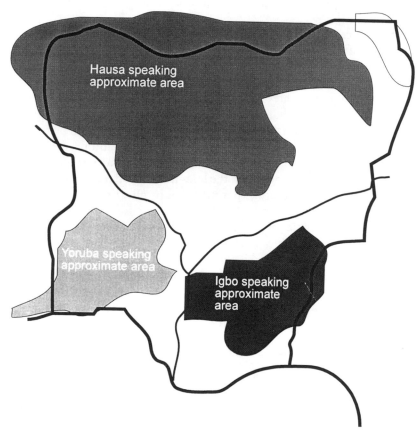

FIG. 9.0. A Map of Nigeria with the Three Major Ethnic Groups.

Colonial Era.   Mungo Park, a British explorer, is generally regarded as the first explorer to set foot on what currently is known as Nigeria, reaching the land through the River Niger. However, the major influx of the British explorers came through the Atlantic Ocean in the South. British explorers encountered stiff resistance from the Yoruba–Benin warriors who had already established the Yoruba–Benin Kingdom in the South.

Whereas the British explorers had to fight wars and conquer the South before establishing the Queen's rulership over the land, the experience in the North was different. Lord Lugard, the first British administrator of the newly conquered land, thought it needless to fight another war in the North, which was already established under the Emirate system. Consequently, Lord Lugard instituted an indirect rule over the North. Thus, the

British colonial government instituted indirect rule in the North but direct rule in the South.

This practice was to have an important implication for the continuing governance of the land even after the colonial era. First, because the local governance system in the North was left undisturbed, the North had the advantage of a stronger local government administration. Second, the northern part of the country projected a more unitary political voice than the South. Third, and perhaps most important, was the psychologic impact of indirect rule on the northerners, (Hausa-Fulani in particular) who took the approach as an indication of their inherent talent and predisposition for public administration. Fourth, the south became more fragmented as the new direct rule was imposed on the less-understood traditional system. The instability of the southern experiment has implications far beyond the colonial era.

However, the struggle for independence was championed in the South, whereas the North became a reluctant partner. This is understandable because the North's rights and rulership were not as violated as those in the south. Perhaps because of the direct rule instituted in the South, and the greater presence of the Christian movement there, more graduates of the British education system come from the South than from the North. This point was made by Beckett and O'Connell (1977):

> It is important to note, however, that production of graduates is not distributed evenly throughout the country. The colonial heritage of differential development, particularly between the North and the South, remains acute in education at every level. A study of student recruitment to the University of Ibadan shows that over the years 1948–1966 students from the northern region accounted for only a little more than 5% of the total enrollment of the university (which, over most of that period, was the only university in the country). When the mainly Yoruba students from Ilorin and Kabba Provinces are omitted, northern students accounted for only 1.9% of total enrollments. Yet more than half the country's total population live in the North. (p. 12)

The new educated elite became the crusaders against the colonial government. The efforts of these individuals both in the country and in Britain ultimately resulted in the independence of Nigeria. Suffice it to say that the North, on realizing the possibility of independence, became very active in working together with the South.

Postcolonial Era.   The British experiment in Nigeria forced many ethnic groups to come in contact with one another. A network of roads was constructed; faster means of transportation were introduced; trading activities escalated; and Africans of different ethnic groups were thrust together. In Nigeria, vertical transportation networks to link the North to the coastal region were created with few or no horizontal networks. As Knight and Newman (1976) observed:

> Despite the shortcomings of the transport and communication systems that have developed from the colonial era to the present, the significant roles these systems have had in inducing social and economic changes should not be overlooked. They played a vital part in the establishment of colonial administration. Railways and roads broke down the friction of distance and ethnic isolation and facilitated the free movement of traders. (p. 351)

Ethnic–tribal differences became less important in the struggle to end the British rule, in the demand for self-rule, and in the condemnation of the British exploitation of Africa's raw materials. It should be noted that the unity of the country ends with these unifying objectives.

The forefathers of the new nation state, Chief Obafemi Awolowo, Chief Nnamdi Azikwe, and Tafawa Balewa (all deceased) were drawn from among the new elite and represented the three largest ethnic groups: Yoruba, Igbo, and Hausa, respectively. In keeping with the aforementioned background, leaders found that people's loyalty was predominantly based on ethnic affiliations. For example, ethnicity was ranked the most important determinant of support during the First Republic (Beckett & O'Connell, 1997). The new ruling class found itself in constant clash with other ethnic groups and also with the traditional ruling system within its own ethnic group, a situation that has continues until today.

Political System

On achieving independence in 1960, Nigeria experimented with democracy and became a republic in 1963. The intraethnic rivalry would soon end this experiment within 5 years with a military coup and a civil war. Several futile efforts have been attempted since to democratize the government of Nigeria. The almost irreconcilable differences among the ethnic groups have prevented democracy from gaining deep root and have made the country susceptible to military dictatorship. Indeed, the background described earlier has made the need for multicultural education the only realistic option for the country. In its absence, the military dictatorship with its uncanny ability to repress dissension and force cohabitation of "unfriendly" ethnic groups continues to wield power over the nation.

Education System

Nigeria experimented with a dualism of education control under the colonial government. The colonial government established schools for the sole purpose of securing trained hands to help them with the trading activities, whereas the missionaries established schools with the sole purpose of converting the heathen to Christianity. The two types of education were neither comprehensive nor responsive to the need of the country.

However, it should be noted that those who became the forefathers of Nigeria's independence were graduates of these schools. But it is accurate to state that the education of these men (women were not included at that time) did not include multicultural initiatives.

The educational structure of Nigeria as it stands today is depicted in Fig. 9.1. Most Nigerian children have access to the elementary education, which is generally called primary education.

A MULTICULTURAL FRAMEWORK FOR EVALUATING DEVELOPMENT IN NIGERIA

The complexity of Africa, especially Nigeria, requires the use of a framework for a better understanding of the intercultural education efforts that have been attempted. A comprehensive examination of a nation's intercultural education should consider both the formal and nonformal education. Formal education would be a preplanned and prestructured socialization system accepted by the political administration of a given state.

As a socialization strategy, formal education becomes an adopted instrument to achieve stability, continuity, economic growth, and social change (DuBey, Edem, & Thakur, 1979). However, nonformal or informal (hereby used interchangeably only for the purpose of this text) education would be characterized as self-help in the form of less structured or unstructured socialization practices prevalent in a particular society. Coombs (1985) described this form of education as

> any organized, systematic, educational activity, carried on outside the framework of the formal system, to provide selected types of learning to particular subgroups in the population, adults as well as children. Thus defined, nonformal education includes, for example, agricultural extension and farmer training programs, adult literacy programs, occupational skill training given outside the formal system, youth clubs with substantial educational purposes, and various community programs of instruction in health, nutrition, family planning, cooperatives, and the like. (p. 23)

In the context of Africa, the need to look at education through both formal and nonformal approaches is underscored by the fact that formal schooling was externally designed and imposed on Africans, and only a fraction of the population has access to formal education. Therefore, the tradi-

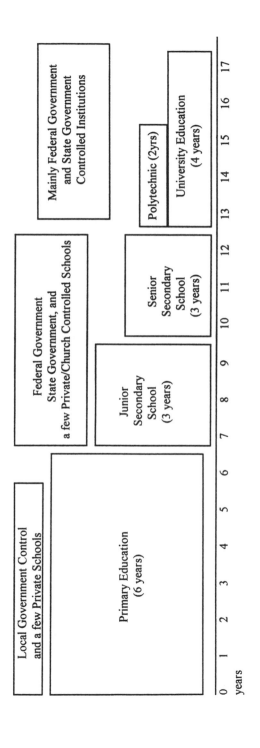

FIG. 9.1. A Simplified Structure of the Nigerian Educational System.

tional socialization process through oral history, apprenticeship, community-based activities, and cultural practices became the nonformal education. Given the limited opportunity of many African children to obtain formal schooling, attempts to understand any educational effort must consider the role of nonformal education.

Nonformal Education Initiatives in Nigeria

DuBey, Edem, and Thakur (1979) noted that

> no other agent of socialization is as important to the total makeup of the child as his family: His primary socialization begins here. The important identifications with ethnic group, culture, religion, social class, and even how he views himself as a male or female have their origins in the family. (p. 22)

Therefore, a child's first intercultural education in Nigeria comes from his or her family. These authors further observed that

> most children in Nigeria do not enter school until they are 6 or 7 years old. Thus they have spent the most crucial foundational years with their parents and other relatives. Their behavior and attitudes are quite well patterned by the time they enter school. (p. 23) Figure 9.2 provides an illustration of a conceptual framework applicable to intercultural education initiatives in Nigeria.

Ethnic–Tribal Socialization

Families are located within their ethnic–tribal cultural domain, and each ethnic group has, over the years, a set of prevailing myths and attitudes toward members of other ethnic groups. As a result, within the family a child quickly learns lessons about such issues as acceptable ethnic rules and practices, acceptable ethnic groups from which to marry, and ethnic groups to avoid. These myths and beliefs are reinforced by the long-established cultural practices of each ethnic group.

Religious Influence. Religious influence plays a crucial role in Nigerian intercultural education. The two main religions—Christianity and Islam—have spiritual injunctions that carry implications for intercultural issues in the country. Although Christianity, as stipulated in the Holy Bible, has an inclusive philosophy, a variety of missionary movements established different types of churches in different areas. The consequence was ethnic-affiliated Christian sects, especially as efforts were made to translate the Bible into different ethnic languages. Therefore, although the Christians proclaim that "we are all brothers and sisters in the Lord," the bond of brotherhood or sisterhood is weakened considerably outside the ethnic group.

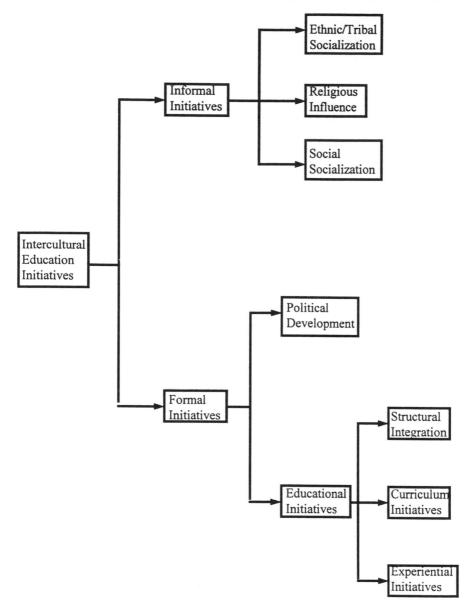

FIG. 9.2. A Framework For Evaluating Intercultural Education in Nigeria.

Although in the Muslim faith sects were less pronounced, patterns of ethnic affiliation of Muslim practices were obvious. Despite the fact that Arabic is the official language of the Holy Quran, several riots that took place in the northern part of Nigeria, notably in Kano and Zaria, between the northern Hausa-Fulanis and the southerners (Yorubas and Igbos) revealed that the Muslim Yorubas were as vulnerable as their Christian counterparts.

However, a neoreligious movement is taking place in Nigeria. This movement is attempting to reeducate believers to accept their religions as a stronger bond that should neutralize ethnic differences. The success of this movement has been limited.

Social Interaction.   Hraba (1979) quoted Robert Ezra Park as saying the following:

> In our estimates of race relations we have not reckoned with the effects of personal intercourse and the friendships that inevitably grow up out of them. These friendships, particularly in a democratic society like our own, cut across and eventually undermine all the barriers of racial segregation and caste by which races seek to maintain their integrity. (p. 35)

Although Nigeria was and is not as democratic as the United States of which Ezra Park was writing, social contact that precedes any cultural understanding has been on the increase in the country. As mentioned earlier, the construction of a network of roads and railways and the centralization of the seat of government resulted in greater movement of people. In addition, trading activities among different ethnic groups and the movement of government workers from one region to another increased social interactions among different tribes and thus necessitated the learning of different languages and an appreciation of different cultural practices.

Although every Nigerian born in the land has had a measure of intercultural education or miseducation through the nonformal channels, it should be noted that these means could also be volatile. For example, a Muslim sect with low tolerance toward other ethnic groups does spring up once in a while in the northern part of the country. Nonformal channels are largely outside the authority of the government, and their effects are less predictable.

FORMAL INTERCULTURAL EDUCATION INITIATIVES

Nigeria is a multiethnic society with three major ethnic groups that constantly jostle for political power and several hundred other tribal languages. Given this scenario, "unity in diversity" becomes the slogan of the government. Indeed, what the colonial powers were able to keep together as a nation became problematic for the indigenes, and even 30 years after independence, the nation is still struggling with its identity.

Formal intercultural education is examined under two headings: the political development and the educational initiatives.

The Political Development

Politics in Nigeria is ethnically based, and loyalty is strongly influenced by ethnicity. Before independence, Nigerians at the forefront of the movement for independence educated their followers (within their ethnic groups) to work with other ethnic groups for the purpose of emancipation. However, a contrary message was conveyed after independence, and today ethnicity plays the most important role in governance, even in the military.

However, several steps were taken to ensure that the unity of the country would be preserved. For example, the first Constitution of the newly independent Nigeria adopted a federal system of government with residual power invested in the federal government. Attempts were made to ensure nationally represented political parties. However, most political parties have been housed in one ethnic group, and a token number of members from other ethnic groups were often invited to join these parties in order to fulfill the legal requirements.

The inability of the civilian governments to keep the nation together resulted in a civil war with a costly, but failed secessionist experiment. The military has ruled over the land for most of the years that Nigeria has been independent. Even though the military, as designed by the British during the colonial regime, was based on seniority, the postcolonial military administration has been careful to take ethnicity and religion into consideration before appointing military governors for the states that comprise the nation.

It is obvious that the political agenda of the Nigerian government is to maintain unity among reluctant groups. With this goal, Nigeria has a federal outlook, but in reality a more unitary system of government exists. This is so because the military as a unitary organization with its uniform rank and power arrangements answers to the head of state who is also the commandant in chief of the armed forces. With this arrangement, dissenting voices can be systematically squelched and resurgence quickly repressed. In addition, all public revenues are consolidated into the hands of the federal government, thus ensuring that the state governments depend very much on the power of the federal government.

Formal Educational Initiatives

To appreciate educational initiatives with respect to intercultural awareness in Nigeria, the country's history of education must be understood. The first efforts to provide formal education to Nigerians were made by missionaries whose intention was primarily to convert the Muslims and heathen to

Christianity. This form of education was essentially limited to the three R's, with the emphasis on reading and understanding the Bible. Schooling was limited to primary education and later extended to the secondary school level. The purpose of secondary school education was to produce a man of God who could serve in various Christian leadership occupations.

Although one school may serve several ethnic groups, the purpose with this arrangement was not to promote cultural diversity nor to enhance cultural understanding and appreciation. In fact, the purpose was to attempt the homogenization of students with different ethnic backgrounds by eliminating or reducing as much as possible their heathen cultural heritage. Because varied Christian sects operated in different regions of the country, each sect attempted to establish its own educational system in its own region. For example, the Sudan Interior Mission operating under the Evangelical Churches of West Africa established primary and secondary schools in the middle belt and the northern part of the country. An example of such schools are E.C.W.A Primary School and E.C.W.A. Secondary School, Mopa (ESMO), both located in Kogi State.

The second phase of development witnessed the role of the government in educating the indigenes. It was expensive for the colonial government to bring in White expatriates mainly for clerical work. Hence, it became imperative that government clerks and interpreters be trained locally from among the indigenes. This need led to the establishment of government schools, whose purpose was limited to providing low-level workers for trading and government activities.

Given this limited government goal, an attempt to provide government schools for all ethnic groups was not made. Schools were located in places such as Lagos, Abeokuta, Ibadan, a region closed to the seat of government (at that time) and close to the Lagos Port. It should be noted that the Muslim communities in the North also established their own formal schools but they came relatively late to the scene.

School systems supported by the government, the Christian missionaries, and the Muslims existed simultaneously for about two decades after the independence. Then the federal military government thought it wise to unify the systems and took control of parochial schools. The last stage of development, therefore, signifies an integrated, government-administered education system. The postcolonial government-administered education system attempted to provide access to all ethnic groups by operating primary and secondary schools close to their geographic locations.

However, two players featured prominently at the scene of the postcolonial government educational endeavor in Nigeria: the state government and the federal government. In the first Constitution of the newly created Republic, education was located in the Concurrent List, meaning that both the federal and the state governments could legislate on this matter. However, the federal government was to supersede over the state government in case of conflict.

Given this background, the federal government established federal government colleges (coeducation) and federal government girls' colleges in almost all the states created subsequent to the Republic. At the same time, the state governments created their own secondary schools, for example, Government College, Ibadan and Government College, Ilorin. Some of the state government colleges were coeducational whereas others offered single-sex education. Some, such as commercial colleges and technical colleges were specialized, whereas others, such as grammar schools, were comprehensive.

The local governments administered the primary school education, although some private schools are currently allowed to function under licensure from the state ministry of education. The secondary schools were admistered by both the federal and the state government. At the postsecondary school level, the federal government at first, and later in combination with the state government, provided the necessary administration. The three premier universities of Nigeria (the University of Ibadan, the University of Nigeria-Nsukka, and Ahmadu Bello University) were established by the effort of the federal government, although the University of Ibadan predated the other two universities and served as an extension campus of the University of London.

In response to the needs of the three major ethnic groups—the Yorubas in the West, the Igbos in the East, and the Hausas in the North—the three universities were located in the lands of these ethnic groups. Although these institutions were federally created, their regional focus was never in question. Consequently, the Beckett and O'Connell (1977) study confirmed that the majority of students who attend these institutions come from the ethnic groups in the regions where they are located.

Although the state had concurrent power over education, university education was left primarily in the hands of the federal government. This was to change about 25 years after independence. The states were invited to participate fully in the university education and, consequently, almost all the states (note that the creation of states has continued to increase) established their own universities, for example, Ogun State University for the then newly established Ogun State, Ondo State University for the then newly created Ondo State, University of Maiduguri for the newly created Borno State, and Anambra State University for the then newly created Anambra State, all created to meet the primary need of specific states. It should be noted that state governments had other avenues for participating in higher education through the establishment of state polytechnics and state colleges of education.

Structural Integration. In the thinking of the federal government, unity was of paramount importance in a country formed by external forces that had limited understanding of the local conditions, and in a country whose inhabitants were reluctant participants in the task of nation building. This unity was to be achieved by "forced contact."

Whereas the federal presence was conspicuously absent in the primary education landscape, secondary and postsecondary education became an important instrument in the hands of the federal government to educate Nigerians, to achieve forced contact among diverse ethnic groups, and to produce (hopefully) "new Nigerians." With the growing economy of the nation, the federal government had plentiful resources for achieving these goals.

Therefore, all the federal government colleges (FGCs) and the federal government girls' colleges (FGGCs) established in each state were to recruit nationally and ensure that each state or each ethnic group was represented. With this provision, FGCs and FGGCs located in the far North recruited students from the far South, and conversely those in the far south recruited students from the far North. The federal government was responsible for transportation and accommodation costs, and tuition costs were minimal.

The secondary education inherited from the missionaries was residential. Boarding schools were necessary because of lacking transportation for busing students to and from school, for providing access to students who lived some distance away from the school, and, most importantly, for exercising total control in reforming and reshaping the minds of these students. By separating the students from their cultural background, it was hoped that clones of the British, modern, "civilized" Christian gentlemen could easily be created. Although these objectives were achieved to some extent, the arrangement created a very expensive education system and, more importantly, an educated elite alienated from their own people, an elite more foreign to their own home than the missionaries themselves, and an elite that would be forever saddled with the task of reconciling their Western thought process with their own motherland.

The shortcomings of residential education notwithstanding, the federal government has continued until now to fund the FGCs and FGGCs as model residential institutions for Nigeria. Although contacts were achieved, religious proselytization was disallowed and, although occasional ethnic celebrations were observed, there was no systematic effort to study cultural issues or enhance cultural understanding and appreciation. Western education viewed African cultural practices with disdain and firmly resolved to exterminate what were regarded as barbaric, heathen customs. The "new Nigerians" were quick to understand this, but as both the missionaries and these new Nigerians would later discover, the products of this education were anything but well-rounded, educated men and women. They were quite British and not fully Africans, a dilemma that has continued to plague the continent of Africa.

Similarly, the federal government expanded its "forced contact" policy to the premier universities and those that were subsequently created. A policy similar to what is known as affirmative action in Western literature was adopted for college admission in Nigeria to ensure representation of all the states in these universities.

The Nigerian education system was heavily oriented toward general, public, external examinations at every level. A common entrance examination for all primary school graduates was required to advance to secondary schools. A General Certificate Examination (GCE), administered from England, and a West African Examination Council (WAEC), administered for all the Anglophone West African countries were required after secondary education. Results from these examination bodies were needed for advanced studies and for subsequent admission to the universities.

Given the heavily examination-oriented education, differential admission criteria had to be established for students from each state. With a fluctuating quota system, each state was assured representation in these institutions and, in spite of all the criticism regarding differential admission criteria, representation was valued as a more important goal. However, as was the case at the secondary school level, universities had no systematic approach to cultural issues. Students were jostled together on campuses with the expectation that they would all get along, and that from interacting with one another, a cohesive nation would be formed.

But ethnicity continued to plague university campuses. Freedoms denied at the secondary school level were gained at the university, and ethnic bashing and intertribal vituperation were not uncommon. At the same time, the university provided these young Nigerians with the opportunity to debate and deliberate about the future of their country.

Curriculum Initiatives. If there is ever a failure of education in Nigeria, such failure could be attributed squarely to the gap between the curriculum and the reality of the people. In 1979, DuBey, Edem, and Thakur wrote:

> The present position of the curriculum in Nigeria is that it has remained largely tied down to curriculum developments in the U.K. and to a limited extent recently in the U.S.A. Innovations which have been brought about are more in the direction of details rather than in basic philosophical assumptions. Furthermore, the primary school curriculum has been responding to the needs of

Nigeria more quickly than secondary, and the secondary somewhat more quickly than the university curriculum. (pp. 57–58)

With major common examinations set in Britain, curriculum matters were geared toward the British reality. With teachers and expatriate professors trained either in the United States or Britain, pedagogic matters reflected what was obtainable in those countries. Local examples were minimal. A comprehensive intercultural education, which was a rarity in both the United States and Britain at that time, could not have been included in the educational agenda of Nigeria. Therefore, this oversight was not deliberate, but rather reflected the prevailing ignorance among policymakers of that era.

Nigerians had a conspicuous appetite for formal education as was revealed by the inability of the system to accommodate the sudden surge in demand when the Western province of the country, under the leadership of the late Chief Obafemi Awolowo, experimented with a universal primary education program. More conspicuous though was the appetite and predisposition toward Western education which, regrettably, the educated elite could not translate quickly enough to meet local needs. Because students with high achievement were selected for the sciences in those days, it soon became generally assumed that the arts must be inferior, and they were regarded with disdain. Therefore, a conducive atmosphere that could have given rise to intercultural education curriculum was lacking. To date, there has never been a well-articulated national policy or effort toward an intercultural education curriculum in Nigeria. However, it should be emphasized that recently, primary education was directed to include a lesson in the native language of the child, and at the secondary school level, students were to be encouraged to study another language.

Experiential Initiatives. What the nation lost in curriculum initiatives, it tried to gain in forced contact. Therefore, the military government under the leadership of General Gowon established a National Youth Service Corps (NYSC) to provide a paramilitary experience for graduates from Nigerian postsecondary institutions. The central goal of the program was to provide the experience in a culture that was different from the ethnic background of the graduate. The program became a precondition for employment after graduating from a postsecondary education institution.

This paramilitary program, one of the most successful forced contact initiatives of the federal government still in existence at this writing, is administered by the military. Under this arrangement, graduates are centrally allocated to states other than their own with some exceptions (e.g., medical condition of the graduate), and hundreds of graduates assigned to each state are provided with basic military training in a camp. After a period of camp experience, they are posted to provide cheap labor to government, business, and nonprofit organizations within their assigned states. The total experience lasts for a year. The hope of the federal government was that graduates would remain in their assigned states to continue their lifelong career and be integrated into the social fabric of that society.

Similarly, federal government offices all over the nation, including federal government institutions, which were once the major employer of the educated elite, provided and continue to provide opportunities for employees to transfer from one state to another. In some cases, it was an expectation that employees would be transferred from one place to another, all for the sole purpose of integration and experiential education.

Although it cannot be denied that the federal government's "forced contact" programs have provided experiential education to graduates, and that these efforts have gone a long way to increase cultural sensitivity, ethnicity has remained the most volatile issue confronting Nigeria. Ethnicity or tribalism has remained intractable to Nigerian leaders and has become a precarious sea of trouble through which the ship of the nation continues to be buffeted by a neverending, wicked storm of life.

THE ISSUE OF NEW IMMIGRANTS

The extent to which a new immigrant to Nigeria can access the opportunity structure of the country depends on a number of factors: racial or ethnic group, knowledge of the major languages, and resources at the disposal of the immigrant. Apart from training sessions provided by foreign embassies and missionary groups operating in Nigeria, there is no government-sponsored program to facilitate immigrant transitions to the country. Because of the historic role of the British, certain expectations await White immigrants, most notably an expectation as to the socioeconomic status of anybody of European descent.

Immigrants from other African countries encounter different problems. Some of the problems include language barriers, except for those from Anglophone countries. There are no official language schools to help integrate immigrants into the social fabric of the country. Immigrants who take it on themselves to acquire a local language will find it easier to participate in the community life of the ethnic group. The indigenization decree promulgated in the 1970s made it difficult for foreign business owners to operate in the country, but those who have adequate resources will find adaptation to the cultures of the country easier.

DIRECTION FOR THE FUTURE

That Nigeria is a troubled nation is reflected in the incessant military coups détat and notorious human rights infractions well documented in the international media. The dream of a peaceful, democratic, and progressive nation has continued to elude Nigeria, a nation actually blessed with enormous natural and human resources. Achebe (1983) attributed the problem to the failure of leadership:

> The trouble with Nigeria is simply and squarely a failure of leadership. There is nothing basically wrong with the Nigerian character. There is nothing wrong with the Nigerian land or climate or water or air or anything. The Nigerian problem is the unwillingness or inability of its leaders to rise to the responsibility, to the challenge of personal example which are the hallmarks of true leadership. (p. 1)

This failure of leadership is reflected in the absence of a comprehensive approach to intercultural education in a land where the bond that holds the various ethnic groups together is pitifully fragile. The same author also observed:

> Our national anthem, our very hymn of deliverance from British colonial bondage, was written for us by a British woman who unfortunately had not been properly briefed on the current awkwardness of the word tribe. So we found ourselves on independence morning rolling our tongues around the very same trickster godling:
>
> Though tribal and tongue may differ, in brotherhood we stand!
>
> It was a most ominous beginning. And not surprisingly we did not stand too long in brotherhood. Within six years we were standing or sprawling on a soil soaked in fratricidal blood. (p. 6)

Intellectuals have failed to agree on a single definition of a Nigerian problem. Hence, a search for realistic solutions have continued to elude the nation. Figure 9.3 attempts to provide another approach in our quest to understand the nation and to appreciate the importance of intercultural education. The first circle represents a nation with a formidable national consciousness such as that found in the United States. Although Native Americans were in the land for hundreds of years before their arrival, Europeans soon conquered the land and firmly established their culture over it. Thus, English became the official language of the land; a democratic form of government was established; and a Constitution that reflects the values and wisdom of the pioneers was adopted. This culture provided the foundation on which the national character or identity was formed,

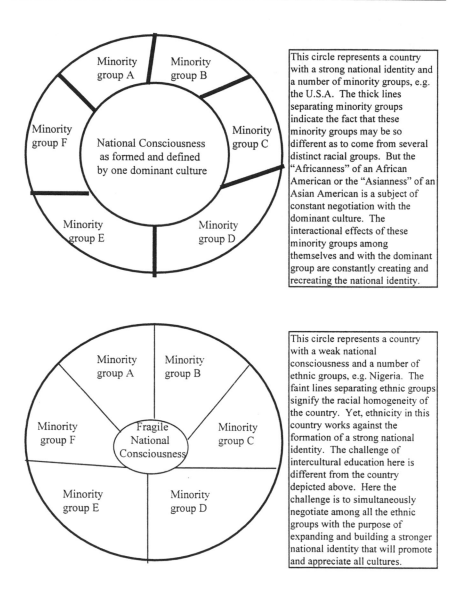

This circle represents a country with a strong national identity and a number of minority groups, e.g. the U.S.A. The thick lines separating minority groups indicate the fact that these minority groups may be so different as to come from several distinct racial groups. But the "Africanness" of an African American or the "Asianness" of an Asian American is a subject of constant negotiation with the dominant culture. The interactional effects of these minority groups among themselves and with the dominant group are constantly creating and recreating the national identity.

This circle represents a country with a weak national consciousness and a number of ethnic groups, e.g. Nigeria. The faint lines separating ethnic groups signify the racial homogeneity of the country. Yet, ethnicity in this country works against the formation of a strong national identity. The challenge of intercultural education here is different from the country depicted above. Here the challenge is to simultaneously negotiate among all the ethnic groups with the purpose of expanding and building a stronger national identity that will promote and appreciate all cultures.

FIG. 9.3. Representations of Ethinic Groups And National identities of Two Countries.

and every immigrant coming to America knew that he or she was coming to live under a European (mainly British) culture. Hector St. Jean de Crevecoeur, as quoted by Franklin (1996), underscored this point:

What, then, is the American, this new man? He is either an European, or the descendant of an European; hence that strange mixture of blood, which you will find in no other country. . . . He is an American, who, leaving behind him all his ancient prejudices and manners, receives new ones from the new mode of the life he has embraced, the new governments he obeys, and the new rank he holds. He becomes an American by being received in the broad lap of our great Alma Mater. Here individuals of all nations are melted into new race of men, whose labours and posterity will one day cause great changes in the world. (p. 29)

Irrespective of the assimilationist view expressed by de Crevecoeur, there is no denying the significance of the European heritage and influence on America. Hence, the size of the inner circle attempts to convey the magnitude and importance of a solid national consciousness in America as compared with the influence of other minority groups. Indeed in the United States, the definition of the marginalized groups goes beyond ethnicity to include race, religion, gender, and lifestyle to mention but a few.

Until recently, the official policy was to open immigration doors to those who could easily assimilate this culture. However, America has evolved, given the presence of millions of non-European immigrants, into its own unique culture. Today, only a few pockets of extremists would question the national identity of the country. It is on this platform that the multicultural/intercultural movements were developed. Consequently, intercultural education in the United States is an attempt to strengthen an already strong nation, to foster cultural understanding, to celebrate the richness of cultural diversity, to minimize cultural barriers to the minority, and to do so because it is the American Way.

However, the second circle in Fig. 9.3 represents a nation such as Nigeria in which national identity is negligible, and ethnicity is of paramount importance. The small size of the inner circle represents the negligible nature of the national identity or national consciousness (NC), whereas the larger outer circle represents the significance of ethnicity. For this reason, many Nigerians doubt if the country could survive without a strong federal government, a theory that was tested during the civil war.

In the absence of one major dominant ethnic group in Nigeria and in the presence of strong ethnic loyalty, the Nigerian consciousness is very weak. The country could not agree on a domestic lingua franca. Hence, English became the official language, and pidgin English evolved for the majority of Nigerians with no formal schooling. National pride is minimal, whereas tribal pride is paramount, a situation that has created reckless use of national resources and nonchalant attitudes to national issues. Indeed, Nigeria continues to be a figment of imagination, having a form of reality only when useful to most Nigerians. Given this scenario, two options are available to the country.

First, the inner circle (national consciousness) may be enlarged by reducing the influence and importance of ethnicity. That means a detribalization process that will achieve the goal of the federal government: the creation of "new Nigerians" whose allegiance would be to the country rather than their ethnic background. Logical as this recommendation may seem, it is a very difficult option for a country characterized by several hundred cultural groups. Each group has only one goal: to consolidate its resources and expand its influence on the country or, at least, prevent its absorption or assimilation by other groups. As long as all the cultural groups have this goal, the impasse is a neverending one.

The second option involves adopting a comprehensive intercultural education that would be compulsory for every Nigerian child. Intercultural education would have to be provided from kindergarten to the postgraduate level. It would have to form the cornerstone of Nigerian education and be seen as a national imperative. Intercultural education in Nigeria would have to go beyond what is commonly found in Western countries. Both the federal and the state governments would need to work together in making intercultural education a national priority and in exposing all Nigerians to the three major languages and cultures, with a view of allowing a voluntary evolution of a meaningful Nigerian identity. The very existence of the country depends on the degree to which a national identity is negotiated and painstakingly actualized. Hence, the country would be wise not to adopt a cosmetic, sporadic, underfunded, ill-conceived, tokenistic, rhetorical intercultural education.

TO CONSIDER

Increasingly, Nigeria is becoming aware of the need to institutionalize democratic practice and make room for all members of its society. Yet it still faces the ever-increasing and very real possibility of civil war. What role can education play in its development?

1. Review current newspapers from Nigeria or listen to news from the BBC and via shortwave radio that may keep you better informed. Search for news items that present issues related to interethnic conflict, the international community, and educational responses to diversity. How do current issues related to diversity within Nigeria relate to what you have just read?

2. What can your nation and schools learn from the experiences of Nigeria?

3. *How can young people in Nigeria be most effectively prepared to interact with others on a global scale? What resources seem to be available within Nigeria to assist young people in developing a global or intercultural perspective?*

4. *Nigeria occasionally receives immigrants and refugees from neighboring African nations. Given what you have just read, how would you respond to the scenario presented in chapter 1. What steps should schools take in responding to the needs of newly arrived immigrant groups?*

5. *Use Figure 9.3 to analyze the ethnic/racial dynamics of any country of your choice. Discuss your analysis and the usefulness of this exercise.*

REFERENCES

Achebe, C. (1983). *The trouble with Nigeria*. London: Heinemann.

Beckett, P., & O'Connell, J. (1977). *Education and power in Nigeria: A study of university students*. London: Hodder & Stoughton.

Coombs, P. H. (1985). *The world crisis in education: The view from the eighties*. New York: Oxford University Press.

DuBey, D. L., Edem, D. A., & Thakur, A. S. (1979). *An introduction to the sociology of Nigerian education*. London: Macmillan.

Franklin, J. H. (1996). Ethnicity in American life: The historical perspective. In C. S. V. Turner, M. Garcia, A. Nora, & L. I. Rendon (Eds.), *Racial and ethnic diversity in higher education* (pp. 29–35). ASHE Reader Series. Needham Heights, MA: Simon & Schuster.

Hraba, J. (1979). *American ethnicity*. Itasca, IL: F. E. Peacock.

Knight, C. G., & Newman, J. L. (1976). *Contemporary African: Geography and change*. Englewood Cliffs, NJ: Prentice-Hall.

Editor's Remarks

The first known contacts between Europeans and South Africans began in the late 1480s, when Portuguese sailors traveled around Africa's southern tip as a result of the spice trade between the East and Europe. By the end of the sixteenth century, the Dutch and English began to replace the Portuguese influence. At first, friendly relationships developed between Europeans and local tribespeople. However, once Europeans began showing signs of permanent settlement, tensions arose and violent clashes between the cultures increased. Years of settlement, development, and clashes continued.

By the late 1800s, Mohandas Ghandi took up residence in South Africa, becoming the leader of the growing Indian population in that part of the world. It was here that he developed his philosophy of nonviolence, which he would use later in his attempt to gain India's independence from Britain. Although racism has operated for along time, it became institutionalized under the apartheid regime of the Nationalist government. Formed early this century the African National Congress attempted during the mid-1900s to ameliorate the grievances of Black citizens by approaching the central government directly, and Nelson Mandela began to get involved in the struggle for Black African rights.

In the 1960s and 1970s, many African nations, as well as others around the world, reacted negatively toward South Africa's continued hard-line position on apartheid. Major civil unrest and violations of human rights were common throughout the 1970s and 1980s. In 1986, Bishop Desmond Tutu encouraged a worldwide effort to apply punitive sanctions against the Botha government until apartheid was abolished, and the United Nations passed 25 resolutions related to the struggle of the South African people. With F. W. de Klerk's government, apartheid was finally dismantled in 1990, and Nelson Mandela was released after being imprisoned for 27 years.

Nelson Mandela's leadership has resulted in the desegregation of the nation's schools, increased use of English as the language of instruction, and a major effort to train Black African teachers for the classrooms.

How would you go about redesigning an educational system that is more equitable and inclusive for all? How would you go about healing the scars and pain that are the result of an exclusive system? How can a core of teachers, all of whom grew up under apartheid, be prepared to teach toward pluralism and inclusion? How can the young people of this vital nation best be prepared for a new tomorrow?

Chapter 10

Breaking Out of a Separatist Paradigm: Intercultural Education in South Africa

ᙏ ◆ ᙎ

John Stonier
South Africa

A BRIEF DESCRIPTION OF SOUTH AFRICA
AND ITS NATIONAL EDUCATION SYSTEM

South African Society

With its remarkably diverse population, South Africa must exemplify an almost unique situation in terms of multiculturalism. The separation of people on the basis of ethnicity in South African civil society has existed for a long time, but it became entrenched in law with the promulgation of various acts of parliament during the apartheid era. The informal apartheid before 1948 and the formal apartheid policies from that date saw the implementation of active programs of social engineering by a White parliament that had as their principal focus the separation of people into racial groups in every facet of society's structures : residential areas and sporting, cultural, recreational, and employment opportunities. This grand design for ensuring the privileged position of Whites was accompanied by the shameless discrimination and humiliation of all other South Africans.

The democratization of the country started in the early 1990s with the unbanning of all previously banned political groupings and the return of large numbers of exiled South Africans. Difficult negotiations finally resulted in a general election in April 1994 when, for the first time since the arrival of Europeans in 1652, Blacks were entitled to vote. This resulted in the first democratically elected government, and the symbolic occasion of the transition of power from the White minority to the Black majority took place on 10 May 1994 when Mr. Nelson Mandela was inaugurated as president of South Africa.

In his inaugural address Mr. Mandela gave an indication of his vision for South Africa by stating, among other things, that "we enter into a covenant that we shall build the society in which all South Africans, both Black and White, will be able to walk tall without any fear in their hearts, assured by their inalienable right to human dignity—a rainbow nation at peace with itself and the world" (Cape Times, 1994). Once the formalities were over, Mr. Mandela "addresse[d] tens of thousands of expectant members of the public attending a 'many cultures—one nation' all-day concert on the lawns of the Union Building" (Johnson, 1994).

The Educational Scene

The Past.   The apartheid ideology applied in civil society was applied just as rigorously to schools and education. The administration of education developed an extraordinary pattern as rigid structures were put in place to accommodate apartheid principles. Children were separated into four main racial groups (Black, used to refer to the indigenous African people in South Africa; Coloured, the term traditionally used to denote persons of racially mixed descent; Indian; and White) each with its own schools. Furthermore, Whites were separated into English-speaking and Afrikaans-speaking schools. Moreover, not only were the students separated into their own schools, but the schools themselves were administered by separate education departments. The isolation of the cultural and ethnic groups was virtually complete, and the "success" of the separation and isolation of the races became very apparent once the move towards a more open society began.

The executive function of education was left to specific but separate education departments of which there were 17; 4 for Whites; 10 for African Homelands (areas set aside under the policy of separate development of a particular Black people, self-governing, and in some cases regarded as "independent") (Branford & Branford, 1991), 1 for people of Indian descent, 1 for Coloureds and one for Blacks who were not resident in any of the 10 Homelands.

The apartheid years resulted in enormous disparities developing between the groups as far as the provision of funding and resources is concerned. The amount of support provided for each group varied from a high of 4,772 rands per White student down to 1,524 rands per Black student in the Homelands. One factor that contributed to this imbalance was the very large difference that existed in qualifications of teachers in the different sectors. Because remuneration is linked to qualifications and because about 80% of an educational budget goes to cover teachers' salaries, the significantly higher qualifications of White teachers were a major factor skewing the per capita expenditure.

The financial disparity is also reflected in the student–teacher ratios, which in 1993 varied from 44.4 students per teacher in Black schools, to about 22 students per teacher in Indian and Coloured schools, to 18 students per teacher in White schools. This data reflects how Black students were severely disadvantaged because they were not able to receive anything like the personal attention enjoyed by the other race groups. Professional attention was hindered even further by the fact that there was a chronic shortage of qualified Black teachers, with 45% of Black teachers being under qualified or unqualified to teach.

The Present. Education is one area of reconstruction to which the government has given a high priority, and the aforementioned disparities and others are being attended to as a matter of urgency. However, it has become clear that effecting a major transformation in every facet of education cannot be achieved overnight. A very complex system has its own momentum, and the authorities have stated that although it is important to effect changes with all speed, care must be exercised to make certain that the system does not collapse. Consequently, the changes taking place have been interpreted by some as being too rapid and by others as being too slow.

These introductory observations indicate that the system of education in South Africa is in a state of flux, with shifts and adjustments taking place month by month. This being the case, it is not possible to describe the present South African position with any precision. The most that can be done is to present a broad outline of the structure and directions that policies seem to suggest.

Policy. In 1994 a new single national Ministry of Education responsible for the establishment of national policy for education at all educational institutions was established. This was the first step towards creating a new system of education for South Africa.

Nine new provinces came into being with the acceptance of the 1993 South African Constitution, and the executive function for formal school education was delegated to the provincial departments of education established in each of these new provinces.

Students who reach 7 years of age in any given year are expected to begin their formal schooling in January, of that year. In the future, students will follow a program of general education for 9 years, which will lead to an examination for a General Education and Training Certificate (GETC). Of those 9 years, the first 7 will be spent in the primary school and the remaining two in a secondary school. It is intended that these 9 years, together with one "reception" (preschool) year will form the basis for 10 years of free and compulsory [1] schooling. The option of 3 further years at secondary school (or other recognized institution), which will not be free, will be available and will lead to an assessment for a Further Education and Training Certificate (FETC) (Department of Education, 1995). A date has not yet been set for the change from the previous structure to the one just mentioned. Although it is true that 98% of all South African schools are state schools, provision has been made for the establishment and recognition of fully independent schools.

Education and Training. Of particular significance is the coupling of education and 'training', not only in the name of the certificates to be awarded, but also for other documents dealing with various facets of the policy and design of a new system (South African Ministerial Committee for Development Work on the National Qualifications Framework Act, 1996). The coupling highlights a major shift toward viewing education and training, not as discrete activities, but as related activities in the development of human resources. The Ministry of Education has committed itself to an integrated approach to education and training in order to remove what are regarded as artificial divisions between knowledge and skills; head and hand; theory and practice; etc. (Department of Education, 1996). The details with regard to this are being vigorously debated at many levels at the time of writing and a final picture is yet to emerge.

Students would be eligible for access to higher education and training (tertiary) if acceptable levels of achievement in the FETC program were achieved. Degrees and Diplomas would be awarded by institutions such as universities, colleges of education, technikons (which place an emphasis on applied studies and disciplines), technical colleges, and other accredited institutions.

Given South Africa's history of minority rule, legislated oppression, and entrenched discrimination, it is not surprising that the 1993 Constitution contains articles of fundamental rights that provide protection against the possibility of anything similar ever taking place again.

---

[1] Schooling for Black students has never been compulsory. Because of the cost involved it is hoped that officials can start phasing in compulsory schooling for Black students beginning in 1997. (Edusource Data News, 1996, p. 5).

It is therefore not surprising that the Ministry of Education's' first White Paper makes special reference to the need for new education and training policies to address legacies of the past and to provide "equal opportunities for all" based on nondiscrimination. Although no specific mention is made of multicultural education,[2] a further statement in the White Paper does give active recognition to the extraordinary diversity that exists in South Africa. It notes that because "all forms of bias (especially racial, ethnic, and gender) are dehumanizing," there is a need for "active encouragement of *mutual respect for our people's diverse religious, cultural and language traditions,* their right to practice them in peace and without hindrance . . . " (Department of Education, 1995; 22, paragraphs 13 and 14)).

DESCRIPTIVE DATA OF DEMOGRAPHICS OF SOUTH AFRICA AND EXPERIENCES OF MAINSTREAM EDUCATION

Population

A key feature of the population of South Africa is its heterogeneity. This will be apparent in the statistics that follow. Unfortunately, the available population figures are not reliable because all births and deaths are not registered (South African Institute of Race Relations [SAIRR] 1995).

The Development Bank of South Africa has estimated that the total population of 40.7 million in 1993 was made up of the following major racial groups: African, 76%; Asian, 2.5%; Coloured, 8.5%; and White, 13%. It is important to note that the use of these categories is a sensitive issue in many quarters, particularly as they formed the basis for the apartheid structures, and their current use is often a reminder of past oppression with its hurt, frustration, and anger. The more pragmatic view holds that unless these categories are used, it will be difficult to establish where the discrimination was most potent and thus where special actions for redress are required.

Of importance to the country as a whole in terms of housing, health, economic growth, education, and so forth is the rate of population increase. The average annual population growth rate between 1985 and 1990 was 2.3%. It is suggested that if this trend continues, the South African population will double in fewer than 30 years, and this has enormous implications for the country's resources (SAIRR, 1995).

[2]There is a continuing debate about the use of terms. I prefer the term "intercultural education" because it implies a more dynamic interchange between different people. However, in this chapter I have stayed with the term "multicultural education" only because it is the one more widely used in South Africa at present.

Religious Affiliations. Not surprisingly, the diverse population reflects a great variety of religious affiliations that includes many of the world's major religions together with a number of independent "African Initiated Churches (AICS)." No reference is made in the official statistics to the practice of any form of indigenous African Traditional Religion (ATR), which hitherto has been denied the status of religion. One reason for this is that in indigenous communities there is no separation of life's activities into those that are religious and those that are secular. The practice of religion permeates all aspects of life, and the various customs, beliefs and rituals all form part of everyday life. Although there are sacred places and symbols, there are no "churches," and neither is there an institutionalized religion as exists in more formalized religions. In spite of the Christian missionary enterprise, the practice of African Traditional Religion has never really disappeared. Its practice, suppressed for centuries, seems to be taking place more openly at present.

Language. Census tables and statistics have tended to group indigenous Black people under the heading of "African." Although convenient, this designation has the capacity to obscure some important differences in Blacks, for example, the variety of home language in use.

Indicating the importance of indigenous languages to the people of South Africa, the 1993 Constitution lists 11 languages as the official languages. Clause 3(1) reads as follows: "Afrikaans, English, isiNdebele, Sotho sa Leboa, Sesotho, siSwati, Xitsonga, Setswana, Tshivenda, isiXhosa, and isiZulu shall be the official South African languages at national level, and conditions shall be created for their development and for the promotion of their equal use and enjoyment."

The following figures indicate the proportion of the total population that uses each language, although it should be noted that speakers of these languages are not evenly distributed throughout South Africa: Zulu, 22.4%; Xhosa, 18.3%; Afrikaans, 14.5%; North Sotho, 9.1%; English, 8.4%; Tawana, 7.7%; South Sotho, 6.4%; Tsonga, 3.7%; Siswati, 3.1%; Venda, 1.7%; Ndebele, 0.7%; and other, 4% (SAIRR, 1995).

The position of the English language deserves special comment. One consequence of the colonial era was the use of English as the lingua franca. The successive National Party governments applied measures to enhance the status and use of Afrikaans in an affirmative way. However, the recent change of government has led to additional impetus for the use of English because it is the common language currency among the African elite. Nevertheless, it is important to note that virtually half of the population can speak neither English nor Afrikaans, which has significant implications for state departments and for education.

SUBGROUPS' ATTITUDE TOWARDS,
AND EXPERIENCES OF,
THE 'MAINSTREAM' EDUCATION SYSTEM

Until very recently the White minority was responsible for determining all aspects of educational policy. Consequently, the word "mainstream," when referring to the education system and the subgroups' experience of it, is placed within quotation marks to indicate the anomalous situation in which the majority of the population had no way of affecting, let alone determining, the pattern of mainstream education. As already noted, significant changes have and are taking place. Nevertheless, to place subgroups' attitudes and experiences regarding the education system in context, a brief historical overview is necessary.

Missionary Education.   Before the arrival of the missionaries, and later the colonial authorities, education was an essential, albeit informal, activity in sub-Saharan Africa, including South Africa. Although formal schooling in special institutions did not exist, there nevertheless was a clear pattern of "schooling" for young people in which formal and informal instruction was given. The focus of this schooling was on nurturing the child so that he or she would learn the strategies necessary for survival, be prepared to undertake the role allocated by the community, and assimilate the values and customs that suited the way of life of the people (Iwuagwu, 1991).

The main purpose of the missionary effort throughout Africa was evangelistic, aimed at effecting conversions to Christianity. However, it soon became apparent that to achieve this aim, rudimentary book knowledge was required. This encouraged the missions to provide basic and elementary schooling. Accordingly, as the expansion of missionary work took place so did the provision of education and schooling. By the 1930s there were very few areas where elementary schooling for Black people was not provided by various missionary societies (Berman, 1974; Boahen, 1987; Scanlon, 1966). This was particularly so in South Africa where, by 1945 "there were 5,360 mission-run schools for Africans in South Africa and only 230 state-sponsored schools" (Berman, 1974, p. 104).

Not surprisingly, the educational policies instituted in the African colonies were projections of European models, which were themselves much influenced by the church (Scanlon, 1996). In a very real sense, the missionary schools supported the assumptions, attitudes, and policies of the colonial governments (Mungazi, 1989). In this way the mission schools displayed all the hallmarks of Western education. These active attempts at the Europeanization of African people had both positive and negative consequences, of which the negative ones had deep pervasive effects apparent still today (Boahen, 1987; Deliwe, 1992).

Reaction to Western Education

With the disparity in power relationships between the colonizers and the colonized, the African was forced to accept Western education in order to survive. The schooling offered was not what the indigenous people would have chosen for their children (Mungazi, 1989). However, these people were powerless to influence the decisions imposed on them.

Consequently, many Africans were schooled in the Western tradition and have adopted many Western styles of living, becoming thoroughly Westernized. Some scholars believe that such Africans have become alienated from their African roots and no longer display genuinely African attitudes, responses, and reactions (Onuoha, 1965). As a result, these Westernized Africans often fail to understand or appreciate the needs and aspirations of less Westernized South Africans.

Referring to the rural people in the Transkei (Eastern Cape Province), Deliwe (1992) noted that Xhosa society came to be divided into two broad categories as a result of schooling, mainly missionary schooling. There were the "school people" who accepted the European way of life and the "red people", called "red" because of the use of red ochre on their faces and the wearing of red blankets. The "red peoples" response to schooling was a rejection of a situation that they interpreted as tampering with the Xhosa social order (Deliwe, 1992).

This view was confirmed in a recent study carried out by the author in an informal settlement (township) in Mpumalanga Province. Schooling was not perceived to have any symbiotic link with the home, but was regarded as something that took place "out there." This view seemed to be rooted in the perception that the schools had rejected family values and customs (Stonier, 1996). Parents came to be alienated from the school because it was not seen as reflecting the worldview held by many Black parents. However, they do recognize that success at school provides the potential for entering well-paid careers and thereby enjoying economic mobility. For this reason, and in spite of the alienation, parents encourage their children to attend school (Stonier, 1996).

Racially Structured Education

In South Africa the colonial/missionary pattern of education was demarcated along racial lines. This pattern was pursued even more vigorously shortly after the conclusion of World War II when the National Party came into power in 1948.

Legislation and policy announcements directed that Blacks would be relegated to a subservient role in society and that they needed to be prepared for that role. This view was clearly set out in the frequently quoted statement made by Dr. H. F. Verwoerd (Minister of Native Affairs at the time) in the South African parliament: There "is no place for him [the Black] in the European community above the level of certain forms of labor. . . ." For that reason it is of no avail for him to receive a training which has as its aim absorption into the European community" (Verwoerd quoted in Malherbe, 1977, p. 546). This view (and others) were taken up in the Bantu Education Act No. 47 of 1953 and formed the basis of the education policy over Blacks for a number of decades.

The curriculum was therefore designed to ensure ethnic differences, and the separation of ethnic groups was emphasized. Budget allocations for Black education declined sharply during the 12-year period after 1953, which resulted in a marked deterioration in the quality of teaching. Subsequent adjustments were made to budget allocations, but Malherbe (1977) expressed some doubt as to whether by 1974 the improved allocations had resulted in any real improvement in the quality of education after 1954.

The Bantu Education Act had its most serious effect on the teacher training institutions, most of which had been under the control of the missions, but were then to be administered by the government. With the closing of the mission training institutions, and because the government was unable to replace them, problems of providing suitably qualified teachers surfaced. The overall result on schools was a steady decline in the quality of education, occasioned by the necessity of using underqualified and unqualified Black teachers, by severe overcrowding in the schools, and by lack of financial support (Malherbe, 1977).

During this period, opportunities were created for parents to become involved in the control of schools through school committees and school boards. However, the areas over which these committees and boards could exercise control were very limited (Malherbe, 1977). In describing this period, Mboya (1987, p. 69) stated that "schools are in fact, under the total control of whites." He noted specifically that the curriculum, the kind of schooling needed by African communities, and the employment of teachers was determined and controlled by White authorities.

The inevitable consequence was a slow but steady buildup of frustration. School students became aware that they were receiving an inferior education, and the humiliation they felt brought into being a new generation of African students who rejected the system of education imposed on them and the values on which it rested, a system aimed at preparing them for a subservient role in society as cheap laborers (Mboya, 1987). This system was rejected because it created a low "glass ceiling" that restricted social, career and economic mobility.

A Crisis in Education

The various measures implemented, particularly in Black education but also in Coloured and Indian education, and the rejection of that education, originally by students and subsequently by parents and communities, resulted in a virtual breakdown of the entire education process. The unhappiness that the oppressed majority felt as a result of their experiences, and their perception of the inhibiting effects of schooling during the last century in general and the last four decades in particular, encouraged some writers to question, not only the content of the curriculum, but all aspects of the school structure, function, and purpose.

The frustration engendered by the Bantu Education Act of 1953 reached a crisis point in 1976 when, on 16 June that year, thousands of school children took to the streets to protest, initially against any attempt to impose the use of the Afrikaans language as a medium of instruction and, subsequently, against the discrimination in education to which they and their parents had been subjected. Similar protests spread to many parts of the country. Anger and frustration was fueled by the heavyhanded military response from the government. Thus began a massive campaign of resistance to apartheid by the young people of South Africa that lasted for more than a decade. One tragic consequence of a deeply politicized school population was the "loss" of a whole generation of Black students who did not receive effective schooling—the "lost generation."

Open Schools Movement

In the same year, 1976, the South African Catholics Bishops' Conference passed a resolution encouraging its private Catholic schools to reject the imposed policies of segregation and to enroll students of all races (Christie, 1990; Gaganakis, 1992). Adopting this stance was a direct challenge to the South African government. This decision meant that for the first time in South African education, Black, Coloured, and Indian children were able to share classrooms with their White counterparts, albeit in private church schools and in very limited numbers.

This shift in the South African education scene came to be referred to as the "open schools movement." It is important to note that even with the active encouragement of the South African Catholic Bishops' Conference, the number of private Catholic schools that "opened" was very limited. Robertson (1994) noted that by 1993, of the 373 Catholic schools in the Republic, only 85 were "open." This meant that very few students were able to take advantage of attending schools in a stable and supportive environment.

Much later, various groups, both civic and political, exercised intense pressure on the government to "open" state schools, and it was in 1990 that the rigid segregationist policy in state schools was relaxed. If a very large majority of parents voted in favor of "opening" their school, the education departments were authorized to allow such schools to determine their own admission policies. Many schools took advantage of this opportunity and developed open admission policies.

The desegregation of state schools started in 1991 and took place very smoothly. The enrollment of Black students in previously White, Coloured, and Indian schools increased rapidly. Statistics for the White sector show an increase from about 8,000 non-White students at the end of 1992 to more than 60,000 in 1993 (SAIRR, 1994). As was the case with the church private schools (Catholic originally and subsequently Methodist and Anglican church schools), Black parents appeared to opt for an open school for two reasons: (a) It was a way of escaping the confusion and disorder taking place in Black schools, and (b) parents viewed education in the open school sector as a way of avoiding the excesses of "Bantu education" (Gaganakis, 1992).

Whatever the reason, the open schools movement was a watershed period in South African educational history because it saw the beginning of significant changes in the classroom composition of White, Coloured, and Indian state schools. The apartheid and segregationist structures started to give way with the anticipation of a more open society. The opening of state schools occasioned a situation in which, for the first time, close interaction between many more students from very disparate cultural and social backgrounds was possible. It must be pointed out that the "mixed" schools constitute a small percentage of schools in South Africa because the overwhelming majority of people are Black. Therefore, most schools are predominantly African.

INTEGRATION, NONRACIALISM AND MULTICULTURALISM

The fact that the desegregation of many schools began smoothly is an important aspect of the process because it suggests the nature of the schools' approach to the new and diverse composition of school and classroom. The early attempts at integration tended to follow a pattern of open enrollment in school policy rather than one essentially multicultural in nature. Even those Catholic schools which had been open for 15 years or more had not shifted from being merely open to actively acknowledging that children bring a worldview to school that needs, not only to be accommodated, but validated as something legitimate. This issue was recognized by Robertson (1994) when he noted that the school of which he was Principal had been open for 17 years, but that the question of handling various cultures in the school had not received the attention it required.

Lack of Preparation. The suddenness with which state schools were allowed to desegregate meant that teachers, as well as educational authorities were completely unprepared to deal with the new situation. The vast majority of teachers had no previous experience of dealing with diversity. The apartheid policy had so effectively segregated individuals that adults had been completely isolated from each other. Thus they were not able to draw on the experience of any previous contact with their fellow South Africans. Added to that was the fact that the teachers were themselves educated in segregated schools and training institutions, so it is very easy to understand the extent to which teachers were unaware of the issues associated with multiculturalism in schools.

A marked degree of euphoria manifested itself when the schools originally opened. It seemed that the guilt felt by many White teachers because of the patently discriminatory system in which they worked could finally be set aside. Schools prided themselves on their ability to take advantage of the new dispensation by becoming nonracial. For the reasons given earlier, however, all the good intentions did not provide the understanding required to resolve the complex issues surrounding the challenge of dealing with students in multicultural and multilingual contexts.

The Assimilation Mode. A prevailing assumption in the early days, which still exists today, is that "all children are the same" or that "children are children", and that to talk about complex issues is to see ghosts where none exist. It became fashionable, and it was thought to be progressive and sensitive, to refuse to indicate how many Black children were enrolled in a previously White class or school. "I have only children in my class" was a refrain often heard. As was experienced in other parts of the world, this blanket statement had the effect of protecting teachers from the difficulty of acknowledging the complexities of the new situation, thus freeing them from the problem of having to rethink and replan their approach to teaching. It meant not having to learn about the worldviews held by Black students and their families. It is not a distortion of the truth to state that most White teachers were socialized within the framework of a colonial mentality without their actual awareness of it.

Some Effects of 'Opening.'   Brenda Cowley (1991) carried out a study to determine the impact of desegregated schooling on 6-year-old children, using directed drawings. She noted, among other things, a significant measure of "misidentification" of Black children, who drew themselves with Caucasian hair and did not depict skin color in their drawings. Cowley acknowledged that the explanation is a complex one, but she felt that the heavy emphasis the school was placing on the directly stated view that "in this school we don't see peoples' colour" or "no matter what colour a person's skin is, people are basically the same" could have caused confusion and a reluctance by the children to depict obvious identification differences. Policies and attitudes that have children depicting themselves with attributes of the dominant group, while understandable, seem not to be doing justice to the development of the child's capacity for accurate self-assessment and, in turn, the child's self-esteem.

Informal observations tend to suggest that Cowley's (1991) findings could be extrapolated to the majority of schools, not only for the age group studied, but for other levels as well. Without conscious realization, the assumption was made that all children are the same and that multicultural education was irrelevant. Adopting this view meant that schools could carry on with business as usual, and therefore did not need to acknowledge any specific goals, aspirations, and needs that the diverse mix of children and their parents may have had. This assimilationist mode implied that the "other" has to become like me. In effect, the open enrollment did nothing to address racist or discriminatory practices.

Adopting an attitude in which obvious differences are ignored was labeled by Halstead (1988) as "colour-blind racism". Flynn and Phoenix (1988) insisted that: "treating black children as if their skin colour is invisible and somehow neutral is to deny their very existence" (Cilliers, 1993, p. 9). These views reflect what is taking place in many of our schools.

The concept of multicultural education is greatly misunderstood in South Africa. It is criticized by both conservatives and radicals because multicultural education deals with sensitive issues. The conservatives fear that multicultural education will "undermine the dominant culture and erode educational standards," and the radicals interpret multicultural education as an incipient form of "apartheid education" in which, once again, the focus is on perceived differences between people (Squelch, 1994, p. 145).

This view is understandable given the emphasis placed on segregated education in the past, but rejecting the theory and practice of multicultural education will not provide the context that enables all children to arrive at a realistic understanding of the worldviews of other South Africans. At the practitioner level, there is little understanding of the field of multicultural education, and the radical view helps to sustain an attitude that is likely to aggravate an area that requires pragmatic and unemotive analysis and handling. At workshops with staff in previously White schools, the author finds himself confronted with comments such as this: "Black parents send their children to our schools because they want what we offer, so why change things?" This statement implies a firm resistance against making the necessary paradigm shift.

Only minimal changes have taken place so far because of the difficulty of making them. Teachers are not really certain what to do. They do not understand exactly what needs to be done, so it is easier to continue with what is familiar (Stonier, 1995). Robertson (1994) expressed a similar view by stating that the "problem lies in the fact that many of us [teachers] do not understand the culture we are supposed to be incorporating into this comprehensive curriculum" (p. 10).

This is a very honest confession and confirms the potent effectiveness of the apartheid machine in keeping various groups so isolated from one another that there is a profound ignorance of each other's cultural values and beliefs. These cultural elements are rooted in the fundamental way in which different people view the world, and it is the deeply entrenched convictions that are misunderstood or not understood at all. Most South Africans know some superficial cultural customs of each other such as style of handshaking, looking or not looking someone in the eye when speaking, and so on. But they are not aware of the deep-seated beliefs, values, and norms underpinning many of the overt customs that easily "come into one's awareness" (Stonier, 1995).

Positive Indications

The main reason for the prevalent assimilationist pattern of multicultural schooling in South Africa lies in the fact that multiculturalism in schools is a relatively recent phenomenon. Those open schools that pursued a policy of assimilation have found that as further desegregation takes place, the issue of multicultural education comes to receive greater attention (Squelch, 1994). As pressure from students, and especially from parents, is exerted, the need to respond in ways characteristic of creative multicultural education is recognized.

Despite a greater interest in multicultural education, students and parents from the minority cultures have had to deal with being assimilated into the dominant culture of the school and are still needing to deal with it.

Black Students and Open Schools.   Gaganakis (1992) reported on a study she conducted during 1986–1987 in six private schools in Johannesburg to determine the perceptions and experiences of Black students in those schools. Some of her findings included the following: Those students whose homes were in the township[3] experienced a "sense of dislocation . . . related to contradictory allegiances . . . as they negotiate their world of school, where they feel safe and secure; and the world of the township with its legacy of violence and deprivation." Associating with White students who take all material accoutrements of privilege for granted highlighted the Black students' feelings of inferiority. Black students' acceptance by the White group was conditional on the extent to which the Blacks assimilated the dominant ethos of the school, and especially the use of proper English. The integration that Black students experienced was confined to the school situation because the social distance between Blacks and Whites outside the school still existed.

Attendance at White schools was also interpreted as providing Black students with educational opportunities that would enable them to fill relatively privileged places in the labor market when the time came for that. School knowledge was perceived as a useful currency in the labor market. The Black students' mode of adaptation to the school was essentially conformist. The exclusive position enjoyed by Black students resulted in their creating their own rules of closure and setting up barriers with their peers in Black state schools. These privileged Blacks experienced threats and various forms of intimidation because they were perceived to be sellouts or traitors.

Various strategies were invoked by open school students to lessen this problem. These included absence from school during organized boycotts, removal of school uniforms before reaching the township; avoidance of using English; careful censoring of their conversation, and so forth. Alienation from the community, social isolation, and becoming a target for abuse by their Black peers is the lot of Black students from the townships who attend White schools. These tensions are lessened for those students whose homes are located in the slowly desegregating residential areas.

Du Toit (1994) referred to some of the results obtained from a research project carried out in 1992–1993 by the Centre of Educational Development at the University of Stellenbosch (CEDUS). The research project attempted to identify, among other things, the "nature and extent of intergroup problems that students had been experiencing" in open schools in South Africa since 1991. Du Toit (1994) noted that the "most important problem experienced by Black students had to do with feelings of alienation and rejection, feelings of not belonging, and of racism" (p. 113). In this connection, the following most disturbing, but not surprising, conclu-

---

[3]Black residential areas are usually marked by poverty as well as inadequate housing and utilities.

sion appeared in the CEDUS report: An analysis of the study revealed that teachers and 'non-Black' students are largely unaware of the feelings of rejection and estrangement experienced by Black students in open schools (Cilliers, 1993).

The author's own observations and discussions with principals and teachers would seem to suggest two things. First, by and large the students were successfully concealing their true feelings from the teachers by keeping in the background and preferring to remain invisible. This could well be due to the fact that the percentage of Black students in the schools concerned was slightly more than 12%, which means that they were a very small minority and understandably reluctant to challenge the situation. The silence encouraged the second reason, namely, that the apparent lack of any problems encouraged a complacent attitude, which seemed to be echoed in the oft-repeated refrain, The sky did not fall in when our school opened and we have no problems with the students as they have all just been accepted.

Black Families and Open Schools.   Sacco (1992) carried out a study in the late 1980s to gain some insight into the impact that an open Catholic school experience had on a small sample of Black families. The reason Black parents enrolled their children at the school was to secure a sound education for their children. By doing so, they often incurred enormous financial burdens. The results of this decision were often unanticipated and painful because many aspects of family life were affected in fundamental ways by the open school experience. In particular, parents suddenly became aware that their children were challenging traditional ways of relating to their elders (Sacco, 1992).

In a study the author carried out during 1995, he noted a similar concern when the desire for a good education at an open school was not balanced against the cost of the erosion of traditional family values. The influence of the open school ethos in this connection was not anticipated, and the reaction to this varies. Sacco (1992) found that parents tended to accept the negatives because of the value attached to good schooling. The author's study revealed a measure of frustration and disappointment among parents. They indicated that in the future parents will have to insist that their family values and traditional customs be recognized by the school (Stonier, 1996). This difference could be accounted for by the fact that the author's study took place about 2 years after the change of government, whereas Sacco's took place several years before.

A shift of power had changed the hierarchy of authority in the family, with the parental authority taken over by what Sacco calls the "princesses" who attended private schools. These "princesses" wielded a new-found power by learning and doing things the Western way (Sacco, 1992). This left the parents and the older siblings impotent to fulfil the roles that the community would traditionally have accorded them. Parents in this context have been robbed of any sense of control or power, not only by being politically disenfranchised, but by their children stripping them of their parental authority. In this way an already low self-worth is further diminished. The acceptance of the child's authority in this context is rooted in decades of discrimination that results in many people living with an attitude of internalized oppression so that what the children learn at a White establishment is assumed to be correct and superior. Having parents' feelings of inferiority endorsed by their children hardly seems to be a desirable outcome of schooling.

On a more positive note, it became apparent that a positive effect of having a democratically elected government was the removal of the constraints Black people had felt previously about expressing their own views. No longer do Black parents need others to speak on their behalf because they are now free to do so themselves. Although it is undoubtedly true that the specter of internalized oppression is widespread among ordinary Black people in South Africa, it is not universal as highlighted by an observation made by Sacco (1992). He noted that two of the families interviewed maintained parental authority, and the "princess" dimension did not operate. He suggested that a strong sense of self by the parents in these cases prevented the loss of parental authority (Sacco, 1992).

Up to the present, Black parents have been caught in a trap that is not of their own making. Parents perceive good schooling as the entry to high-earning occupations for their children. However, sending them to open schools at present means accepting assimilation into another culture with its inherent consequences. The alternative is to keep their children at schools that were sites of contestation and struggle for two decades, but in which schooling progress and achievement is questionable for the reasons referred to earlier. By leaving their children in Black state schools, however, there is still no guarantee that family values and customs will be preserved because those schools are expected to adhere to curricula with a distinctive Western orientation.

The establishment continues to view the Western model of schooling as the legitimate model for the people of Africa that will enable them to enter the modern economic, social, and cultural world. This attitude seems to be at the heart of the assimilationist position. The needs of the modern industrialized world are given as the rationale for maintaining the status quo. It has become apparent that African leaders brought up and steeped in a Western tradition think likewise, primarily, it is suspected, because formal schooling is essentially a Western concept, and there seems to be a reluctance to tamper with it in any way. Agyakwa (1976) observed that "one of the standing ironies or rather puzzles in the history of African education generally, is that at certain stages the Africans themselves resist any effort to introduce nonwestern curricula for fear that this would result in inferior education" (p. 14).

However, very definite moves are being taken at present to see that the African worldview is not only acknowledged, but that it takes its rightful place in education. Two of these voices are those of Mboya (1993) and Vilakazi (1995), who represent a small lobby at present. The author's 1996 study suggested that a strong desire exists in the hearts and minds of ordinary Black parents that the schools their children attend should incorporate many aspects of the African worldview. In this connection suggestions were made about the physical appearance, the furnishings, and the curriculum. It is puzzling that concepts such as "Ubuntu" or "humanness," which are frequently used in the South African context, seem not to be featured as an intrinsic part of education policies being developed at present.

It is suspected that with a new-found confidence in the heritage of Black Africans, and once enrollment numbers in previously White schools reach the critical figure of 35% as suggested by Christie (1991), the demand for a truly multicultural handling of the school curriculum and structures will be made. When this stage is reached, schools will be challenged to review their previous practices seriously and to effect appropriate shifts.

PERCEIVED OBSTACLES TO MULTICULTURAL ISSUES AND POSSIBLE SOLUTIONS

In reviewing the South African education system and in describing the very early stages of the desegregation of schools, the main obstacles facing the establishment of a pattern of multiculturalism in schools becomes apparent. The description indicates very clearly that South Africa is at an embryonic stage of developing an appropriate approach to multiculturalism. The overseas literature seems to suggest that the pattern that took place in Europe and North America 30 or 40 years ago is the same one that South Africa is experiencing at present. The obstacles are not likely to be significantly different from those experienced by other countries, especially the United Kingdom and the United States. The lessons learned in those countries should serve South Africa well, but it will not be possible to import ready-made solutions from elsewhere because of the unique circumstances that exist in South Africa.

The fact that this discussion focuses mainly on the position of multicultural education in White schools and on the position of and reaction to heterogeneous class and school compositions by White teachers requires comment. It may appear that a distorted and one-sided picture is being presented. The explanation for this apparent imbalance lies in the fact that it is the previously White schools with their White teachers that have found themselves at the vanguard of multiculturalism in schools, although Coloured and Indian schools and teachers are in a similar position as they, too, grapple with a new and different context. The diversity of cultural groupings is a phenomenon that has so far been confined to these schools. As was noted, the White sector, in particular, was well resourced in terms of facilities and manpower and had developed a stable educational environment that proved an attraction for Black parents. It is doubtful if more than a handful of parents of White students have opted to enrol their children at Black schools staffed by Black teachers. Consequently, multicultural education issues have not had to be dealt with by those schools and teachers with any immediacy.

In time it seems that the teachers in all schools will reach the position in which most White teachers now find themselves. However, it is important to acknowledge that the size of the Black population is such that a large number of Black schools will remain Black and monocultural for a long time to come. The future task of such schools clearly will be to approach multicultural education in a way that enables students to understand the concept of multiculturalism and some of the significant dimensions of the worldviews held by other South Africans. It seems unlikely that the previously White state schools will ever be anything but multicultural, and thus the main thrust of any initiatives in connection with multicultural education may have to be directed towards that sector.

It has to be remembered that White South Africans as a group have lost the political power they previously held. The impact of this loss of control is felt day by day in many unanticipated ways. To accommodate this dramatic change in a constructive way requires a paradigm shift of major proportions, a change for which most White South Africans received no effective preparation. The response to the change in the distribution of political power has been met by many Whites in the same way that any dramatic change in life is met, namely, by resistance.

A similar response can be detected within the ranks of teachers, and although the responses and fears are real and understandable, it will not be sufficient to ignore them. It will be important to invoke strategies that enable teachers to come to terms with the inevitability of all the facets of the new dispensation. This dilemma is well encapsulated in the following observation: "Apartheid as a formal model will end; apartheid as a mental and social model will persist" (Ohlson & Stedman in Meyer, 1994, p. 27). This observation effectively describes the 'dying of the old but the new not yet born' and also the entrenched nature of the socialization that took place during the apartheid era.

It would seem that the major challenge for Whites is to reconcile the resistance to change from apartheid as a mental and social model with the demands of a new society in which apartheid as a political model has ended. Most teachers, and a large proportion of White South Africans, are struggling to come to terms with the shift of power.

There are many other issues to obstruct the process of multicultural education, and although they are important, the author believes their resolution does not hold the key to widespread tolerance and an understanding of multiculturalism as it applies to schools. One such issue is the assumption that if students from disparate backgrounds come together, their prejudices and stereotypes will disappear of their own accord. Research and experience has shown that this is not a viable assumption and that special strategies for active intervention are required if there is to be a reduction of negative consequences between students themselves and between students and teachers. Little research has been done on the "contact hypothesis" in South Africa, but there would seem to be no reason why the overseas research is not applicable to South Africa (Foster, see Cowley 1991).

White, Coloured and Indian schools use either English or Afrikaans as the medium of instruction. A large percentage of Black students enrolled at these schools whose mother tongue is not English or Afrikaans do not have a sufficient command of either language (especially in secondary schools) for coping with the academic demands made on them. If Black students are to cope in languages that are not their home languages, then special programs for accelerating the acquisition of the language used as the medium of instruction at an open school is an urgent necessity. Lack of proficiency in either English or Afrikaans often results in Black students being regarded as linguistically inadequate. This is obviously a false assumption because a poor performance in a second or third language does not imply general linguistic deprivation. Nevertheless the tendency to make such an assumption affects the teachers' general expectation of the students' chances of success, with the implied consequences of the Pygmalion effect.

The multilingual nature of South Africa is going to present schools with unique challenges for which resolutions are not going to be easy. Squelch (1994) confirmed the problems related to language by noting that teachers in open schools often refer to "cross-cultural communication differences" as a major obstacle to building positive teacher–parent relationships. This communication includes both the spoken and written word.

A major area of concern is the lack of contact between Black parents and White teachers in open schools. Often Black parents feel alienated from the school and are reluctant to make contact because of feelings of inadequacy (the internalized oppression operating again). It is also true that teachers are not sure what approach to adopt when dealing with Black parents because they feel uneasy when having to engage with someone who comes from a very unfamiliar cultural milieu.

The inadequate preparation of teachers was mentioned in the previous section. Students currently leaving the training institutions are somewhat better prepared for the teaching situation into which they are going. However, a serious problem remains unless current teachers are provided with specialized help.

Suggested Solutions

Need for a National Policy.   In many schools, valiant efforts are being made to cope with the situation. In some cases appropriate school policies in connection with multicultural education have been developed to give a general direction. In other cases, individual teachers in isolated pockets have been responding very creatively. The reaction to these initiatives by school management structures ranges from active encouragement to deep suspicion.

Nevertheless, many valuable lessons are being learned as conscientious, enthusiastic, and committed teachers tackle the issues. Unfortunately, these efforts are not coordinated. Neither do they follow any kind of integrated pattern because no goals have been set at a national level that are deemed to be in the best interests of the country as a whole. There is clearly an awareness of the issues of diversity, and reference is made to them in government policy documents. An important reason why multicultural education is relegated to the back burner is the fact that the education authorities have given priority to issues such as the governance and financing of schools, a more equitable distribution of teachers and resources, the amalgamation of the separate departments of the old dispensation into new unified nonracial ones, curriculum development and the like. All these are necessary, laudable, and urgent initiatives, each with its own complexity, but they do mean a measure of neglect, at both national and provincial level, of those issues related to smoothing the tensions inherent in a diverse society such as that of South Africa. This has resulted in the multicultural, multilingual, multifaith, and multiethnic aspects of society being addressed in a somewhat ad hoc way in the schools.

Research.   Foster (cited in Cowley, 1991) pointed out that surprisingly little research on the development of racial awareness and racial attitudes has been carried out in South Africa. The tendency was to rely on research carried out in other countries. Nevertheless, sincere attempts are being made in a number of schools to reach a real understanding of multicultural education. Unfortunately, it seems that the findings tend to remain in academic journals, and because there is no national policy, the results are not substantially influencing the work being done in the classroom.

Nonformal Assistance. Because multiculturalism is something that White teachers (and to some extent Colored and Indian teachers) face day by day, various teachers' organizations and other nongovernmental agencies such as the Open Schools Association (the precursor of the Resource Unit for Intercultural Education in South Africa [RUIESA]), the Centre for Cognitive Development, the Centre for Conflict Resolution, the Early Learning Resource Unit, and many others have prepared material, run workshops, and published documents and guidelines on aspects of multiculturalism, antiracist education, desegregation of schools, and so on. A useful and helpful contribution has been made by these agencies, but they have not been able to reach many teachers. These agencies mentioned are funded by donations from the private sector or overseas foundations. Unfortunately, however, one of the results of the new democracy was the demise of many self-help organizations because funders believe that what they supported during the apartheid regime is now the responsibility of the democratically elected government. Sadly, the government has not been able to take over the work done by these agencies, and neither has it been able to provide financial support for their continued existence.

Immediate Requirement. There is an urgent need to articulate a national policy on multicultural education at a depth beyond references to the need to satisfy the human rights taken up in the South African Constitution. Making this suggestion implies the existence of a disturbing gap in educational planning for multicultural education at present, but one that needs to be addressed. It will have become apparent to the reader that South Africa's experience in multicultural education and its response to it is at an embryonic stage. Given the fact that the country has only recently come out of its apartheid shackles, we have not had sufficient time to develop positions that reflect the newly acquired status of an open society and that show how this should be dealt with at the school level.

Teacher Training and Multicultural Issues

To provide a reasonably composite picture of the way that multicultural education is handled by teacher preparation institutions, an invitation was extended to the appropriate person in each of 22 South African teacher training institutions of various kinds to give a brief outline of the approach used in his or her particular institution. Fourteen institutions responded and, apart from the author's own informal observations and experience, the following description relies heavily on the comments received from them. The responses received came from a useful cross-section of institutions responsible for teacher training.

The term multicultural education is bandied about somewhat loosely, and it does not mean the same thing for all those who use it. It is not, therefore, at all certain how training institutions are interpreting intercultural or multicultural education. It may be that there is no alternative to the uncertainty at this stage in South Africa's educational history as educationalists struggle to define what multicultural education means in the South African context.

From the institutions consulted, one respondent held the view that placing a heavy focus on multicultural education could cause "further fragmentation of South African society," whereas another suggested that multicultural education could be useful for "breaking down barriers and building bridges." These views highlight two extreme interpretations given to the concept multicultural education, with many positioned between these two.

With a move towards a more open society, there seems to have been a rush towards considering how to deal with this new and unique situation. There is a sense that it is important for institutions to become actively involved in a new "invention". There are those who believe that multicultural education is nothing more than good education. By this they mean that cultural differences should be handled with the same sensitivity and understanding as any other differences, such as between boys and girls, or between those intellectually well endowed and those who are not. People holding that view do not see the necessity for placing any emphasis on multicultural education.

What comes across clearly in the responses is that although the overseas experience in multicultural education is valuable, it cannot be imported and applied in South Africa without an examination of the specific circumstances that obtain in the country before the appropriate adjustments are made. Not surprisingly, the curricula as outlined in the submissions contain many common threads and, almost always, reference is made to an exploration of the following issues:

Culture and the Difficulty of Defining It. Particular concern was expressed about the definition of culture and cultural differences. To many, the use of these terms seems to have the inherent danger of communicating that "culture" implies a fixed intransigent way of looking at and dealing with the world. It is felt that unless the dynamic nature of culture and the continuous ways in which individuals negotiate their changing cultural positions is taken into account, the danger of entrenching stereotypes and prejudices is very real.

Diversity.   It seems that at the undergraduate level in most teacher training institutions, a module on cultural diversity of varying lengths and intensity is included in at least one of the following courses: sociology of education, foundations of education, historical and comparative education, perspectives of education and training, or educational studies. Whereas attention to multicultural education at the undergraduate level is confined to specific modules, at the postgraduate level there has been a remarkable level of interest. Many people are pursuing programs of study at Master's degree level with obviously fewer at the doctoral level.

Overall, it would seem that a useful start has been made at the teacher preparation institutions in South Africa to introduce prospective teachers to the theory and practice of multicultural education. The tertiary institutions in South Africa are generally autonomous, so coordinating the work in this field is difficult. It can be assumed that a measure of coordination takes place through informal contact between teachers/lecturers responsible for multicultural education programs. However, the emphasis is left entirely to the institutions themselves. The feeling is inescapable that multicultural is still in its early days and that further development will take place in due course. It could well happen at some stage in the future, before teacher training courses are accredited, that certain minimum requirements in connection with multicultural education could be laid down, in which case, some control would be exercised in connection with content and time allotted at the undergraduate level.

I (the author) give a final thought in connection with teacher training courses. Although I have no evidence other than my own observations at three tertiary institutions, I suspect that the topics in the multicultural education modules are dealt with at the cognitive level only. This means that the various aspects of diversity rooted in the affective domain are not addressed: race, prejudice, oppression, cultural differences, and so on. Differing religious beliefs, deeply entrenched convictions, customs, and behavior rooted in long periods of socialization have a link with an individual's psyche that is not exclusively cognitive. My experience sug-gests that individual students (and practicing teachers) are more than willing to deal with these complex issues at a "thinking" level but not at an emotional or "feeling" level. I believe that attention will need to be given to the important dimension of feelings in this context.

An approach in which head and heart are integrated when dealing with multicultural issues would provide an essential balance and create the right climate for individuals to examine their attitudes and, where necessary, to modify them. It is relatively easy to acknowledge at a cognitive level that an attitude or view needs modification, but it is far more difficult to internalize that new attitude in such a way that it results in a change of heart so that the "other" can be viewed in a deeply sensitive and constructive way. If teacher training, as far as this component is concerned, remains at the cognitive level, students could easily slide into sympathizing with the "other," when in actual fact what is needed is for students to empathize with the "other" (i.e., to feel themselves within the "other"s' worldview). None of this means rejecting one's own worldview. Rather, it means moving towards a real and full understanding of the "other." Doing so will be immensely difficult, but I have no doubt that it is imperative. Designing courses that plumb the depth of students' feelings requires great skill, but not doing it means approaching the "left brain" only. Dealing with South Africa's diversity clearly requires the use of the "right brain" as well.

CONCLUSION

I am of the view that there really are no effective short-term solutions to problems in multicultural education. Invoking makeshift adjustments here and there may satisfy a temporary need, and will need to be done, but that is rather like treating a medical problem that requires chemotherapy by prescribing an aspirin. The only effective solutions are those that are long term, in which intense and prolonged programs are mounted and aimed at bringing about appropriate changes of attitude—changes of "heart" and changes of "head," so that what I understand in my head is integrated with what I feel in my gut.

TO CONSIDER

Bishop Desmond Tutu, at the inauguration of Nelson Mandela, made the following remarks; "Bless this beautiful land with its wonderful people of different races, cultures, and languages so that it will be a land of laughter and joy, of justice and reconciliation, or peace and unity, of compassion, caring, and sharing" (1994). As Dr. Stonier has suggested, the necessary changes that must take place in South Africa with regard to people's understanding, acceptance, and ability to interact more effectively with one another will take considerable time to achieve.

1. *The situation in South Africa is changing almost daily, and it would be next to impossible for a book of this type to be up-to-date with the most current changes. Review current newspapers from South Africa, which can be found on the World Wide Web at www.vol.it/UK/EN/EDI-COLA/quot_str.htm#menu. Search for items related to reconciliation, multicultural education, intergroup relations, and so forth. How do current issues related to diversity relate to what you have just read? What is the current state of affairs in South Africa regarding the changes that are underway? What struggles continue?*

2. *What can your nation and schools learn from the experience of South Africa?*

3. *How can young people in South Africa be most effectively prepared to interact with one another? With others on a global scale? What resources seem to be available within South Africa to assist young people in developing an intercultural perspective?*

4. *What steps should schools take in responding to the need to fully integrate the educational experience of all young people? What plan of action would you propose?*

5. *On occasion, South Africa receives refugees or immigrants from neighboring nations. Given what you have just read, how would you respond to the scenario presented in chapter 1. What steps should schools take to respond to the needs of newly arriving immigrant groups?*

REFERENCES

Agyakwa, K. O. (1976). *Akan epistemology and Western thought: A philosophical approach to the problems of educational modernization in Ghana.* Unpublished doctoral thesis, Columbia University, New York.

Berman, E. H. (1974, December). African responses to Christian mission education. *African Studies Review, 17*(3), 527–540.

Boahen, A. A. (1987). *African perspectives on colonialism.* Baltimore: John Hopkins University Press.

Branford, J., & Branford, W. (1991). *A dictionary of South African English* (4th ed.) Cape Town: Oxford University Press.

Christie, P. (1990). *Open schools: Racially mixed Catholic schools in South Africa, 1976– 1986.* Johannesburg: Ravan Press.

Christie, P. (1991, May 23). *Open schools: The challenge of numbers.* Unpublished paper presented to the Open Schools Association, Cape Town, South Africa.

Cilliers, C. D. (Ed.) (1993). *A support programme for teachers in multicultural schools.* Stellenbosch: Centre for Educational Development (CEDUS), University of Stellenbosch.

Cowley, B. B. (1991). *The assessment of the impact of desegregated schooling on young children, utilizing their drawings.* Unpublished Master's dissertation, University of Cape Town, Cape Town.

Deliwe, D. (1992). *Responses to Western education among the conservative people of Transkei.* Unpublished Master's Thesis, Rhodes University, Grahamstown.

Department of Education. (1996). *The organisation, governance and funding of schools.* (white paper No. 2). Pretoria: Department of Education.

Du Toit, P. J. (1994). Building bridges in multicultural classrooms through structured discussion groups. In: J. L. Van der Walt (Ed.), *Multicultural education : New challenges for South Africa* (pp. 112–125). Potchefstroom: Faculty of Education, Potchefstroom University for Christian Higher Education.

Edusource Data News. (1996, April). *Edusource data news.* (12). Craighall, South Africa: The Education Foundation.

Flynn, R., & Phoenix, A. (1988). Racism and the child care services. Update: *Current Issues in Early Childhood,* (25), 1–3.

Gaganakis, M. (1992). Opening up the closed school: Conceptualizing the presence of Black students in White schools. In: D. Freer (Ed.), *Towards open schools: Possibilities and realities for non-racial education in South Africa* (pp. 73–93). Johannesburg: University of Witwatersrand.

Glory, hope to have liberty. (1994, May 8). Cape Times, p. 11.

Halstead, M., (1988). *Education, justice and cultural diversity: An examination of the Honeyford Affair, 1984–1985.* London: The Falmer Press.

Iwuagwu, A. O. (1991). African traditional education: Its emphasis on religion and morality. In E. M. Uka (Ed.), *Readings in African traditional religion. Structure, meaning, relevance, future* (pp. 257–268). Bern: Peter Lang.

Johnson, A. (1994, May 11). *SA's great day. Cape Times,* p. 11.

Malherbe, E. G. (1977). *Education in South Africa, Vol. II 1923–1975.* Cape Town: Juta.

Mboya, M. (1987). Community control of Afrikan (sic) schools. In D. Young & R. Burns (Eds.), *Education at the crossroads* (pp. 67–76). Rondebosch, South Africa: School of Education, University of Cape Town.

Mboya, M. M. (1993). *Beyond apartheid: The question of education for liberation.* Cape Town: [s.n.].

Meyer, G. (1994, December). The new is not yet born. *Track Two, 3*(4), 27–28.

Mungazi, D. A. (1989). *The struggle for social change in Southern Africa.* New York: Crane Russak (Taylor & Francis Group).

Onuoha, B. (1965). *The elements of African socialism.* London: Andre Deutsch.

Robertson, D. (1994). Conference: Multicultural education: New challenges for South Africa. In J. L. Van der Wa (Ed.), *Multicultural education : New challenges for South Africa* (pp. 7–12). Potchefstroom: Faculty of Education, Potchefstroom University for Christian Higher Education.

Sacco, T. (1992). "Princesses" and others: Parental and sibling perceptions of Black students attending a Roman Catholic, nonracial primary school. In D. Freer (Ed.), *Towards open schools: Possibilities and realities for nonracial education in South Africa* (pp. 136–155). Johannesburg: University of Witwatersrand.

Scanlon, D. G. (1996). Introduction. In D. G. Scanlon (Ed.), *Church, state, and education in Africa* (pp. 3–22). New York: Springer.

South African Institute of Race Relations (SAIRR). (1994). *Race relations survey 1993/94.* Johannesburg: SAIRR.

South African Institute of Race Relations (SAIRR). (1995). *Race relations survey 1994/95.* Johannesburg: SAIRR.

South African Ministerial Committee for Development work on the National Qualifications Framework (1996). *Discussion document: Lifelong learning through a national qualifications framework: Report of the Ministerial Committee for Development work on the National Qualifications Framework.* Pretoria: Deptartment of Education.

Squelch, J. (1994). The multicultural classroom: Problems and future challenges. In J. L. Van der Walt (Ed.), *Multicultural education: New challenges for South Africa* (pp. 143–155). Potchefstroom: Faculty of Education, Potchefstroom University for Christian Higher Education.

Stonier, J. L. (1995). Some challenges facing multicultural schools. *Stimulus, 2*(6):2–3.

Stonier, J. L. (1996). *Implications of "Africanness" for educational planning in the Republic of South Africa: A qualitative study of educational needs.* Unpublished doctoral thesis, University of Stellenbosch, Stellenbosch.

Vilakazi, H. W. (1995, May 24). *On the transformation of our education.* Unpublished paper presented at University of Cape Town, Cape Town, South Africa.

Editor's Remarks

Anthropologists argue that there is evidence of human settlement along the coast of Ghana that goes back 30,000 to 40,000 years. Later, slave traders from Portugal, Holland, Spain, Britain, and Denmark were among the first Europeans to begin settlement in Ghana. Britain retained control of Ghana's forts and castles once the slave trade was finally outlawed.

Traditional Ghanaian education has its roots in the various microcultures that make up Ghana. Although different from the European model, traditional Ghanaian education focused on ethnic taboos, mores, and other aspects of the various microcultures. Western education came to Ghana in the 1500s to facilitate European evangelistic efforts. Ghana always had a reputation as having some of the finest schools in all of Africa. In fact, the University of Ghana, established in 1948, allowed young Ghanaian students to receive a higher education degree at home without the need to study abroad which had been the case for many other Africans.

Ghana's attempt to address the issue of multicultural education has been overshadowed by the need to provide a basic education for all. Although English became the official language because of the colonial experience with Britain, the preferred languages of communication are the various ethnic tongues spoken throughout the country. As a result, only the most highly educated are able to speak, read, and write English as well as they can communicate in their ethnic language.

Ghana, and most African countries, have been revising and improving their textbooks since the 1960s, thanks to support from the United States, Britain, and the IMF. There has been regular introduction of new textbooks written by Ghanaians in the 1970s, 1980s, and the 1990s.

Chapter 11

Ghana: Education in a Multicultural Context

ᚮ ◆ ᚯ

Benjamin A. Eshun
University of Cape Coast

THE EDUCATION SYSTEM

Ghana (then known as Gold Coast) was the first Black African country to gain, on March 6, 1957, independence as a British colony. Its education system was modeled on the British system and was similar to those of former British West African colonies: Nigeria, Sierra Leone, and the Gambia. There had been only minor educational modifications to its structure until the educational reform in 1987. The current ongoing reform has changed both the structure and content of education. There are now 6 years of primary, 3 years of junior secondary, 3 years of senior secondary, and 3 or 4 years of tertiary or university education.

In the old system, at the end of primary six, children were selected for a 5-year secondary education through a national common entrance examination. Children who did not enter secondary schools continued in the 4-year middle schools. At the end of 5-year secondary school, there was further selection through the General Certificate of Education (GCE) Ordinary Level into the 2-year Sixth Form. Students who did not gain admission into the latter entered the teacher training college (TTC) or the polytechnic school. Admission into the universities is still through the GCE Advanced Level or the Mature Entrance Examination for persons over 30 years.

238

Currently, all children proceed after primary six to the 3-year junior secondary school (JSS). There is selection after the JSS for the 3-year senior secondary school (SSS) through the Basic Education Certificate Examination (BECE), then later from SSS for the TTCs, polytechnics, and the universities through the Senior Secondary Certificate Examination (SSCE). Ghana's national school examinations are conducted by the West African Examinations Council (WAEC). There are large numbers of private primary, junior secondary, senior secondary, and vocational schools, mainly in the urban towns. The public schools are administered by the Ghana Education Service (GES) under the Ministry of Education (MOE). Schools established by the missions (Christian churches and Islamic religion) are now under GES administration, but whereas the teachers are paid by the GES, they are managed by the education units of the religious bodies.

Formal education in Ghana was not introduced to pass on the knowledge and culture of the society to the young as the current notion of education demands. Early attempts at educating the youth in Ghana were carried out in the forts and castles along the coast as missionary enterprises from the 15th century through the early part of the 19th century (McWilliam, 1962). In 1835, the Wesleyan mission (now Methodist Church) began to establish schools outside the castles in the coastal towns mainly "to spread the Christian faith" (McWilliam, 1962, p. 7).

Growth and Enrollment in Education

The provision and growth of education was very limited in the colonial period from 1844 through 1951. Ghana had its first African government in 1951, and by that time there were only about 300,000 children in primary and middle schools, and fewer than 7,000 students in secondary schools. Only one university college had been established then with a small enrollment of 208 students.

Pre University Education. The African government under Dr. Kwame Nkrumah pursued a vigorous expansion of education and made generous budgetary provisions. The rapid growth was achieved through the government's Accelerated Development Plan (ACP) introduced in 1951, which ushered in universal free primary education . The Education Act of 1961 by the same government consolidated the free provision of primary education and in addition made it compulsory. The plan also produced a modest expansion of secondary education, which continued to be selective.

In 1966 when the first independent government under President Kwame Nkrumah was overthrown, there were nearly 1.5 million children in primary and middle schools, a fivefold growth over enrollment in 1951. Successive governments continued the expansion, but not at the same pace as the first republic. In 1987 the Provisional National Defense Council (PNDC) under its Chairman, Flt. Lieutenant Jerry John Rawlings, made a major policy change in education, introducing the 3 years of compulsory and nonselective JSS and the phasing out of the middle schools.

The effect of the new policy and the increased awareness of the value of education is evident in the provision of schools and the enrollment at all levels. By 1995 there were more than 11,200 primary schools and 5,240 junior secondary schools with a total of enrollment nearly 2.6 million children, a growth of more than 70% over the 1966 enrollment and more than 750% over the 1951 enrollment. The 7-year secondary schools, which were redesignated as 3-year SSSs in 1987, have grown to 450 with an enrollment of more than 200,000 in 1995, a growth nearly 30-fold over 1951 enrollment and about fivefold over 1966 enrollment, mainly due to the establishment of new SSS. However, the increases could have been larger if it had not been for the boarding and selective nature of SSS that restricts expansion. The PNDC reform in 1987 emphasized the establishment of day SSS, but the convenience of the boarding schools and their academic successes continue to attract students and their parents as observed by Foster (1965). Because the SSS are tuition free, the only major cost to parents are the fees for boarding and meals, which lags behind the cost for food in middle-class homes. Thus parents in the capital of Accra and the urban cities of Kumasi, Takoradi, Cape Coast, and Tamale prefer to send their wards to boarding schools inside or outside their cities.

Teacher Education.   Teacher training colleges (TTCs) were the first form of higher education in Ghana. Their function, which has not changed over the years, was to train primary- and middle-school teachers. In 1951 there were only 20 TTCs with nearly 2,000 students. The colleges offered Certificate (Cert) B and A to post–middle-school students after 2- and 4-year programs respectively, and Cert A to postsecondary students after a 2-year program. The ACP of 1951 caused corresponding expansion in teacher education to meet the demands of teacher supply for the large increases in the number of primary schools and growing enrollment. By the 1971– 1972 school year, there were 74 TTCs with more than 19,200 students. In the late 1970s 3-year postsecondary colleges were introduced. The postmiddle colleges were phased out, and many were turned into secondary schools. Thus, in 1995 there were only 38 TTCs preparing 20,290 teachers for the new JSS and primary schools.

The unprecedented and sudden increases in primary school expansion in the 1950s contributed to the large number of untrained (student) teachers in the education system. Whereas there were only 3,430 untrained teachers in 1951, by 1966 the number had increased to 32, 865 (George, 1976, p. 128). However, the percentage of untrained teachers increased only from 47.6% to 64.5% in the same period. In 1984, there was a total of 78,746 primary- and middle school teachers, and more than 40% of them were untrained (Antwi, 1992, p. 124). The current policy of the GES is to replace untrained teachers with newly trained teachers. As a result, in 1991 72% of the teachers in both primary and junior secondary schools were trained (MOE, 1994, p. 52).

University Education.   Ghana had three universities by 1966. But it took 30 years before two more were added in 1993/1994. The first three were the University of Ghana, the Kwame Nkrumah University of Science and Technology, and the University of Cape Coast, established in 1948, 1951, and 1962, respectively. The last two universities established were the University College of Education at Winneba and the University of Devel - opmental Studies. In 1966 the three universities had a total enrollment of 4,301, which was 10% of the secondary enrollment and only 1% of the primary enrollment. The student enrollment in 1995 was about 18,000.

All five universities have separate missions directing their major areas of study. The designated areas are degrees in pure science and in the arts and humanities at the University of Ghana; degree courses in engineering, applied science, and technology at the University of Science and Technology; degrees in education for teaching in secondary school and training colleges at the University of Cape Coast and the University College of Education at Winneba, and degrees in developmental studies at the fifth university. The first two universities have medical schools, and the first in addition has a law school. The decision to assign specific programs to each institution can be traced to the following remarks of the Minister of Education in 1963 (George, 1976):

> The need for national planning in every country in the world is reinforcing the need for separate institutes for both training and research. Clearly in the case of a socialist country where planning is basic to the structure of the society, institutes of higher education must be flexible and responsive to planned social needs. Where these do not exist or where they exist as low-priority departments in established Universities, there are grounds for setting up separate or mono-faculty institutions in order to produce a rate of growth which is related to the overall plan. (p. 170)

University education had remained completely free to students until the recent educational reforms. A student loan scheme was introduced in 1970 by the Busia government to shift some of the burden of university education to students and their guardians. But the scheme had to be aborted a year later as a result of both student protest and public outcry. However, the loan scheme was reintroduced in 1987, and students now bear the cost of their food, whereas the government continues to bear all other costs including tuition and accommodation in halls of residence on campuses.

CULTURAL GROUPS AND EDUCATION

Ghana is a country in West Africa bounded in the South by the Gulf of Guinea. It has a land area of 238,540 km ^{2} and a population of about 18 million. It is rich in mineral and agricultural resources, the major ones being gold, diamonds, bauxite, manganese, cocoa, timber, and rubber. The people of Ghana can be classified into two main groups: the Kwa language speakers of the southern section and the Mossi-Grusi or Gur language speakers of the northern section. There are five culturally distinct and dominant subgroups within the Kwa peoples: the Twi-, Fante-, Guan-, Ga-Adangme-, and the Ewe-speaking peoples. The first three in addition to other smaller language speakers are called the Akan, which together constitute 44% or 45% of the total population (Antwi, 1992; Foster, 1965; Grimes, 1996). The Ewe people are 13% and the Ga together with the Adangme and Krobo peoples constitute 8% of the population. The Gur people of the North constitute about 30% of the population and belong to one of four subgroups: the Mole-Dagomba (Dagbani), Grusi, Gurma, and Senufo (Antwi, 1992, p. 10; Rattray, 1932, quoted in Foster, 1965, p. 19).

Ghana is currently divided into 10 administrative regions, each of which is further divided into districts. There are a total of 110 such districts in which the dominant indigenous groups have their own culture, traditional religious beliefs, and practices as well as distinctive Ghanaian Languages (GLs). In the colonial period, the country had three divisions, the Colony (now Western, Central, Eastern, and Greater Accra regions), Trans-Volta Togoland (now Volta region), Ashanti (now Ashanti and Brong-Ahafo regions), and Northern Territories (now Northern, Upper East and Upper West regions).

Early Educational Efforts

The coastal peoples were in close contact with the Europeans who occupied the castles and forts from the 15th century through the early part of the 19th century. They permitted the Wesleyan and Basel (now Presbyterian Church) missions to establish schools for their children. The hostilities between the Ashantis and the Fantes prevented earlier European contacts and expansion of education to the former and the people in the Northern Territories. The Ashantis were initially not interested in education, which they feared could lead to rebellion and political unrest (Southon, 1935, quoted in Foster, 1965, p. 60). A treaty in 1831 between the Asantehene (the ruler of Ashanti) and Governor George Maclean, which led to the education of two sons of Ashanti chiefs in Britain, did not open any doors for schools. The Ashantis thought "their children had better work to do than to sit down all day idly to learn Hoy! Hoy! Hoy!" (unintelligible sounds; Groves, 1948, quoted in Foster, 1965). In 1941, Reverend Thomas Birch Freeman, a Wesleyan missionary, took the two sons of the Ashanti chiefs to Kumasi, but although he was given a plot of land for a mission station, he was refused permission to open a school (McWilliam, 1962).

The nature and provision of education was unequal in the four administrative divisions of the Gold Coast, the Colony, Trans-Volta, Ashanti, and the Northern Territories. Education was mainly in the hands of the missions with no government control but some financial aid. The growth in the provision of schools and enrollment in primary and middle schools occurred mainly along the coastal urban towns and declined from the coast to the North with Ashanti in the middle. This situation persisted throughout the colonial period, which ended in 1951.

Education Under Ghanaian Governments

As mentioned earlier, Ghana was granted self-government status in 1951 under an African Minister of Government Business, Dr. Kwame Nkrumah. In 1984 the three regions with the largest groups of people in order were Ashanti, Eastern, and Greater Accra. The size of the population in the five regions—Volta, Brong-Ahafo, Northern, Central, and Western—was about the same, and the area with the least people was the Upper East region with less than 20% of the people in Ashanti.

There is disparity in the enrollment of children in the various regions in comparison with their total populations. In 1952 the Northern and Upper regions constituted 25% of the country's population, but they had only 2% of the total primary enrollment and only 1.3% of the total middle school enrollment. The other three areas, the Colony, Trans-Volta Togoland, and Ashanti, each had more children in both primary and middle schools than their proportions in the population. The Colony had the highest enrollment of 12% more than its proportion in the population, and Ashanti had an enrollment of about 7% more than its proportion in the population.

The disparities in the regions began to equalize a little by 1970 and quite a bit by 1994/1995. Several factors could be attributed to the current even distribution of enrollment in the primary and middle schools. First, the Accelerated Development Plan of 1951 ushered in a universal primary education, and this influenced parents throughout the country to change their attitudes toward schooling for their children, especially in Ashanti, Northern, and Upper regions. Second, all the African governments since 1951 have provided special financial assistance to children in the Northern and Upper regions, and in some parts of the Brong-Ahafo region, which has resulted in rapid educational expansion in these areas (George, 1976). Third, the Education Act of 1961 made primary and middle school fee free and therefore affordable to the majority of parents. Fourth, the 1987 educational reform introduced 3 years of junior secondary school as a basic right of all Ghanaian children. This made education more valuable. In 10 years primary grade one enrollment increased by more than 100,000 from about 295,000 in 1980 to about 390,000 in 1990 (MOE, 1994).

The Northern and the two Upper regions have made remarkable improvement in the provision of schools and enlarged enrollment, although they continue to lag behind the rest of the country. Factors contributing to the low enrollment in the Northern and Upper regions are the use of boys as cattle herdsmen and the traditional practice of men marrying girls at very tender ages. Girls who stay at home with their mothers and learn to run a home, farm, and sell produce in the markets are considered more ready for marriage than their counterparts in school. Also, the educated girls attract higher dowries which discourages suitors. But the most important factor is that brothers are eager to see their sisters marry so that they could use their dowries to obtain wives for themselves.

GHANAIAN LANGUAGE ISSUES IN EDUCATION

Before the missionaries established formal schools, there was informal education of young people in Ghana with the main objective of passing on the vocations of the adult males and the role of motherhood. Busia's (1964) description captures adequately the type of training that went on in most communities for the young people:

> The young were taught how to cope with their environment; how to farm, or hunt, or fish, or prepare food, or build a house, or run a home. They were taught the language and manners, and generally the culture of the community. The

methods were informal, the young learnt by participating in activities alongside their elders. They learnt by listening, by watching, by doing. In many ways they learnt how to live as members of their community. (p. 13)

The informal training or education that young people received was in the medium of the ethnic language and very much related to their environment, cultural group, and the traditional religious beliefs. Some boys were sent to other adults to learn trades and skills not practiced by their fathers or family members. But the upbringing of the boys and girls contributed to the achievement of a "relative cultural homogeneity of their populations" (Foster, 1965, p. 34).

Recent work has identified 70 distinct languages spoken in Ghana including English, but excluding the Ghana and Adamorobe sign languages (Grimes, 1996). Table 11.1 shows the major Ghanaian languages (GLs) with at least 100,000 speakers and the region(s) where the latter are predominantly located. The table shows that the Volta region has the most linguistically homogeneous population in Ghana, although there are different dialects of the Ewe language. On the other hand, the Northern and the two Upper regions have the most heterogeneous population with 14 languages spoken by at least 100,000 people and five languages (Dagbani, Gurenne, Dagaari, Kusaal, and Konkomba) spoken by at least 400,000 people (Grimes, 1996).

The very large number of distinct GLs clearly poses a challenge to the education system. The MOE would require considerable human, material, and financial resources to provide appropriate and adequate instruction in the first or mother tongue of each child. Fortunately only 20 GLs have more than 150,000 speakers (Grimes, 1996). Also, each of the 10 regions, except the Northern and Upper regions could be associated with one major GL (see Table 11.1). Thus, using the major GL in a region as the medium of instruction in the lower primary grades would cater to the cultural needs of the greater proportion of children. However, the various colonial or postindependence governments have shifted from one language policy to another because of broader political or philosophical considerations and because of educational objectives (George, 1976).

Language Polices

Instruction of Ghanaian children in the coastal castles and forts was in the language of the European settlers (Portuguese, Dutch, Danes, and British). As Wiltgen (quoted in McWilliam, 1962) wrote: "In 1529 the Portuguese king, John III, laid plans for the conversion of the Elminas to the Catholic faith. As part of this programme a Portuguese teacher was to teach reading

TABLE 11.1

Major Ghanaian Languages Spoken by Region, and Population of Speakers

Region	Language	Speakers	Population %
Eastern Ashanti Brong-Ahafo	Akwampim Twi Asante Twi Abron, Gua	5,530,000	34.8
Central	Fante, Awutu	1,270,000	8.0
Volta	Ewe	1,615,000	10.2
Greater Accra	Ga-Adangme-Krobo	1,125,000	7.1
Western	Nzema, Anyin, Sehwi, Wasa Ahanta	960,000	6.0
Northern Upper East Upper West	Dagbani, Gurenne, Dagaari Kusaal, Konkomba, Gonja Mampruli, Sisaala, Ntcham Bissa, Kasem, BiriforBuli, Wali	3,703,200	23.3

Source: B. F. Grimes (Ed.) (1996). *Ethnologue: The languages of the world* (13th ed.). Dallas, Texas: Summer Institute of Linguistics.

and writing (in Portuguese) to African boys living in the village of Edina near the fort" (p. 8).

The Wesleyan mission that took over the castle school at Cape Coast under Reverend Joseph Dunwell in 1835 established schools in the coastal towns in which English was the language of instruction. However, the Basel mission used the Akwapim Twi to instruct primary students in Akropong in the Eastern region (Foster, 1965). Governor Gordon Gug - gisburg (1919 to 1927) was the first to pass an Education Ordinance (1925), which set forth the provision that in the infant classes (the first 3 years of schooling) "the vernacular shall be the medium of instruction whenever the nature of the subject permits its use"(Chinebuah, 1970, quoted in George, 1976, p. 115). However, the African government under Dr. Kwame Nkrumah in its Accelerated Development Plan of 1951 placed more emphasis on instruction in English, although it recognized the appropriateness of using the local vernacular at the beginning of the primary grades. Whereas Guggisburg's policy was specific about how long the vernacular was to be used as a medium of instruction, the Nkrumah government's policy left the timing to the discretion of teachers and schools.

The Busia government in 1970 reverted to a policy similar to that of Guggisburg but with greater clarity, specifying the type of GL, the timing, and the grade levels concerned as follows:

> The *main* [author's emphasis] Ghanaian Languages provided for in the elementary curriculums should be used as the medium of instruction throughout the first 3 years of elementary education, and, where the subject makes it possible, in the 4th through the 6th years as well" (Chinebuah, 1970, George, 1976, p. 119).

The changing policies on the use of GLs for instruction in the first 3 years of primary education has negatively affected education at this level because teachers do not change their habits of teaching as quickly as policies are formulated and thrown out by governments. Also, for the most part, teachers tend to teach only what they know, but they are capable of teaching new things according to their willingness to adapt to new situations.

Recent studies have shown that Ghanaian children after 6 years of primary education have very poor literacy (in English) and numeracy. The criterion referenced test (CRT) conducted in 1995 by the Primary Education Project (PREP) on a national sample of primary Grade 6 students revealed that only 1.8% and 3.6% had mastered the items in mathematics and English, respectively (Primary Education Project, 1995). The Ghana Living Standards Survey of 1989 reported that only 11% of the children age's 9 through 14 were able to write a letter. The new education reform of 1987 set forth the same language policy for instruction as did the Busia government. The MOE (1994) has noted that the medium of instruction contributed to the children's poor literacy rate. According to the MOE,

> The poor performance of children in language competency after six years of schooling can be attributed in part to the problem of language of instruction. The greater majority of students in primary grades are not able to read or write in either a Ghanaian language or English well enough so that it can be a tool for learning. (MOE, 1994, p. 20).

> The Curriculum Review Committee (CRC) set up in 1993 pointed out the urgent need to implement the language policy (MOE, 1994). The CRC recommended the following:

> The prescribed language policy in the early primary grades must be *implemented as a priority* [author's emphasis], so that children first gain literacy and communication skills in a familiar Ghanaian language, before moving on to English as a medium of instruction in [primary grade four]. (MOE, 1994, p. 20)

The problem of constant changes in the language policy and its implementation is not due only to political and educational considerations but also to the social expectations of middle-class parents and their children. First, the official language of Ghana is English, and proficiency in it is important for social interaction and employment opportunities. Second, the medium of instruction in secondary schools and higher education is English, so literacy in English is necessary for academic success, which is very crucial for the middle class. Third, students from private primary (preparatory) schools have a record of high success rates of gaining admission into the secondary schools through the Common Entrance Examination. Many middle-class parents have patronized these preparatory schools in preference to the public schools in which the language policy applies. The preparatory schools use English as the medium of instruction. Thus other parents who cannot afford the high fees of the private schools encourage teachers in public schools to use English for instruction. But whereas public school students study nine subjects, their counterparts in the preparatory schools study mainly the two subjects English and mathematics. The few hours devoted to the learning of English in the public school negatively affect children because they experience difficulties in coping with English as a medium of instruction.

The use of a GL that is the first or second language of children has positive benefits because it enables children to draw on their prior knowledge and experiences, which are crucial for their learning. Also, there is research evidence that good bilingual programs tend to raise academic achievement and impart English more effectively than English programs (Cummins, 1989). The issue of language policy for instruction and for achieving appropriate multicultural education for Ghanaian children is very important and discussed further in the next section in relation to teacher preparation and classroom practice.

TEACHER PREPARATION AND INTERCULTURAL EDUCATION

Teachers play a central role in the implementation of any curriculum reform. Preservice teacher preparation influences to a large extent how they, in turn, teach their students. Owing to technologic and social advances and the need for education reform, teachers are constantly called on to teach children differently than they themselves were taught. In the colonial era, Ghanaian teachers regarded themselves mostly as working for the foreign government and missionaries rather than educating their own people to build a better tomorrow. In postindependent Ghana, many teachers realized that only relatively few children in the public primary schools had a chance of proceeding to secondary schools, so they continued to teach as they were taught aiming for the few bright ones to succeed.

The objectives of the 1987 educational reform provide 9 years of compulsory basic education to prepare children to be literate and numerate, to appreciate their cultural identity and heritage, and to contribute to the development of their communities and the country. The new reform is therefore an attempt to provide a multicultural education "that builds on previous knowledge and experiences in the first culture [of the child] . . . and develops more extensive knowledge and awareness of other cultures" (Jung, 1996; Nieto, 1992). The challenge to teachers is to provide a type of multicutural education that their own primary and secondary education might have denied them. The question then is: How do teacher education institutions in Ghana prepare teachers to teach intercultural groups of children to satisfy the challenge of multicultural education? We now consider four issues in teacher preparation programs that relate to this challenge.

The Issue of Religion

The early missionaries established teacher training colleges (TTCs) to train teachers for their primary schools, but curriculum, although considered important, was not the thrust of their education, but rather character training. Thus preservice teachers were instilled with Western European patterns of behavior and Christian morality. Attendance at a teacher training college meant accepting the code of behavior and religious observance of that college. The boarding nature of the TTCs made it possible to enforce college regulations relating to cultural and religious practices.

The majority (about two thirds) of the TTCs in Ghana have affiliation with a major Christian or Islamic religious organization. Thus religious observance and attendance at college worship were strictly enforced by the missionaries and their Ghanaian counterparts. The Education Act of 1961 set forth the policy stating that no student can, if the parents object, be required to attend or abstain from attending any form of religious worship or observance. This provision has led to TTCs relaxing their rule requiring compulsory attendance of all students at church services. It is now possible for protestant students in Catholic TTCs to arrange for protestant preachers to organize separate church services, and vice versa for Catholic students in protestant institutions. Muslim students may be granted leave from the college campuses to attend worship in town. However, students with traditional religious beliefs are not permitted to engage in their religion on college grounds. If they stay on campus, they are expected to join the protestants or the Catholics.

Demographic information on Ghana indicates that at least 30% of the population practice a traditional religion. The greater majority of the people live in smaller towns and villages where the traditional religion is usually practiced publicly during festivals, funerals, and naming of infants. Chiefs and traditional leaders as well as elders of families (extended) are the custodians of the traditional religion.

In the past, nearly all of these chiefs and elders were uneducated, but the situation has rapidly changed with the expansion of education to these areas. Many teachers therefore have been enstooled or enskinned as chiefs or appointed as family elders. Some Ghanaian Christians, including teachers and the clergy, find it no hindrance to their Christian faith to participate in the Akan custom of pouring libation as a way of achieving a sacramental communion with the ancestors and thus a way of maintaining filial ties with the dead. But others regard the practices as against Christian beliefs and would object strongly to participating in them.

It is significant that the curriculum of the 1987 education reforms for basic education included culture, which involved the practice of traditional religion. But as a result of protest from the Christian and Muslim communities, the culture has been merged with the Ghanaian language and traditional religion but studied as an academic subject only together with Christian and Islam religions.

Teachers who have been denied the practice of their traditional religion at the TTCs are less likely to promote such practices for their students. Also, because the teachers' own primary and secondary education has given them no knowledge and experience in the practice of traditional religion, they are less able to teach it adequately to their students. Thus teacher education programs do not provide appropriate multicultural education in terms of traditional religious experiences for their students. Thus TTCs are contributing to a situation in which teachers are unable to accept the premise that participation in traditional religion is compatible with their Christian faith.

The Role of Language

By policy, no TTCs may deny admission to students on ethnic or religious grounds. Students are free therefore to apply for admission to the TTCs of their choice. However, TTCs can provide only Ghanaian Language (GL) courses for which they have sufficient number of students and staff.

Ghana has about 28 languages with a sizable number of speakers, yet only nine are studied in TTCs. By policy, all preservice teachers are required to study one GL. Twi courses, for instance, are offered in the TTCs in seven regions, and Ewe is offered in four regions. Thus students whose mother tongues are Twi or Ewe have a number of TTCs from which to select, whereas students who are speakers of the other seven GL's (except Ga) have no alternative choices. In fact, only one TTC offers three GL courses, whereas 22 (58%) TTCs offer only one GL course. The implication is that many students have to study GLs that are not their mother tongues. The expectation that preservice teachers will select TTCs offering their first GL or that students could successfully study any GL is not realistic.

In practice many students choose to attend TTCs not offering their first GL for various reasons. The student's choice may be based on religious affiliation, academic prestige of the college, parental and peer influence, the college that offered them admission, or the proximity of the college to home. This situation results in some students failing their GL courses. In 1995, for example, 444 students (7%) from a total of 6,509 failed their GL courses. It appears at the moment that many preservice teachers are willing to forego or suppress their ethnic language needs and cultural background to attain teacher education. One implication is that TTCs are preparing teachers capable of teaching one of the nine GLs. Thus teachers should be able to implement the language policy for the early primary grades. However, in reality some teachers cannot implement the policy because they are assigned to areas in which they are not speakers of the local GL, or they have not studied it at college. Such teachers are likely to require that their students in primary schools forego their cultural identity and learn to speak and write another GL or English, even if the latter would contravene education policy.

We may deduce that teacher education providers in Ghana recognize the need for preservice teachers to receive training in their mother tongues, but circumstances and lack of resources make this unattainable. Similarly, many teachers may recognize the need to educate young children in their mother tongues, but they as teachers lack the ability and resources to do so. Such teachers could put forth extra effort or enlist the help of able children who can speak both the local GL and English, but some are unwilling and unaware of alternatives to provide instruction in an appropriate language to benefit children's education.

The behavior of such Ghanaian teachers is consistent with Craig's (1990) observation that teachers represent a major obstacle to the implementation of new policies due to teacher quality (Adetoro 1966, cited by Craig, 1990). Also, teachers may doubt that putting such policies into practice is worth the effort (Adams, 1983 cited by Craig, 1990). Policymakers in Ghana have decided that young children should receive appropriate education relating to their diverse language and cultural backgrounds, yet significantly large numbers are being denied such multicultural education that draws on their strengths as well as provide them with useful knowledge, attitudes, and skills. The low literacy rate of Ghanaian youth, as mentioned earlier, and the nonimplementation of the language policy calls for a critical look at the objectives, curriculum, and participation in teacher education.

Teacher education institutions should introduce new courses that prepare students to use the GLs as media of instruction. As mentioned earlier, policymakers have noted that many children are unable to read or write a GL or English. The MOE (1994) therefore recommends dividing TTCs into two categories and charging one group with the responsibility for preparing teachers who will be competent to implement the language policy appropriately. The recommendation is as follows:

> Fifteen of the existing Group 2 colleges (which teach literature, social studies, and life skills) be devoted to training teachers for *lower primary grades*, and offer training in one or more regional Ghanaian languages. Trainees would be *selected from the area*, and would be posted to *teach within the area* [author's emphasis].
> ... Group 1 colleges (which teach sciences, math, and technical subjects) would train teachers for *upper primary* and junior secondary schools. They would recruit and post teachers throughout the country. And they would concentrate training in English [author's emphasis]. (p. 24)

The preceding recommendation is very important and should be implemented. But to achieve the expected outcome, the 15 TTCs for GL instruction should be distributed evenly throughout the 10 regions. Better still, the number should be increased to 20 and each region allocated two TTCs. This would make it possible to promote at least two major languages in each region and cater to the GL of the students. Also, preservice primary schoolteachers should be attracted to their local TTCs and should see themselves as not only learning to teach students to be literate and numerate, but also serving as role models and community leaders. The communities and their leaders should encourage their youth to pursue teacher education in local TTCs and support them when they become teachers.

The Issue of Textbooks

Currently teacher education programs do not include methodology in using a GL as a medium of instruction to teach primary school subjects such as mathematics, social studies, science, religion, and moral education. The situation is made worse by the lack of textbooks written in the GLs for these subjects. Teachers use textbooks written in English and their own methods or devices to provide instruction in these subjects using the GLs. Many teachers therefore opt for the easier option and use English as the medium of instruction. The children also have to read and understand the textbooks written in English. The effect is that very few children succeed, as the CRT results for English and mathematics have shown (PREP, 1995).

As teachers are given their teaching assignment without reference to their competence in the GLs, it is possible for some to be posted to areas in which they cannot read or write the local GLs. For example, a teacher the author once observed could speak the local GL which was Fanti. She therefore knew that the Fanti word for 12 (twelve) is "duebien," but could not write it on the chalkboard for the primary grade one children. She therefore refused to accept the Fanti words as appropriate names for mathematical numerals. Many of the children apparently did not know the English names but knew the Fanti number names very well because they kept mentioning them against the teacher's direction. The unfortunate teacher could easily have been helped if there had been textbooks for mathematics in Fanti.

The lack of textbooks in GLs therefore contributes to the predominant use of English in instruction and denies children appropriate education in their local languages at a crucial stage in their cognitive development. The MOE (1994) realizes the problems and the effect that the absence of such textbooks has on student achievement and has recommended that textbooks and instructional materials should be developed in Ghanaian languages for use in lower primary school. It is hoped the recommendation would be translated into policy and implemented. However, an immediate start could be made at the TTCs to assist preservice teachers until the books and materials are produced.

The Issue of Student Teaching

Ghana's 1987 educational reform has involved the provision of considerable inputs (textbooks and infrastructure) with support from the World Bank and some donor countries (MOE, 1994). Between 500 and 800 new schools have been established since 1990 (MOE, 1994), many of them in rural areas. Another aspect of the reform is the replacement of student teachers with newly trained teachers from the TTCs, sometimes in preference to filling vacancies. The TTCs have been organizing student teaching in urban schools over the years for practical reasons. Such schools are nearer to the colleges, are easily accessible by road transport, have trained teachers (under whom the student teachers can work), have many children of high ability, have reasonable teaching resources and facilities, and have parents and guardians eager to support their children's education. On the other hand, rural schools lack many of these human and material resources. Thus, preservice students gain experiences working with urban students, whose parents approve English as a medium of instruction and have adopted a lot of Western European norms of behavior and the Christian religion. The newly trained teachers sent to rural areas therefore find that their training experiences have not adequately prepared them for their new reality. Some of these teachers may be total strangers in the areas in which they have to work and may not be able to speak the local languages. In such circumstances the rural children may be better off with intelligent student teachers who are local people.

Teacher education programs need to include student teaching in the rural areas as an important field experience. This will enable new teachers to have training and later job satisfaction in rural areas. But more importantly, rural children would be offered appropriate multicultural education that builds on their cultural experiences and thus enables them to succeed in school. Whereas children ages 9 through 14 in Accra (the capital of Ghana) have a literacy rate of 34% and other urban areas together have a rate of 15.5%, rural areas have only a 6% literacy rate. The proposed recommendation, discussed earlier, of assigning 15 TTCs to train in GLs for lower primary schools, would have to address two issues. First, the preservice teachers must be exposed to teaching and living in rural areas. Second, serious efforts should be made to recruit students from the rural areas themselves for training as proposed.

CONCLUDING REMARKS

Ghanaian children have diverse cultures, languages, and religions that their education cannot continue to ignore. Teacher education programs in Ghana, especially for primary school certification, in many respects lack adequate programs and student field experiences to prepare preservice teachers for multicultural education in the schools. The current programs in many respects contribute to the perpetuation of the Western type of education that the early missionaries provided. Inappropriate multicultural programs in the TTCs affect the preservice teachers' own achievement at college, which in turn affects the achievement of the students they later teach.

There is a need to provide proper bilingual education in Ghana, which according to Cummins (1989), is likely to raise academic achievement and make students better at learning English. Also, there is still the need in Ghana to redesign teacher education course work to prepare preservice teachers who can respond better to the diverse array of students they are likely to be teaching in their schools. The programs should prepare and equip Ghanaian teachers realistically to work in the rural, multicultural settings. The locus of that preparation should shift from the urban to the rural schools and to greater interaction with the leadership of rural communities as well as other agencies that serve these communities. Finally, the production of textbooks for mathematics, science, social studies, religion, and moral education written in the Ghanaian languages for lower primary school children is needed urgently. The MOE recommendation on this is appropriate and should be implemented to achieve effective bilingual education in Ghana.

TO CONSIDER

Ghana has long been known as an educational leader throughout Africa. But like many developing nations, it has struggled to find the resources necessary to build effectively, especially in the area of multicultural or intercultural education. Ghana, as many nations in Africa, has many distinct tribal or ethnic groups placed within its artificial boundaries and is wrestling with issues of nationalism versus ethnicity. Fortunately, with few exceptions, Ghana has been spared the bloody massacres that have made recent front-page headlines in such places as Somalia and Rwanda. However, Ghana has yet to launch a sustained multicultural education program in its schools and communities. It is increasingly obvious, in travels through the country, that the preferred means of communication among people is the ethnic language.

1. Review current newspapers from Ghana (and other nations of Africa). Search for news items that present issues related to ethnic rights, the international community, interethnic conflict, and educational responses to diversity. How do current issues about diversity relate to what you have just read? What struggles continue around tribal issues?

2. What can your nation and schools learn from the experiences of Ghana?

3. How can young people in Ghana be most effectively prepared to interact with others on a global scale? What resources seem to be available within Ghana to assist young people in developing a global or intercultural perspective?

4. Ghana occasionally receives immigrants and refugees from other African nations. Given what you have just read, how would you respond to the scenario presented in chapter 1. What steps should schools take in responding to the needs of newly arrived immigrant groups?

REFERENCES

Adams, R. S. (1983). Research into educational innovation: A possible case of educational transfer. *Compare, 13,* 69–70.

Adetoro, J. E. (1966). Universal primary education and the teacher supply problem in Nigeria. *Comparative Education, 2,* 209–216.

Antwi, M. K. (1992). *Education, society and development in Ghana.* Accra: Unimax.

Busia, K. A. (1964). *Purposeful education for Africa*. London, The Hague, Paris: Mouton.

Chinebuah, I. K. (1970). The education review report and the study of Ghanaian languages. *Ghana Journal of Education, 1*(2), 22.

Craig, J. (1990). *Comparative African experiences in implementing educational policies* (World Bank Discussion Papers, No. 83) Africa Technical Department Series. The World Bank, Washington, DC.

Cummins. J. (1989). *Empowering minority students*. Sacramento, CA: California Association of Bilingual Education.

Foster, P. (1965). *Education* and *social change in Ghana*. Chicago: University of Chicago Press.

George, B. S. (1976). *Education in Ghana*. Washington, DC: U.S. Government Printing Office.

Ghana. (1962) *Education Act 1961*. Accra: Government Printer.

Gold Coast. (1951). *Accelerated Development Plan for Education*. p. 1.

Grimes, B. F. (Ed.). (1996). *Ethnologue: The languages of the world* (13th Ed.) Dallas, TX: Summer Institute of Linguistics.

Groves, C. P. (1948). *The planting of Christianity in Africa* (Vol. 1, p. 73). London and Red Hill: Lutterworth Press.

Jung, B. (1996). *Multicultural education and mono-cultural students: Curriculum struggles in teacher education*. Unpublished manuscript, Texas Tech University, Lubbock, Texas.

McWilliam, H. O. A. (1962). *The development of education in Ghana: An outline*. (2nd Ed.). London: Longmans.

Ministry of Education. (1993). *List of post secondary training colleges: Composition of subject grouping, and Ghanaian languages being taught in the various colleges* (undated document in 1993). Accra: Ministry

Ministry of Education. (1994). *Towards learning for all: Basic education in Ghana to year 2000* (Education sector paper as a follow-up to the National Programme of Action). Accra: Ministry.

Nieto, S. (1992). *Affirming diversity: The sociopolitical context of multicultural education*. New York: Longman.

Nieto, S. (1996). *Affirming diversity: The sociopolitical context of multicultural education* (2nd Ed.). New York: Longman.

Primary Education Project. (1995). *Results of the 1995 criterion-referenced tests*. An unpublished report, Ministry of Education, Accra, Ghana.

Rattray, R. S. (1932). *The tribes of Ashanti hinterland* (2 vols.). Oxford: Clarendon.

Southon, A. E. (1935). *Gold Coast Methodism: The first hundred years, (1835–1935)* (p. 70). London: Cargate.

Editor's Remarks

Multicultural education is a relatively new field that has faced a constant struggle for legitimacy, even though the issues it addresses regarding human difference, social justice, and the form education should take in a pluralistic society are as old as the United States. Sleeter, 1996[1]

Before Europeans ever set foot in the Americas, educational activity was carried out by hundreds of Native American tribes scattered throughout the land. The curricula of these groups, in aiming to help the young become contributing members of their specific group did not contain the traditional subjects we think of today. In fact, it was not until much later that a written language existed for any of the Native American peoples, and that was in 1846 when Sequoia wrote a language for the Cherokee.

Jefferson and others in the postrevolution/constitution-creation period argued for the importance of establishing an education system that guaranteed a free education for all citizens (excepting African American slaves and freedmen, Native Americans and Asian immigrants) as a means of perpetuating the basic principles of a participatory democracy. The issue of educational equality for Blacks and other people of color did not appear in the courts until the 1896 Plessy v. Ferguson decision allowed for segregation. It was not until the 1954 Brown v. Board of Education of Topeka, Kansas decision finally declared segregated schools unconstitutional that the nation was ordered by law to provide education for all.

From the early post-Columbian days until the present, a variety of educational approaches have evolved in each of the 50 states. This state-directed and locally controlled approach to education is a hallmark of the American educational system today. The 20th century also saw the passage of such laws as Public Law 94-142, which mandated "mainstreaming," programs allowing for children with special needs to participate in heterogeneous classrooms.

Like the nations of Western Europe, the United States, enjoying a high standard of living, has become a haven for the oppressed and an attraction for opportunists. This, coupled with the need for cheap labor, results in a highly pluralistic society. Its unique constitutional guarantees of equal educational access for all has created a tremendous challenge to the system.

---

[1]Sleeter, C E. (1996). *Multicultural education as social activism*. Albany, NY: State University of New York Press (SUNY), p. 1.

In response, many of the states now have formal multicultural education programs, with 28 states with a person appointed who is directly responsible for such efforts. In addition, 27 states require prospective teachers to meet certain requirements in multicultural education before they can be certified or licensed to teach. Although significant initial efforts have been made, children still exist who do not receive all the educational opportunity available, and instances of racism seem to be on the rise. Apparently, quite a bit of work needs yet to be done.

Chapter 12

Multicultural Education in the United States

80 ◆ C3

Vilma Seeberg
Beth Swadener
Marguerite Vanden-Wyngaard
Todd Rickel
Kent State University

FOUNDATIONS OF MULTICULTURAL EDUCATION IN AMERICA

The American civil rights movement, beginning with the Niagara Convention in 1906, saw the fruits of its labors rewarded in 1954 when the highest court of the United States ordered nationwide school desegregation to fulfill the constitutional promise of equal protection under the law. School desegregation stands as one of the major efforts at social engineering launched by any government in the 20th century. Albeit not as massive or violent as the socialist revolutions, it reorganized modern human society by insisting that people of color be included as equal citizens in a multiethnic United States—a country proclaiming itself the melting pot of nations welcoming to its shores the "tired, poor, huddled masses yearning to be free".

A century earlier, the nation had opened her first public schools to unite the citizens of the land, but from 1790 on denied all but "the class of persons [known to be] White" the "privilege of citizenship" by order of the Supreme Court as late as 1923. Schooling for Native Americans, post-emancipation African Americans, and Asian Americans, if they were provided schooling at all, was in legally segregated establishments.

After the 1954 Supreme Court Brown vs. Topeka, Kansas enforcement decree, desegregation of schools occurred at a snail's pace and only through the use of federal government and military force. White flight and backlash turned affected schools into zones of hostility. By the mid-1980s, resegregation was nearly complete in most northern areas, and the reality and concept of desegregation was in danger.[2] It became clear that integration alone could not bring about equality of opportunity, that it must be accompanied by its twin concept: respect for the other and his or her self determination. Integration was acceptable to the White American to the extent that it stood for assimilation, a state difficult to attain in a racially diverse population. The White American had not counted on extending respect to an "other" who would be him- herself, who would be content to think, feel, and behave according to a self-determined collectively held identity, not only an "other" appearance. Self-determination, philosophically speaking, is a precondition for the generation and acknowledgment of a unique ontology, epistemology, axiology, and social knowledge, the whole of socially constructed reality of a group of people. Without the right to "bring along" one's culture, an invitation to be included is hollow: One is invited to join but not to participate. The failure of school integration fostered this radical reconceptualization of the equality principle. From it have emerged new sociocultural reform movements as well as a new backlash, engendering what has been called the "culture wars."[3]

Thus was born the multicultural education movement in the United States. Pioneers such as G. Baker (1977), James Banks (1973), Geneva Gay (1971), and Carl Grant (1978) began to explore how education could attend to multiple sources of cultural experience. Activists and intellectuals in racially and otherwise marginalized communities as well as multiculturalists propose that education that reflects multiple canons rather than only that of the dominant, elite, and mainstream America is a fuller expression of the pluralism that is American democracy. Conservatives, however, see America as a land of immigrants whose common cultural

---

[2]Gary Orfield (1993) of Harvard University School Desegregation Project conducted a study for US. School Board Association, that was much quoted in the popular press. The study revealed that the United States has been slipping back into school segregation, even "hypersegregation" in northeastern metropolitan areas. These schools have "debilitating" proportions of poor students, whereas only 5% of heavily European-American schools, mostly located further out of the inner cities, are marked by poverty (Teepen, 1997).

[3]For description of the issues involved in the culture wars, see Gates (1992), and West (1993b).

core is shaped by the Anglo-Western tradition. They see the multicultural trend as the "disuniting" of America.

Democratic pluralism lays the foundation for the theory of education that is multicultural. Grassroots reform activism is the foundation of its practice, continuing the tradition of its parent, the civil rights movement. Education that is multicultural is a continuation of the great human social movements pressing for fuller equality and freedom and a more balanced culture and society.

Due to its heritage, multicultural education in the 1970s at first attended to issues of a racial and social class nature. By the 1980s, gender, social class, religion, language, exceptionalities, and finally sexual orientation were recognized as parallel threads in the tapestry that form the interwoven patterns in education that is multicultural.

Cultural Pluralism and Segregation in Society

The antecedents of multiculturalism in the "new" world are in part similar and in part dissimilar to those from the "old" world.[4] Cultural pluralism has been called the central problem of the 20th century. The setting of the old world is one of continuous traditions, in which nations tend to embody largely an ethnically homogeneous population. The idea of the new world is posited on the discontinuity of culture, the annihilation of the previous indigenous cultures, the creation of a synergistic amalgamation of several imported traditions, and the exclusion of other ethnic and particularly race-related cultures. By the end of the 20th century, however, both old and new worlds encountered colonization, many waves of immigration, and internal multiple nationalities.

United States Population Diversity at the Turn of the Millenium

According to the 1990 census, the U.S. population was reported to be 248.7 million, and in the 5 years that followed, it grew an additional 13 million (5.2%; Deardorff & Montgomery, 1997). It is the increasingly ethnically diverse pattern of this growth that has been noted throughout American society. In 1990, 75.7% of the population was of European descent, 12.3% of African descent, 9% of Hispanic origin (by name, hence of any descent), 3% of Asian and Pacific Island descent. Only 0.8% of the

---

[4]The "new world" refers primarily to Australia and North America, but also includes Central and South America, although there the indigenous traditions and peoples have a greater presence even today.

population consisted of Native Americans (Fig. 12.1). Only a decade earlier, in 1980, Americans of European descent made up a much larger majority of 84% and Native Americans were a significantly larger 3.2% minority. All other subgroups had a smaller share of the population: African Americans a slightly smaller 11.8%, Hispanic-named 6.4%, and Asian and Pacific Island Americans 1% (U.S. Census).

In census projections of the population, the non-Hispanic White population will decrease from 76% in 1990 and to 52.5% in 2050. All other groups are expected to increase in numbers, with Hispanics providing the largest growth figures from 9% in 1990 to 22.5% in 2050 (Cheeseman Day, 1997; see Figure 12.1). The increase in diversity and the growth in minority populations coupled with the dwindling share of the European-descent population suggests that the influence of the mainly Anglo-protestant cultural dominance is diminishing. The fact that a substantial share of the growth and diversification of the population is being contributed by immigrants (e.g., 30% in 1994) who bring with them, at minimum, another language, strongly suggests a consequent diversification of the culture and an attenuation of the Anglo melting-pot mentality.

Growth rates are closely associated with school enrollments because the largest share of growth (e.g., 70% in 1994) comes from natural births and because immigrants tend to be of childbearing age or younger. In 1994

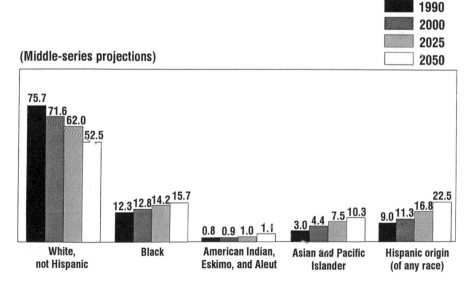

FIG. 12.1. Percent of population by race and origin.
Source: U.S. Bureau of the Census (1997, May 9) National population projections.
Cited in Cheeseman Day (1997). [On-line] Available at
Http://www.census.gov/population/www/pop-profile/natproj.html

for the first time, growth in the Hispanic population was larger than in the White, non-Hispanic population. The Hispanic population grew by 3.5% in contrast to the White, non-Hispanic population growth of 0.4%. The Hispanic population is typically younger than the general population, presaging continued greater natural increase. As a side note, but one of some urgency for the American schools, in 1992, 40% of all Hispanic children in America ages 18 years or younger lived in poverty compared with 13.2% of non-Hispanic White children (Pinal, 1997).

The growth rate of the African-American population, a steady 1.5% in the mid-1990s, will result in doubling this population from its present size by 2050. A closer examination of the American-Indian, Eskimo, and Aleut population reveals that this population has grown significantly since 1970, more than doubling its numbers in two decades from 827,000 in 1970 to nearly 2 million in 1990 (Paisano, 1997), although its share of population has decreased.

The newest widely felt contribution to diversity is coming from the fastest growing "race group," Asian and Pacific Islanders. This continued trend will result in this group doubling its 1997 size by 2010. In the 1990s, more than 60% of that growth is contributed by net international immigration (Cheeseman Day, 1997), with the bulk of the immigration coming from Asia. It should be noted as well that this is a very heterogeneous group.

Net immigration is projected to remain near current numbers (about 880,000 a year), and the total population in 2050 is expected to reach 392 million, in increase of 50% from the 1990 census numbers. With the aging of the present majority population and the increasing growth in the present minority populations, this nation is being catapulted into a state of diversity unprecedented in human history, and the American school's ability to provide education multiculturally and equitably will be the litmus test of democratic pluralism and survival of the nation.

HISTORY OF A SEGREGATED SOCIETY AND SCHOOLING

The United States has been a pluralistic and segregated society from its very beginning. Thirteen small former colonial enclaves, composed of a variety of European nationalities and religious sects, were surrounded by a vast land sparsely populated by many Native American nationalities practicing a great assortment of languages, cultures, and economic activities, all grouped in a variety of political units. The founders of the United States bestowed the privileges of citizenship on only a few landed European-descent males, and thereby enshrined the notion of exclusion in the new land's notion of democracy. Not only were Native Americans "removed" or eliminated as heathen wherever Europeans wanted land, but imported slaves were considered less than human. Various European nationalities practiced blatant discrimination against each other, and women of any descent were considered unworthy of citizenship until 1920.

The Anglo-Protestant Roots of Segregated Schooling

Education as a differentiated institution from childrearing was introduced in North America by early European colonizers. The protestant religious elites had brought along the scholastic tradition of Europe to train the next generation's theocratic leadership from among their own. As protestant converts, the early settlers rejected the harsh social class distinctions of the Catholic old world society, and included or pressed the children of the poorer classes into schooling to instill in them Protestant discipline and virtue and to "drive out the devil." Children of the Native-American population were heathen to these settlers, and hence excluded from schooling. The early schools for village folk were quite separate from the elite schools, a pattern still visible in the public–private school separation even today. With the founding of the American state, the European and American paths diverged.

Schooling for the American Dream

During the 1800s, the period of nation building, with the continuing incorporation of expropriated Native-American territories and the increasing numbers of immigrants from a variety of lands, schooling in America came to occupy a singularly important place in society. "Common schooling" began to take on the form and ideology still in place today: publicly funded by the community members, universal as far as social class background, and based on a common curriculum furthering a protestant morality[5] The communities still defined themselves rather strictly as Christian and of European-American ancestry, with the occasional inclusion of African-American freed men and Native-American farmers or settlers. Politicians found the schools a convenient, broad-based policy mechanism for addressing the vast social, economic, and political problems of the new state, which was not yet a nation nor a unified economy.

---

[5]The historical outline in this section owes its basic concepts and references primarily to Joel Spring's (1997) as well as Steven Tozer's (1993) presentation of the history of American schooling.

Political reformers embraced the old-world, romantic ideology that human nature can be formed, shaped, and given direction to create a better society, but they gave it an American, pragmatic cast. Local communities would watch over the socialization of their young to create a better tomorrow. The separate states found they could enforce compliance with social imperative on the schools rather than by regulating the many individual families. For example, schooling could unite the nation by compelling all citizens to use a common language. It could improve the lives of the "huddled masses" arriving from Europe by raising their social and human capital.

Ever since those days, American common schooling has been enlisted to reduce crime and poverty, to increase the skills of the future workforce, to reduce tensions between social classes and European ethnic groups, to assimilate immigrants, and to prepare citizens for the vote in a representative democracy (Cubberly, 1934). In the mid 19th century, the economic juggernaut that became 20th century America was built from the product of the schools: an orderly, dependable work force. Although the notion of a common school appeared to enjoy broad popularity, political interests differed ideologically in their support.

Then as now, new industrialists, status-anxious parents, and middle-class educators believed the rightful function of the public schools was to ready youth for a specific civic and economic adult role (Katz, 1968). Liberal democratic reformers, however, have emphasized another aspect of public schooling: the assurance of equal access to knowledge deemed appropriate by society or equal educational opportunity (Curti, 1935). Social reconstructionists, whether from among the working and poorer classes or among the educators, have continued to characterize the common schools as an attempt by the state to impose a bureaucratic order that protects the wealthy and assimilates potentially rebellious outsiders into the Anglo-American protestant culture (Kaestle, 1983). They call on the schools, instead, to enhance the political and economic position of the marginalized sectors of the society by assuring equal access to knowledge. Multiculturalists of the day have added the premise that all, regardless of social status, be involved in the creation of "legitimate" or "school" knowledge and the acquisition of equal access (Banks, 1993; Grant, 1992).

The dominant mythology regarding the American common school, either as a reality or an ideal, however, has continued to be embraced by most Americans regardless of their secular political differences. An exception has been those seeking religiously based education or socialization into elite status. It is public education that has furnished the unifying principle of mainstream society, the American dream.

For conservatives, to achieve the American dream, the poor had but to learn how to exercise restraint, rationalistic mental disciplines, Anglo-

Protestant morality, and family life values. Individual effort would result in achievement in school, which would ensure everyone the right and ability to acquire property and economic success (Kaestle, 1983, Spring, 1997) is a belief proclaimed by both liberal reformers and conservatives such as William Bennet (1984), E.D. Hirsch (1987), and Diane Ravitch (1990), even today[6]

All along, however, and often well after persons affiliated with traditions other than that of Anglo-European were outsiders until and after the granting of citizenship. To those who were thus excluded, such as former slaves, Asian immigrants and indentured servants, and Native Americans, a more fundamentally critical and social reconstructionist view of the common school was obvious and necessary. They questioned the selection and deselection practices of the school, and, after desegregation, its social normalizing and assimilationist agenda. The experience of school desegregation over the last three decades of the 20th century made it clear that integration with compensatory education, such as that instituted as part of the "War on Poverty," cannot undo the unfair advantage from a century of Anglo-Protestant schooling, the socioeconomic dominance of the European mainstream, and the reification of elite Anglo-Western traditions. Those privileged by race and generations of economic well-being are now poised to take advantage of information-age technology to guarantee their place at the top of an ever-more bifurcated economy and society while those visually distinct from the people of the historic mainstream are relegated to caste-like sociocultural status and, as a majority, condemned to secondary job markets. As the end of the 20th century approaches, the unfinished struggle for democratic pluralism in the United States has become crystalized in the call for education that is multicultural.

The 20th Century Identity Crisis

In many parts of the world, the foremost political issue remains the question of peaceful national ethnic pluralism. Will different people and nations share the resources of the globe in a balanced and sustainable fashion, or will competition continue to drive people into ethnic wars (Havel, 1994; Wynter, 1992a)? Moreover, have the rivers of refugees and immigrants mixed the global people-stew so profoundly as to make of multiethnicity or multiraciality a new identity group, a veritable people of

---

[6]On the need for a common Western cultural core, see also Allan Bloom (1988) and Arthur M. Schlesinger, Jr., (1992). On the conservative view of the culture wars in academia and schools, see William J. Bennett (1984), and Dinesh D'Souza, (1991).

color? In the meanwhile, even the terminology is still in dispute, evidencing the tenseness of the ideological dispute.

In the American cultural dialogue as reflected in the popular media of the 1990s, the term *democratic pluralism* is used as an accusation of wrong-headedness. When used by conservatives, democratic pluralism means "collaboration in the disuniting of Americica," but when used by Afrocentrists, it is yet another excuse "to deny the white-supremacist core of American culture" (Asante, 1990; Hilliard, Payton-Stewart, & Williams, 1990; Mazrui, 1986; and Wynter, 1992b).

The term "minority" has been resisted by different racial and ethnic groups because it artificially separates "people of color" in the United States from the global majority. Furthermore, minorities together number nearly one third of the U.S. population, and, in the 20 largest school districts, approximately 60% to 70% of the students are people of color (Grant & Secada, 1990, p. 403). The term minority is also seen as an essentializing label lumping numerous, heterogeneous groups of people, distinct ethnicities, blended cultures, and linguistic groups into a monolithic "other," defined primarily by what it is not (e.g., non-white).

Issues of minority rights, in the meantime, have grown to include members of other oppressed groups (e.g., persons with disabilities and persons who are gay, lesbian, or bisexual known as "sexual minorities").

To a growing number of people—teachers, students, families, and others—so-called minority issues are rather a matter of equity and pluralism, social justice, and anti-oppression praxis (Ladson-Billings & Henry, 1990; Shade, 1989; Sleeter & Grant, 1987). In the 1990s *social justice pedagogy* is the term coming into use to describe multicultural educational practice in the United States, a practice based on educational theories of social reconstructionism and *critical multiculturalism* (McLaren, 1994; Sleeter & McLaren, 1995), and drawing as well on the concurrently developing *critical race theory* (Bell, 1987, 1992; Crichlow, 1991; Hadjor, 1993; McCarthy & Crichlow, 1993; Tate, 1997; and West, 1993a).

It is interesting to note how the issues of national identity developed in unique paths in the different national discourses of the "new world." For example, the concepts of *multicultural* or *intercultural* have come into use only recently in the education literature of Australia, the United Kingdom, and Canada. Instead, here in the United States the discussion was framed first as *anti-discriminatory education, antiracist/antisexist pedagogy*, and *first people's education*. In Great Britain, the antiracist theory was centered in neomarxist critiques, very structural in nature, and perhaps most similar to that of the U.S. social reconstructionist multiculturalists. Pedagogic parallels can be drawn to "antiprejudice" and "antibias" education in the United States. The groundwork for this direction in U.S. multicultural education, however, was laid by scholarship in psychology on racial attitude beginning in the 1940s (Agnes, 1947; Jackson, 1944), prejudice reduction (Katz, 1973; Williams & Edwards, 1969), the intercultural curriculum of the 1950s and 60s, and racial identity development theory (Cross, 1985, 1991; Helms, 1990; Tatum, 1992).

In the late 1990s, the different national discourses are converging, and the social reconstructionist perspective is gaining ground among multiculturalists in the United States, certainly in part because of the continued intolerable structural inequalities in the educational system.

A brief description of the system and its present conditions with regard to these inequalities will throw light on the urgency of the reconstructionist movement in education.

COMMON SCHOOLING AND SEGREGATION: THE SYSTEM AT THE TURN OF THE MILLENIUM

In the United States, each of the 50 states provides free education that is compulsory. States determine the years that students must attend, which in most states is until the age of 16. Formal schooling for youth is divided into primary (years 1 through 6) and secondary schools (years 7 through 12), culminating in a universal diploma. School districts may join in offering specialized secondary schools, such as vocational high schools (ages 14–18) or arts or science magnet schools, whereas regular high schools offer comprehensive curricula. Most schools, from primary through high schools, despite mainstreaming and other reform efforts, separate students into tracks of ability groups.

In 1993, 65.4 million students were enrolled in pre-kindergarten through college. The number of students enrolled in kindergarten through Grade 12 mirrors the population of 5 to 17 years old because nearly all persons in that age group are enrolled in school. Between 1973 and 1993, enrollment in kindergarten through 12th grade declined by 3%, nursery enrollment more than doubled, and college enrollment increased 55%. Nine out of 10 elementary and secondary enrollments were in public institutions (Bruno, 1997).

The distinctive feature of the educational system of the United States is that it is proudly decentralized to reflect local customs and socioeconomic conditions. Strong sentiments center on the notion of grassroots control of the socialization and education of a community's youth. Although all areas of government, federal, state, and local, have a variety of responsibilities for schools, there is no federal mandate for education.

The federal government does have an influence in education. Under the Fourteenth Amendment of the U.S. Constitution, which guarantees equal protection of the laws to any and all persons, the federal government has responded, often belatedly, to citizen initiatives and mass struggles by creating federal legislation mandating policies tied to financial support, and even by sending in Federal armed forces to resolve local conflicts. School desegregation has occasioned the most massive intervention by the federal government in decentralized schooling. Mass mobilization by African Americans and allies finally brought the federal government to the table to lay out policy affecting all localities.

The 1954 federal Supreme Court decision Brown v. Board of Education of Topeka was enforced by federal police and military forces and led to the passage of the Civil Rights Act of 1964 and other legislation stipulating financial penalties and incentives for desegregation of schooling during the 1970s in the northern states. In 1975, the Education for Handicapped Children Act, which mandated and paid for services for their special needs, was enacted. Further legislation stipulated that students with disabilities must be educated in the least restrictive environment along with nondisabled students. This participation by the federal government, however, does not indicate the existence of a federal system of education or a national curriculum.

Decentralization, Financing, and its Devastating Consequences

Decentralization is often hailed as a basic principle of American grass-roots democracy. This section shows that decentralization in public schooling has resulted in institutionalized inequality that some have characterized as "caste-like" (Ogbu, 1986). Hypersegregation by race, hyperconcentration of poverty, and bordered cities-fenced suburbs have become fused together permanently by and in the institution of the school district. Race, poverty, and urban location are merged into one factor, which determines of the greatest schooling inequality and inequity as well as access to opportunity—in short, a good proportion of Americans' life chances. Decentralized school districts, as enforced by the U.S. Supreme Court, particularly since 1974[7] give the technoeconomic bifurcation of American society its racial, income, and locational character.

In most states, the immediate control of the schools is delegated to local school boards. These boards are elected by voters within the geographic proximity of a high school and its set of feeder schools, the school district. The boards are responsible for the operation of the school, including curriculum decisions, school finance, and contract negotiations with

---

[7] San Antonio Independent School District v. Rodriguez (1973) and Milliken v. Bradley (1974).

faculty and staff. In 1990–1991, there were 15,358 local school districts in the United States, each with its own board (Husen, 1994). In the decades since the civil rights movement and escalating with the accountability movement of the 1990s, the state departments of education have assumed growing control over curriculum and standards, which they enforce through ever more standardized examination systems, licensing of educators, and funding of school reform mandates.

Although state governments also have increased their share of school funding to an average 45% by 1992–1993 (U.S. Department of Education, National Center for Education Statistics, 1995, Table 154, p. 151), the primary source of revenue for schools remains local, raised from property taxes (47.4%, 1992–1993, Table 154, p. 151). This reliance on local property taxes as the basis of revenue for schools has created considerable inequities between school districts because property values are not equally distributed across any state or the country. "Poor school districts [primarily urban and rural] are often able to levy only modest sums per pupil despite high property tax rates, whereas rich school districts are able to raise considerable sums per pupil despite low tax rates" (Husen, 1994, p. 6544). There are indeed "savage inequalities" (Kozol, 1991) in U.S. public schools and other social service programs.

In the state of Ohio, with 1.8 million pupils attending 611 school districts, the existing school finance system was thrown out by a state court in the spring of 1997 on the basis of its "equity gap" and inability to meet "even the most basic educational needs of many of its students" (Judge Sweeney wrote Ohio, *Coalition for Equity and Adequacy of School Funding v. State of Ohio*, March 1997). A comparison of two not very distant school districts' tax revenue and school allocation in 1996 illustrates the problem. An inner city school district was able to raise $21 from a 1-mill property tax and, in turn, allocate $7,200 per pupil per year, 75% of which came from supplementary funding from the state and federal government. On the other hand, in the shiny new outer-ring suburban school district, 1 mill of property tax brought $582, which constituted 93% of the $13,000 annual per pupil expenditure (Ohio Department of Education, March 25, 1997, p. 9-A, Table: The Equity Gap). Many rural school districts reached the state mandated $3,500 minimum only by virtue of an 80% or more subsidy of its expenditure (Ponessa, 1997, p. 3). Although dollars invested are not the lone cause of differential opportunities in education, these large financial discrepancies must produce substantial inequalities in outcome, and they do, as is seen in the following section.

The consequences of such inequities have been loudly deplored in the media, in the courts, even by politicians, and yet they persist. Most recently, Jonathan Kozol (1991) succeeded in focusing national attention through his acclaimed book *Savage Inequalities*, public appearances, and other publications in 1994. He described the squalor of poor school districts in which many American school children find themselves, including typical schools in East St. Louis, Chicago, Detroit, Cincinnati, and the Bronx of New York City which lack basic materials including textbooks, literature, laboratories and desks, while contending with broken furnaces, windows, and walls, as well as unequipped playgrounds and backed-up sewers, schools that are unsafe and filled with demoralized staff and students. In the most concentrated urban areas, schools could not operate for overcrowding if half their students were not absent on a regular day.

Inequality in School Performance

The distribution of poverty not only strikes unequally by region and by inner city versus outer ring suburb, but also by racial and ethnic status. People of color, notably African Americans and Hispanic Americans, are particularly hard hit by poverty. The increase in poverty among children and female-headed families adds a further dimension to the school district equity gap. Among Hispanic and African American children, 38.4% and 44%, respectively, live below the official standard of poverty (U.S. Bureau of the Census, 1991).

During the fall of 1995, the National Education Goals Panel convened by President Carter released its annual report at the midpoint of the national reform, National Education Goals 2000. In all areas assessed by the National Assessment of Educational Progress[8] (NAEP), at three grade levels, in 1992, fewer minority students—African Americans, Hispanic, and Native Americans/Alaskan Natives—met the performance standard (as "proficient" or "advanced") than White students. They scored from 20 to 30 points lower in reading, math, history, and geography (see Table 12.1 for reading scores). In 1992, 24% fewer minority students met the performance standard set for Goals 2000 than did their White counterparts (Educational Testing Service, 1992). "White students are dramatically pulling away from African-American and Latino students in measures of achievement, after two decades where African-American students significantly narrowed the gap" (Jackson, 1997).

The U.S. Department of Education National Center for Education Statistics also published student scores on the NAEP disaggregated by the area of the school district. Reading scores of "disadvantaged urban"

---

[8]The National Assessment of Educational Progress (NAEP) is one of the most visible and comprehensive standardized tests given in the United States at randomly selected public and private schools for students ages 9, 13, and 17 years. It is sponsored by the National Center for Education Statistics of the U.S. Department of Education and administered by the Educational Testing Service.

TABLE 12.1

1992 Average Student Proficiency in Reading Scores* by Race–Ethnicity, Type of Community

	9-yr-olds	13-yr-olds	17-yr-olds
Race–Ethnicity			
White	217.9	266.4	297.4
Black	184.5	237.6	260.6
Hispanic	191.7	239.2	271.2
Type of Community			
Advantaged urban	233.6	280.8	302.6
Disadvantaged urban	183.5	230.9	266.7
Extreme rural	206.5	257.2	285.3

*Note: NAEP 1992

Source: Educational Testing Service: (1992). National Assessment of Educational Progress: Trends in Academic Progress. In U.S. Department of Education, National Center for Education Statistics. *Digest of Education Statistics 1995* (p. 113). Washington, DC: U.S. Government Printing Office.

graduating students (17-year-olds) are 27 points lower than the national average, 35.9 points lower than their "advantaged" urban peers, and still 18.6 points lower than their rural peers (see Table 12.1).

The criteria for the performance standard used by the U.S. Department of Education National Center for Education Statistics (1995, p.113) indicate that the students of color, when completing high school, have the ability to make generalizations and to seek specific information, but do not have the ability to read complicated materials, then synthesize and generate meaning. Obviously, on the average, these students are ill prepared for advanced study or a stable career in the generally high-technology primary job market.

The third element of the inequality web, poverty, seals the trap. Socioeconomic status (SES) factors generally continued to have an impact on school achievement and attainment. Across the United States, 7.5% of high school dropouts were from families earning less than $20,000 annually compared with 1.5% from families earning more than $40,000 in 1993 (Bruno, 1997). Those with lower incomes have lower scores on standardized tests. In Ohio, for example, where the average income in 1992 was $15,367 (vs. $16,227 nationally), only 47% students from homes with less than a $17,500 annual income (i.e., the majority of students), passed the Ohio nineth-grade proficiency examination.

As the annual income of the home rose, more students passed the examination. At $22,500 to 25,000, 62% passed, and at $27,500 to $30,000, as many as 78% passed. We do not know how many of the students from the 15.2% of Ohio families officially designated as in poverty (vs. 14.8 percent nationally) passed, but the figures suggest that the large majority did not (Bracey Report, 1997, based on the U.S. DOE National Center for Education Statistics compilations; Bracey, 1997).

Increasingly, testing mandates are driving curriculum decisions in the United States at the end of the 20th century. Teachers in urban districts are teaching from a deficit position, lacking materials, facilities, and student preparation in the early grades needed to reach the testing goals. High-stakes testing contributes greatly to the early rigidification in the bifurcation of the postindustrial U.S. economy, casting students who are urban, of color, and poor into the lower realm, beneath a barrier that is less and less possible to cross.

Schooling for Groups by Race and Culture

Educational attainment has steadily improved for the three major race groups over the postdesegregation decades: In 1993, 41% of all high school graduates ages 18 to 24 years were enrolled in college (42% of men, up 7 points from 1973; 41% of women, up 16 points from 1973). By race group, 42% of European Americans, 33% of African Americans, and 36% of Hispanic-named Americans graduating from high school ages 18 to 24 years were enrolled in college (Bruno, 1997). However, in 1993, fully 40% of college students were older than 25 years (Bruno, 1997), and the share of persons with minority "race" status thus enrolled has been greater than that of European Americans. Hence, the overall college enrollment share of African Americans and Hispanic-named Americans likely was a few points higher, thus narrowing the educational gap at the high end of the educational pyramid. However, schools have reversed the 1950–1970 court-ordered desegregation trend and, since then with the assistance of the Nixon–Reagan Supreme Court decisions have even reversed the course. The schools have become ever more segregated by race, where Hispanic-named Americans are included, to levels higher than in 1972. In 1993, two thirds of all African American children attended mostly Black schools, and the other one third attended nearly all-minority schools.

Metropolitan areas that have school districts separating city and suburbs, such as most of the older cities in the former industrial centers of the northeastern states, are the most racially divided. Hispanics have suffered a consistent rise in segregation since 1978, and nationally are the most segregated of any minority group. In 1992, 73.4% attended mostly minority schools. The segregation studies also show that African Americans and Hispanics are far more likely than European Americans to attend the poorest schools in the nation (Orfield, 1993).

Given the anticipated increase in the number of Hispanic-named school-age Americans, the disadvantages this group experiences in the schools call for special attention. In recent years, improvements regarding educational attainment are encouraging: among Hispanics ages 25 years and older, the share of persons with less than a fifth-grade education decreased from 15.6% in 1983 to 11.8% in 1993; the share of persons with high school diplomas increased from 1983 rates of less than 48% to just more than 53% in 1993, although the gap reported in March 1993 between high school graduation rates of young Hispanic adults (60.4%), compared with non-Hispanic Whites (91.2%) remains highly discriminatory (Pinal, 1997).

Reflection

In the U.S. educational system, although the desire to teach all children well regardless of socioeconomic background, race–ethnicity, or religion may be robust among educators and parents, the political will to do so does not express itself in the voting process, in the legislatures, or in the courts. Those that care about the education of the urban poor and children of color have continued the fight for a reform agenda in common schooling. Thus the call for education that is multicultural and social reconstructionist is an attempt to redress the whole cycle of social marginalization and oppression. It aims to rectify the most egregious of historic educational segregation that goes back to the first formal school in the first American colonial settlement. At the turn of the millenium reform for equitable schooling must be mindful of human group diversity, including culture and cultural status, social class status, gender, religion, and exceptionality.

We are beginning to hear calls to include the as-yet taboo issue of sexual orientation diversity and its stigmatized population in the American cultural dialogue. Extending equal social and civil rights to those who have not been granted the right to full expression of self is particularly relevant to the schools. It is during the school-age years that humans acquire and come to terms with their sexual identity, and the schools must provide a safe and encouraging environment for the unfolding of this as well as every other human characteristic. Although included in the literature of multiculturalism, it is fair to state that the cultural dialogue of America has yet to develop a language of appreciation for persons who are bisexual, gay, or lesbian.

INTEGRATING MULTICULTURAL EDUCATION INTO SCHOOLS

The following section discusses the very complex and challenging question of whether and how U.S. public schools are grappling with the issues raised in this chapter. We explore how U.S. schools are meeting the current common school challenge to educate multiculturally and democratically.

Multicultural Education Policy, the State and Teacher Education

This section briefly reviews the state of the policy for education that is multicultural at the state level and some related demographic issues.

The State. Federal initiatives have focused mainly on helping students with disabilities and culturally diverse students to provide equal educational opportunity in preschool, elementary, and secondary education. States have generally followed the federal lead through state grants to implement federal policies, although some have moved beyond federal efforts, especially in the area of curriculum development.

The federal government maintains records to assess state performance on staff employment and student equal opportunity measures. A number of state initiatives have addressed making education more reflective of cultural diversity and providing the equal education opportunities the federal government mandates. These efforts at multicultural education policy have often addressed curriculum reform through adding courses or inserting units (Gollnick, 1995). Because policy studies give accurate state level data, we rely on a somewhat older report (Mitchell, 1988). Mitchell found that 27 of 50 states had initiated some kind of multicultural education program: 28 having a person responsible for multicultural education, 27 having multicultural teacher certification requirements, 25 requiring textbook screening, and 21 having specific laws or policies pertaining to multicultural education. The next step must be policies on cultural diversity and equity being used as the lenses through which all educational reform is viewed.

Teachers and K–12 Enrollment. A most urgent issue that the state must address is the startling gap between the makeup of the teacher corps and that of the students. The increase in diversity of the immigrant populations and natural population growth was accelerated in the 1990s in sharp contrast to a decline in diversity of the teaching force. In 1990–1991, 9.2% of public school teachers were African American, 3.1% Hispanic, and 1% Asian/Pacific Islander American as compared to enrolled students 16% of whom were African American, 12% Hispanic, and 3% Asian Pacific Islander Americans (Table 12.2).

It is expected that the overall demand for teachers will increase into the 21st century. Professional associations as well as the federal government

TABLE 12.2

Student Enrollment and Teacher Employment by Race, 1990

	Enrollment Students (%)	Teachers (%)
European American	68.0	86.0
African American	16.0	9.2
Hispanic American	12.0	3.1
Asian/Pacific Islander	3.0	1.0
American Indian/Alaskan	<1.0	0.7

Source: U.S. Department of Education. (1990) Elementary and Secondary School Civil Rights Survey, 1990: *National and state summary* of projected data. In T. M. Smith, G. T. Rogers, N. Alsalam, M. Perie, R. P. Mahoney, & V. Martin (1994). *The condition of education, 1994.* Washington, DC: National Center for Education Statistics, U.S. Department of Education, and National Data Resource Center, National Center for Education Statistics, 1990–1991 Schools and Staffing Survey: Teacher Questionnaire.

have responded by stressing the importance of and funding for some initiatives, such as the U.S. Department of Education Office of Post Secondary Education Minority Teacher Recruitment Program, to recruit minority professionals to enter the educational field (American Association of Colleges for Teacher Education, 1987; American Council on Education, 1988).

However, at this time, teacher education students show as little diversity as the teacher corps. In 1991, 84.7% of teacher education students were European American, 6.9% African American, 3.6% Hispanic, 1% Asian or Pacific American, 0.3% Native American, and 3.3% other. A small note of optimism is sounded by the fact that these proportions did represent some increases in diversity since 1989 (U.S. Department of Education, National Center for Education Statistics, 1992).

There is also concern about the growing social and cultural distance between students and teachers. Teachers live in existential worlds different from those of their charges. Only 37% of teachers live in the attendance area of the school in which they teach, and in large urban systems, which have the highest concentrations of ethnically diverse and poor populations, even fewer (17.3%) of teachers live in proximity to the school neighborhood or attendance area (Gay, 1993).

Other factors increasing the sociocultural schism include gender (72% female teachers), educational level as compared to the parents, technological and media adeptness favoring the student, and an aging teacher corps. As Gay (1993) pointed out, the "conduits of personal meaning" (i.e., the examples or illustrations provided by the teacher to make abstractions meaningful to the student) tend to come from a neighborhood totally unfamiliar to the teacher's charges. "Preparing teachers to connect meaningfully is the ultimate challenge of teacher education in an ethnically and culturally pluralistic and technologically complex world" (p. 46). Are the colleges of education preparing a teaching force adept at creating culturally compatible classroom procedures, norms, and learning styles and environments[9]

The Education of Educators[10]   Teacher education is influenced by licensing regulations promulgated by state education agencies subject to the legislatures (see earlier discussion) and by the policy of two national organizations: the Association of Colleges of Teacher Education (AACTE) and the National Council for Accreditation of Teacher Education (NCATE). The AACTE in 1968 turned its attention to multicultural education policy and undertook measures that led to NCATE adopting multicultural education standards in 1979. Of the approximately 1,200 colleges and universities that prepare teachers, 514 were accredited by NCATE in 1992, and were thereby subject to a 5-year review to determine whether they meet NCATE's standards. From 1981, teacher education institutions were required to provide multicultural education.

NCATE integrated multicultural education concepts into seven compliance criteria and four standards: professional studies, clinical and field-based experiences, student and faculty diversity, faculty qualifications, and assignments. Itself composed of 26 professional and learned societies associated with various program areas in colleges of education, NCATE also enforces their curriculum guidelines, including those on multicultural education stipulated by 13 societies. "These are the only national policies to which colleges and universities may be held accountable, and then it is a voluntary process" (Gollnick, 1992, p. 230).

NCATE (1990) defines "cultural diversity" and "multicultural perspective" as referring to "cultural membership based on ethnicity, race, religion, class, gender and exceptionality," (cited in Gollnick, 1993, p. 230) but it does not refer to inequality, discrimination, racism, sexism, or prejudice. The standards also do not recommend active involvement in changing those conditions present in the schools.

Although it would appear that the standards are rather unobjectionable, performance data seem to indicate otherwise. By 1989, 8 years after the required implementation of multicultural education, among the 59 institutions reviewed, NCATE found only 8 (13.6%) in full compliance, and

---

[9]For theoretical and applied explanations of issues of cross-cultural learning see Boykin, 1986; Holiday, 1985; Shade, 1989; Spindler, 1987; and Trueba, Guthrie, & Au, 1981.

[10]This section is based on an article by Donna Gollnick, a staff member of NCATE, published in 1992 in C. A. Grant, (Ed.), *Research and Multicultural Education*. Bristol, PA: Falmer.

51 institutions were cited for one or more weaknesses or standards not met. In summary, NCATE found that after 12 years of standards, nearly half of its member institutions (250 of the 514) had not responded by incorporating multicultural education into the professional education program. Gollnick (1992) concluded that many "faculty and administrators have not accepted the underlying ideology and assumptions for multicultural education. They are not convinced of its contribution to the major goals of schools, or they are afraid that it actually might change the traditional goals of schooling" (p. 237).

School Reform Models. Given the decentralized nature of schooling in the United States, school reform for education that is multicultural and equitable usually is locally initiated. In the metropolitan centers, the fact that schools were in crisis precipitated the first steps in major systemic school reform. The East Harlem school district in New York City encompasses one of the poorest and most devastated neighborhoods in the United States, the place where the term "mean streets" was coined. In this most unlikely place, 26 small, new public schools were opened within existing facilities and organized around new and diverse philosophies. The alternative concept schools grew incrementally between 1973 and 1987 and became institutionalized in the district. Although achievement statistics cannot measure the impact on equity and diversity, we give them here to show that school reform can improve the achievement of the poorest students most of whom are Hispanic and African American in East Harlem. In 1974 only 15% of the students read at or above grade level; in 1988, 62.5% did so (Fliegel & MacGuire, 1993).

The city of Chicago has been undergoing system reorganization through site-based management of schools. Several national initiatives started by educators (e.g., the James Comer Schools Project [1988], accelerated schools project, and Schooling For All), address multicultural education in various ways. The National Association for Multicultural Education that began in the 1980s is a growing professional organization directed toward the practice of schooling.

We turn now to exploring the major tendencies in ideologies and assumptions for multicultural education found in the literature and practice of multicultural education.

Approaches to and Theory of Multicultural Education in the United States

One of the most comprehensive reviews of the practice and literature of multicultural education, which has become seminal work, was published by

Sleeter & Grant (1987, 1988). These authors identified five distinctive approaches or models of multicultural education used widely in the United States at that time: (1) *teaching the culturally different*, (2) *human relations approaches*, (3) *single group studies*, (4) *inclusive multicultural education*, and (5) *education that is multicultural and social reconstructionist*. The authors of this chapter would argue that the most prevalent forms of multicultural education practiced in the United States are the first and second: *teaching of the culturally different* and *human relations* approaches. Both of these approaches can be adopted by those who hold an assimilationist view paralleling the views held by conservatives and liberals during the first common school movement in the 19th and early 20th century. As opposed to these ethnocentric approaches the following three approaches are based on an assumption of the right to self-determination of each cultural group. These approaches are based on the notion of democratic cultural pluralism. Only *single group studies* and *education that is multicultural and reconstructionist* acknowledge the need for a shift in social power relationships for the realization of cultural parity and the abolition of racism, sexism, classism, and the like. The chapter authors would argue that *education that is multicultural and social reconstructionist* incorporates all of the other approaches and allows for the fullest realization of individual enrichment and social justice for the common good.

Model 1, *teaching the culturally different*, is posited on the notion that those who differ culturally from the mainstream are at a disadvantage in American society and economy. The conservative approach is to neglect the cultural differences and expect conformity to the Anglo mainstream because it offers "the classic canon"[11] and core creed of America. The liberal approach is to provide programs to compensate for the "cultural deficiency" of the student. A progressive version of this notion would add that students need to be taught the skills to move at will in the "culture of power," while being given the skills to maintain their distinct cultural practices (Delpit, 1988). Many of the increasing number of programs for at-risk students, early intervention programs, bilingual programs, and other compensatory strategies instituted since the civil rights laws of the 1960s, which are used mainly with students of color, low-income students, and children with developmental differences, are based on the liberal version of this model. A smaller number of increasingly more successful Headstart, bilingual, and early intervention programs are based on the

---

[11]See authors such as Terrell Bell, William Bennett, Allen Bloom, Lynne Cheney, Diane Ravitch, and Geroge Will, whose educational theories are in large part based on the work of the essentialists such as Robert Hutchins (1936), as well as *The Great Books* series and curriculum.

progressive version. The debate started by the Oakland School Board in 1997 on the school use of "ebonics" crashed on the rocks of the afore-mentioned liberal-progressive ideological conflict.

Model 2, the *human relations* approach, also called intercultural edu-cation, is perhaps an even more pervasive practice among educators. This approach views good communication between people of different cultures as the goal. Cross-cultural communication in both the teacher– student relationship and the student–student relationship can be taught by parlay-ing practical knowledge that fosters a deeper understanding of the ways and beliefs of the other and the skills to face the self in order to understand the deep structure of culture in the human psyche and behaviors. A fundamental goal is prejudice reduction and increased empathy for an "other." This approach posits individual change and border crossing for all participants as the path to change. Educators with counseling sensibility recommend this approach to be used as early as preschool and at all levels of schooling thereafter. Those who otherwise have a conservative view toward maintaining the system and core content of education see much good coming from this approach. The limitation of this approach is its lack of addressing institutionalized oppression and privileges per se and systemic change.

Model 3, *single group studies,* refers to educational approaches that focus on the culture of a single marginalized demographic or affinity group. Such curricula continue to persist in the form of secondary school courses (African American history) and even thrive at the post-secondary level (women's studies, pan-African studies, Native-American studies, Jewish studies, etc.). These courses or academic programs, according to Cushner, McClelland, and Safford (1996), have two purposes. The first is "to develop a content dimension, as exclusion from the mainstream material typically resulted in lack of information readily available about certain groups," and the second purpose is, "to help individuals develop a more positive perception and self-image" (p. 39). Such programs also have represented a form of resistance to the assimilationist demands of educational institutions and educators. They also have been resistant to critique advocating infusion instead of focused study. Infusion, however, has often resulted in superficial or no coverage at all, so that content matter was reduced to a perfunctory summary (i.e., coverage "a mile wide and a half inch deep").

Critiques of single-subject education include the concern that, although such programs serve group members, they often do not reach nongroup members (e.g., Anglo or European American students do not typically enroll in African-American studies courses, and men rarely take women's studies courses). They may do little to take the discussion across race, gender, linguistic, and other borders. However, scholarship in successful praxis with African American youth, for example, has contributed substantially to the development of multicultural pedagogic designs (Gordon,1982; Hilliard,1992; Hollins & Spencer,1990; Ladson-Billings, 1992; Lee, Lomotey, & Shujaa, 1990).

The single-group or *ethnic studies'* approach to multicultural education takes the form of culture-centric pedagogy. It is a curriculum and schooling movement. Included in this group of education initiatives are Afrocentric education and some supplementary schools such as freedom schools or weekend programs (e.g., cultural immersion Sunday schools for Korean, Hmong, Japanese, Chinese, and other children, for whom language and culture maintenance are highly prized by families). Indigenous or Native Americans also offer K-12 education programs and schools, a growing number under direct tribal control. Many are conducted in the native language. Native American colleges are developing culturally consistent and relevant educational approaches for K-12 and higher education.

Gender issues have intersected some of these culture-centric models. For example, some work of African-American writers and activists such as Asante, Hilliard, and Kunjufu, has found expression in rites of passage programs for African-American males only (and more recently females only) and in aforementioned Afrocentric males-only schooling in some metropolitan areas.

A special case of single-group education is emerging in the late 1990s mostly in urban American settings such as Detroit, Chicago, Milwaukee, and Baltimore. In the chronically violent surroundings experienced by young, urban African American and Hispanic males in particular, a call for Afrocentric males-only schooling has arisen. Defenders have argued that the social and cultural oppression combined with economic hyper-isolation of inner city African-Americans requires the creation of programs focused on protective and reconstructive socialization. These programs have argued that they are addressing the need for male role models and cultural connections to students' lives, experiences, and futures because they offer culturally relevant curriculum, teaching, and learning styles; opportunities; and human relations experience. The apparent de facto resegregation of urban housing and schooling perhaps makes Afrocentric schooling feasible and constitutional, however, the courts have insisted that these programs admit female students as well.

The last two models of multicultural education described by Grant and Sleeter offer more systemically transformative practices and goals. The *inclusive multicultural education* model is one that many teacher education programs in the U.S. attempt to support. Its goals are to promote (a) the strength and value of cultural diversity, (b) human rights and respect for those who are different from oneself, (c) alternative life choices for people, (d) social justice and equal opportunity for all people, and (e) equity in the distribution of power among groups.

This approach often focuses primarily, or only, on race and ethnicity, or only on gender, and can include multiethnic education (Banks, 1991). It is intended for all students, across the curriculum, but does not argue for an active questioning of oppression or an attempt to transform the status quo beyond advocating that equal opportunity be afforded all members of the society. It includes many antibias education practices, such as gender-fair language, more inclusive curriculum regarding different groups, and endorses bilingual or multilingual curriculum. Diversifying in the staffing of schools is considered part of *inclusive multicultural education* (Gollnick & Chinn, 1990; Sleeter, 1992; Sleeter & Grant, 1987).

Model 5, *education that is multicultural and social reconstructionist*, offers the most comprehensive and activist approach to multicultural education in the United States. "Education that is multicultural" was a framework advocated by Carl Grant (1978) highlighting the redesign of the entire education program to reflect the concerns of diverse cultural groups and the comprehensive infusion across not only the curriculum, but all aspects of school. This construct also includes issues of gender, class, religion, language, sexual orientation, disability, and other forms of diversity often marginalized in existing multicultural education approaches, as discussed in the previous paragraph. The addition of "social reconstructionist" evolved as Grant, Sleeter, and others incorporated conflict theory and critical theories, based in part on Freire's work and that of earlier progressive educators such as Dewey and Counts, as well as on the work of educators in the tradition of transformative, liberatory pedagogy[12] Critical theory allows this approach to deal more directly than other approaches with oppression and social structural inequality based on the interaction of race, social class, and gender (Sleeter & Grant, 1987). Social reconstruction speaks "the language of possibility," (Aronowitz & Giroux, 1985) and does not accept the status quo. It questions typical Anglo-protestant educational values, such as individual competition, and encourages democratic and transformative classroom and educational practices.

Culturally Relevant Pedagogy: Maintenance of Cultural Integrity. A concept raised consistently by progressive educators as far back as John Dewey is being revitalized in the development of multicultural pedagogy. Educational writers are advocating maintenance of cultural integrity

---

[12]For a pedagogic perspective of critical theory, see Crichlow, Goodwin, Shakes, and Swartz, (1990), and O'Connor (1989). For critical theory in multicultural education, see also Banks (1991 and later), Bennett (1990), Gay (1993), Nieto (1992), and Adams, Pardo, & Schniedewind (1991, 1992).

within systems of oppression such as schools and school systems. Scholars advocate enhancing the cultural continuity between home/community and school (Shade, 1989; Sleeter, 1996; Swadener & Lubeck, 1995). Francesca Jackson's (1994) discussion of culturally responsive pedagogy is similar to the work of Gloria Ladson-Billings (1995) emphasizing "culturally relevant pedagogy." These researchers share the view that the responsibilities of educators include creating an environment that fosters positive intercultural interactions and reflects teachers' "cultural literacy," particularly in the cultures that their students bring to school. This could include sensitivity to oral literacy and different perceptual and learning styles, as well as many of the intercultural communication issues addressed throughout this volume.

Another way to frame this issues of cultural continuity–discontinuity between home culture and school is found in Shirley Brice Heath's book *Ways with Words* (1983), which examines communication patterns used in classrooms and homes of both children from low income and African American homes and teachers typically from White middle-class backgrounds. Although the cultural continuity framework has been critiqued (Banks, 1991; Bloch & Swadener, 1992; Sleeter, 1995; Tabachnick & Bloch, 1995), it is useful when examining issues critical to the academic success of children from marginalized cultures in U.S. schools (Boykin, 1986; Delgato-Gaitan, 1990; Ramirez & Castaneda, 1974). Learning more about the cultural expectations (Clark, 1991; Nelson-LeGall & Jones, 1991), preferred learning styles (Gilbert & Gay, 1989; O'Neil, 1990), and contrasting rhetoric (Cooper, 1989; Delpit, 1988) across cultures is considered critical to effective pedagogy in culturally and linguistically diverse classrooms and other education and care settings.[13] It is important, however, to address deep structures of the culture and not artifices of style, which are superficial (Flanagan & Miranda, 1995; Taylor, 1991). In the 1970s, so-called culture-fair testing and related pedagogical efforts were unsuccessful and caused backlash because style was mistaken for culture (Ogbu, 1986).

A well-documented experiment in using the cultural continuity approach to enhance indigenous children's academic success can be found in Hawaii's Kamehameha Early Education Project (KEEP), in which the school environment and culture was modified to be more congruent with the home culture of the children (Au & Jordan, 1981; Vogt, Jordan, & Tharp, 1987). For example children were seated and taught in groups,

---

[13]The theories of knowledge construction and transmission and canon formation (Gates, 1992) have been translated into cognitive pedagogy by educational scholars such as Shade (1989) and into cultural pedagogy by Banks (1993) and Ogbu (1992).

avoiding the elevation of one achiever over others, which embarrassed and frightened the children.

A Freirean approach often provides the theoretical base of such community- or family-centered literacy projects. The object is to reach the learners in their zone of comfort, and by providing literacy skills and critical insight into their position in the larger society, to allow them to liberate themselves from their forced exclusion. However, family-centered programs (e.g., within Head Start, the national comprehensive early childhood program, or family literacy programs) still often operate from negative assumptions about families, rather than directly address structural oppression and education as liberation there from.

Other voices in multicultural pedagogy have included Janice Hale-Benson's (1986) early work and Lisa Delpit's (1986, 1988, 1995) much-cited work on understanding the language and culture of power. Delpit argued that the implicit rules and expectations for success within dominant European American, middle-class culture need to be made more explicit to children from marginalized subordinate class backgrounds such as many children of color. Ladson-Billings' work (1992) on successful teachers of Black children focused heavily on both culturally relevant pedagogy and relational work with students. In other words, successful multicultural education in the view of Ladson-Billings would require knowledge of and comfort with students' lived culture(s), as well as a relational approach to interacting with students and their families.

Culturally relevant pedagogy is consistent with a *critique of Western ideologic hegermony* on the schools that Africentric scholars have developed. Whereas Gordon (1995) advocates the advancement of Africentric scholarship as on *autochtonous science,* K-12 educators address crosscultural and bicultural pedagogy. Authors in related disciplines, such as Bell Hooks in philosophy and Ira Shor and Christine Sleeter in critical pedagogy, add a political perspective. These authors frame multicultural pedagogy as struggle against patriarchal and White supremacist values and structures and as transformative learning, which together form a liberatory process.

Global Education. The National Council for the Social Studies (1982) urged teachers in all fields to assist students in developing a global perspective, to use "the knowledge, skills, and attitudes needed to live effectively in a world possessing limited natural resources and characterized by ethnic diversity, cultural pluralism, and increasing interdependence." For some instructors, global education includes intercultural education and global ecological awareness. However, other social studies teachers remain centered in the traditional world issues perspective. This approach emphasizes cognitive studies in international politics, economics, and foreign trade.

Proponents of intercultural global education practice an approach very similar to that of the *human relations* model of multicultural education described earlier. Hanvey (1978) identified five elements of a broad and transformative global perspective curriculum frequently cited in global or international education: perspective consciousness, state of planet awareness, cross-cultural awareness, knowledge of global dynamics or world systems, and awareness of human choice (Cushner et al., 1996).

Multiple Language Issues.   Bilingual education for students with a native language other than English is funded by legislation passed after a Chinese family in 1974 won a U.S. Supreme Court case under the Fourteenth Amendment (see earlier discussion). Included are Native Americans, Spanish-speaking Americans, and recent immigrants. Non–school-age immigrant schooling is addressed in the section on immigration. Bilingual education is intended to assist students, some monolingual and some bilingual, in learning English and mastering content. How students can best reach those goals has become a divisive political battle in the education arena. The State Board of Education of California, the state with the largest bilingual school program and limited-English-Proficiency (LEP) population, in March, 1998 rescinded its decades-old policy requiring that students with limited English be taught in their native language.

Three types of bilingual education have become established throughout the United States. *Submersion* means simply that students learn everything in English, in other words, they "sink or swim." Sometimes, if there are enough students, they may be "pulled out of regular classes" for English as a second language instruction—again in English—geared to language acquisition. *Transitional bilingual education*, most frequently offered in larger urban districts, provides intensive English language instruction, while offering the students some portion of their academic courses in their native language. The goal is to prepare students to join mainstream classes taught in English without letting them fall behind in subject areas. In theory, students are transitioned out of these programs within a few years by advancing through three levels of gradually increased in-English instruction. *Maintenance*, or developmental, bilingual education, the most intensive and least practical bilingual education model, aims to preserve and build on the students' native-language skills as they continue to acquire English as a second language. Bilingual scholars such as Collier (1992), Snow (1992), Hakuta (1990), Diaz (1985), and Cummins (1981) claim the *maintenance* model is the most effective method.

In the early 1970s, limited-English speakers and educators argued that if schools were not teaching students in a language they understood, the students were being deprived of an education. But more recently, even some Hispanic parents—who historically have been bilingual education's strongest supporters—are expressing doubts. Civil rights and cultural advocacy are now being opposed by concerns of practicality and a backlash against immigration. Opponents argue that the government should save valuable resources—and make an important cultural statement— by mandating an official language. Sixteen states had done so by the mid-1990s. Critics argue that many nonnative English speakers are coming out of the school system with poor reading skills in both English and their native language, pointing at test scores on standardized examinations.

Advocates of bilingual education call the opposition movement unnecessary and xenophobic. They cite research indicating that instruction in the native language concurrent with English instruction actually enhances the acquisition of English (Willig, 1985). They insist that the problem is not bilingual education, but that becoming proficient in any second language takes longer than 1 or 2 years. There is a shortage of well-qualified, fully bilingual teachers, so in many cases the problem with bilingual instruction is not the curriculum, but the instruction.

The issue has become emotionally charged, and pedagogic concerns often become secondary to political ones. The controversial English Only movement has transformed the idea that English should be the only language taught and spoken in the United States into an election-year staple.

Immigration and Schools.   The rapid rise in new immigrants poses an overwhelming challenge for the schools. Immigration in the 1990s has averaged ¾ million people per year, an increase of 100,000 on the average from the previous decade. Immigration rates are highest for Hispanics and Asian/Pacific Islanders (Deardorff & Montgomery, 1997).

Of course, children must be integrated into ongoing schooling. School children from 250 countries of origin have come into U.S. schools since 1984, with Mexico providing and California receiving the greatest number. Districts in California have as many as 55 home languages to address, not to mention other issues related to cultural diversity and discrimination. Even Cleveland, Ohio, a city in the middle of the country, has more than 35 home languages for which the district must provide expert tutors and bilingual teachers. (See chapter 14 on Mexico in this volume for a discussion of binational programs designed to integrate children who regularly move between schools in the United States and Mexico.)

By the mid 1990s, several U.S. government reports had shown that poor children and those with Limited English Proficiency (LEP) are more likely than others to experience academic failure. Most recent immigrant students bring a double disadvantage being both poor and limited in English proficiency. The GAO estimated that the number of children in immigrant households grew by 24% during the 1980s. The federal government funded language related services to 348,000 immigrant students in 1984 and 767,000, which is double that number, in 1994. (US Department of Education, 1995).

The Emergency Immigrant Education Act (EIEA) of 1984 was enacted by Congress in response to the financial challenges facing school districts with large numbers of immigrant students. Although immigrant students in 1994 encompassed only about 5% of the overall school-age population, their geographic concentration in some school districts represented a significant burden for some local communities.

Through the EIEA program, Congress reimburses school districts for part of the cost to educate these children. To have its immigrant children included in the state count, a school district must have either a minimum of 500 eligible immigrant students, or eligible immigrant students must comprise 3% or more of its total student population. The funding for the programs, however, has decreased in contrast with the growth in students served. Whereas the allocation allowed an average expenditure of $86 per student in 1984, it allowed only $36 in 1994. Here, too, the conservative mood of powerful elements in society is reflected.

Let us examine for a moment, however, the educational challenge presented by adult immigrants. For example, in 1997 alone, Montgomery County Schools in the state of Maryland, just outside of Washington, D.C., provided free classes in English for speakers of other languages (ESOL) to 12,000 foreign-born nationals. In 1990, the U.S. Census Bureau announced that 14 million foreign-born U.S. residents did not speak English well or at all. Over the next 15 years, 17 to 20 million immigrants with limited English are expected to arrive in the United States. The Federal Department of Education's Office of Vocational and Adult Education at the present is paying for only 1.4 to 1.5 million adults in locally sponsored ESOL courses each year (Strauss, 1997).

Newspapers nationwide report that poor language integration in the workplace, public services, and the schools has affected not only public civility, but also transportation safety and economic development. While immigration and illegal inflows are accelerating, the public mood is becoming ever more fiscally conservative, tilting in the direction of English-Only laws and anti-immigrant restrictions on public services (see earlier discussion).

For reasons of limited space, other exciting topics relevant to multicultural education cannot be discussed here, such as advocacy roles of parents, children with special needs, sexual orientation, and religious diversity. We find it most instructive to present a brief report of a multicultural education project in action in order to show ideas in practice.

MULTICULTURAL REFORM IN ONE SCHOOL[14]

The photo showed the end-of-the-year advancement assembly for the fifth grade, revealing the lineup of the National Presidential Academic Achievement Awards recipients. Eleven glowing faces—10 White and 1 Black—stared at us. "It has always been like that," we groaned, all of us teachers trying to ignore the contradictory truth that most of our students were African American. This was a moment of epiphany that led a team of teachers to undertake a multicultural change process that still continues to transform the school 6 years later. The story is told in the voice of the teachers on the multicultural core team.

Our school had received an invitation from a group of education faculty at a nearby state university to join a collaborative project called the Institute for Education That Is Multicultural. As a team, five motivated teaching and support staff, including the principal, participated in an intensive summer workshop series that laid the foundation for us to "reinvent" our school community.

The workshop got us involved in reading about culture, social context and education, multicultural schools, and change processes. We learned methods to assess our strengths and needs as a school in a community and the process of designing a 5-year strategic plan of multicultural change. We learned how to be a team of key players in the school. We practiced ways to reflect on our personal biases and the role these might play in the school. We were given the conceptual tools and the time to envision ourselves "as is" and how we could be. The workshop leaders had asked each of us to consider what we would do, if it were possible, to fundamentally change things. It was an eye-opener for me to think about what I *could* do, rather than what I *should* do. No longer was I the object of a reform, but the subject coming up with the answers!

One afternoon, as the team met over a meal at a local restaurant, discussing the racist impact of standard assessments and testing, the opening scene suddenly popped up before our eyes. Wasn't it crazy to keep on doing the same thing over and over again, yet expect different results?

---

[14]A long report of this project was published by V. Seeberg, & L. Chapman (1994, spring).

We had never before been asked collectively to consider the consequences of our actions, however well intended or professional we thought we were. We had not taken an honest, hard look at such patterns of racial exclusion. We had hidden from it, isolated in our classrooms, guilty of not knowing how to change things, afraid to admit the obvious.

New visions emerged in our excited discussion and chased away the paralysis we all felt had dragged us down. We consistently considered the following dimensions of school change: What were to be our new goals and standards (norms)? How would we structure new political relations, and what technical changes did that imply? Sometimes we approached this last question the other way around. Although we did not know it at the time, our process followed the school change model observed by Jeannie Oakes (1992) in successful detracking reform.

With the searing memory of our awards assembly, we suddenly realized a host of related shortcomings. We knew very few of our students' parents: our parental contact was largely reserved for trouble-shooting, the communications were almost solely in writing; the PTA was almost exclusively European American; the overall school achievement levels were very low; our grading process was cumbersome, time consuming, and confusing; and the parent conference was uninspiring and poorly attended. Particularly grating was our grading process. The grading period rather than the internal dynamics of the instruction seemed to drive our teaching schedule. Furthermore, grading had a highly competitive effect. It didn't translate well into some of the more cooperative educational methods or the whole language process that we had been exploring recently.

Relatedly, we teachers had felt a sharp need for better communication with the student's homes. Doing our school scan, we had found little social contact between parents and school. It struck us that parents were not satisfied just to receive a grade in the mail. Parents probably wanted to be included in the process of educating their children. It seemed that our grading methods themselves were exclusionary. Not only were more conferences with parents needed, but these had to allow for meaningful participation by parents and students. The conferences could no more continue in the old form, the teacher-dominated, one-way communication of grade averages.

The thought of more conferences immediately raised the specter of an increased workload. Including parents as authentic partners sounded like long conferences and conversations at night when we stole moments of rest. The team, however, was not eager to return to the paralysis of old. In our deliberations we had gotten a taste of creating our vision for our new future. Hence we pushed on. What if . . . we were to move away from grades? We would be freed from the time-consuming job of closing out books and averaging grades eight times a year. Perhaps that would give us the time for more conferences. The notion of tossing out the grades opened the door to another idea: direct performance assessment. Perhaps we could trade some of the time from computing grades for time compiling portfolios and evaluating with parents in conferences.

So it went. One creative solution led to another. We found that the predominant style of instruction had tended to be linear providing a step-wise, sequential presentation of content and skills, largely in written format. In our school too, by third grade, student–teacher relationships had typically become less personalized, with emphasis shifting to individual achievement and competition among students (Eccles, Midgley, & Adler, 1984). We had felt but had not understood how exclusive reliance on this style did not give equal opportunity to African-American students to demonstrate their achievement. Our instructional style had discriminated against the more holistic, orally based, kinesthetic (Hale-Benson, 1986; Madhere, 1989), cooperative and social learning style of many African-American students (Boykin, 1986; Clark, 1991; Nelson-LeGall & Jones, 1991; Patchen, 1982; Shade, 1989).

In summary, we felt that the change to an alternative assessment method could be seen as a solid first step to changing pedagogic practices overall. The technical shift would necessitate changing the roles for the participating players and the new assessment norms. The parents and students would hold the power, and the teacher would act as a learning coach. The new performance norms would value progress toward a multiplicity of goals, including both learning tasks and personal development. On the basis of the need for a normative change, we had moved from considering the technical and the political dimension. With a bit of nudging from the Institute faculty, we had zeroed in on a moment of discomfort and discovered a general unease with our practice. We had taken a deep breath and reframed the whole discussion into "what if." We were veterans; we had confidence in our intentions; and we imagined the vision in its holistic form. We formulated a consistent plan, and we on the team felt we could do it.

From Holistic Theory to Making It Happen

Having decided to give the alternative assessment project a try, we set up a pilot team: three members of the multicultural core team and two other interested classroom teachers. We constituted the alternative assessment team in the second part of the summer and contributed some planning time. The team designed the goal-setting form to be used at the initial parent– student–teacher conference in September. We pulled key educational objectives from the district, state, and national objectives, including the new National Council of Teachers of Mathematics standards, and allowed for personal development goals to be suggested by the parents and student. This gave us a four-page educational performance assessment form.

The assessment would read "in progress" or, if at 80% of objective or above, "proficient." All of the following activities were put into effect throughout the first year in the two fifth-grade classes with 42 students. The material for the assessment was collected in a portfolio for each child, which included traditional tests and quizzes as well as compositions, experiments, cooperative learning activity products, project evaluations, oral presentation notes, art samples, and work selected solely by the students. For the fifth-grade classes, teachers kept separate records of incomplete work, a common occurrence at this grade level.

Interim reports, traditionally mailed home, were replaced with telephone calls. We also sent home low-score tests for signatures in order to alert parents immediately of possible problems. Three conferences, punctuated by interim phone calls, placed the student's in-class learning experience within a framework of multifaceted home–school communication.

The Multicultural Institute workshop encouraged us to move away from the traditional basal reading program into a theme-based literature and whole language program. This was a direct result of research we had done on using more effective instructional methods with African-American learners. The themes were selected from the State social studies curriculum, Native Americans, colonial America, and early African-American history. We integrated an enriched skill series text, choosing what had previously been the top group's skill series and theme literature for the whole fifth-grade class. We were applying cooperative, enriched learning methods throughout the curriculum, doing away with ability grouping. Together, the instructional style would go a long way toward creating more equal access for all students.

After finishing the design of the pilot project, we turned to planning the political tasks. Because the key players, including the principal, had been in on the pilot project from the beginning, we needed to get approval only from various district level agencies. After the summer workshop, the principal got the support of the district superintendent, in part due to the latter's involvement since the beginning of the Institute. The district's curriculum advisory council, consisting of teachers, and the executive board of the teachers union also approved the pilot project.

The final and most important approval was yet to come— from our parents. During the first few days of school we called our parents to introduce personally ourselves and invite them and their child student to attend an open house to be held the second week of school. In class we also invited the students and asked them to bring their parents to the open house. The turnout was excellent. Nearly all the parents (95%) came.

We presented the pilot project to the parents and opened up the forum to entertain their comments, questions, concerns, and fears. After much lively discussion, the parents agreed by consensus to give the plan a try, understanding that they would have the opportunity to evaluate the pilot project at the end of the year. Then we went on to explain the instructional and curricular changes in reading and language arts.

In planning for the meeting, our major fear had been that parents of the traditionally "top" students would object to heterogeneous instruction. But apparently in the public forum and consensus-making process, the parents felt their concerns were heard and that the favorable opinions were persuasive. It was also important that we had chosen the theme-based literature approach, which had previously been taught only to the "top" group. As a result, apparently no parents felt that their child would be missing out, and all felt included.

In the classroom, we faced some further technical problems. Could we use a program ranging from at grade level to above grade level with children who historically had functioned far below that level? Among "special needs" children, 16% had been identified as learning disabled and were on individualized education plans. Another 20% of our students qualified for the federally guided Chapter One remedial reading program. Working together with the special education teachers and the remedial reading teachers was the solution. They requested the literature books and supplemented the classroom work by giving one-on-one instruction to the children with special needs. We had fundamentally changed the way both learning and teaching were done. We had gone further than we had been able to imagine.

High Five Results

We began to see results almost immediately. First and foremost was the attitude change evident in students, parents, and us. There was a new focus on the individual student and not on his or her placement. Instruction, conditions, and school resources, for the first time, were consistent across the class and equal for all students. This changed the atmosphere enormously. Things seemed fair to the students and they expressed this often. The cooperative education models used in language arts spilled over into the other curriculum areas. Teaming occurred more often. Social studies, science, and special programs and curriculums were taught together.

Daily, we saw improved individual performance, enhanced communication with parents, and much better relationships between students and teachers. As students set goals for themselves, they got excited about reaching them. Because of the more democratic norms in the classroom, the student conflict managers felt comfortable in mediating conflicts. Parents who had previously been uninvolved began volunteering and coming into our classrooms for special activities.

To assess the results of the pilot project convincingly, we felt we had to use normed statistical achievement data (Iowa Test of Basic Skills). In the fall only 50% of the students had scored above the 51st percentile in reading comprehension, whereas in the spring 63% did so. In math concepts, the change was from 38% to 48%, and in math computation from 19% to 21%. In math problem solving, the improvement occurred in the middle set, from the 26th to 51st percentile. There was no change in vocabulary scores. This last result was what was expected on normed standardized tests—the improvements were unexpected bonuses.

The gains in points were also astounding. In every category, an average two thirds of the students gained more than 15 points. The gains, illustrated by the reading comprehension scores, were significant and supported our starting hypothesis that there is a better way to instruct and assess.

The African-American students demonstrated by far the largest gains, which is exactly what we hoped and envisioned. Before this year, we had always taught a tracked ability level in language arts and math. These students spent most of their elementary years in tracked settings and the results were always the same. This pilot project removed the tracks and allowed equal educational opportunities for all our students. The results speak for themselves, and they represents only 180 days of instruction.

Reflecting on the Simplicity of Fundamental Change

On reflection, the following programmatic and attitude changes account for much of the encouraging results:

- Having an ongoing relationship with parents
- Assessing goals democratically and in a way that it maintains self-esteem
- Instructing everyone in the accelerated mode and cooperative, child-centered style.

For us, this was only the beginning. Two years of piloting behind us, we are now moving to school-wide adoption of the changes. After the first year, we shared these results with the site- based management council, and they proposed implementing these strategies throughout the school. During the first year, the core team duplicated the Multicultural Institute summer workshop process for the whole school faculty and professional staff. In the second year, we held in-services to share our pilot project processes, ideas, techniques, and results as they were being reported.

Most educators want improved achievement scores, with no race- or social class-related gap in scores. Yet each teacher needs to arrive at his or her encounter with the paradigm question in his or her own time. Our multicultural core team can keep coming together, questioning, experimenting, evaluating, and improving. In the process, we must share our questions and experiences on a daily basis and during in-services with our colleagues. We can nurture our hope.

Hope for the future arrives in my room daily as my students walk through the door—your hopes, my hopes, their and their parents' hopes. For us, too, now, they are the children of promise.

The university faculty of the Institute may have offered the faculty a hand, but the team grabbed the whole cake too—and therein lies the answer. It is all the same, no matter where we start the process of multicultural change. As long as we complete the whole circle from instruction through assessment to empowerment; as long as we make all three kinds of change, the normative, technical, and political ones; and as long as we weave it all together by the common thread of democratic resolve, we will realize what we promise.

TO CONSIDER

The United States, more than many nations in the world, has made a solid beginning in its attempt to address education from a multicultural perspective. Its constitution, although originally written for Europeans, has now been interpreted as a document that applies to all, regardless of race, ethnicity, gender, religion, or national origin. This move to an education that is less Eurocentric takes time and may create tensions along the way.

1. Review current newspapers from the United States (such as The New York Times or The Washington Post) which, if not available in your library, are available on the World Wide Web. Search for news items that present issues related to Native people's rights, the international community, interethnic conflict, and educational responses to diversity. How do current issues concerning diversity relate to what you have just read? What is the current state of affairs regarding issues such as racism? What struggles continue around indigenous issues?

2. What can your nation and schools learn from the experiences of the United States?

3. *How can young people in the United States be most effectively prepared to interact with others on a global scale? What resources seem to be available in the United States to assist young people in developing a global or intercultural perspective?*

4. *The United States frequently receives immigrants and refugees from many nations of the world. Given what you have just read, how would you respond to the scenario presented in chapter 1. What steps should schools take in responding to the needs of newly arrived immigrant groups?*

REFERENCES

Adams, B. S., Pardo, W. E., & Schniedewind, N. (1991/1992). Changing "the way we do things around here." *Educational Leadership, 49*, 37–42. Cited in Gay in Banks & McGee Banks (1995) (p. 32–41). *Handbook of Research on Multicultural Education.* NY: Macmillan Publishing.

Agnes, M. (1947). Influences of reading on the racial attitudes of adolescent girls. *Catholic Educational Review, 45*, 405–420. Cited in Banks (1995). History, goals, status, and issues. In Banks, J. A. & McGee Banks, G. A. (Eds.) p. 3–24. *Handbook of Research on Multicultural Education.* NY: Macmillan Publishing.

Aronowitz, S., & Giroux, H. A. (1985). *Education under siege.* South Hadley, MA: Bergin & Garvey.

Asante, M. K. (1990). *Kemet, Afrocentricity, and knowledge.* Trenton, NJ: Africa World Press.

Au, K. H., & Jordan, C. (1981). Teaching reading to Hawaiian children: Finding a culturally appropriate solution. In H. T., Trueba, G. P. Guthrie, & K. H. Au (Eds.), (1981) *Culture and the bilingual classroom* Rouleu, MA: New Bury House (pp. 139–152).

Baker, G. (1977). Multicultural education: Two preservice approaches. *Journal of Teacher Education, 28*, 31–33.

Banks, J. A. (Ed.) (1973). *Teaching ethnic studies: Concepts and strategies* (43rd yearbook). Washington, DC: National Council for the Social Studies.

Banks, J. A. (1991). *Teaching strategies for ethnic studies* (5th ed.). Boston: Allyn & Bacon.

Banks, J. A. (1993). The canon debate, knowledge construction, and multicultural education. *Educational Researchers, 22*(5), 4–14.

Banks, J. A., & McGee Banks, C. A. (1995). *Handbook of research on multicultural educaiton.* New York: Macmillan.

Bell, D. (1987). *And we are not saved: The elusive quest for racial justice.* New York: Basic Books.

Bell, D. (1992). *Faces at the bottom of the well: The permanence of racism.* New York: Basic Books.

Bennett, W. J. (1984), *To reclaim a legacy: A report on the humanities in higher education.* Washington, DC: National Endowment for the Humanities.

Bloom, A. (1988). *The closing of the American mind.* New York: Simon & Schuster.

Boykin, A. W. (1986). The triple quandary and the schooling of Afroamerican children. In U. Neisser, (Ed.), *The school achievement of minority youth: New perspectives* (pp. 57–92). Hillsdale, NJ: Lawrence Erlbaum Associates.

Bracey, J. (1997). *The condition of public education in Ohio: Bracey Report 1997 to the Ohio School Funding Cooperative, the Ohio School Boards Association.* [Online]. Available: http://www.ode.ohio.gov/.

Bruno, R. (1997, May). *School enrollment.* US Census Bureau. [Online]. Available: http://www.census.gov/population/www/pop-profile/schenrol.html

Chapman, L., & Seeberg, V. (1994, spring). Multicultural education change: The simplicity of enacting a vision. *Equity and Choice, 10*(3): 45–53.

Cheeseman Day J. (1997, May). *National Population Projections.* US Census Bureau. [Online]. Available: http://www.census.gov/population/www/pop-profile/natproj.html

Cheney, L. E. (1987). *American memory: A report on the humanities in the nation's schools.* Washington, DC: National Endowment for the Humanities Office of Publications.

Clark, M. L. (1991). Social identity, peer relations, and academic competence of African-American adolescents, *Education and Urban Society* 24(1), 41–52.

Coalition for Equity and Adequacy of School Funding v. *State of Ohio.* (1997, March). Ohio Supreme School Court.

Collier, V. P. (1992). A synthesis of studies examining long-term language minority student data on academic achievement. *Bilingual Research Journal, 16*(1 & 2): 185–210.

Comer, J. (1988, November). Educating poor minority children, *Scientific American, 259*(1988, November): 42–48.

Cooper, G. (1989). Black language and holistic cognitive style. In *Culture, style and the educative process.* Shade, B. R. (Ed.). Springfield, IL: Charles C. Thomas.

Counts, G. (1932). *Dare the schools build a new social order?* Carbondale: Southern Illinois University Press.

Crichlow, W. (1991). *Theories of representation: Implications for understanding race in the multicultural curriculum.* Unpublished manuscript, University of Rochester, School of Education.

Crichlow, W., Goodwin, S., Shakes, G., & Swartz, E. (1990). *Cultural pluralism and common curriculum.* Melbourne, Australia: Melbourne University Press.

Cross, W. E., Jr. (1985). Black identity: Rediscovering the distinction between personal identity and reference group orientation. In M. B. Spencer, G. K. Brookins, & W. R. Allen (Eds.), *Beginnings: The social and affective development of Black children* (pp. 155–171). Hillsdale, NJ: Lawrence Erlbaum Associates.

Cross, W. E., Jr., (1991). *Shades of Black: Diversity in African American identity.* Philadelphia: Temple University Press.

Cubberly, E. (1934). *Public education in the United States: A study and interpretation of American educational history.* Boston: Houghton Mifflin.

Cummins, J. (1981). The role of primary language development in promoting educational success for language minority students. In *Schooling and language minority students: A theoretical framework* (pp. 3–49). Los Angeles: California State University, National Evaluation Dissemination and Assessment Center.

Curti, M. (1935, 1974). *The social ideas of American Educators.* Totowa, NJ: Littlefield, Adams.

Cushner, K., McClelland, A., & Safford, P. (1996). *Human diversity in education: An integrative approach* (2nd ed.). New York: McGraw-Hill.

Deardorff, K. E., & Montgomery, P. (1997). *National population trends.* US Census Bureau. [Online]. Available: http://www.census.gov/population/www/pop-profile/nattrend.html.

Delgado-Gaitan, C. (1990). *Literacy for empowerment: The role of parents in children's education.* London: Falmer.

Delpit, L. D. (1986). Skills and other dilemmas of a progressive Black educator. *Harvard Educational Review, 56*(4): 379–385.

Delpit, L. D. (1988). The silenced dialogue: Power and pedagogy in educating other people's children, *Harvard Educational Review, 58,* 280–298.

Delpit, L. D. (1995). *Other people's children: Cultural conflict in the classroom,* New York: The New Press.

Diaz, R. (1985). Bilingual cognitive development: Addressing three gaps in current research. *Child Development, 56,* 1376–1388.

D'Souza, D. (1991) *Illiberal education: The politics of race and sex on campus.* New York: Free Press.

Eccles, J., Midgley, C., & Adler, T. (1984). Grade-related changes in the school environment: Effects on achievement motivation. In J. Nicholls (Ed.), *Advances in motivation and achievement* (pp. 283–331). New York: JAI.

Educational Testing Service. (1992). National Assessment of Educational Progress: Trends in Academic Progress. In U.S. Department of Education, National Center for Education Statistics, *Digest of Education Statistics 1995.* Washington, DC: U.S. Government Printing Office.

Flanagan, D. P., & Miranda, A. H. (1995). Best practices in working with culturally different families. In Nuttall, E. V., DeLeon, B., & Valle, M. (1995) (Eds.), *Best Practices in School Psychology, III.* (pp. 1049–1060). Washington, DC: The National Association of School Psychologists.

Fliegel, S., & MacGuire, J. (1993). *Miracle in East Harlem*. New York: Random House.

Gates, H. L., Jr. (1992). *Loose canons: Notes on the culture wars*. New York: Oxford University Press.

Gay, G. (1971). Ethnic minority studies: How widespread? How successful? *Educational Leadership, 29*, 108–112.

Gay, G. (1993). Building cultural bridges: A bold proposal for teacher education. *Education and Urban Society, 25*, 287–301. Reprinted in Schultz, F. (1996). *Multicultural Education 96/97* (pp. 45–51). Annual Editions Series. Guilford, CT: Dushkin Publishing Group/Brown & Benchmark Publishers.

Gay, G. (1995). Curriculum theory and multicultural education. In J. A. Banks, & C. A. McGee Banks (Eds.), *Handbook of research on multicultural education* (pp. 32–41). New York: Macmillan.

Gilbert, S. E., II, & Gay, G. (1989). Improving the success in school of poor Black children. In *Culture, style, and the educative process*. Springfield IL: Charles C. Thomas. B. R. Shade (Ed.), (pp.275–283).

Gollnick, D. (1992). Multicultural education: Policies and practices in teacher education. In C. A. Grant (Ed.), *Research and multicultural education*. (pp. 219–239). Bristol, PA: Falmer.

Gollnick, D. M. (1995). *National and state initiatives for multicultural education*. Washington DC: ERIC Clearinghouse UD030382. ED382698.

Gollnick, D. M., & Chinn, P. C. (Eds.). (1990). *Multicultural education in a pluralistic society* (3rd ed.). Columbus, OH: Merrill.

Gordon, B. M. (1982). The marginalized discourse of minority intellectual thought in traditional writings on teaching. In C. Grant (Ed.), *Research in multicultural education: From the margins to the mainstream* (pp.19–31). New York: Falmer.

Gordon, B. M. (1995). Knowledge construction, competing critical theories, and education. In *Handbook of research on multicultural education*. J. A. Banks, & C. A. McGee Banks (Eds.), pp. 184–199. New York: Macmillan.

Grant, C. A. (1978). Education that is multicultural—Isn't that what we mean? *Journal of Teacher Education, 29*, 45–49.

Grant, C. A. (Ed.). (1992). *Research in multicultural education: From the margins to the mainstream*. New York: Falmer.

Grant, C. A., & Secada, W. G. (1990). Preparing teachers for diversity. In W. R. Houston (Ed.), *Handbook of research on teacher education* (pp. 403–422). New York: Macmillan.

Hadjor, K. B. (1993). *Another America: The politics of race and blame*. Boston: South End Press.

Hakuta, K. (1990). Language and cognition in bilingual children. In A. M. Padilla, H. H. Fairchild, & C. M. Valdez (Eds.) *Bilingual Education: Issues and Strategies* (pp. 47–59) Newbury Park, CA: Sage Publications.

Hale-Benson, J. (1986). *Black children: Their roots, culture and learning styles* (rev. ed.). Baltimore, MD: Johns Hopkins University Press.

Hanvey, R. (1978). *An attainable global perspective*. New York: Center for Global Perspectives.

Havel, V. (1994). *Address of the President of the Czech Republic, His Excellency Vàclav Havel, on the occasion of the Liberty Medal Ceremony*, July 4, Philadelphia.

Heath, S. B. (1983). *Ways with words: Language, life, and work in communities and classrooms*. New York: Cambridge University Press.

Helms, J. E. (Ed.). (1990). *Black and white racial identity: Theory, research and practices*. Westport, CT: Greenwood.

Hilliard, A. G. III (1992). Behavioral style, culture, and teaching an learning. *Journal of Negro Education, 61*(3), 370–377.

Hilliard, A. G., III, Payton-Stewart, L., & Williams, L. O. (Eds.). (1990). *Infusion of African and African American content in the school curriculum*. Morristown, NJ: Aaron.

Hirsch, E. D., Jr. (1987). *Cultural literacy: What every American needs to know*. Boston: Houghton Mifflin.

Holliday, B. G. (1985). Towards a model of teacher–child transactional processes affecting Black children's academic achievement. In M. B. Spencer, G. K. Brookins, & W. R. Allen (Eds.), *Beginnings: The social and affective development of Black children* (pp. 117–130). Hillsdale, NJ: Lawrence Erlbaum Associates.

Hollins, E. R., & Spencer, K. (1990). Restructuring schools for cultural inclusion: Changing the schooling process for African American youngsters. *Journal of Education, 172*(2), 89–100.

Hooks, B. (1994). *Teaching to transgress: Education as the practice of freedom.* New York: Routledge.

Husen, T. and Postlethwaite, T. N. (Eds.). (1994). *International Encyclopedia of Education.* New York: Pergamon.

Hutchins, R. M. (1936). *The higher learning in America.* New Haven: Yale University Press.

Jackson, D. Z. (1997, January 7). White jive: The outrage over ebonics. *Akron Beacon Journal.* (Tuesday, January 7, 1997) (p. A9).

Jackson, E. P. (1944). Effects of reading upon the attitudes toward the Negro race. *The Library Quarterly, 14*, 47–54. Cited in Banks (1995). History, goals, status, and issues. In Banks & McGee Banks (Eds.) (pp.3–24). Handbook of research on multicultural education. New York: Macmillan.

Jackson, F. (1994). Seven strategies to support a culturally responsive pedagogy. *Journal of Reading, 37*(4), 298–303.

Kaestle, C. (1983). *Pillars of the Republic: Common schools and American society, 1780– 1860.* New York: Hill & Wang.

Katz, M. B. (1968). *The irony of early school reform.* Cambridge, MA: Harvard University Press.

Katz, P. A. (1973). Perception of racial cues in preschool children: A new look. *Developmental Psychology, 14*, 295–299.

King, J. E., & Wilson, T. L. (1990). Being the soul-freeing substance: A legacy of hope in Afro humanity. *Journal of Education, 172*, 9–27. Cited in Gay (1995) *Curriculum theory and multicultural education.* New York: Macmillan. In Banks & McGee Banks (Eds.) *Handbook of Research on Multicultural Education.* New York: Macmillan (pp.32–41).

Kozol, J. (1991). *Savage Inequalities.* New York: Harper Perennial.

Ladson-Billings, G. (1992). Liberatory consequences of literacy: A case of culturally relevant instruction for African American students. *Journal of Negro Education, 61*(3), 378–391.

Ladson-Billings, G. (1995). *Dream keepers: Successful teaching with African-American children.* San Francisco: Jessey-Bous Publishers.

Ladson-Billings, G., & Henry, A. (1990). Blurring the borders: Voices of African liberatory pedagogy in the U.S. and Canada. *Journal of Education, 172*(2), 72–88.

Lawton, M. (1996, December 11). U.S. is big education spender in global study. *Education Week, 16*(15), 3.

Lee, C., Lomotey, K., & Shujaa, M. (1990). How shall we sing our sacred song in a strange land? The dilemma of double consciousness and the complexities of an African-centered pedagogy. *Journal of Education, 172*(2), 45–62.

Madhere, S. (1989). Models of intelligence and the Black intellect. *Journal of Negro Education 58*(2): 189–201.

Mazrui, A. (1986). *The Africans: A triple heritage.* Boston: Little, Brown. Cited in Gordon, B. (1992). The marginalized discourse of minority intellectual thought in traditional writings on teaching.

McCarthy, C., & Crichlow, W. (Eds.) (1993). *Race, identity and representation in education.* New York: Routledge.

McLaren, P. (1994). Multiculturalism and the postmodern critique: Towards a pedagogy of resistance and transformation. In Giroux & McLaren (Eds.), *Between Borders: pedagogy and the politics of cultural studies.* (pp. 192-222). London: Routledge.

McLeod, B. (1994). Linguistic diversity and academic achievement. In B. McLeod (Ed.) *Language and Learning: Educating linguistically diverse students.* Albany, New York: State University of New York.

Michael-Bandele, M. (1993). *Who's missing from the classroom: The need for minority teachers.* (Trends and Issues Paper No. 9). Washington DC: ERIC Clearinghouse on Teacher Education and American Association of Colleges for Teacher Education. ED352361.

Mitchell, B. (1988). *A national survey of multicultural education.* Cheney, WA: Western States Consulting and Evaluation Services.

Morrison, T. (1992). *Playing in the dark: Whiteness and the literary imagination.* Cambridge, MA: Harvard University Press. Cited in Gordon, B. (1995). Knowledge construction, competing critical theories, and education. In Banks & McGee Banks (Eds.) (pp. 184–199).

National Council for Accreditation of Teacher Education. (1990). *NCATE standards, procedures, and policies for the accreditation of professional education units.* Washington DC: NCATE.

National Council for the Social Studies. (1982). *Position statement on global education.* Washington, DC: National Council for the Social Studies.

National Education Goals Panel. (1995). *National Education Goals Report: Building a nation of learners.* Washington, DC: U.S. Government Printing Office.

Nelson-LeGall, S., & Jones, E. (1991). Classroom help-seeking behavior of African-American children. *Education and Urban Society, 24*(1): 27–40.

Nieto, S. (1992/1996) *Affirming diversity: The sociopolitical context of multicultural education.* New York: Longman.

Oakes, J. (1992, May). Can tracking research inform practice: Technical, normative, and political considerations. *Educational Researcher, 21*(4): 12–21.

O'Connor, T. (1989). Cultural voice and strategies for multicultural education. *Journal of Education, 171,* 57–73. Cited in Gay Curriculum theory and multicultural education. In J. A. Banks & C. A. McGee Banks (Eds.), *Handbook of research on multicultural education* (pp.32– 41). New York: MacMillan Publishing.

Ogbu, J. U. (1986). The consequences of the caste system. In *The school achievement of minoity children: New Perspectives.* Neisser (Ed.). The school achievement of minority youth: New perspectives (pp. 19–56). Hillsdale, NJ: Lawrence Erlbaum Associates.

Ogbu, J. U. (1992, November). Understanding cultural diversity and learning. *Educational Researcher, (21),* 5–14.

Ohio Department of Education. (1997, March 25). School funding ruling: The equity gap. *The Plain Dealer,* p. 9-A (Table).

O'Neil, J. (1990). Making sense of style. *Educational Leadership* 48(2): 4–9.

Orfield, G. (1993). *The growth of segregation in American schools : Changing patterns of separation and poverty since 1968.* Report of the Harvard Project on School Desegregation to the National School Boards Association. Alexandria, VA: National School Boards Association, Council of Urban Boards of Education.

Paisano, E. (1997, May). *The American Indian, Eskimo, and Aleut Population.* U.S. Census Bureau. [Online]. Available: ttp://www.census.gov/population/www/pop-profile/amerind.html

Patchen, M. (1982). *Black-white contact in schools: Its social and academic effects.* West Lafayette, IN: Purdue University Press.

Pinal, J. (1997, May). *The Hispanic population.* U.S. Census Bureau. [Online]. Available: http://www.census.gov/population/www/pop-profile/hisppop.html

Ponessa, J. (1997, April 2). Justices reject Ohio system of school finance. *Education Week, 16*(27), 1, 31.

Ramirez, M., & Castaneda, A. (1974). Cultural democracy, bicognitive development, and education. NY: Academic Press.

Ravitch, D. (1990). Multiculturalism: E pluribus plures? *The American Scholar, 59,* 337–354.

San Antonio Independent School District v. *Rodriguez* (1973). Washington, DC: U.S. Supreme Court.

Schlesinger, A. M., Jr. (1992). *The disuniting of America: Reflections on a multicultural society.* New York: Norton.

Shade, B. R. J. (1989). Afro-American cognitive patterns. In B. R. J. Shade (Ed.). *Culture, style, and the educative process.* (pp. 87–115). Springfield, IL: Charles C Thomas.

Shor, I. (1987). *Culture wars: School and society in the conservative restoration.* Boston: Routledge & Kegan Paul.

Sleeter, C. E. (1992). *Keeper of the American dream: A study of staff development and multicultural education.* New York: Falmer.

Sleeter, C. E. (1995). An analysis of the critiques of multicultural education. In J. A. Banks & C. A. McGee Banks (Eds.), (1995) (pp. 81–98). *Handbook of research on Multicultural Education.* New York: Macmillan

Sleeter, C. E. (1996). *Multicultural education as social activism.* Albany, NY: State University of New York Press.

Sleeter, C. E., & Grant, C. A. (1987). An analysis of multicultural education in the United States. *Harvard Educational Review, 7,* 424–444.

Sleeter, C. E., & Grant, C. A. (1988). *Making choices for milticultural education: Five approaches to race, class, and gender.* 2nd ed. Columbus, OH: Merrill.

Sleeter, C. E., & McLaren, P. (Eds.) (1995). *Multicultural education, critical pedagogy, and the politics of difference.* Albany: SUNY.

Snow, C. E. (1992). Perspectives on second-language development: Implications for bilingual education. *Educational Researcher, 21*(2): 16–19.

Spindler, G. D. (Ed.). (1987). *Education and cultural process: Anthropological perspectives.* Prospect Heights, IL: Waveland.

Spring, J. (1997). *The American school, 1642–1990.* (4th ed.).NY: McGraw-Hill.

Strauss, G. (1997, February 28). Survival 101: Learning English. *USA Today,* 9A.

Swadener, B. B., & Lubeck, S. (1995). *Children and families "at promise": Deconstructing the discourse of risk.* Albany, NY: State University of New York Press.

Sweeney, J. (1997, March). *Coalition for Equity and Adequacy of School Funding V. State of Ohio.*

Tabachnick, R., & Bloch, M. N. (1995). Learning in and out of school: Critical perspectives on the theory of cultural compatibility. In B. B. Swadener, & S. Lubeck (Eds.), (pp.187–209). *Children and families "at promise": Deconstructing the discourse of risk.* Albany, NY: State University of New York Press.

Tate, W. F. IV. (1997). Critical race theory and education: History, theory, and implications. *Review of Research in Education, 22,* p. 437.

Tatum, B. (1992). Talking about race, learning about racism: The application of racial identity development theory in the classroom. *Harvard Educational Review, 62*(1), 1–24.

Taylor, S. (1991). Social competence and the early school transition. *Education and Urban Society, 24*(1).

Teepen, T. (1997, April 13). Rebuilding the racial divides. *The Plain Dealer,* 2 H.

Tozer, S. E., Violas, P. C., & Senese, G. (1993). *School and society: Educational practice as social expression.* NY: McGraw-Hill.

Trueba, H. T., Guthrie, G. P., & Au, K. H. (Eds.). (1981). *Culture and the bilingual classroom.* Rowley, MA: Newbury House.

U.S. Bureau of the Census. (1991). *Statistical Abstract of the United States* (111th ed.) Washington, DC: Department of Commerce, Bureau of the Census.

U.S. Bureau of the Census (1997) *National population projections.* Cited in Cheeseman Day (1997). [Online] Available at Http://www.census.gov/population/www/pop-profile/nat-proj.html.

U.S. Department of Education. (1990). Elementary and Secondary School Civil Rights Survey, 1990, National and State Summary of Projected Data. In T. M. Smith, G. T. Rogers, N. Alsalam, M. Perie, R. P. Mahoney, & V. Martin (1994). *The condition of education, 1994.* Washington, DC: National Center for Education Statistics, U.S. Department of Education, and National Data Resource Center, National Center for Education Statistics, 1990–91 Schools and Staffing Survey, "Teacher Questionnaire."

U.S. Department of Education, National Center for Education Statistics. (1992) [Online]. Available http://www.ed.gov/offices/OERI/#NCES.

U.S. Department of Education, National Center for Education Statistics. (1995). Table 154, p. 151. [Online]. Available http://www.ed.gov/offices/OERI/#NCES.

Vogt, L., Jordan, C., & Tharp, R. (1987). Explaining school failure, producing school success: Two cases. *Anthropology and Education Quarterly, 18,* 277–286.

West, C. (1993a). *Race matters.* Boston: Beacon Press.

West, C. (1993b) *Prophetic reflections: Notes on race and power in America.* Monroe, ME: Common Courage Press.

Williams, J. E., & Edwards, C. D. (1969). An exploratory study of the modification of color and racial concept attitudes in preschool children. *Child Development, 40,* 737-750.

Willig, A. (1985). A meta analysis of selected studies on the effectiveness of bilingual education. *Review of Educational Research, 55,* 269–317.

Wynter, S. (1992a, April). *The challenge to our episteme: The case of the California textbook controversy.* Paper presented at the annual meeting of the American Educational Research Association, San Francisco, CA.

Wynter, S. (1992b). *Do not call us Negroes: How multicultural textbooks perpetuate the ideology of racism.* San Jose, CA: Aspire Books.

Editor's Remarks

A close look at the early beginnings of Canada's education system readily reveals a number of similarities between its own history and that of the United States and Australia. Native Canadians had their own form of education before the arrival of the Europeans. In addition to the number of European immigrants populating Canada in the early years, many freed American slaves found their way to Canada via the Underground Railroad. The education systems thus changed dramatically over the years as the French Canadians and English Canadians made major changes in the concept of an education needed by a rapidly changing society such as Canada.

Compared with many other nations, Canada has fared rather well economically, thus enabling the country to generate a number of special programs addressing the needs of some of its microcultures, such as the 70 or more different groups found in New Brunswick alone. Issues related to language and ethnicity have been topics of great controversy throughout the history of Canada's education system. In particular, the questions of whether English or French should be the language of instruction in schools, and the degree to which indigenous issues should be addressed frame the debate. Section 23 of the Canadian Charter of Rights and Freedom guarantees French- and English-speaking Canadians the right to be educated in their mother tongue. In recent years, Canadian educators also have debated a number of issues related to private schools, and, whereas in the United States separation of church and state has been decided by the Constitution, in Canada, this decision has been left to the individual provinces. One particularly interesting controversy in Canada pertains to the "mosaic versus melting pot" theme. Many in Canada suggest that compared with the United States, Canada subscribes more to a mosaic or pluralistic approach to education than to an assimilationist ideology, which has tended to permeate much of the education experience in the United States.

Chapter 13

Intercultural Education in Canada: Glimpses from the Past, Hopes for the Future

৪০ ◆ ৫৪

Robert Fowler
University of Victoria

ESTABLISHING THE FOUNDATIONS

Historically, Canada is a land of immigrants. Sprawling 6,000 km from east to west and encompassing seven time zones, Canada has attracted settlers ever since, as scholars speculate, aboriginal peoples traversed the land bridge from Asia millennia ago. The earliest inhabitants, aboriginals, or as they call themselves, the First Nations, over thousands of years evolved a variety of linguistic and cultural groups. However, it was the coming of the Europeans in the 16th century that initiated the process of intercultural interaction that characterizes the Canadian confederation in the 1990s.

The demographic and cultural mosaic of contemporary Canada was pieced together gradually in the centuries after Samuel de Champlain planted a French colony at Quebec in 1608 and the North American hinterland was subsequently explored by the French. In this process of settlement and exploration was initiated a process of intercultural relationships between Europeans and aboriginals characterized in turn by violence, mutual economic collaboration and, on the part of the Europeans, vigorous proselytism (Magnuson, 1992).

However, the defeat of the French forces by British troops at Quebec City in 1759 initiated a new phase of cultural interaction between French colonists (numbering 60,000) and their Anglo-Celtic conquerors. Thus, through the next two centuries after the conquest the multicultural mosaic of Canada unfolded.

A crucial stage in this evolution was reached by the mid-19th century when the Anglo-Celts achieved parity with the French within a confederation of heretofore disparate British colonies. The remainder of the century unveiled expansion of the new confederation to the Pacific coast; continued immigration, mainly from the British Isles and the United States; and the final subjugation of most aboriginals into enclaves called reserves.

The dawning of the 20th century witnessed new waves of immigrants, primarily from eastern and central Europe to prairie homesteads in the West. By the middle of the century yet more people were drawn by the Canadian dream. From the Middle East, southern Europe, East Asia and the Indian subcontinent, they came chiefly to metropolitan centers across the land. In the latter half of the 20th century, fresh waves of immigrants from China (mainly Hong Kong), Vietnam, the Caribbean, and Latin America engulfed Toronto, Vancouver, and Montreal. All contributed to the mix of ethnicity, languages, and heritages characteristic of contemporary Canada.

CONTEMPORARY CONTEXT

Contemporary Canada embraces a population of 30 million distributed among 10 provinces and 2 northern territories. Since the 1950s, the Canadian confederation has become increasingly urbanized and industrialized. The heartland of Ontario and Quebec serves as the manufacturing and financial hub of the nation. However, economic health of Canada still rests to a considerable degree on the export of commodities: grain and oil from the prairie provinces; forest products from northern Ontario, British Columbia, and New Brunswick; fish from Atlantic and Pacific coastal regions; and minerals from the pre-Cambrian shield of the North.

Politically, Canada is served by a federal system of government with chief political powers divided between the federal (national) government and provincial governments. With reference to the issues arising in this chapter, powers relating to immigration lie with the federal government (except for a devolution of power in this sphere to Quebec which is discussed later), whereas responsibility for education is held by the provinces.

In social and cultural terms, Canada has evolved as a multicultural mosaic grafted on a bilingual framework. The bilingual nature of Canada has had considerable influence in the evolution of multiculturalism both in terms of settlement patterns of new immigrants and development of policies on immigration and multiculturalism in Quebec as contrasted with the rest of Canada. It is important to note that *francophones*, (French-speakers), constitute about 23% of Canada's population and over 80% of the province of Quebec. Relationships between francophone Quebec and the rest of Canada have been strained from time to time over the years. These strains have become more acute since the 1960s with the emergence of francophone national consciousness and a separatist movement now supported by a majority of francophones. In efforts to diffuse the independence movement, successive federal governments have established French as the second official language in the federal system and devolved certain powers to Quebec, including considerable control of manpower training and immigration (Whitaker,1991).

Revival of aboriginal self-consciousness also plays a significant role in the evolution of Canadian multiculturalism. Aboriginal peoples have been marginalized over the centuries as wards of the federal government and submerged either in enclaves called reserves or within poor neighborhoods in cities. However, over the last two decades, although very diverse among themselves in terms of language and tradition, aboriginals have become more assertive in voicing cultural self-awareness and reviving ancient claims to land and resources. On occasion, the more militant among them have manned barricades in defiant expression of cultural self-awareness. In terms of multiculturalism, although enjoying a prolific birth rate (Census Canada, 1991b, p. 165), aboriginal leaders disdain official policies on multiculturalism as, at best, not relevant to their concerns and, at worst, detrimental to their self-perceived special status as the original settlers of Canada.

Cultural interaction between Europeans and aboriginals continues to play an important role in the evolution of the Canadian confederation. Less significant in terms of scope, but increasingly important in the light of recent immigration has been the evolution of relationships between the dominant cultural groups and long-standing communities of African Canadians, descendants of former slaves who emigrated with their masters chiefly to Atlantic Canada and of runaway slaves from the United States who settled in southwestern Ontario. Small in numbers (Table 13.1), these communities have been relatively ignored in Canadian history, except when a few gifted members have distinguished themselves in various fields, or when interracial tensions have exploded in violence. With the emergence, however, of growing communities of Black immigrants, chiefly from the Caribbean, and the benefit from increasing societal

TABLE 13.1

Population by Ethnic Origin

British	5,611,050
French	6,146,600
Western European	1,355,485
Northern European	213,600
Eastern European	946,810
Southern European	1,379,030
Other European	251,140
Asian and African	1,633,660
Pacific Islands	7,215
Latin, Central, and South American	85,535
Caribbean	94,395
Black	321,035
Aboriginal	470,615
Other	780
Multiple origins	7,794,250
Total Population	26,994,045

Source: *Canada., Ethnic Origins, the Nation,* Ottawa: Statistics, Canada, 1991, pp. 12–13.

awareness of these communities in the aftermath of the civil rights movement in the United States, indigenous Blacks are beginning to assert their presence in the Canadian multicultural mosaic.

As the dominant cultural groups struggle for mutual reconciliation and endeavor to deal with marginal groups, they have gradually acclimatized themselves to the reality of a multicultural Canada. Moreover, their cultural hegemony has been eroded by successive waves of culturally diverse immigrants. The story begins with the arrival in eastern Canada of thousands of poor Irish Catholic and Highland Scots in the 1840s and 1850s. It was in western Canada, however, that the impact of foreign arrivals was most striking.

At the turn of the 20th century, the federal government of the day actively recruited immigrants from the steppes of eastern Europe as prospective farmers for the prairies. Offered homesteads in a land pictured in glowing terms as the new Canaan, by steamer and railroad they came, Ukrainians, Russians, Poles, Serbo-Croatians, Scandinavians, and Germans, along with Anglo-Celts from Ontario (Table 13.2). With them came persecuted religious sects, most notably Mennonites and Hutterites. Like

TABLE 13.2

Ethnic Origins of Population: Alberta, Manitoba, Saskatchewan 1911
(Aboriginals excluded)

	Alberta	Manitoba	Saskatchewan
English	97,955	122,798	124,091
Irish	36,739	58,463	53,865
Scotch	54,881	82,861	70,753
Other British	2,571	2,293	2,301
French	19,825	30,944	23,251
German	36,862	34,530	68,628
Austro-Hungarian	26,427	39,665	41,651
Bulgarian/Rumanian	1,956	123	2,336
Polish	2,243	12,310	3,785
Russian	9,421	8,841	18,413
Scandinavian	28,047	16,419	33,991

Source: *Census of Canada*, Ottawa: King's Printer, 1911, Vol. II, pp. 332–340.

their Scotch-Irish predecessors they trekked, poor, mainly illiterate and ill-prepared for the harsh winters and treeless vistas of the Canadian West. Their homesteads, clustered in ethnic enclaves, dotted the landscape from Red River to the foothills of the Rockies.

Inevitably, the various groups interacted in commercial transactions and collaborative support. Unable to speak either English or French, they communicated in various tongues, evolving a patois of local dialects mixed with English. They lived in sod homes, built their churches in Catholic or Orthodox fashion, and lived their dream of freedom. Some, like the Hutterites, pursued a communal way of life in the Anabaptist biblical tradition (Lehr & Katz, 1994).

It was in the scattered agricultural communities of the prairie West that the roots of multiculturalism took hold, at first tenuously but by mid-20th century with vigor. Likewise, later, in metropolitan centers across the country, immigrants from southern and eastern Europe, the Middle East, and Asia forged similar communities within the urban marketplace. The Vancouver suburb of Richmond, for instance, displays the face of its new demographics in the presence of neon signs in Cantonese beckoning a burgeoning Chinese population. Restaurants specializing in Vietnamese and Thai cuisine tantalize palates in most cities alongside more familiar Italian and Greek culinary houses. Sikh temples and Muslim mosques augment traditional centers for worship. Black Canadians of Jamaican and

Haitian ancestry populate classrooms in Toronto and Montreal that in decades past dispensed knowledge and wisdom to young Anglo-Celts, Jews, Irish Catholic, Italians, Germans, and Slavs.

IMMIGRATION POLICY AND NATIVISM

The persistence of *nativism*, the attitude of cultural superiority of an established group, reflected either in exclusionism of other cultural groups or discriminatory activity, historically can be detected both in official policy of government and in the actions of individual Canadians. Official immigration policy, for example, has vacillated between exclusion and openness. At times, exclusion reflected outright racism, as in the exclusion of Asiatic immigration during the heyday of imperialistic sentiment in the first decades of the 20th century. A residue of this sentiment no doubt in part prompted Mackenzie King's government to deny admission of German Jews fleeing Nazism in the 1930s (Whitaker, 1991).

Furthermore, in time of crisis, whether economic depression or war, federal governments from time to time have shut off the flow of "undesirable" immigrants and have even interned suspected "enemy aliens" (Kostash, 1977). Moreover, during these times of turmoil, nativist racism has emerged in the form of anti-immigrant publications and demonstrations of blatantly racist organizations, such as the Ku Klux Klan, which enjoyed some notoriety in the 1930s (Robin, 1992).

After 1945, however, nativism was gradually expunged from policies of government as Canada once more opened its doors to the world. By the 1960s and 1970s, spurred by economic growth requiring an extensive skilled labor force, the federal government enacted legislation to encourage immigration from all parts of the world, subject only to the exclusion of "persons who [were] likely to engage in criminal activity" (Whitaker, 1991, p.20). By the 1980s Canadian immigration policies ranked among the most liberal in the world, although amendments passed in 1987 placed some restrictions on the flow of refugees by providing sanctions against ships illegally dumping immigrants on Canadian coasts and provisions for the expeditious deportation of arrivals whose claim for refugee status had been denied (Whitaker, 1991).

Overt nativist activities by individual Canadians also have receded over time. Deprived of institutional bases for expression (all significant institutions are committed to liberal immigration policies and the principle of nondiscrimination), nativism has diminished. This is not to say that it has disappeared. Subtle episodes of economic and social discrimination occur sometimes in the workplace, in social gatherings, and even in schools.

Restiveness about the inroads of non-White immigration in particular is still evident (Peirol, 1996). Moreover, racial relationships have been strained in the inner cities where Black communities, in particular, claim undue harassment of their young people by members of police forces (Came, 1995).

PERCEPTIONS OF MULTICULTURALISM

Pernicious nativism aside, some Canadians perceive that undue emphasis on multiculturalism threatens national cohesion. Conservatively oriented politicians in particular have raised concerns about the potentially destabilizing effects of emphasis on ethnic pride (Peirol, 1996). Similarly, individual Canadians or groups have expressed outrage when, in their view, national symbols are compromised by cultural imperatives, as for instance, when a Sikh recruit in the Royal Canadian Mounted Police refused to doff his religious headdress to accommodate the traditional stetson (Gualtieri, 1995).

Perceived threats to national unity arising from multiculturalism derive, in part at least, from confusing multiculturalism with potentially divisive cultural pluralism. Kallen (quoted in Lawson & Ghosh, 1986) emphasized that multiculturalism, unlike cultural pluralism, cultivates social cohesion but it, "includes the idea of sharing and building together in a spirit of acceptance and equality" (p. 452).

The development of multiculturalism in Canada encompasses three major components outlined by Kallen: cultural integration, ethnic or heritage preservation, and antiracism. *Cultural integration*, the process of equipping citizens from diverse ethnic backgrounds with the appropriate knowledge and skills required for success in an industrialized state (Moodley, 1995), has characterized Canadian education policies since the 1840s. In this process, ethnicity and linguistic differences are not necessarily denigrated, but are viewed as barriers to successful integration of individuals into the mainstream of economic life. Hence, the emphasis on acquisition of linguistic competency in either of Canada's two official languages.

Multiculturalism in contemporary Canada, however, entails much more than linguistic enculturation and reluctant acceptance of cultural diversity. Indeed, respect for diversity and the right of freedom from cultural and other forms of discrimination is enshrined in the Canadian Charter of Rights and Freedoms of 1982. Moreover, the Canadian Multiculturalism Act of 1988 officially recognized Canada as a multicultural country and allocated modest funds to encourage interracial harmony, promote cross-cultural awareness, and preserve heritage language and traditions.

In essence, Canadian multiculturalism attempts to blend preservation of diverse cultural heritages with social cohesion on the basis of a common values framework, which Lawson and Ghosh (1986) pointed out constitutes the "glue" of bonding. Specifically, this framework consists of a high value on industrial–corporate organization, a highly developed sense of social responsibility and acceptance of cultural diversity, commitment to the ideals of justice, equality and good order, commitment to the freedoms and processes of parliamentary democracy, and finally, an emphasis on nonviolence and peaceful resolution of disputes (Lawson & Ghosh, 1986).

The reconciliation of cultural diversity and social cohesion is a highly complex exercise in Canada, the product of history, demographics, altruism, and economics. In the end, the Canadian "glue," of commitment to the values of a social democratic society, in spite of powerful centripetal forces, seems to cement the mosaic in place.

Concerns of Quebec and the First Nations

Reservations about multiculturalism have surfaced more readily from francophone Quebecers and aboriginal peoples because of the concerns from both groups that the federal government's preoccupation with multiculturalism might preempt its address of their particular grievances (Moodley, 1995; Talbani, 1993). In anglophone Canada, resistance to multiculturalism has been overcome gradually in view of the hegemonic position the English language holds in world affairs. Thus, the ethnic newcomer poses little threat to the preeminence of English in the public forum (Moodley, 1995).

However, francophone Quebecers, enjoying no sense of linguistic preeminence amid a continental sea of anglophones, have been engaged in a struggle for linguistic and cultural survival (Ryan, 1985). Successive provincial governments, therefore, have focused primarily on legislative guarantees for the preeminence of the French language within government and the public market place. This drive for linguistic preservation and increased provincial autonomy has prompted successive governments of Quebec to reject federal policies on multiculturalism and to construct parallel policies of interculturalism, which emphasize the integration of ethnic newcomers into a francophone society (Talbani, 1993). However, toleration of cultural diversity has not been discarded in Quebec, despite occasional outbursts of francophone nativism, and the values that constitute the "glue" of the Canadian cultural mosaic are mirrored in Quebec (Moodley, 1995).

Aboriginals, engaged as they are in pressing for mainstream recognition of their cultural heritage and wresting some form of self-determination from the federal government, also have stood aloof from federal efforts to enshrine multiculturalism. Indeed, aboriginals in general do not view themselves as a mere strand within the cultural mosaic. In their view, aboriginal peoples enjoy special status as the original inhabitants of Canada and as subjects of historical oppression (McMillan, 1992). Their leadership often has viewed official multicultural policies as unfortunate distractions from government's consideration of aboriginal concerns and grievances. However, in the main, aboriginal leaders support the ideal of cultural toleration and respect as well as the values of parliamentary democracy and the rule of law inherent in the Canadian "glue" (McMillan, 1992). In essence, aboriginal peoples do not oppose multiculturalism as much as they view it as irrelevant to their concerns.

Multiculturalism and Schooling

Historically, Canadian schools have served as the chief means of inducting newcomers into the Canadian way of life as interpreted by the dominant cultural group. That story in anglophone Canada begins in the 1840s with the creation of a publicly funded system of schooling in Ontario. Its impetus derived from the vision of a Methodist clergyman, Egerton Ryerson, who envisioned a system of common or elementary schools for all children to promote literacy and the evolution of a productive, loyal, and healthy citizenry. Moreover, Ryerson hoped that such a system would, to a large extent, integrate recalcitrant Irish into the dominant Anglo-Celtic ethos, an important objective for the maintenance of social stability (Katz, 1976).

In the end, Ryerson, like his visionary counterparts in the United States, succeeded in establishing a system of public schools with himself as superintendent. However, the system that evolved in Ontario after confederation differed significantly from Ryerson's dream inasmuch as it accommodated, to a greater extent than the superintendent espoused, the expression of the Irish Catholic tradition in schools. Publicly funded separate elementary schools were created in response to Irish demands expressed through an articulate and forceful episcopate (Wilson, Stamp, & Audet, 1970).

The battles over the forms of schooling in the new confederation were enjoined at the provincial rather than federal level because the British North America Act of 1867 reserved jurisdiction for the provinces, a reservation demanded by all the colonies. Within the Act, however, along with guarantees for francophone schooling, the specific right of the anglophone protestant minority for education in English was enshrined. Hence, the door was ajar for parallel systems of schooling in other provinces—thus the success of the Irish Catholics in Ontario.

Similarly, Alberta and Saskatchewan, on achieving provincial status in 1905, opted for a dual-track publicly funded system in the light of sizable Roman Catholic populations (Wilson, Stamp, & Audet, 1970). In Atlantic Canada, various informal arrangements were made to accommodate sectarian religious instruction in schools, as was done also in Manitoba after very contentious disputes in the 1890s over language and religious instruction in schools (Coates & McGuiness, 1987).

Alone among the provinces, possibly because of a more homogeneous Anglo-Celtic Protestant majority, British Columbia adhered to a unitary system of schooling devoid of religious affiliation, with provisions for minority religious groups to establish private schools (Sutherland, Barman, & Wilson, 1995). In the two territories north of the 60th parallel, mission schools, Anglican or Roman Catholic, were founded and maintained as a dual-track system by the federal government when it assumed control of territorial education in the 1940s (Kach & Mazurek, 1992).

In many systems of schooling the language of instruction at times became the focus of heated acrimony. In Quebec the issue had been resolved as part of the original constitutional package quaranteeing instruction in either French or English to the respective linguistic communities with the provision of public funds for Roman Catholic schools (French-speaking) and Protestant schools (English-speaking). However, in other provinces francophones fared poorly in securing the establishment of francophone schools or even instruction in French. Indeed, public disputation over the issue in Manitoba during the 1890s and in Ontario during World War I exacerbated yet again the cultural chasm between the two major linguistic groups.

The Ontario case, in particular, underscored the hesitation of anglo - phone provincial politicians to maintain policies accommodating linguistic differences in schools. A hard-line position was adopted in that province when the government of the day enacted the infamous (from francophones' point of view) Resolution 17 at the height of Anglo-Celtic imperialistic fervor in 1917. Resolution 17 summarily abrogated previous approval of instruction in French "where circumstances warranted" (Wardhaugh, 1987, p. 143).

Similarly, on the prairies, Ukrainian and Polish communities by 1914 had lost tenuous rights for instruction and even teacher education in the vernacular language (Wilson, Stamp, & Audet, 1970). Children of the polyglot farming settlements were instructed in English with a view to integrating them more closely into the mainstream of a Canadian way of life.

In effect, the public schools in Canada were engaged during the early 20th century (francophone Quebec excluded) in transforming a polyglot population into a reasonably literate citizenry obedient to King and

Country; respectful of authority; committed to values of diligence, thrift and social responsibility; and imbued with assurance of the superior value ascribed to European society and particularly British civilization. Roman Catholic schools, inspected by provincial departments of education to ensure adherence to curriculum, appropriate teaching practice, and use of authorized texts, also served to transmit these values, leavened as they were with a healthy dose of militant Roman Catholicism (Curtis, 1988).

Francophone Quebec, by way of contrast, ensured that its schools emphasized "la survivance" (survival) of French language and tradition along with ultramontane Roman Catholicism as a counterpoise to Anglo-Celtic hegemony and the growing spirit of secular liberalism permeating Europe and North America (Henchney, 1987). The clergy who controlled the schools, culturally introspective though they were, counseled neither revolution nor abnegation of the Canadian status quo. They viewed the umbrella of the British connection as an antidote to the assimilative republicanism of the United States (Henchney, 1987).

For the aboriginals, however, schooling offered dimmer prospects. Decimated in population over the decades through disease and deprivation, and largely confined to reserves, aboriginals were designated by the pact of confederation as wards of the federal government. Their schooling at the turn of the 20th century continued to be entrusted to missionaries, mainly Roman Catholic and Anglican, in a tradition established by the Recollets and Jesuits of the 16th century.

The missionary school, often residential, became the instrument of assimilation wherein aboriginal children, more often than not, were forbidden to converse in their native tongues while learning English or French, basic literacy, skills in "industrial arts," and hygiene (Bull, 1991). They were taught, most importantly in the eyes of their cleric teachers, the means to achieve eternal salvation and in the process were exposed to a "superior" culture. Although usually with benign intent, mission schools practically extirpated ancient values of traditional societies in pursuing the goal of integrating new generations of aboriginals into an increasingly industrialized and highly technical world (Perley, 1993).

By the end of World War I, a framework for multicultural education had evolved in Canada. It entailed elements of both assimilation and accommodation of diversity. Francophone Quebecers maintained, through schooling, separate traditions of language, religion, and values. Anglophone Roman Catholics outside Quebec were generally accommodated in their aspirations for sectarian-flavored schools. Measures of accommodation were overshadowed, however, by increased efforts across the land to instill into recent immigrants the requisite values of an Anglo-Celtic imperialistic world. First Nations' children, moreover, were confronted by intense immersion efforts at assimilation, often in residential schools far removed from family and familiar surroundings.

As Canada's multicultural mosaic evolved in the 1970s, each provincial and territorial school system attempted to deal with problems inherent in cultural and linguistic diversity, generally by attempting to provide equality of opportunity for all students, combat racism, and promote positive interaction among cultural groups (Kehoe, 1994).

Equality of opportunity has been the goal of Canadian public education since Ryerson opened schools to the illiterate Irish. Implementation of this worthy goal, however, has become increasingly more difficult as linguistic diversity has proliferated among the populace. Hence, primary education has become focused on immersion in either of the two dominant languages, an emphasis applauded by immigrant parents who recognized its importance in future prospects for their children (Lawson & Ghosh, 1986).

More recently, however, given the predominance in some inner-city schools of non-English or French speakers, immersion in the dominant language has been replaced or supplemented by the teaching of English or French as a second language. Use of vernacular languages is becoming more prevalent, especially in the primary grades (Henley & Young, 1981). Nonetheless, development of fluency in the dominant language remains a primary goal, and its success depends on a variety of local conditions such as the availability of appropriate learning materials, well-trained teachers, and parental support.

In attempting to educate a linguistically and culturally diverse population, schools have also tried to eradicate racism, which continues to resurface both in the classroom and on the playground. Racist incidents have involved either violent interactions among individuals or groups of students and, more pernicious perhaps, of individual teachers promulgating intolerance (Moodley,1995; School violence, 1994). Schools in all provinces and territories have responded generally through antiracist policies, guidelines for teachers, and the development of antiracist curricular materials (Werner, 1993). Teachers' unions have also taken the lead in developing anti-racist learning materials and suggestions for teaching (Moodley, 1995). However laudable these efforts, they have failed so far to eradicate racism. Nonetheless, the struggle continues and is reinforced by renewed emphasis on schools promoting respect for cultural diversity and pride in heritage.

As a matter of policy, not necessarily always of practice, respect for cultural diversity has gradually been introduced into Canadian schools. Provincial jurisdiction over education established in 1867 serves as implicit recognition of differences in local contexts for schooling, especially recognizing the legitimacy in Quebec of instruction in French. The Canadian Charter of Rights and Freedoms of 1982 has confirmed and extended this tradition. Section 29, for example, reaffirms the constitutional right of all Canadians to establish denominational or separate schools.

By the late 1970s, most provinces and territories had provided for the establishment of independent schools by various religious groups and had to a modest degree entertained teaching in vernacular languages, a reversal of long-held assimilationist views on instructional language. The prairie provinces, in particular, have encouraged teaching of so-called "heritage languages" in public schools (in most cases, Ukrainian or aboriginal) (Henley & Young, 1981). Similarly, in eastern Canada, Ontario's Heritage Language Program has encouraged teaching in heritage languages, a practice adopted in Quebec as well (Henley & Young, 1981). At this writing British Columbia has announced consideration of secondary courses in Punjabi, Hindi, and Mandarin, which may be used for completion of a second language requirement.

Emphasis on the preservation of heritage languages has been accompanied by curricular emphasis on heritage cultures. Most school jurisdictions have developed multiculturally focused curricula in social studies (Werner, 1993). Ministries of education, teachers, university professors, and publishers have cooperated both in the development of appropriate learning resources and pedagogy (Moodley, 1995).

The schooling of aboriginals also has changed with the evolution of multicultural awareness. Teaching in aboriginal languages has been promoted, as noted previously, in the prairie provinces and in the Northwest Territories (Jewison, 1993). Native studies, benefiting from curricular renewal, have been legitimized as a field of study for aboriginals and nonaboriginals alike. (Goddard, 1993). It seems ironic that although aboriginals have held themselves aloof from Canada's multicultural mosaic, they have benefited from a societal drift from ethnocentrism.

CONCLUSION

Canadian schools daily wrestle with problems in implementing noble goals of multicultural education. Although in the last decade, particularly, Canadian society can be judged to have shifted significantly from ethnocentrism and become more tolerant of cultural diversity, difficulties remain in implementing successful multicultural education in the classroom. First, prioritization of goals at times is flawed. Second, often local contexts impede successful implementation. Finally, there remains a compelling need to reform programs to prepare teachers to teach in the multicultural school.

Misplaced prioritization of goals occurs whenever school personnel fail to emphasize survival skills (primarily in acquisition of literacy and fluency in the dominant language) in well-intentioned attempts to encourage acquisition of knowledge about minority cultures. Undue emphasis on the latter not only can detract from teaching skills that the immigrant parents themselves demand (Moodley,1995), but can result in the romanticizing of "exotic" cultures by inauthentic cultural transmitters (Kehoe, 1994; Moodley, 1995; Werner, 1993).

Effective multicultural education also can be thwarted by undue emphasis on racism, which can serve to accent color differences and reify race (Mansfield & Kehoe, 1994). However, as Moodley (1995) suggested, generally Canadian multiculturalism has been correct in keeping relatively silent on race and focusing on the more valid concept of ethnicity and culture. As Kehoe (1994) pointed out the necessity of balancing goals to afford equality of opportunity, promote positive group interaction, and develop pride of heritage. He and Mansfield (1994) suggested that teaching about racism with emphasis on observing discrepancies in power and institutional contexts can be a valuable component of multicultural education.

However, as Moodley (1995) observed, policies and guidelines do not ensure sound classroom practice. Although curricula in schools have become less ethnocentric and multicultural, and even though pedagogy is much enhanced through in-service workshops, multiculturalism does not always flourish in the schools. Instead as Tator and Henry (1991) reported, all too often multicultural education is superficial, providing a veneer of change.

Reasons for ineffective pedagogy arise from the contexts of school and classroom. Occasionally, nativist-oriented teachers still promote ethnocentrism. Limited resources constrain curriculum development and innovations in teaching. Mainstreaming of pupils with learning and behavioral problems absorb teachers' energies. Moreover, problems arise from within the bureaucratic and professional contexts of schooling. The former can often obfuscate lines of communication and serve as an insensitive obstacle to pedagogic innovation. The latter, in the guise of academic freedom and professional prerogative, can at times accord only desultory, discretionary attempts at multicultural pedagogy and frustrate efforts to establish systems of accountability vis-à-vis goals of multicultural education.

Given these contexts, it remains to be seen whether changes in programs of teacher education can lead to improvements in multicultural education. The direction for changes in teacher education seem clear. First, as Moodley (1995) suggested, successful multicultural education requires that prospective teachers conceptualize culture as dynamic rather than static, display sensitivity to and promote respect for diverse cultures, and focus on teaching survival skills required of a highly technologic society. Second, programs in teacher education need to focus on developing skills in innovative pedagogy, establishing standards, and evaluating achievement (Goodlad, 1991). Finally, prospective teachers must be initiated into a professional context that emphasizes skills in collective decision making, community building, conflict resolution, and interpersonal, intercultural relationships.

To effect these changes, however, requires significant modification of programs in teacher education. For example, it has been well documented by Goodlad (1991) that emphasis on group cohesion or collective consciousness (in the opinion of the author, important attributes in establishing a multicultural school), is inhibited by programs in teacher education that offer primarily a collection of discrete courses. Furthermore, in many of these courses preservice teachers must listen to exhortations about pedagogy rather than do pedagogy, an approach to teaching and learning that McGregor and Ungerleiter (1993) postulated as a superior approach to developing an understanding of multicultural education. Moreover, emphasis on passive absorption of information, which in the observation of Ginsberg and Clift (1990) characterizes many programs in teacher education, seriously undermines the development of the proactive, enthusiastic teacher–leader required for the multicultural classroom. Without a doubt, effective classes in multiculturalism, pedagogy, evaluation, and the like do serve in the development of successful teachers. However, efforts of solitary instructors all too often are not reinforced in a coherent programmatic sense. Finally, development of expertise in community building, collective decision making, and conflict resolution generally is lacking in teacher education.

Reform of teacher education is a necessary prerequisite for successful multicultural education. There is some optimism because as Fullan (1993) suggested, the forces of change are afoot, and research on teaching and learning in the multicultural classroom has afforded insights and guidelines. Canada has made great strides in the accommodation of cultural diversity. Despite difficulties in resources and contexts, Canadian schools are becoming sensitized to the needs of a culturally diverse populace.

TO CONSIDER

Canada is becoming an increasingly multicultural society, and it is easy to see that educators have made great strides, especially in the last four decades, to recognize and respond to this diversity. Schools apparently have become quite active in preparing young people for their place in a society that is pluralistic and culturally diverse.

1. *Review current newspapers from Canada that, if not available in your library or local news stand, are available on the World Wide Web at www.vol.it/UK/EN/EDICOLA/quot_str.htm#menu. Search for news items that present issues related to indigenous land rights, the international community, interethnic conflict, and educational responses to diversity. How do current issues concerning diversity relate to what you have just read? What struggles continue around indigenous issues?*

2. *What can your nation and schools learn from the experiences of Canada?*

3. *How can young people in Canada be most effectively prepared to interact with others on a global scale? What resources seem to be available within Canada to assist young people in developing a global or intercultural perspective?*

4. *Canada frequently receives immigrants and refugees from many nations of Southeast Asia. Given what you have just read, how would you respond to the scenario presented in chapter 1. What steps should schools take in responding to the needs of newly arrived immigrant groups?*

REFERENCES

British North America Act (1867) In J. M. Bliss (Ed.), *Canadian history in documents, 1763–1966* (pp. 132–142). Toronto: McGraw-Hill. Ryerson, 1967.

Bull, L. (1991). Indian residential schooling: The native perspective. *Canadian Journal of Native Education, 20,* 1, 118–127.

Came, B. (1995). Montreal police under seige: Four officers convicted in a brutal beating add to a force's woes. *Maclean's, 108,* 28, 14–15.

Census Canada. (1991a). *Ethnic origin: The nation.* Ottawa: Statistics Canada.

Census Canada. (1991b). *Fertility.* Ottawa: Statistics Canada.

Census of Canada. (1911). Vol. II. Ottawa: King's Printer.

Coates, K., & McGuiness, F. (1987). *Manitoba: the province and the people.* Winnipeg MB: University of Manitoba Press.

Curtis, B. (1988). *Building the education state: Canada West 1836–1871.* London ON: Althouse Press.

Fullan, M. (1993). *Change forces: Probing the depths of educational reform.* London: Falmer.

Ginsberg, M. & Clift, R. (1990). The hidden curriculum of teacher education. In W. R. Houston (Ed.), *Handbook of Research on teacher education* (pp. 329–348). New York: Macmillan.

Goddard, J. (1993). Band-controlled schools: Considerations for the future. *Canadian Journal of Native Education, 20,* 1, 163–167.

Goodlad, J. (1991). *Teachers for our nation's schools.* San Francisco: Jossey-Bass.

Gualtieri, R. (1995). Multiculturalism and modernity: The Sikh turban and the RCMP, *Policy Options, 16*(2), 27–31.

Henchney, B. (1987). *Between past and future: Quebec education in transition.* Calgary AB: Detselig.

Henley, R., & Young, J. (1981). Multicultural education: Contemporary variations on a historical theme, *History and Social Science Teacher, 17*(1), 7–16.

Jewison, C. (1993, Spring). Our students, our future, innovations in first nations' education in the Northwest Territories, *Education Canada, 35*(11), 4–12.

Kach, N., & Mazurek, K. (1992). *Exploring our educational past: Schooling in the Northwest Territories and Alberta.* Calgary AB: Detselig.

Katz, M. (1976, Winter). Origins of public education: A reassessment, *History of Education Quarterly, 16,* 381–407.

Kehoe, J. (1994). Multicultural education versus anti-racist education: The debate in Canada, *Social Education, 58*(6), 354–357.

Kostash, M. (1977). *All of Baba's children.* Edmonton AB: Hurtig.

Lawson, R., & Ghosh, R. (1986). *Education and Urban Society, 18*(4), 449–461.

Lehr, J. C., & Katz, Y. (1994). Ethnicity, institutions, and the cultural landscape of the Canadian prairie west, *Canadian Ethnic Studies, 26*(2), 70–85.

Magnuson, R. (1992). *Education in New France.* Montreal: McGill-Queen's University Press.

Mansfield, E., & Kehoe, J. (1994). A critical examination of anti-racist education, *Canadian Journal of Education, 19*(4), 418–430.

McGregor, J., & Ungerleiter, C. (1993). Multicultural and racist awareness programs for teachers: A meta-analysis of the research. In K. A. Mcleod (Ed.), *Multicultural education: The state of the art.* (National Study Report No. 1 pp. 59–63). Toronto: Faculty of Education, University of Toronto.

McMillan, A. D. (1992). Native peoples and cultures of Canada: A book review, *Canadian Ethnic Studies, 24,* 1, 33.

Moodley, K. (1995). Multicultural education in Canada: Historical development current status. in J. A. Banks (Ed.), *Handbook of research on multicultural education* (pp. 801–819). New York: Macmillan.

Peirol, P. (1996, October 18). Ottawa fails to sell multiculturalism, *Globe and Mail.*

Perley, D. (1993). Aboriginal education in Canada as internal colonialism, *Canadian Journal of Native Education, 20*(1), 118–127.

Robin, M. (1992). *Shades of right: Nativist and fascist politics in Canada 1920–1940.* Toronto: University of Toronto Press.

Ryan, E. (1985, February). Bilingualism and biculturalism in Canada. *Social Education, 49*(2), 114–115.

School violence: its roots, interventions and challenges (1994), *Orbit, 25*(3), 28–31.

Sutherland, N., Barman, J., & Wilson, J. D. (1995), *Children, teachers, schools in the history of British Columbia.* Calgary AB: Detselig.

Talbani, A. (1993). Intercultural education and minorities: Policy initiatives in Quebec. *McGill Journal of Education, 28*(3), 407–419.

Tator, C., & Henry, F. (1991). *Multicultural education: Translating policy into practice.* Ottawa: Multiculturalism and Citizenship Canada.

Wardbaugh, R. (1987). Education of the new Canadian 1918 and 1981: Persistence of certain themes, *TESL Talk, 13*(3), 141–154.

Werner, W. (1993). Considering new guidelines for multicultural curricula, *Canadian Social Studies, 27*(4), 154–155.

Whitaker, R. (1991). *Canadian immigration policy since Confederation.* Ottawa: Canadian Historical Association.

Wilson, J. D., Stamp, R., & Audet, L. (1970). *Canadian education: A history.* Scarborough ON: Prentice-Hall.

Editor's Remarks

Mexico can be described in two words: diversity and immensity. It has been said that there is no one Mexico, but many; that Mexico is a land of contrasts. As a nation, it has its strongest roots in indigenous traditions of distinct cultural antecedents, whose cultural migrations and transformations constitute the main process in the early history of central Mexico. For various reasons, some of which have not been analyzed, the population distribution took a specific modality due to the contraction of the mesoamerican border, resulting in movement toward the central valleys and to its southern regions. Thus, the greatest population concentration is in the southern half of the Mexican Republic, where the Aztec Empire settled and became strong. The Spanish conquest succeeded in capturing the key places of the Aztec empire, and colonization began by capitalizing on the forms of domination and paying of tributes already in place in the Aztec empire.

The Conquest influenced Mexican culture in an important way. The arrival of the Europeans broke the ecological and psychological balance of the mesoamerican world. It broke a system of life in order to install another in which the indigenous people were left in a totally unprotected position, without social compensations that could justify their role within society. Within these indigenous societies a phenomenon of apathy was generated toward life itself, which does not seem to have a parallel in history. The Conquest also amplified the multiethnic condition of the Mexican population—Mestizo, Indigenous, White, Black—and set up diversity and contrast as a condition of life. The wars of Independence and the Revolution led to the Constitution of modern Mexico with its liberal position but with a strong conservative tradition.

Modern Mexico has encountered many stumbling blocks, and has not been able to resolve its social inequalities and regional disparities. Trapped in the myth of modernity, it has related its identity to poverty, to its past—which it wants to discard. Thus, Mexico has not been able to resolve the tensions between tradition and modernization in the best possible manner.

Today, at the threshold of the 21st century, with the slow and difficult death of a political system supported by the thesis of supposed or manipulated consensus, Mexico is moving toward a political system based on democratic principles. This is taking place at a time of financial crisis but historically strengthened. Mexico is a nation that keeps looking at the past and its diversity as well as the global tendencies of the contemporary world.

How to maintain sovereignty and independence in a world directed towards globaliztation but with marked assymetrical relations? How to grow without deepening social inequalities and the unfair distribution of resources? Mexico does not yet have the answer for this, but count on their tenacity and preseverance, their paticence and creativity in order not to repeat history but to be able to signal a new era in their history.

Chapter 14

Intercultural Education:
The Case of Mexico

ଛ ◆ ଔ

Aurora Elizondo Huerta
Universidad Pedagógica Nacional, Ajusco

Norma Tarrow
California State University, Long Beach

Gisela Salinas Sanchez
Universidad Pedagógica Nacional, Ajusco

INTRODUCTION

In terms of intercultural education, Mexico is a very special case. Educators within the country have to deal with the fourth largest population growth rate in the world, a long-overlooked and disadvantaged indigenous population with its own languages, political and economic refugees from the south, and emigration from the poor rural countryside to its major cities or border cities and then across the porous border with its northern neighbor. Thus, this chapter follows a different format than most of the others in this volume and includes the following: a description of the demographic dynamics of Mexico, an overview of the Mexican education system, the indigenous population and current programs for indigenous education, policies for dealing with immigrants from the south, characteristics of emigration to the north, and, examples of binational intercultural education programs on both sides of the border as both the Mexican and U.S. governments recognize their respective responsibilities. The chapter concludes with some policy guidelines for intercultural education in Mexico.

THE DEMOGRAPHICS OF MEXICO

Mexico is a complex cultural and ethnic mosaic. Its population of 91.6 million inhabitants is growing at a rate of approximately 2% annually. Even though its annual growth rate decreased in the last 30 years from 3.4% to 2.05%, the population underwent an increase from 42.5 to 91.6 million inhabitants in that same period (Poder, 1995a).

At the beginning of the 1990s Mexico experienced the illusion of becoming a First World country, canceling out its past and, for the first time, setting its eyes on the future. The former mood of revolutionary nationalism with a strong "anti-North American matrix" turned into the notion of solidarity, which accompanied the idea of "a union for change". This circumstance, together with changes in the international system of world and regional power, meant that the differences between Mexico and the United States were not entirely insurmountable. The Free Trade Agreement was like an "arranged marriage" decided at the highest level and accompanied by a strongly supportive media campaign. Mexico joined the First World countries through a commercial association with the "big ones up north." At the end of 1993, the Mexican economy was a very open one, and its process of integration with the North American economy was already sufficiently advanced to the point of being irreversible. Revolutionary nationalism—political and economic—seemed like ancient history. At the beginning of the last decade of the 20th century, the future of the Mexico–United States relation was being built on new foundations very different from those that had prevailed since World War II, which had lasted from the conclusion of the Mexican Revolution until the end of the Cold War (Meyer & Zoraida, 1994)

The outbreak of the Chiapas uprising on New Year's Day of 1994 brought Mexico back to reality. It was a sharp reminder that Mexico cannot exist if it forgets that it is a *mestizo* (mixed-race) and pluricultural country with a strong Indian heritage in which tradition and modernity exist side-by-side. Within its borders, Mexico contains 56 officially recognized different indigenous groups living and communicating in a totally different manner from the mestizo population. To this should be added those Mexicans who live beyond its frontiers, especially those working in the United States and who, in one form or another, conduct their lives as if they were still part of their homeland, its identity, and its heritage. Fuentes (1994) pointed out that Mexico cannot be one of its parts, but all of them. Solidarity, as an indicator of modern Mexico's identity, must signify the acknowledgment of its cultural and linguistic plurality where diversity is respected and can be openly displayed.

In the struggle to achieve greater democracy for the country, Mexico must abandon the modernity-without-a-past myth and accept what it is and what it has been, recognizing its multicultural character in a world ever more varied and pluralistic. It is precisely this neglected multicultural character that has resulted in the elementary school doing a disservice–service to the Mexican population as a whole. Current educational enrollment stands at 14,754,202 children in elementary school and 4,493,173 in secondary education (Poder, 1995b). These figures might lead to the belief that Mexico has been able to assure universal attendance at elementary school as it enters the modern world. However, in 1990 there were more than 20 million disadvantaged people living in poverty, of whom about 2 million were under the age of 15 and had not completed elementary school. This fact, added to the estimated dropout rate for the 1980s of nearly 50%, indicated a major failure to achieve the goal of elementary education for all with quality and efficiency (Muñoz & Suarez, 1996).

The situation of the disadvantaged varies, depending on the proportion of the population living in a rural environment. The 1990 census reported that the national percentage of people ages 6 to 14 years who did not attend school was 13.3%. However, the census also indicated that in some states, such as rural Guerrero and Chiapas, this rate goes up to 19.1% and 27.3%, respectively, whereas the rate for the Federal District (Mexico City) was less than 6.9%. The data on the indigenous population is overwhelming. Even though they represent only 7% to 10% of the national population, they account for 46% of the illiterates in the country (Poder, 1995a).

According to the 1990 census, there were 156,602 towns and villages in the country, of which more than 108,000 have fewer than 100 inhabitants. The great majority of the communities lacking educational services are found in this group. Nevertheless, the situation just described cannot be explained only in terms of lacking services, but also as a consequence of a lacking relation between formal education and the actual needs of small and isolated populations of indigenous people. Another issue is the migrant population. Due to the working situation of their parents, children may spend part of the year living with their parents and part of the year in their native villages. This concerns those adults who leave the country as well as those who migrate internally to find better employment opportunities.

MEXICO'S EDUCATIONAL SYSTEM

Mexico's education system is at present undergoing a process designated as "federalization" that, in its first stage, has had significant effects, such as administrative decentralization of its services. This process has become associated with a struggle on the part of state entities to break the strong controlling tendency of the federal government.

The system's organization at the national level consists of two main parts: the elementary school subsystem, which includes preschool, elementary school, and junior high school, covering a total of 10 years of schooling and the higher education subsystem, which includes high school education, bachelors' degrees, teacher training schools, and graduate programs such as those for masters' and doctoral degrees.

Elementary school education, nevertheless, demonstrates a number of serious deficiencies in satisfying the population's education demands with quality and equity due to high rates of failure, repetition, and dropout. Current education policies for this sector place high priority on increasing equity, quality, and pertinence. With this end in mind, for the year 2000 the school population reaching the age of 15 years could have received 7.5 years of education— compared with 6.5 in 1990—and in the future, the indicators for elementary school education should allow it to achieve an average 9 years of education by the year 2010.

During the 1994–1995 educational year, secondary education's approximately 4.5 million students included 2.3 million students in *educación media superior* (middle higher education) with an academic staff of more than 167,000 teachers. Higher education continues after high school and is composed of bachelors' degrees, specialization, masters' and doctoral programs, and terminal options connected with the bachelor's degree. It also includes technical and vocational education and normal schools in which teachers receive accreditation for all levels and specialties. The subsystem that accredits and trains teachers at the elementary and intermediate school level is made up of 508 teacher-training schools dedicated to preservice education (Poder, 1995b). Here the presence of the National Pedagogic University stands out as part of the university subsystem concerned with the in-service professionalization of teachers in the general subsystem, in the indigenous subsystem, as well as postgraduate studies for professional improvement

Education policies face a serious paradox at present. A significant proportion of the population possesses an advanced level of education, but at the same time there are high illiteracy rates, and a large number of people do not complete primary school. The expansion of education does not respond to the requirements of the economy, nor does it correspond to satisfying the demand of the population. Education faces the double challenge of prioritizing the service of disadvantaged social groups that suffer from neglect and supporting the development of economic competitiveness by strengthening higher education.

In the plan of education development for 1995–2000, greater priority is given to elementary education. The more vulnerable social groups such as those living in rural and urban marginal zones, those who are handicapped, and migrant seasonal workers are also receiving special attention. The indigenous populations will benefit from a particular commitment giving special emphasis to the recognition of their cultural and ethnic diversity, and providing bilingual education.

The subject of indigenous education is particularly important. Its services will be adapted to the needs, demands, and circumstances of local culture and language, urban development, social organization, and forms of production and work. At the same time, fundamental skills will be taken into account, as well as the attitudes and values required in a modern and democratic nation characterized by high population mobility and rapid cultural transformation. The use of electronic means—audiovisual, telecommunications, and computers—is suggested as a basic strategy for remote communities that are difficult to reach. In this way, the equity of education services can be improved without reducing quality.

This policy faces a number of difficulties: an economic crisis in which the education sector has suffered a budgetary cut, and a crisis in the power exerted at different levels such that political motives predominate over the planning of services. It needs to be recognized that decentralization may represent a policy enabling the adaptation of national programs to local and regional requirements. However, the social, cultural, economic, and politically heterogeneous situation that prevails in the country suggests that inequalities will continue and may even get worse. For example, a weakening of federal institutions responsible for indigenous education is observed. These institutions no longer undertake concrete action to tackle the situation of the disadvantaged in an intercultural perspective, and local or state agencies apparently do not have the resources to take up the challenge.

THE INDIGENOUS POPULATION AND THEIR EDUCATION

An introduction to the indigenous populations of Mexico is provided in the first part of this section. This is followed by a discussion of issues related to their education in general. A third part describes recent attempts to resolve some of the problems related to indigenous education, including the Program of Educational Development (PED), and provides a realistic description of the educational background of most of the teaching force. Finally, an innovative program implemented by the National Pedagogic University (UPN) to upgrade the preparation of indigenous teachers with specific bilingual and intercultural emphasis is presented.

Indigenous Populations

Today 56 officially recognized indigenous groups exist in Mexico. Each has its own cultural values, language, and identity, as well as forms of social organization, customs, and traditions. The differences between the groups are also expressed in terms of number, location, and their relationship with the national society. Diverse opinions prevail in relation to the existing groups, their demographic composition, the enormous linguistic variety, and the criteria determining who is to be classified as indigenous. Data derived from many sources suggest that the population involved fluctuates between 7 and 11 million people, of whom approximatly 20% are monolingual (Dirección General de Educación Indigena [DGEI], 1994; Poder, 1995b). According to data from the National Indigenous Institute, 62% are concentrated in five states: Oaxaca (21.76%), Veracruz (11.58%), Yucatan (11.48%), Puebla (11.12%), and Chiapas (9.26%), whereas in Aguascalientes, Baja California Sur, Nuevo Leon, Colima, Tamaulipas, and Zacatecas the indigenous population is almost nonexistent. In the Federal District, Baja California Norte, and Sinaloa the indigenous population has had a tendency to increase because of people searching for employment. More recent data from the National Institute of Statistics, Geography, and Information Systems indicate that, in the Metropolitan Zone of the Federal District, 1 out of every 20 inhabitants comes from an indigenous group—approximately 446,000 people (Poder federal ejecutivo, 1995a).

As previously noted, 26% of the total illiterate population of Mexico comes from indigenous communities. Furthermore, 51% of indigenous women do not know how to read or write, a fact that is one cause of the high mortality rate for infants, undernourishment, frequent pregnancies, and marginalization. In 1990, the mortality rate for infants of the total population that speaks particular dialects surpassed that for the rest of the country by 70%. In some indigenous regions the depressed economic and social situation is much more noticeable, although recently an incipient reduction in child mortality rates has begun (Poder, 1995b).

The presence of indigenous groups is closely related to poverty and socioeconomic disadvantage, which is generally characterized by a pattern of thinly spread and isolated populations, high pregnancy rates, agricultural backwardness, and a lack of housing, medical services, fresh water, electricity, drainage, and schools. Moreover, there is also an epidemiologic profile with a relatively short life span and a high mortality rate due to intestinal and respiratory infections, injuries, and malnutrition.

Indigenous Education in General

Even though there have been some advances in the realm of indigenous education in Mexico, they have not been very encouraging. In 1990 an alarming dropout rate of 21 per 100 students for elementary education was reported. It also became evident that national education was of poor quality and provided insufficient coverage. There was a strong tendency to ignore indigenous languages and cultures. Indigenous teachers were trained in a few weeks with limited attention to their languages and cultures, with the result that schools and teachers that promoted indigenous culture were rejected by their own communities. Parents wanted those indigenous children who spoke no Spanish to be made literate in Spanish. Nowadays, in many cases, the indigenous school is a place where the indigenous teacher is devalued, a place where parents themselves hope that their children will stop being indigenous, and a place where they "learn," because schools start with the notion that "they do not know anything at all."

School is viewed then as a place to be "de-Indianized" (i.e., to lose the indigenous culture), a place where students stop being Indian, and are introduced to the language and national culture "that matters," thus allowing them to improve their lives. It is still common practice that teachers use only Spanish as a teaching language. In some cases, they rely on indigenous dialects for the very minimum (e.g., instructions and discipline). The teacher working in an indigenous community may assume a progressive attitude toward education but still will always be oriented to following the national curriculum.

Bilingual and bicultural education were tried by teachers employed by indigenous organizations in the 1970s, but did not achieve the hoped-for expectations. Even when there were several teachers who assumed the duty of introducing bilingual education, the bicultural aspect resulted in failure. How do you make a dominant and overbearing national culture compatible with cultural minorities that are dominated, stigmatized, and unappreciative of their own culture? Mexico deals with an asymmetric relation that cannot be resolved simply by an official decree.

Even today, teachers committed to making indigenous education a reality have, at times, been severely reprimanded by the communities for which they provide their services. On one occasion, a man belonging to a Mixteca community made the following comment: "School is so that our children can be better than we are, so that they can have an education in order to escape from poverty. And teachers insist on the fact that our children should *not* stop speaking our language and should cherish our customs. In that way they will *not* stop being poor. That is why we send them to school, so that they will not suffer as we did. This is also why I switched them to another school." (personal communication to Gisella Salinas, April 20, 1995).

Therefore, after centuries of domination and stigmatization, many indigenous parents believe that their community is not cultivated, and that its culture and language represent an obstacle to achieving access to the benefits of the national society. This is evidenced by the large number of indigenous teachers who send their own children to nonindigenous schools and, based on their own mastery of Spanish, make sure that their children do not use their native languages. Neither political declarations nor advances in legislation have encouraged the generalization of education practices by which cultural diversity is effectively recognized and given value, and a balanced bilingualism sought.

Often, the imparted education does not recognize the fact that indigenous children (as well as all other children) have acquired knowledge outside school that will stay with them for life. That is why such knowledge is valuable and meaningful, even when it is different or even contradictory to the knowledge mandated by the national curriculum. Some examples of this knowledge would be the cultivation of plants, the way to carry out the harvest, the relation of movements between the sun and the moon, the working organization of society by gender or generations, and the qualities that distinguish between good and evil. At times, indigenous languages are not appreciated and are considered by some teachers as dialects. They are repeatedly described as languages that cannot be used in teaching because textbooks for them do not exist, and because there are difficulties in standardizing their spelling. These languages may also be restricted by a lack of words to describe some subjects.

On many occasions, forms of appropriation and transmittal that indigenous communities possess are not recognized as valid. In other words, it would seem that the only education process that is valued is the one provided by academic communities, and that the education strategies of indigenous communities are not considered meaningful, as far as what they teach and the way they are taught, even when they represent learning for life. The indigenous school is considered as a place that intends to erase differences and looks for the formation of an integrated individual who possesses a certain mastery of knowledge, competence, and behaviors that do not necessarily place value on cultural diversity and the respect of values typical of other communities.

The indigenous school, an intercultural place by nature, seems occasionally to convert itself into an authoritarian place in a double sense. An attempt is made to eradicate differences in identity, from the beginning, by the predominance of national content, and by resorting to teaching and learning processes that are foreign to the community. It is also a place where the teachers' authoritarianism comes to the fore, particularly those who claim to have committed themselves to the reevaluation of languages and indigenous cultures. If the population does not place any value on what is theirs; if it does not find the essence of its culture; if the "others" do not stop looking at indigenous culture as something different, inferior, or subordinate because its knowledge only forms part of folklore and not of the nation's cultural riches, then the teacher's good intentions for insisting on the richness of what belongs to the community might be considered as authoritarian attitudes that can lead to conflicts between the school and the community.

Indigenous Education: Current Issues and Special Programs

According to data from the first report of the government of Ernesto Zedillo, at the initial education level 23,743 indigenous adults and 21,007 children between the ages of 0 and 4 were served in the 1994–1995 school cycle. At the preschool level, 252,260 indigenous children received education in 7,254 centers in the same number of villages and towns, with 11,663 teachers serving a population speaking 41 indigenous languages in 23 states. At the elementary school level, 669,000 students from 44 different language groups and some variants were enrolled in 7,521 indigenous communities or 7,581 schools, with a staff of 27,382 teachers working in different kinds of schools (Zedillo,1995).

The indigenous primary education schools are attended by 351,983 boys and 317,026 girls, but boys are more likely to reach the sixth grade (31,844 boys, 27,646 girls). However, statistics show that girls have a lower failure rate than boys, with 50,715 boys and 40,767 girls dropping out at the beginning of the 1994–1995 school year. Indigenous children's ages at the elementary school level range from 5 to 15 years. In adult education, 69,391 Indians became literate, 33,195 of them in their own language and in dialectical variants of 15 groups in the country (DGEI, 1995).

To resolve the complex problems of educating indigenous children in accordance with Article 4 of the Constitution, which states that the Mexican nation has a pluricultural composition originally represented by its indigenous communities, and in keeping with the Federal Education Law (Ley General de Educación, 1994), which establishes the right of indigenous people's to have an education that responds to their linguistic and cultural characteristics, the Program of Educational Development (PED) for 1995–2000 was created. This program proposes an education that would be adequate to face life's circumstances and the great necessities of indigenous people, and that, at the same time, would lay the foundations of the fundamental skills, attitudes, and values required by a modern democratic nation. A nation characterized by the intense mobility of its population and rapid cultural transformations due to the cultural and linguistic diversity of its indigenous people requires great flexibility in educational actions, according to the needs and expectations of populations at the community and microregional level. Thus, the Program of Educational Development is willing to combat manifest or latent forms of racism and intolerance, and to promote a just appreciation of indigenous contributions to the historic construction of the nation, recognizing through these contributions that Mexicans carry out their lives in diverse ways.

Many shortcomings in the education of indigenous groups derive from an inadequate educational and cultural approach that simply reproduces the type of teaching used in urban schools. Seldom are the knowledge and behaviors pertaining to each ethnic group incorporated into the curriculum as learning content, and only on rare occasions are indigenous languages used to provide instruction. With respect to these problems, the Program of Educational Development proposes to promote the initial learning of reading and writing in the mother tongue during the early grades and to advance, when the first improvements allow it, to the teaching of oral and written Spanish as a second language. In the higher educational grades, the use of Spanish will be consolidated, but the program also will maintain mother tongue. To launch this strategy, teachers' linguistic competencies must be improved as a means of recognizing the situation of a particular community, together with its educational aspirations.

An additional highly significant outcome of current efforts in indigenous elementary education is book production. The Ministry of Education (SEP), in collaboration with educational experts and indigenous representatives, has produced books in 47 languages and dialectical variants. These materials are designed to transmit literature, to inform, and to support practical goals in promoting indigenous languages, contributing to limiting linguistic attrition in many regions. However, these materials are not always available to or used by teachers.

Last, but by no means unimportant, a fundamental element in indigenous education is its teachers, for whom some training problems need to be recognized. Some teachers have benefited from teacher training school studies (generally open or semi-institutionalized), but most of them were accredited in 3- to 6-month courses called Introduction to Teaching Practice. Some teachers had no more than 15 days of teaching practice before they were sent to work after receiving their certificate of enrollment!

Putting the indigenous education system together was not an easy task. Among other things, there were not enough young people available who met the required academic standards and could be enrolled as teachers. In the beginning, secondary school graduates were certified to teach, whereas there were some who had barely completed elementary schooling. Little by little the teachers' level of schooling reached the level of the high school certificate, and more teachers with "normal" school studies were also recruited. One outstanding fact mentioned on numerous occasions by teachers in indigenous education, however, is that most of their teacher education courses did not take place in teacher training centers. There still exist some practicing teachers who have completed only elementary school studies. Others have intermediate studies, whereas only the smallest percentage has university studies or certification.

On many occasions, aspirants have succeeded in becoming teachers by their own personal efforts, a fact that demonstrates the difficulties facing the indigenous population in obtaining access to education. Some enter schools late; some attend schools with incomplete classes; some have to live in hostels away from their families; some go to cities to work as waiters or waitresses so they can complete their elementary schooling and then undertake their secondary education in night school. Even so, their schooling may be irregular. On many occasions in the past, they did not have textbooks, and their teachers took on the task of *castellanizarlo* (i.e., obliging them to learn Spanish by using such methods as fines, extra duties, corporal punishment, shaving heads, suspension, etc.) Unfortunately, some of these experiences still occur today.

Almost none of these teachers had access to preschool education. Most of them remembered the stigma of being indigenous and of finding in education a way of not being indigenous anymore. Perhaps because of this, they adopt similar attitudes in their own teaching. In many communities, they are considered *Ladinos,* that is people of indigenous culture who have used their government positions at the expense of their own culture. However, in spite of the influence of *Ladinas,* the contribution at many teachers has been very significant in the construction of indigenous education.

Teacher Preparation: The Innovative Program of the National Pedagogic University

At the national level, teachers involved in the education of indigenous people are those with a more diverse professional profile. With the purpose of raising the education level of indigenous working teachers, in 1990 the National Pedagogical University (UPN), in collaboration with the General Directorate of Indigenous Education, designed a program that would cater to their training needs. During the 1994–1995 school year, the UPN enrolled 11,304 teachers (26.5% of the total staff for indigenous education) in 73 centers located near the indigenous communities with the intention of raising the quality of education provided to indigenous groups, thus attempting to launch intercultural and bilingual education.

Initial evaluation of the program has illustrated the great importance of professional education for indigenous teachers. One outcome has been increased appreciation of their ethnic identity. Since these teachers were incorporated into the university teaching programs (not without conflict from some sectors), they have taken another look at their indigenous identity. This is manifested by their participation in diverse cultural, community, and institutional activities resulting in the promotion of indigenous languages and the production of texts, and their use in diverse ceremonies and public activities. The results of this process also account for the strengthening and revival of some languages and indigenous cultures. In different forms and levels, some teachers who did not speak their native tongue or had an incomplete knowledge of it are now relearning it.

Some reports inform us that as parents (and most indigeuous education teachers are), they are beginning to teach their children in their native tongue. Furthermore, indigenous education teachers who were incorporated into this program have begun to project a different self-image and to identify with particular characteristics of their teaching career. They have begun to feel more secure as teachers, to give more value to their work with children and in indigenous communities, and to visualize the possibility of a worthy professional career as teachers within the indigenous system. At the same time, they have improved their relationship with the community and have strengthened academic quality in the school zone and region (Salinas, 1996).

However, it must be pointed out much still needs to be done. Of the total number of teachers working in indigenous elementary schools, 66.18% have not benefited from higher education, and within the pre-school staff, this percentage reaches 64% (DGEI, 1995). Moreover, the teacher training processes do not lead to immediate changes, and deeply rooted education practices of indigenous teaching, such as resorting to Spanish, are difficult to eradicate, not necessarily because of teachers' actions but due to community pressure. At the same time, a period of university attendance does not guarantee that language and indigenous cultures will be viewed favorably. Mexico needs to recognize the limits of educational action. The training of indigenous teachers and the creation of indigenous schools cannot overcome by itself the stigma of "Indianidad", and the expression of racist and discriminatory attitudes toward the indigenous population.

Finally, attention has been given to the vast numbers of indigenous children and teenagers living in urban zones. This implied the training of urban teachers to provide adapted education services that give due heed to their origins, needs, and circumstances with respect to their language and culture and the use of indigenous materials developed by the Ministry of Education.

Indigenous education cannot be removed from the ongoing national debate about indigenous people's rights in the context of the January 1994 uprising and the subsequent peace negotiations. Some of the proposals by the 56 ethnic groups forming the Mexican indigenous mosaic are attempts to consider plural or intercultural education as a constitutional right or as concepts that surpass bilingual education and imply the respect of cultural values. Fulfilling this initiative would require an amendment to the third article of the Constitution to include, among other rights, access to intercultural and bilingual education (Instituto de investigaciones juridicas, 1996).

The subject of indigenous education includes the way that urban nonindigenous children regard those who are indigenous. Soon after the Chiapas uprising, many teachers had to revise lessons about indigenous groups that mentioned them solely as a feature of the past. Teachers and nonindigenous children were amazed to discover that there were still "live" Mayans surviving in situations of extreme poverty, far removed from the way "historic Mayans" were portrayed in school books as people enjoying an era of great cultural splendor.

Political speeches and education practices seem to be pointless if there is no national recognition of cultural and linguistic diversity. Mexico should stop thinking about indigenous people as human beings without knowledge or values who simply are waiting for what nonindigenous people can give them, and waiting to become part of the nation that denies them their identity, waiting to stop being indigenous and without any rights to their own culture and values being expressed in different spheres (not only at school). There is also a desperate need to resolve socioeconomic differences while respecting cultural and linguistic diversity.

As Hererra (1995) pointed out, one of the most obvious "bottlenecks" in intercultural–bilingual education is in the move from theory to practice, from intentions to reality, and from rhetoric to an implementing of the law and a changing of daily community life. But without any doubt, the most fundamental element is the involvement of the indigenous community itself in the definition of educational projects for children and youth in accordance with their expectations and realities. In this respect, Gigante (1994) noted that even though Mexico has been a leader in linguistics and education policies for the indigenous population, educational situations as well as the different curricular proposals show that there is a great gap between the setting forth of that fundamental program and its educational implementation.

Put another way, the stigma of "Indianization" will not disappear merely with the introduction of educational projects because to be able to offer a true intercultural–bilingual education, the involvement of others—nonindigenous partners—is required as well. This is especially true of those who, in the past, have negated and patronized the indigenous people, their languages, and their culture. Why not teach nonindigenous children something about the culture, values, and language of existing indigenous groups and not just tell them about Indians in the great classic civilizations of the past? That is the major challenge of indigenous education.

In this sense, the Program for Educational Development also has a vision that is still in the proposal stage: to ensure that the different syllabi and curricula convey a just and balanced vision of the actual situation of indigenous groups and show the significance of the indigenous groups in the conformation of Mexico as a mestizo country.

MIGRATION INTO MEXICO
AND RELATED EDUCATIONAL POLICIES

Foreigners entering Mexico are not as numerous as Mexicans who emmigrate. The major flows of immigrants have been refugees from the Civil War in Spain at the end of the 1930s, political refugees expelled by military governments in South America at the beginning of the 1970s, and exiles from the political conflicts and violence in Guatemala, El Salvador, and Nicaragua during the 1970s and 1980s. Foreign residents amounted to 280,000 in 1980 and not more than 400,000 in 1990. Whereas Mexicans who travel to the United States do so because there is a demand for manual labor, Central Americans arrive in Mexico as a transitory destination or seeking a political refuge, but hardly with the expectation of improving their economic situation. Their language, physical features, and customs are not so different from Mexican characteristics, a fact that makes it very difficult to distinguish between immigrants and Mexicans.

Thus, it is very easy for immigrants to enter the country unnoticed looking for lodging and some kind of manual labor. Given the very lax procedures in the country regarding the issuance of birth certificates and identity papers, it is not difficult for these immigrants to acquire all the necessary documentation to survive in the country. In addition, they do not encounter racist attitudes or strong discrimination in the communities where they reside. In the 1980s Mexico received a massive exodus of Guatemalans, and as a result of agreements between the two countries, a new program was launched that would locate these groups at camp sites where they would receive general services, housing, formal education, access to land in order to cultivate crops, and so on. Their physical movement was limited to a small zone with a sign indicating that they would forfeit their rights if they went outside this area. Residents could work in nearby areas. This precipitated a crisis in the Chiapas region because Guatemalans, in order to survive, had cornered the labor market, a situation that made life difficult for Chiapans. The situation, however, never degenerated into open conflict.

These living conditions have generated painful and contradictory situations. On the one hand, these immigrants enjoy good living conditions due to their isolation, maintaining their identity with their own ethnic groups and their country and expressing a strong desire to return, even though they may legally stay in Mexico. On the other hand, their children are granted Mexican nationality and do not identify themselves with their parents' nationality. They are happy to stay in Mexico. The situation is attributable in part to the formal education provided by the Mexican Government to the children at the camp sites, which lacks any intercultural perspectives and is strongly in favor of assimilation.

Nongovernmental organizations, relying on foreign support, have dedicated themselves to offering informal education, with consent from the respective authorities, establishing rescue programs for the Guatemalan culture, bilingual education, education for the promotion of mental health and communal organizations, and so forth. All this has been done with the sole idea of giving these migrants an education so they could return home without being faced with a contradiction between the desires of the parents and their offspring, and without the rejection that the Guatemalan community in the country of origin felt toward those living in camp sites. This rejection was based on the idea that these refugees had escaped the Guatemalan War and its consequences, that they had enjoyed "good living conditions" and would now return home to a piece of land promised by the government, protected by infrastructures, training, and the like. Meanwhile, those who had stayed behind may have sacrificed life, family, land, and work, and were now treated as subjects with no rights compared with the well-being afforded the groups of returning refugees (Jascott, 1993).

The National Migration Institute considers Mexico a country that while losing migrants, is also a country of destination and transit. It claims to sustain a comprehensive policy of protecting migrants both inside and outside the country. Such a policy is supposed to be upheld through the protection of human rights and people's physical integrity. Mexico believes that crime rates are not necessarily a responsibility of migrant groups, but of criminal groups that see migrants as easy victims due to their psychologic and material circumstances.

In 1990, the BETA Group was created to protect migrants and respond to the crime rate that had risen around transient geographic zones. This group was described by the National Commission on Human Rights as an honest and efficient police body. These qualifications were derived from its way of operating, which included training, salaries, and permanent supervision. At present, the Institute ostensibly has three main objectives: encouragement of migratory flows that benefit national development, safer borders, and improvement of the quality of migratory services through respect for the law and human rights.

In regard to the first objective, there is an ample margin of discretion in deciding whether immigration complies with these principles or not. In regard to the second objective, the Mexican authorities maintain political contacts on both sides of the border, with particular attention to the southern zone due to the permanent state of war in Central America and the ease of crossing the border. Regarding the third objective, there is talk about giving a permit to the agricultural seasonal worker who travels across the border to work in coffee fields mainly in Chiapas, Veracruz, and Tabasco. This scheme would establish treaties and agreements with national producers. The objective seems to be more a future goal than an achievement because there are serious conflicts in the region between the rural owners (*latifundistas*) and the rural indigenous population. These conflicts are connected with exploitation of the work force accompanied by unfair human rights practices, a situation that today has become serious due to the power crisis of the PRI (Partido Revolucionario Institucional) government and the advancement of the democratic movement.

Mexican legislation does not facilitate the procedures to legalize residence. In fact, Mexico has not signed the United Nations Declaration recognizing economic refuge. In July 1990, Mexico adopted the General Population Law under strong pressure from nongovernmental organizations (NGOs) so as to include the category of action refugee after the enactment of restrictive regulation in 1992. However, not everyone coming from Central America into Mexico is a political refugee. Many claim the right to live and not to starve, arriving in Mexico as a bridge for passing on to the United States. These people, in many instances, are arrested, abused, and deported as common criminals by the immigration authorities. Such actions are seen by nongovernmental organizations as a result of agreements with the U.S. government seeking a more efficient control of migratory flows (Elizondo, 1996).

EMIGRATION FROM MEXICO
AND INTERCULTURAL EDUCATION

The migration of Mexicans toward the United States started in the first half of the last century and began to intensify during the revolutionary period, reaching its highest levels in recent years. Between 1910 and 1919 about 200,000 people, mainly natives from Jalisco, Michoacan, and Guanajato, moved to Texas, Arizona and California to work in agricultural activities, to lay railroad tracks, or, on a lesser scale, to enter industry. Two events that took place between 1920 and 1940 restricted both the Mexican ingress to the United States and the exit of a large number of Mexican workers from that country: the end of the World War I and the economic crisis of 1929. These circumstances led to the reduction of Mexican immigration between 1930 and 1940. Mexicans began migrating to the United States again during World War I.

According to recent estimates, in 1950, 1960, and 1970 the number of Mexicans living in the United States was approximately 630,000, 834,000, and 1,399,000, respectively. From the 1970s on, the number of residents multiplied rapidly. In 1980, there were more than 2.5 million, and by 1990, 4.5 million. This figure amounts to slightly more than 5.4% of the total population of Mexico. In 1990, it was calculated that there were about 15 million Mexican Americans, between 2 and 3 million illegal workers and that this figure was increasing by 100,000 to 200,000 per year (El Financiero, 1996).

The evolution of Mexican migration toward the United States shows that the stereotype about immigrants is no longer correct: Mexican immigrants are coming from not only rural areas in the center, the north, and the west of the country, and they are not just agricultural workers with little or no schooling in search of temporary or seasonal work. It is possible that the change in the immigrant composition had begun to take place toward the latter part of the 1960s and the beginning of the 1970s, but it intensified during the 1980s due to four main factors: (a) the Mexican economic crisis during 1980–1990 accented migratory pressures, (b) changes in the North American economy affecting the magnitude and profile of the demand for migrant workers in the United States, (c) legislation passed by the United States Congress in 1986 precipitating decisions to emigrate that perhaps would not have taken place without this law, and (d) the consolidation of social functional networks linking places of origin to places of destination. Regarding this last factor, it has been pointed out that once the Mexican population in the United States reached a certain level, the continuous expansion of social networks produced a reduction in costs and risks associated with international movement and increased the probability of a successful outcome, thus giving the migratory movement a powerful impulse.

The concurrence of these factors has helped to bring about some significant changes in the dynamic composition of the illegal immigration phenomenon: A growing regional diversification of migration toward the United States is evident. It is now accepted that the geographic origin of

Mexican immigrants has extended beyond traditional migration origins: Jalisco, Michoacan, Zacatecas, Durango and Chihuahua. Particularly noteworthy is the contingent of people coming from the metropolitan zone of Mexico City. The migration of women and children has reached a peak. More frequently, complete families move, stimulated by the desire for family reunification.

A growing occupational and sectarian diversification is evident among immigrants in both the United States in Mexico. It is evident that immigrants who carry out an agricultural occupation in their place of origin are no longer a majority. The stays of immigrants in the neighboring country gradually have been getting longer. Almost two thirds of Mexican immigrants who reside in California, protected by the 1986 immigration law, have 10 years or more of residence in North America. The economic impact of this migration is not to be overlooked because, according to data from the Bank of Mexico, the country receives U.S. $3,763,000 of revenue per annum sent "home" by 2.5 million illegal Mexican immigrants (El Financiero, 1996).

The following profile of this migration emerges: (a) the majority of immigrants are male (83%), (b) The age range of the immigrants is concentrated at the time of life when economic activity is fundamental: between the ages of 15 and 44 (96.2%), with 6 out of every 10 (57.7%) between the ages of 20 and 29, (c) It can be noted that only 5.4% of the immigrants have no schooling; 21.9% have 1 to 5 years of schooling; 33.5% have 6 years of elementary school; and the remaining 40% has 7 or more years of schooling. Thus, the average years of schooling for immigrants is 6.44, (d) The city of Tijuana acts as the hub, because 6 out of every 10 illegal immigrants start from there on their way north. The city of Juarez is next in importance with 19.4%, followed by Mexicali with 10.4%, and finally Nuevo Laredo and Matamoros through which the remaining 12.1% of immigrants pass.

Almost half of illegal immigrants head toward California (48.9%), mainly the city of Los Angeles, where 23.5% of all immigrants end up staying. The state of Texas is second, with 20.5% of all immigrants headed there, although most of them stay in the border city of El Paso. The remaining 18.3% do not have a fixed destination.

As far as children of immigrants are concerned, it is not easy to determine the total number with precision. However, the National Program of Agricultural Workers of the Department of Social Development (SEDESOL) estimates that 1.2 million minors under the age of 14 are the children of seasonal migrant workers (Lopez, 1996).

In the United States, particularly in California, it is believed that public education has not been able to successfully handle adequate assimilation of the Mexican population. The problem of lower academic achievement by students with Latino origin is evident. Data regarding Latino students from the California Assessment Program allow us to see that in 1990 in the Los Angeles School District, they represented 63% of the total student body. On the average, third-grade elementary students, for both reading and mathematics, attained a score of 500, whereas the average for White and non-Latino was 614.

In the eighth grade, the gulf was even wider. The average scores were 414 for Latinos and 567 for Whites and non-Latinos. Also, 45% of Latino teenagers entering ninth grade in California do not graduate. A third of them drop out of school in the 10th grade. Throughout the whole state of California, the dropout rate for Latinos is double that for Whites and non-Latinos. Equality and adequate attention for this sector face two great challenges (Rothstein, 1995). On the one hand, there is the need to confront the problem of an illiterate environment in the home. On the other hand, it would be an advantage to offer not only bilingual but intercultural education that would break prejudices and favor assimilation policies while generating significant changes in the way the Mexican population is viewed and views itself, so that it can be more competitive with regard to the rules of North American society. Both cultural sectors would need to keep an open attitude toward change and make intercultural education available. Hayes-Bautista (1995) pointed out that in 1990 59% of the first generation born in the United States finished secondary school, and 70% of the second generation did so. However, some reports indicate that students' academic performance declines as the distance from Mexico increases with each generation (Vigil & Long, 1986). Moreover, data about the increase in academic achievements by generation show a significant improvement only until the completion of high school. University completion rates for the grandchildren of Mexican immigrants are not much higher that those of their parents' generation (McCarthy & Burciaga, 1985). As Rothstein (1995) pointed out, solving this problem would demand intensifying the participation of students' parents, expanding bilingual education, launching an educational reform, and achieving a greater transition from school to the work market.

INTERCULTURAL EDUCATION: BINATIONAL PROGRAMS

Because of the particular relation between Mexico and the United States, a number of binational intercultural and bilingual programs have been initiated. Some have a history of more than two decades, whereas others are relatively new. Some are directed at the elementary school population, whereas others focus on the preparation of teachers to work with these children. The next section describes several of these programs.

The Binational Educational Program

The Binational Educational Program was created in 1966 by a group of concerned teachers who sought support from the governments of the two countries through the respective departments of education. They established a series of actions intended to reduce limitations thought to affect the enrollment of students. Believing that education has no borders, they decided they were faced with the challenge and commitment to provide education to all children.

For 22 years, officials of these two countries have dealt with the effects of such programs as the Bracero (day-laborer) Program, which allowed guarantees to be extended to Mexican workers. In the last three decades, those who primarily benefited were the rural groups searching for better living conditions and moving seasonally or temporarily to the United States. This situation has a fundamental consequence of dislocating the education of school-age children and teenagers.

The Binational Educational Program has tried since 1966 to provide support in such situations. It first turned its attention to the children of fishermen and agricultural immigrants, but it was not until the first information exchange between Pajaro Valley of California and Gómez Farías of Michoacan that blue-collar workers also began to benefit from this program. In 1987, the Department of Migrant Education in California took up this project and, in conjunction with the state of Michoacan, agreed to some actions tending to guarantee access and educational continuity to immigrant students. This program has been well received in states with the greatest migratory flows: California, Colorado, Arizona, and Oregon in the United States, and Michoacan, Zacatecas, Chihuahua, Sonora, Mexico, Baja California Norte, Jalisco, and Guanajuato in Mexico.

The state of California receives approximately 63% of the Mexican students that migrate to the United States. According to statistics, 40% of these children go back to Mexico for periods of 2 to 6 months each year, a fact that in most cases limits them to receiving only 3 months of education in the United States. It is during the months of November to January, when there is a great influx of Mexican families into California, that the greatest enrollment of migrant students in education institutions occurs.

The major objective of the Binational Educational Program is the establishment of a system that allows migrant children and teenagers to enroll in American schools and schools in Mexican states that participate in this program, so they can continue with their studies even when the annual school cycle has already started. It must be realized that these children have been profoundly affected by the Mexican norm requiring a formal evaluation of their studies for enrollment, a problem they did not need to face during their stay in the United States.

In the context of the actions executed by the Mexican Ministry of Education (SEP) and the Ministry of Foreign Affairs, the administrative procedures for the enrollment of migrant children have been greatly simplified. The aim is to encourage incorporation of the students into the grade corresponding to their age while guaranteeing their immediate acceptance by schools in their respective communities, regardless of the time of year when they arrive. Also, in the context of the federalization of the Mexican nation, it has been possible to publish a document entitled *Transfer Document for the Binational Immigrant Student*, which allows students coming from the United States to provide their Mexican teachers with minimum required academic information. This affords the Mexican side an idea about the education level already achieved by the migrant or immigrant child.

Although popular initiatives such as California's Propositions 187 and 209 reflect a general attitude of rejection toward the immigrant population, in schools children not only have found acceptance, but many also have found the opportunity to achieve their educational goals through binational cooperation.

Binational Intercultural–Bilingual Programs for the Preparation of Teachers

This section describes two innovative programs for the preparation of teachers to work with California's diverse population, one based in California and directed at former Mexican teachers who have emigrated to California, and the other directed at California credential candidates and carried out in Mexico. This is a response to a very real influx of people across a common border. But first, we must examine the data on the Mexican presence in California schools as well as the exacting standards established for issuance of the new cross-cultural credentials that establish parameters for both of these programs.

The ever-changing demographics of California have posed a critical demand for qualified, competent teachers who are better prepared to address the multifaceted needs of diverse student population. Schools are faced with increasing numbers of students, of whom a great portion require instructional services to help develop academic skills in English. California's total enrollment of school-age (K–12 and ungraded) children in public schools is approximately 5.5 million. Of these, 23.6% or 1,262,982 are classified as limited english proficient (LEP). In 1995, Spanish-speaking LEP students made up 78% (990,801) of the overall LEP population in California. The needs of these language and culturally diverse students attending urban public schools go far beyond the obvious academic areas of language development and acquisition of core content knowledge. Language-diverse students face a multitude of challenges both in school and in the outside community that can have devastating consequences on their ability to succeed in school and society in relationships with peers and school staff. The academic success or failure of language-diverse students can be greatly influenced by the quality of their interactions with teachers.

Colleges and universities in the areas most heavily affected by LEP students do not have sufficient minority enrollments in teacher preparation programs to meet fully the demand for teachers in school districts with high numbers of minorities. The lack of minority candidates in teacher preparation programs exacerbates the ethnic difference between the teaching force and the communities they serve as well as the lack of educational services and opportunities for an increasingly diverse student population. The fact that there are too few minority teachers affects the type of schooling available to minority students. Students need a variety of cultural perspectives via a multiethnic teaching force in which racial and ethnic groups are included at a level of parity with their numbers in the student population (Marcoulides & Heck, 1988). Dash (1988) notes that although college enrollments have grown, proportions of Black and Hispanic high school graduates in college have changed little during the 1980s. Of all the teacher training candidates applying for admission to teacher programs in the California State University (CSU) system in September 1986, only 3% were Black and 5% Hispanic.

Language minority students preparing for the teaching profession are often constrained by limited resources as they strive to complete college. This lack of resources especially hinders language minority students who may possess bilingual skills. In addition, many are intimidated by bureaucratic procedures or standardized examinations outside their realm of experience. The California Basic Education Skills Test (CBEST) is administered to all teacher credential candidates in California, and has greatly diminished the pool of eligible minority teacher candidates. The California Department of Education LEP Issues Task Force (1991) reported that candidates from the pool who have been identified as having the best potential for becoming bilingually certified (Hispanics and Asian Americans) continue to have a low rate of passing the CBEST. Only 51% of Hispanics passed the CBEST during the 1989–1990 school year. The types of results obtained from standardized teacher examinations has not been very favorable and have had a severe impact on the supply of language minority candidates to the teaching profession (Quexada, 1992).

As the need for effective teachers of diverse student populations has grown more obvious, some schools and teacher education programs have begun to respond by rethinking their strategies for supporting the development of both bilingual and monolingual teachers with cross-cultural preparation. Perhaps the most far-reaching effort was California's 1992 decision to create two new credentials for elementary school teachers with state-wide standards established by the Commission on Teacher Credentialing (CTC). In California, teacher credential programs are considered professional preparation or "fifth-year programs." Thus, all teacher preparation programs are built on the foundation of an earned baccalaureate degree in Liberal studies or the combination of a baccalaureate degree in an academic discipline and an examination to assure a broad liberal studies background.

California's new Cross-Cultural, Language, and Academic Development Credential (CLAD) is based on the recognition that the responsibility for teaching children from a variety of linguistic and cultural backgrounds whose primary language is not English is part of all mainstream teachers' jobs, not just the terrain of special teachers. The goal of the credential is to equip teaching candidates with skills and knowledge in three areas: language acquisition and development, culture, and pedagogic strategies for teaching new English language learners in the content areas. The second credential adopted by the Commission on Teacher Credentialing is the Bilingual Cross-Cultural, Language, and Academic Development Credential (BCLAD), which delineates additional requirements that address a grounding in primary language instruction and a specific culture of emphasis.

Although California's system of teacher credentialing assures high quality teacher preparation programs, it obviously places severe constraints on those that differ from the norm either in the population they serve or their locale for program delivery. Despite this, in 1994, two innovative programs were created through collaboration of the National Pedagogic University of Mexico (UPN) and the California State University (CSU) system: a baccalaureate degree delivered by UPN, Mexicali at CSU, Long Beach to former Mexican teachers now residing in southern California, which provides the prerequisites for admission into a CSU teacher education credential program; and a teacher education credential program to prepare bilingual teachers for California delivered by UPN and CSU international programs to California State University students in Mexico at UPN, Ajusco, and in California at San Diego State University.

The National Pedagogic University Mexicali–California State University Long Beach Program

Designed to provide teachers sensitive to the needs of Mexican immigrants, and largely supported by Mexican funding sources, the UPN Mexicali program intends to integrate Mexican teachers residing in Los

Angeles into the California education system through a bilingual–bicultural approach. It is a partnership between the Mexicali unit of the National Pedagogic University and California State University, Long Beach. Its target population is the large number of Mexican teachers living in California who, due to the state's teacher certification requirements, are unable to practice their profession. They survive by accepting any kind of employment or, rather, subemployment. Because they are legal residents of California with previous professional experience and knowledge of the language and culture of Mexicans, they could help alleviate the shortage of bilingual and bicultural teachers (Bocanegra, Elizondo, Gomez, & Vazquez, 1994).

The first cohort began in 1994 and displays the following profile: Most of the participants in the program (72%) are between the ages of 25 and 35 years and the majority are women. Only 20% come from urban areas, which means that most of them have pursued their teaching career in rural areas. At the start of the program, the majority (70%) earned lower salaries than the average teacher in Mexico. Only seven had achieved the status of teaching assistant, and the remainder were unemployed until entering this activity. The cost of education explains their own disadvantaged situation.

During the program, all of the participants were placed in positions as teacher aides. Despite the fact that they have lived in California, the majority did not speak English well. Some even showed an aversion for the language. However, it is true that only a few of them have ever had any contact with American citizens, because most of them have had dealings only with Hispanic communities.

Because both countries have developed different traditions with respect to teacher certification, the bilingual education programs have had to face problems of identity, concepts, and methods, and they present a challenge to pedagogic creativity, requiring great effort to promote human development.

A central problem was the difference in preparation of teachers in the two countries. In California, a student intending to become a teacher must obtain a university degree and then complete a postgraduate credential program. In contrast, the professional preparation of these teachers in Mexico consisted of the equivalent to a community college degree. Thus, the approach adopted was to provide coursework that would grant them a licenciatura (or equivalent of a baccalaureate degree) from the UPN. This coursework was specifically designed to parallel the baccalaureate in liberal studies usually completed by most teacher education candidates. On attainment of this degree, and appropriate English language skills, these students will be eligible for the credential program at CSULB, which as previously explained, is a postgraduate education program.

Intercultural Challenges

Development of a teacher training curriculum for multicultural contexts theoretically should adopt the best of both educational traditions. However, it must be remembered that these former Mexican teachers will be teaching in U.S. schools, serving children of varied ethnic and racial backgrounds. Thus, the curriculum is heavily based on the California standards that teachers and their future students must achieve.

Content and Strategies

The Mexican and American curricula demonstrate a number of divergencies derived from conceptions and practices unique to each country. In the first place, the proposed curriculum raises fundamental problems regarding teacher training to which there is no consensus in either country. Four fundamental issues must be clarified.

- *Different Approaches*: In each country, teacher education uses different content and strategies. What should the content be? Over what period of time? In what way should it be taught? How should multiculturality be tackled? And, more concretely, by what teaching methods?
- *The recognition of experience*: The program starts by recognizing and valuing the acquired professional and cultural experience of its students. However, neither country has an adequate mechanism that would allow the bureaucracy to recognize such experience in formal terms.
- *Teacher trainer qualifications*: This aspect is the most complex, because it involves subjective decisions as to what is required in the way of a profile and qualifications for a teacher trainer. Even though each university has defined its criteria, profound reservations remain about the suitability of those who do not belong to the same academic guild.
- *Cost*: The financial conditions under which this education program is actually offered in California would make it almost inaccessible to those for whom it is intended without its current level of binational support.

Institutional Barriers

Time and institutional space have not allowed the cultural and academic exchange to take place as had perhaps been anticipated. For example, with the program limited to weekends, the relationship between the Mexican faculty team (that commutes to offer classes at the CSULB campus) and the faculty in the Teacher Education Department at California State University Long Beach is practically nonexistent, and student contact with the institution is limited to meeting their teachers and some Mexican officials that come to visit them from time to time. The shared teaching program has faced a multitude of difficulties, mainly because of administrative criteria in force at California State University Long Beach, such as the assignment of teaching loads and teacher pay per class. But there has also been a lack of knowledge about how to design a course employing two cultural and professional traditions, except for those faculty with experience in both cultures.

Design and Redesign of Courses

Even when parameters exist for each course in the curricula of each university, it has been necessary to redesign them. This has been especially difficult for the teaching staff at California State University Long Beach, who have long experience in the courses they teach. Both universities have different conceptions with respect to creating a course study plan, a fact that leads to unevenness.

Multicultural Education

Multicultural education cannot be reduced to specific courses, so a series of strategies present in all of the courses has been designed: These include:

- Resorting to the social and cultural context in teaching practice. (Most of the teaching assistants in bilingual education live in Latino communities.) Contextualization of the education process provides relevance and pertinence.
- Strengthening cultural identity and encouraging self-esteem by allowing time and space in the curriculum to converse and to establish an ongoing relationship between teachers and students.
- Aiming for bilingualism more than the mastery of one language (English) in relation to the other (Spanish). This aim is promoted throughout the courses offered in English and Spanish by teachers who master their own language and encourage reading and writing in both languages.
- Promoting group work with the aim of identifying the obstacles that make communication difficult by encouraging respect for differences in the search for consensus and, above all, by developing common tasks.
- In addition, requiring students to take a three-unit course entitled Social and Cultural Diversity in Educational Settings. This course provides experiential opportunities to examine personal attitudes toward distinct groups of persons, to develop multicultural competences, and to examine racism. Study of cultural, historical, social and psychologic factors that promote equal human worth and consideration of content and process issues related to interculturalism in school and community are an integral part of the course.

The BCLAD in Mexico Program

Whereas various programs offer (either in Mexico or the United States) intensive Spanish language training or extensive knowledge of Mexican culture, the BCLAD program is unique in offering both in addition to what its designers consider critical: the adjustment experience required of an immigrant student. Its major student objectives, in addition to those for the regular BCLAD credential programs, are to achieve fluency in the Spanish language as written and spoken in Mexico (particularly as used in school settings) to the level of competency required to teach Spanish-speaking children all subjects in Spanish; to achieve an understanding of Mexican history, civilization, and current political, economic, and social issues within the context of the Mexican family; and to live the experience of being an immigrant in Mexico with all the adjustments that their future students will go through in their adaptation as immigrants to California.

For this innovative program, the CSU has combined the resources of its teacher education faculty with those of the international programs of the Chancellor's office to provide a unique systemwide credential program designed to prepare teacher candidates to meet the challenges of the contemporary multicultural classroom. The program combines professional education coursework conducted in California and Mexico with the experience of cultural immersion and intensive language study in the Mexican milieu.

The program is conducted with the full participation of the Ajusco campus of the National Pedagogic University (UPN) in Mexico City, at which participants spend an academic year, and San Diego State University, at which they complete a pre- and postsummer session. Under the terms of a special agreement for academic cooperation between the CSU system and the Mexican Ministry of Education (SEP), students have access to exemplary private and public (urban as well as rural indigenous) schools, for field experiences and student teaching (Tarrow, 1994, 1995).

The program is undergong continuous review and development under the close supervision of an International Teacher Education Council (ITEC) comprised of faculty from all the participating CSU campuses and the formal evaluation of CTC during its review of credential programs offered at or by each CSU campus (Sutter & Tarrow, 1993). Assessment includes formal evaluations completed by students and faculty at the end of each course, summaries of information from student journals, summaries of meetings with teachers, observations of visiting ITEC faculty, and reports of the resident director and program administrators at Ajusco and San Diego.

Some of the challenges that participants faced in the first 3 years, include difficulties in adapting to student teaching in Mexican public schools and in assuring adequate supervision for the participants; difficulties related to the wide variation of Spanish language competency on the part of the participants; unrealistic expectations based on inadequate explanation and orientation to the program before entry; difficulties in securing comfortable housing with families willing to include participants in family and cultural life; different expectations of Mexican faculty about the amount of required reading, the writing of papers, and the balance of theoretical and practical elements in their courses; and problems in the student teaching experience related to value differences. This has led to a major international research project on value conflicts between teachers and students coming from different cultures (Tarrow, 1996).

Three cohorts of students have successfully completed the program and are now teaching in bilingual, primarily Mexican–American classrooms, in California and Arizona. Other positive outcomes include the close bonds that have developed between the California and Mexican faculty. Joint research projects have been undertaken; opportunities for academic exchange have been explored; and opportunities have provided for interchange of ideas between students and faculty in both of the programs described in this section. As a direct outcome of this project, all of the faculty and students involved have testified to their personal growth in intercultural understanding and communication, and to their greater understanding of the linguistic and cultural problems faced by students being educated in schools and by teachers from cultures other than their own. Program participants report that they will never forget the frustrations they felt in learning a new language and adapting to life in another culture as they deal every day with children in their classrooms facing such difficulties. Their journals reflect the fact that they lived intercultural education on a daily basis and are committed to it for the rest of their lives.

INTERCULTURAL EDUCATIONAL POLITICS

This chapter dealt with intercultural education issues affecting Mexican children on both sides of the border. The following is clear:

> The United States must pay attention to indicators, research, and the borne-out wisdom of experts who maintain that lines in the dirt do not impede the aspirations of people in search of a living. Border educators contend that Mexican students will continue to cross the border to attend U.S. schools—whether they have to sneak across at the risk of being detained in border patrol offices, or drive boldly across each morning in cars with Mexican license plates to the school bus stops. For the schools, this is a bi-national education issue, not an immigration issue" (Council for Educational Development and Research (n.d.)). p. 8

Mexico is rapidly being integrated into the global economy marked by a new international division of work. No country can distance itself from this process. It can be seen that by the end of this century, isolated cultures will perish and only cultures in communication, open to trade and the inevitable integration, will become wealthy and survive. This survival, however, depends on a relationship of mutual respect and joint effort. We should not only be able to live together in spite of our differences, but also to live with each other while respecting our differences.

It must be stressed that in Mexico an intercultural vision in this field does not exist because the defense of national sovereignty comes before the interest of integration. Mexico is a country too enclosed in itself, a situation that at the beginning of the 21st century is about to change. Neoliberal government politics, the decline in ideological discourse about the Mexican Revolution, the growing interdependence of nations, and the political influence that migratory flows have over the country today have begun to generate new policies.

The government recognizes that the only way to keep in their own country those Mexican workers who do not wish to emigrate is by reintroducing dynamism and new political expectations for the Mexican economy through exports and foreign investments. No country can afford to remain isolated today, especially in the field of information. To choose isolation means remaining on the fringe of events and losing the capacity to respond to social aspirations. Change is calling each nation to find a course toward the front of the world stage opening up toward the future. Our scale of values will need to be reconstructed so as to allow human beings to live together, encouraging the principles that adequately govern relationships between individuals, and founding and strengthening the new institutions that would ensure peaceful and mutually rewarding relationships between nations. To accomplish this, a new formula needs to be found, one that would preserve territorial integrity, culture, and national values in the midst of a permanently interrelated world, and in ways that guarantee reciprocity (Elizondo, 1996).

Confronted with this situation, Mexico moves ahead, attempting to reconcile change with tradition and practicing its form of democracy while participating in a competitive international market that makes it impossible to live in isolation. Mexico's history speaks to us about a permanent tension between the modern world's dynamism and tradition. Nothing can be ruled out for the future in the Mexican experience. Life styles and legal claims that date to the pre-Hispanic or from the colonial centuries are still valid in our time, and the cultural aspect has again become a priority, thus forcing us to recognize that culture is what makes a nation and not vice versa.

For a country with evident multiculturality, an intercultural educational policy for the whole population is necessary. It should aim to avoid any discriminatory or intolerant behavior and thus require the following: launching the design, development, and evaluation of curricula for the education system, teacher training, and professional education that would give an impetus to intercultural–bilingual education; stimulating research programs that analyze the particularities of minority groups indigenous or migrant and their relationship to the national context; developing programs for evaluation of education at all levels in relation to cultural and linguistic diversity; stimulating educational innovation that responds to the requirements of intercultural education; and stimulating interchange of experiences at the national and international levels concerning intercultural education.

Intercultural–bilingual education is necessary for developing an education that respects and accepts knowledge and values of minority groups. This education should promote a new attitude concerning what it means to be indigenous or immigrant. Such education should be fair and of good quality. This education should be addressed not only to indigenous and immigrant groups but also to members of the dominant group. It should be an education that integrates the characteristics and potential of a multicultural country, an education for all Mexican children, giving them similar opportunities without discrimination or marginalization.

TO CONSIDER

Unlike its neighbor to the north, there has been little division along racial lines in Mexico. Nonetheless, Mexico has had to confront numerous problems similar to those of many other developing nations, including a long occupation and dependence for cheap labor by Spain, thus keeping it from making the kinds of advances experienced by some other nations. Although Mexico is responding to the need to internationalize, it is doing so with less advantage than many other nations hold.

Mexico is becoming an increasingly multicultural society, and educators are beginning to recognize and respond to this diversity. A number of innovative programs between Mexico and the United States have recognized the realities experienced by students who regularly move across the border. Schools seem to have become quite active in preparing its young people for their place in a society that is pluralistic and culturally diverse.

1. Review current newspapers from Mexico that are available on the World Wide Web at www.vol.it/UK/EN/EDICOLA/quot_str.htm#menu.

Search for news items that present issues related to native land rights, the international community, interethnic conflict, and educational responses to diversity. How do current issues concerning diversity relate to what you have just read? What struggles continue around indigenous issues?
    2. *What can your nation and schools learn from the binational experiences of Mexico and the U.S.?*
    3. *How can young people in Mexico be most effectively prepared to interact with others on a global scale? What resources seem to be available in Mexico to assist young people in developing a global or intercultural perspective?*
    4. *What has been learned about creating professional training opportunities for indigenous teachers that has relevance in your situation?*
    5. *Mexico also receives immigrants and refugees from other Central American nations. Given what you have just read, how would you respond to the scenario presented in chapter 1. What steps should schools take in responding to the needs of newly arrived immigrant groups?*

ACKNOWLEDGMENTS

The authors thank Norma Bocanegra Gastélum for her contribution to this chapter.

REFERENCES

Bocanegra, N. (1994). Formación de docentes bilingües-biculturales: en el filo de la utopia [Preparation of bilingual-bicultural teachers: Reaching Utopia]. In *Diversidad en la Educación*. México.: SEP/UPN.
Bocanegra, N., Elizondo, A., Gomez, G., & Vasquez, M. (1994). *Licenciatura en educaciónn bilingüe y bicultural* [Bilingual and Bicultural B.A. in Education]. México: National Pedagogic University.
California Department of Education. (1991). Remedying the shortage of teachers for limited-english-proficient students. Report to the Superintendent from The Task Force on Selected LEP Issues, Sacramento, CA.
Council for Educational Development and Research. (n.d.). *Schools along the border: Education in the age of NAFTA*. Washington, DC: Author.
Dash, R. (1988, September). *Roundtable report: The challenge—preparing teachers for diverse student populations*. Far West Laboratory for Educational Reach and Development. San Francisco.
Dirección General de Educación Indígena. (1994). *Orientaciones para la enseñanza bilingüe en las primarias de zonas indígena* [Orientation for bilingual teaching in the elementary schools of intigenous regions]. México: SEP/DGEI.
Dirección General de Educación Indigena. (1995). *Estadística básica de educación indigena, inicio de ciclo escolar 1994–1995* [Basic statistics of indigenos education, beginning at academic year 1994–1995]. México: SEP/DGEI.
El Financiero. (1996, April 21) *Informe especial* [Special edition]. México.
Elizondo, A. (1996). *Política migratoria en México* [Migration policies in Mexico]. México, UPN.
Fuentes, C. (1994). *El espejo enterrado* [The buried mirror]. México: FCE.
Gigante, E. (1994). *Formación de maestros para la educación intercultural* [Preparation of teachers for intercultural education]. (preliminary version). Geneva, Switzerland: OIE-UNESCO.
Hayes-Bautista, D. (1995). Mexicanos en el sur de California: ¿Enriquecimiento social u oportunidad desperdiciada? In A. Lowenthal, & K. Burgess, (Eds.), *La conexión México–California* (pp. 159–176) [Social enrichment or wasted opportunity]. México. Siglo XXI.

Herrera Peña, G. (1995). *Detección de los cuellos de botella en todos los programas de educación intecultural bilingüe* [Detection of bottlenecks in all the bilingual intercultural education programs]. Paper presented at the Congreso de Educación Intercultural Bilingüe américa Indigena, Antigua, Guatemala.

Instituto de Investigaciones Jurídicas. (1996, May). *Memoria de la consulta nacional sobre derechos y participación indígenas* [Record of the national discussion about indigenous rights and participation]. UNAM/IIJ, México.

Jascott, M. (1994). *1993: El fenómeno de la migración en México* [The phenomenon of migration in Mexico]. México: Comité del D.F. Dirección Nacional de las ONG's.

Ley General de Educación [General Law of Education]. (1994). México: Secretaría Pública de Educación.

López, M. L. (1996). *Reforma*, April 20, p. 8.

Marcoulides, G. & Heck, R.. (1988). Teacher education reform: Issues of equity and accountability. *The Urban Review*, 20(2), 125–133.

McCarthy, F., & Burciaga, V. (1985). *Current and future effects of Mexican immigration in California: Executive summary*. Santa Monica, CA: Rand Institute.

Méyer, L., & Zoriada, V. (1994). Los años recientes: De la búsqueda de la diversidad al nuevo acercamiento. In L. Meyer & V. Zoraida (Eds.), *México frente a Estados Unidos: Un ensayo histórico, 1776–1994* (3rd ed.) [The recent years: From the search for diversity to the new approaches]. México: FCE.

Muñoz, G. & Suárez, H. (1996). *Perfil educativo de la población mexicana* [Educational profile of the Mexican Population, Vol. IV]. México: INEGI-ISS-UNAM.

Poder Federal Ejecutivo. (1995a). *Programa nacional de población, 1995–2000* [Federal executive power National population program]. México, D. F.: Department of Communications, Office of the President.

Poder Federal Ejecutivo. (1995b). *Programa de desarrollo educativo, 1995-2000* [Federal executive power Educational development program]. México, D. F.: Department of Communications, Office of the President.

Quezada, M. S. (1992). District remedies to eliminate the shortage of qualified teachers of limited-English-proficient students in selected districts in California. Unpublished Doctoral Dissertation, University of Southern California.

Rothstein, R. (1995) En búsqueda del sueno americano: Obstáculos para los latinos en la educación [In search of the American dream: Obstacles for *Latinos* in education]. In A. Lowenthal, & K. Burgess (Eds.), *La conexión México–California*. México: Siglo XXI.

Salinas, G. (1996). *Informe nacional de evaluación y seguimiento* [National report of evaluation and follow-up: B. A. program for preschool and elementary teahers in indigenous environments]. LEPYPEMI. México: UPN/SEP.

Sutter, R., & Tarrow, N. (1993, November). *An innovative international program for the preparation of bilingual–crosscultural teachers*. Paper presented at the Comparative and International Education Society, Western Regional Conference, Los Angeles, CA.

Tarrow, N. (1996). *Report: BCLAD in Mexico*. Mexico: CSU/UPN.

Tarrow, N. (1995, September) *Transformation in teacher preparation in the context of NAFTA*. Paper presented at International Symposium Formación docente, modernización educativa y globalización. Mexico: UPN.

Tarrow, N. (1994). Evaluación y práctica docente en el marco del proyecto académico de la UPN. In *Diversidad en la educación* (pp. 111–122) [Evaluation and student teaching in the context at the academic project of the National Pedagogic University]. México: SEPUPN.

Vigil, J., & Long, J. (1986). Unidirectional or nativist acculturation: Chicano paths to school achievement. *American Journal of Educaition*, 95(1), 233–255.

Zedillo, E. (1995). *Poder Ejecutivo Federal: Primer informe de gobierno* [Federal executive power]. (Vol. 11). Desarrollo Social. México, D. F.: Department of Communications, Office of the President.

Chapter 15

Intercultural Education from an International Perspective: Commonalities and Future Prospects

ಐ ◆ ಛ

Kenneth Cushner
Kent State University

This volume has explored how the educational establishments in various nations understand and attempt to resolve some of the complex and critical multicultural issues that they confront. The various chapters have surveyed such issues as historical developments that have influenced the present cultural landscape of the nation, the experience of minorities within the society at large, the clash between the culture of the school and the culture of the home, indigenous approaches to cultural maintenance and revitalization, and approaches to teacher training.

As reflected in the various experiences reported in this volume, most nations around the world are becoming increasingly multicultural. But just because a nation is multicultural does not guarantee that it is an effective intercultural one. Intercultural implies a give and take: a multilateral appreciation, understanding, accommodation and ability to interact effectively with people different from oneself. It is this emphasis on the intercultural dimension, including intercultural interaction and understanding, that will move people closer to a time when not only tolerance, but collaboration is the norm.

The nations surveyed represent a varied and complex array of population dynamics with respect to diversity. At least four scenarios seem to be present, each presenting unique educational needs and responses, and not all mutually exclusive.

1. In one context are nations that are home to oppressed indigenous or First Nation people. Nations standing out in this category include Australia, Canada, Mexico, New Zealand, South Africa, and the United States. South Africa with its recent transition from minority rule through apartheid to a democracy presents a unique situation that many around the world will anxiously watch.

2. In another context are nations that have significantly high voluntary immigrant populations. Nations in this category include Australia, Britain, Canada, Mexico, the Netherlands, New Zealand, and the United States.

3. Involuntary immigration into the United States presents a rather unique category. African Americans represent a population forced into the country in its early history as a direct result of the slave trade. The nation struggles with this legacy still today.

4. Finally, there are the smaller, multicultural nations that have responded to their cultural diversity in various ways. Ghana, Nigeria, and Malaysia present special cases in which European colonization imposed an artificial nationalist structure atop a previously existing multiethnic landscape. Identification with one's ethnic group (tribe or clan) still has little legitimacy in the eyes of many, and thus remains in conflict with the idea of a nationstate. Also, the European nations of Spain and Romania have demonstrated relatively little in terms of attention and direction in relation to multicultural policy and practice. Each of these nations is home to a number of different minority groups whose specific needs are not well understood nor addressed by the mainstream. Something these nations have in common with each other are the Gypsies who live within each of their borders.

In addition to these four scenarios, most of these nations confront increasing internationalization in their business communities. There is a great need to prepare young people for the certainty of diversity both from within, and from outside national borders.

COMMON ISSUES AND PROBLEMS

The problems, issues, and opportunities facing nations and educators are numerous and complex. Although most of the specifics experienced by any one nation will not be reiterated here as they have been presented in the various chapters, there are some similarities which are apparent across the spectrum that can be instructive to others. Analysis of schools that are successful with diverse populations, or that actively address issues related to diversity in a changing society confirms that many commonalities are faced across the globe.

Appropriate efforts at education reform can be found that will bring about positive change and lead to effective schools. Some of these efforts have been reported in these pages. Obviously, no formula has been developed and applied across the board that will work in all schools or situations. Successful innovation is more likely to occur when educators make the effort to adapt what is known about specific cultural issues and effective schools to their own situation. Furthermore, the school often is not the sole initiator or actor in such a process. Rather, some partnership or collaboration with others outside the school has proven to be an essential element in a successful change process.

In many cases, an important change may not seem very dramatic, but may still be what is necessary in a given place, at a given time, and in a given circumstance. For instance, the teaching of Italian in a traditional manner from a traditional textbook is not particularly innovative in and of itself. But simply offering Italian as a foreign language option in a school on the outskirts of Melbourne, Australia that has a large Italian population might be enough to help bring about a desired climate precisely because the needs and identity of a certain set of students and their families are recognized and appreciated. Sweeping, dramatic changes are not often necessarily a key element. Indeed, such changes often can be doomed from the start. Moreover, the key element is not necessarily the infusion of large amounts of additional money. Often the most effective are small, shared, relatively unobtrusive innovations that are closely monitored for their results and implications, such as those related in many of the preceding chapters.

The commonalities evident in the nations surveyed tend to center around five major issues: (a) the tension between cultural maintenance and cultural pluralism involving indigenous people, refugees, immigrants, and relationships between majority and minority populations in multiple contexts; (b) linguistic preservation, diversity, and training; (c) curriculum practices that are exclusive, ethnocentric, and restrictive and thus require expansion, representation, and balance; (d) teacher readiness and preparation; and (e) issues of national policy. Each of these five issues is considered in the following discussion.

Cultural Pluralism, Including Indigenous People, Refugees and Immigrants, and the Relationships between Majority and Minority Populations

It is obvious that each nation surveyed confronts issues of increasing cultural complexity and pluralism within its borders, and that relationships between majority and minority groups are often times quite strained.

Having different cultural groups living in a society can result in quite difficult and painful circumstances for immigrants and minorities who, at any given moment, may confront tremendous problems due to cultural or linguistic differences. Efforts to participate in a society made up of people with differing and sometimes opposing value systems as well as dissimilar patterns of communication and thinking are frequently not well understood by members of the dominant culture. Minorities, even in nations that espouse a pluralistic as opposed to an assimilationist ideology, are oftentimes forced to either modify their own values and behavior or adapt them to new cultural and social conditions.

It is also quite evident that a tremendous gap often exists between the culture of the home and the culture of the school, a gap too great at times for many students to bridge. In many instances, children come from a home and community whose values, beliefs, and practices are in direct conflict with those of the Western-oriented school, a situation in which the children are left to struggle and mediate between the two. The effective school recognizes this dilemma and aids the child and family in understanding that the two realities, with effort, can be accommodated. Such efforts can be directed at particular stationary communities, as has been the case in some projects directed at the education of Navajo and Hawaiian children in the United States or, as in the case with the unique program developed in Mexico, those efforts can serve the needs of children who regularly move between the United States and Mexico.

Building a sense of community from within the school as well as from without assists in removing barriers of access to knowledge, to the mainstream society and culture, and to one's own identity. By accepting and integrating various cultures, languages, and experiences, all may begin learning to negotiate life in a society characterized by multiple layers of identity and affiliation. Equally important is the dialogue that can develop between a community and its schools, particularly with regard to negotiating between the purposes of the school and community expectations.

Many nations struggle with the relationship between their indigenous people and a culturally different mainstream society. New Zealand, for instance, struggles with relationships between the Maori and the Pakeha (European) communities. The integration of these two peoples has not been realized to the extent imagined and desired since the signing of the Treaty of Waitangi, with the Pakeha remaining in a dominant role and an assimilationist ideology still quite pervasive. New immigrants to New Zealand, as reported by Russell Bishop and Ted Glynn in Chapter 3, also face considerable obstacles as they enter a society dominated by one group. Immigrants are typically viewed as having deficiencies and in need of remedial attention, thus stressing the need for more proactive measures by the schools. Even the Asian student often is viewed more in terms of an economic benefit than as a means to increase cultural diversity and sensitivity in New Zealand.

Australia, today, is one of the most ethnically diverse nations in the world, claiming to have more people born outside the country than any nation except Israel. But this present reality follows extreme initial resistance to pluralism. The White Australia policy in existence until the 1950s disappeared, and by the 1980s, all states had adopted multicultural education policies. A nation of immigrants, Australia also must come to grips with the conditions its indigenous Aboriginals confront. On almost any socioeconomic indicator, Australian Aboriginals are the most disadvantaged group in Australia, and the outlook for immediate improvement does not appear to be bright. Aboriginal children have faced problems in schools for almost as long as they have been allowed to attend. As late as 1972 in New South Wales, school principals could remove Aboriginal children from school if any White parent objected to their presence. Moreover, it was only in 1997 that the government came forth to apologize for the forceful removal of Aboriginal children from their families, a practice that occurred since the early 1900s when the common belief among the European population was that the Aborigines were a doomed culture and people.

Canada, too, is a land of immigrants with more than 70 groups in New Brunswick alone, who interact with a significant indigenous population claiming special status as First Nation people. Canadian aboriginal self-consciousness is significant today, and people are showing ever greater assertiveness and disdain toward government policies on multiculturalism that seem irrelevant or, at worst, detrimental to their needs. Until the 1950s, there was pervasive nativism, an attitude of cultural superiority expressed by one established group that operated to the exclusion of others. Since the 1950s, Canada has witnessed greater openness, in part due to an economic need for a larger labor pool. With this has come increased racial tensions, especially in the urban communities. Reservations about multiculturalism are especially strong among the francophone Quebecers as well as among many aboriginal groups out of fear that their specific grievances may not be met.

South Africa certainly exhibits a unique situation in the world today as it undergoes changes from apartheid and four separate school systems administered by separate educational authorities to a single more unified system. In the struggle to overcome a strong separatist ideology, a Western model of schooling still seems, for many, to be the one best system for all. This extremely heterogeneous society must confront cultural, social, religious, and linguistic differences of untold complexity. In addition, South Africans speak of the "lost generation," a group of young people who received little schooling as a result of the decade-long campaign of resistance against apartheid that began in 1976. Multiculturalists around the world keeping a close watch on the various developments that unfold in South Africa are especially challenged as the change from Apartheid as a political model shifts to the needed change in the cognitive and social domains. Other parts of Africa, too, particularly Nigeria and Ghana, struggle to integrate hundreds of languages, numerous ethnic groups, and varied religions.

Other nations also regularly confront indigenous or immigrant issues that have been poorly addressed by the education establishment. Throughout Europe, as evidenced in the chapters on Romania and Spain, and even in parts of the United States although not as well known, the unique needs and experience of the Gypsy communities challenge even the most open and inclusive of educators. The United States, a land established by immigrants primarily from Europe to the chagrin of its native peoples, now welcomes people from such diverse regions of the world as Asia, Central America, the Middle East, and Africa, and also boasts a population of about 1 million Gypsies. Moreover, decolonization of such countries as the Netherlands and Britain has resulted in the entry of many from such former colonies as India, Indonesia, and Africa, to name a few. Racism in the greater society is often reflected in problems experienced in school.

Linguistic Diversity, Preservation and Training

The languages of many of the indigenous peoples around the world, as well as the first language of many immigrant children, are disappearing at a far greater rate than ever before. Questions seem to abound concerning the role of the school in the maintenance and preservation of students' home languages, the degree to which a host school should be responsible for responding to and maintaining the linguistic needs of its community, and the determination of the preferred language of instruction. The cultural landscape in the United States, for instance, has become increasingly diverse over the past decades, to the extent that some urban school districts work to integrate students representing more than 60 different languages.

Although some community-based efforts to develop and maintain local and indigenous language exist, anxiety over linguistic issues in general are high. In response, nearly one third of the states in the United States, for instance, have voted English as the official language, even though the United States has become the fifth largest Spanish-speaking nation in the world. Furthermore, linguistic diversity is increasing in many schools, reflected by the fact that 184 different languages are spoken in the homes of school children in London. At the other extreme, as experienced in

Mexico, the push for integration is so strong that many indigenous people desire to give up their primary language because it is perceived as lacking value in the greater society.

New Zealand has witnessed a steady decline in the number of Maori language speakers due to pressures of assimilation, urbanization, and modernization. Aggressive efforts in Maori-medium schools since the early 1990s seems to have had an influence in revitalizing and reestablishing Maori as a legitimate language base. In terms of language maintenance and revitalization, these community-based efforts seem to be far ahead of the more traditional teacher education programs, which teach a minimal amount of the Maori language, limiting a teacher's use to surface- or tourist-level functionality.

In a similar manner, many educators in Canada, Australia, and the United States are committed to language preservation and maintenance, and when possible, strive to provide bilingual instruction programs. In particular, francophones in Canada have been quite successful at ensuring that the population in general, not only children in schools, live in a context that recognizes and maintains French as a critical language. In addition, the Canadian Heritage Language Program enables children to study their primary language, be it Punjabi, Hindi, or Mandarin. In Australia, because most schools serve more than one language group, community language schools providing instruction after school hours have been established. In Hawaii, language immersion schools have proven effective in the development and maintenance of the Hawaiian language, a language that was all but lost merely one generation ago. Recent debates about the role of Ebonics in American education continue to fuel controversy.

In Romania, the lack of education in their mother tongue has resulted in an increasing school dropout rate for Hungarian students. Although official government documents state that minorities have the right to an education in their mother tongue, this policy often is not put into practice. In Malaysia, however, the picture seems to be quite different. Malaysian schools are required to offer education in any language when more than 15 parents make such a request.

Curriculum Practices which are Exclusive, Ethnocentric, and Restrictive

Curriculum inclusion and expansion are key problem areas identified by many of the authors. It is a perenniel question whether a standard, universal curriculum is best for all students and teachers or if diversification is more effective. The former choice rests on the assumption that teachers and students are more alike than different. For many who adopt such a view, a universal curriculum serves all learners by assuming that all can and should learn what is taught. The latter choice is based on the assumption that differences between people are closely tied to learning, and that a rich, expanded, and diverse curriculum encourages plurality and facilitates not only subject matter learning, but also the development of respect for and understanding of, difference. An inclusive curriculum focuses on all students. Unlike some approaches, which introduce specialized content aimed only at minority students, educational objectives emphasizing pluralism in an increasingly interdependent society seek lifelong learning for everyone, which is characterized by change; diversity of ideas, values, and behaviors; and rapid technological development. An emphasis on flexibility, creativity, human rights, and shared values becomes the core of such efforts.

Likewise, integrating an indigenous or "other" perspective receives perhaps less attention than it should given the high degree of success that some have experienced. Examples of efforts in the United States, such as the Afrocentric movement within the African American community, suggest that it is possible to bring community members, teachers, and parents together to develop curricular experiences that are inclusive and transformative in nature. As already discussed, community immersion schools adopting the language of a particular group, from indigenous to immigrant, have formed in many different parts of the world. Such schools serve multiple purposes, from providing a language-rich environment in which children can grow and develop to adopting an instructional approach that is more similar to the learning style preferences children typically bring with them from their homes and communities. In Mexico, books in 47 indigenous languages and dialectical variants have been produced.

Many are concerned with issues of bias and balance in textbooks and curriculum materials. In Romania, many textbooks contain stereotypes that serve only to sustain a nationalistic-oriented education. In the Netherlands, there is a concerted effort underway to screen material for prejudice and discrimination, and in Spain, racism and xenophobia in instructional material seem evident by the exclusion of certain groups, the stereotyping of others, and the denial of racism in the country's past and present.

Australian educators, like many others, struggle with the dilemma of where an intercultural perspective fits in the curriculum, questioning if it is best linked to the social sciences, the language arts, or the fine arts. In Canada and the United States, much of a multicultural focus is concentrated in the social studies and the language arts. Regardless of where it is presented in the curriculum, one goal of an intercultural perspective is to focus on the development of a positive self-esteem, with particular emphasis on the inclusion of ethnic-specific groups across the board. Education strategies proposed in Australia for improving the identity and self-esteem of Aboriginal students are increasing, for instance, and include courses in traditional Aboriginal culture taught by elders in the community, the use of kinship organization in the teaching of mathematics, and the use of traditional knowledge about plants in teaching botany. Similar efforts are underway in Hawaii, where Hawaiian elders are an integral part of the public school instruction program in Hawaiian studies.

Perhaps, however, an intercultural perspective is best developed when it is infused across the discipline areas and not seen as separate or as an add-on to an already overcrowded curriculum. The goals of the Swann Report in England, as reported in Chapter 6, can only be realized if the school curriculum is permeated by a multicultural perspective. If the goals of a good intercultural education are to be achieved, its concepts should be seen as relevant in all areas of instruction. Thus, concepts that effectively cut across the disciplines should be identified and developed.

Teacher Readiness and Preparation

Multiple issues present themselves in relation to the category of teacher preparation. For one, the range of teacher preparedness in general is quite extensive. In Ghana, many teachers are untrained or sent to areas of the country in which they have little preparation to teach. In Mexico, many teachers, especially those in the rural areas, have only 3 to 6 months of training, some having barely completed elementary school themselves, with few having university training.

Everywhere, however, most teachers are not well trained in the complexities of multicultural classrooms and societies. As a result of poorly understanding issues of diversity, new immigrants and minorities may be labeled with negative attributions by teachers because they do not appear to speak correctly, dress appropriately, or behave as expected. Thus a self-fulfilling prophesy may be established. By not confronting the situation up front, public education may serve only to exacerbate the reproduction of racist or xenophobic ideas.

In Romania, as in Malaysia, intercultural education is poorly addressed, if at all, in the teacher education curriculum. In Spain, many teachers agree that intercultural training is necessary in schools and in teacher education, but themselves seem to display little sensitivity toward others. Multicultural understanding is felt to be more important for members of minority communities than for those in the majority. Intercultural understanding and training has been introduced in varying degrees into teacher education in the Netherlands, Canada, the United States, Australia, New Zealand, and in parts of Britain.

The literature in the field of culture learning suggests that it is only through significant and long-term experiences with people different from oneself can one become effective at living and working across cultures (Cushner & Brislin, 1996, 1997). Culture learning is just not effective when a cognitive-only approach is used. This is echoed at the end of John Stonier's discussion on South Africa (this volume, Chapter 10). Teachers, as in most of the countries surveyed, tend to represent the majority group. In addition, most teachers have had limited meaningful experiences with people different from themselves. Such a scenario presents quite a dilemma for teacher educators who are often at a loss in knowing how to provide foundational experiences from which their students can later grow. Although numerous strategies which have been developed have proven effective at increasing sensitivity and awareness of potential problems in cross-cultural communication and interaction, achieving change in behavior--in this case teachers' abilities to interact more effectively with others, in work across cultures, and to modify existing instructional material to be more inclusive--is far more difficult to achieve. The most effective methods seem to link cognitive inputs with extensive affective and/or experiential encounters (Cushner & Brislin, 1996, 1997; Cushner, McClelland, & Safford, 1996), something many institutions or nations are not yet prepared to actualize.

Most teachers are not sure how to go about making the necessary changes. In particular, people often lack an understanding of culture's influence on behavior and thinking, and of how subjective or deep culture differs from objective or surface culture. Thus, teachers are ill-prepared themselves for the diversity in their classrooms, making it twice as difficult for them to effectively reach their students. Educators today are on a precarious tightrope. On the one side, they must become better to work with the diversity of children in their charge, while on the other transferring this cultural content and new knowledge to their students curriculum concept in such a manner that they become skilled with others in the highly diverse and interdependent world in which they will live. This is no easy task, especially given what we know of the culture learning process.

Much criticism has been leveled against teacher educators for their inability to offer substantial intercultural curriculum for preservice teachers. Teacher preparation institutions in many have been criticized particularly for the rather superficial treatment and culture contact in the preparation of teachers. In preservice teacher education has a tendency to touch such issues, particularly with regard to the use of the Maori language in the schools. Such a surface level or "tourist-curriculum" approach to language learning leads to little substantial learning about Maori ways, history, and language. The call throughout New Zealand is for both groups, Maori and Pakeha, to work together in addressing one another's needs. This scenario is repeated in many of the nations surveyed.

In the Netherlands, the majority of today's teachers received their training before the current reforms that affect schools in regard to diversity. The nation has witnessed a strong policy initiative, but like so many other nations, has experienced little in the way of concretes. The importance of moving intercultural education from a topic to be included in a few areas of study to one which underlies all areas, including teacher relationships with parents, is becoming more evident.

One major problem faced by many nations is the lack of teachers who represent the various communities of their students. Bachellor Institute in the Northern Territory of Australia, for instance, has developed specialized programs in training leaders from traditional Aboriginal communities to become teachers. Numerous programs throughout the United States have focused on the recruitment and retention of under-represented groups in teacher education and have demonstrated that with a concerted and focused effort, great strides at diversifying the teaching force can be made.

Education Policy

Perhaps more critical than any of the issues already presented is the degree to which attention to intercultural issues is seen as a priority at the national level and thus addressed at the level of policymakers. Many nations are in a state of infancy in terms of addressing such issues, perhaps due to the great expanse of space in some nations, which has allowed separatism to survive for so long, and in other nations due to a variety of political or social forces. Over the years, European settlement in the United States, for instance, saw a great westward expansion, partly in response to people's desire for space and partly as the expression of individualism. In Australia, people have tended to congregate in the relatively few large urban centers scattered along its coast leaving much of the nation sparsely populated. Canada, too, has had the luxury of tremendous space, providing ample room for its population to grow and expand.

Although space may have been the great multicultural problem solver for some nations, the intercultural issues were not resolved. Rather, these critical intercultural issues played out and perhaps even exaggerated in the schools today, may have been ignored and postponed quite easily and comfortably for some time. Today, we witness the tensions from years of frustration and anger on the part of many people, and the inability of some, due to poor intercultural education and experience, to adequately address these problems. Many smaller nations have been forced to confront multicultural issues earlier, or to squelch them through force. Some, as in the case of Nigeria, have, as a direct result of colonialization, neglected to confront these issues, and as Michael and Michael suggest in their chapter, may not be able to move forward as a nation–state until attention is given to these issues.

Victor Neumann, in his chapter on Romania, points out that one of the obstacles to promoting interculturalism is evident when people become urbanized, a phenomenon experienced across the planet today at an ever-increasing rate. That is, people in transition from village-like and relatively collectivist settings to more urbanized and individualistc environments face quite a different social context. People adopting a more collectivist orientation may have a tendency to blend into the crowd, to be suspicious and fearful of the unknown, and to be relatively close-minded. The idea of sacrifice is promoted only in the name of the collective good. Individualism, then, is often mistaken as selfishness, protectionism, and a self-serving mentality. A society structured on collectivist village ideals tends to reject urban behavioral rules. The transition from village to city, rural to urban, collectivist to individualist requires crossing from one set of rules to another—something most people are ill-prepared to do. A collective identification and way of life tends to be perpetuated in people's behavior and expectations, but may not be easily transferred to an individualistic context, and thus may work against integration and an intercultural perspective. The frustrations felt by many may be traced to this transition.

Intergroup contact does not always lead to positive interactions, and this is obvious. Increasing intercultural interaction can lead to conflict in communities, schools, and the workplace. It can result in miscommunication and misunderstanding and can lead to increased mistrust. This is the point at which intercultural and multicultural education become critical. Through careful and thoughtful planning, intercultural goals and concepts can be developed.

It is clear that public education (often in combination with social service or other community or government agencies) can play a critical role in building societies that are inclusive of all people, nonracist, and ultimately proactive in addressing some needs of new immigrants, refugees, indigenous people, and cultural minorities. It is through such approaches as multicultural and intercultural education that elements essential for developing a democratic, inclusive society can be addressed, thus enabling all communities to learn to live peacefully with one another; to maintain their unique cultures, languages, and religions without facing discrimination; and to develop mutual solidarity and undertake common activities aimed at solving shared problems. It is unfortunate that in most countries, public education, as yet, has not been very successful in fulfilling this role. As presented in the various chapters in this volume, there is often a wide gap between theory and practice. That is, many, but not all of the nations surveyed in this volume, promote multicultural education and an intercultural perspective in policy and theory. The gap between policy and the day-to-day reality, however, is often quite wide. We see evidence of successful practice, but it is often sporadic. What is needed is a more comprehensive application of the practice and principles known to be successful.

Although there still is an obvious need for continuous effort, some nations have made considerable strides. In many nations, particularly Australia, New Zealand, the Netherlands, Britain, the United States and Canada, attention to intercultural education receives support, at least in terms of either policy directives from the state or federal government or an emphasis from numerous professional associations. The Australian government, for instance, has supported intercultural efforts by mandating a multicultural perspective in the curriculum for all schools since the 1980s. People the world over watch closely as events change and unfold in South Africa.

There are no policy directives and little apparent support for intercultural education in the nations of Malaysia, Romania, Spain, Mexico, Ghana, or Nigeria. In Spain, the Spanish Education Law and the objectives of LOGSE (Law of General Arrangement of the Educational System) imply an intercultural perspective, but attention to such is not required in teacher training. In Romania, the central government pays no attention to intercultural issues, stressing instead an assimilationist ideology, and although there is no national policy in Mexico, the indigenous population wants the government to consider intercultural education as a constitutional right. In Malaysia, education policy does not spell out attention to intercultural or multicultural education. Rather, related issues are assumed to be covered through the social studies curriculum.

It is precisely in some of these contexts that attention to intercultural education may be the most critical. In their discussion on Nigeria (this volume, Chapter 9), Michael and Michael suggest that the lack of attention to such issues may in fact underlie the problems that many African nations face. The inability of people to reconcile their interethnic (or tribal) differences may make it nearly impossible to identify with a superordinate nation–state. Such a warning, perhaps, should be communicated to many other nations that have yet to openly address and consider their multicultural reality.

RESPONSES TO THE REFUGEE SCENARIO

To tease you, the reader, and to encourage you to apply the content presented in this volume to a possible real-world situation, you were introduced to a refugee scenario in the first chapter. At the end of each chapter you were encouraged to respond to the scenario from the perspective of the nation you had just studied. A review of this scenario follows:

> Global conditions are such that there are at the present time more than 24 million people that the United Nations identifies as refugees, that is, people presently in transition from their country of origin to a potentially more hopeful situation. Your country has suddenly found itself host to a rather large number of political refugees. There is no hope that these people can return to their homeland, and your government has obligated itself to provide them with a home.

> A large group of these refugees have been settling in a part of your country that traditionally has been relatively culturally and linguistically homogeneous. The refugees prefer to settle in one of two settings: a relatively major city where work opportunities seem plentiful, or along a major source of water where they hopefully can continue their traditional farming and fishing activities. This represents an unexpected and unplanned change for the local population. Few of the people in either of these settings have any knowledge of the refugees' language, culture, or religious beliefs.

> Over the past 5 years in which this influx has been occurring, considerable tensions have arisen in the local communities, especially in the schools. Locals complain about the refugees' loud behavior, their strange language and inability or unwillingness to learn the local language, the way they raise their children, and even their health practices. Refugees in turn complain that the local communities do not open their doors to them, that they are unwilling to do business with them, and that their own young people are being forced to do things in school that go against their culture and religion. Teachers have become increasingly frustrated with their apparent inability to work well with many of the students. Tensions in schools between young people have also increased, as the secondary schools have seen an increase in vandalism and fighting between members of the two groups.

> You are on a team of education officials who have been asked to provide a plan of action to address the current situation. Using the practices and thinking that reflect the perspective of your own nation, please respond using the following questions as a guideline. How will you go about your work? What major obstacles do you anticipate? How will you go about overcoming these obstacles? What long-range actions do you propose? What major issues or concerns guide your proposal? How might teacher training be affected? How might you overcome any negative attitudes that teacher education students might have?

Chapter authors also were asked to respond to the refugee scenario. Their responses were, for the most part, idealized responses, so, almost without fail, they all reflected a number of similarities: a sincere concern for the individual dignity of the refugee or immigrant, an attempt to ease the transition experience, a need to link with community agencies, and a desire to maintain the refugees' home culture and language where possible.

Most nations, it appears, would provide some means of support for the refugees as new arrivals. Some nations, Australia in particular, may pay for some or all of the transportation expenses incurred by the refugees or new immigrants. Limited social security benefits including health care and assistance in locating work may be available, as well as counseling services, the availability of language interpreters, and language training in the language of the host country.

For the most part, it is recommended that all parties be involved in all aspects of the design and delivery of the various programs and experiences. That is, not only should public officials and school personnel play a role in resettlement, but representatives of the refugee community should be consulted as well. Religious and other community leaders from the refugee community should be sought out for their knowledge and ability to communicate effectively with the majority of their community. As soon as possible, representatives of the refugee community should be placed on most, if not all, of the school staff committees. In addition, those representing the host community should reflect a diversity of viewpoints in order to adequately represent the diversity of the community at large.

Language-related issues present another critical dilemma for both the new settler and the host community. In most instances, it is recognized that maintenance of a primary or home language is essential to one's ability in adequately adjusting to a new setting and developing competence in a second language. A variety of language-maintenance programs were proposed by the authors, including the use of parents and community leaders to assist school personnel with curriculum and teaching as required. It was suggested in some instances that school personnel would aim to use the refugee's language in school both as a bridge for new students and as an educational tool for the host community. Bilingual teachers were seen as essential to the process because that teachers might have to be recruited from the refugee community itself. Translation of school notices and other documents were deemed essential by many, as were bilingual signs posted throughout the school for students and parents alike. English as a second language (ESL) courses or other host-second language classes would most certainly need to be established.

In many cases, the authors recognized that the resettlement of refugee populations demands that agencies beyond the schools become involved. Many propose working closely with a variety of social service agencies with the school serving as the central place where the various communities come together. In many cases, a significant amount of culture learning would have to take place. That is, refugees would have to understand the education structures that exist in the host nation, the role of parents and community in school operation, and perhaps even the history of intercultural relations in the nation as well as the local community. In addition, the authors proposed a variety of professional development activities for school personnel. Because of the relatively poor preparation most teachers have had on topics and issues related to diversity, many proposed that school staff gain experience and expertise in such areas as identifying discriminatory practice, reviewing the relevance of the curriculum, modifying curriculum as needed, promoting antiracist practice in the community at large as well as throughout the educational establishment, and using a second language.

Curricular modification also is something that most nations would propose. There appears to be a great need for schools to provide curriculum materials that adequately reflect the various groups served by the schools. Recommendations suggest that curriculums be infused with new perspectives and additional content while becoming more inclusive. All levels should adopt pluralism as the goal and avoid an assimilation ideology. In particular, modification of the social studies or social education curriculum was seen as the most relevant arena in which to begin. How did your responses compare?

NEXT STEPS

Where are we headed? What is needed to improve the human condition? In what ways have we progressed? What gaps remain?

The intercultural education needs across the planet are many, and it appears that for the most part we have a long way to go. Local and national stability rests on a foundation that at one level provides a knowledge base so that all members of a society develop a fundamental understanding of the pluralistic nature of their nation while it offers support for a diversity of opinions, behavior, thinking, and communication styles. The next level, however, demands that understanding and support of others be translated into action and skill between individuals in communities, across a nation, and between nations. That is, young people today must be equipped not only with an awareness and knowledge of cultural diversity, but with the skills and abilities to interact more effectively across cultural boundaries and to collaborate with others in the solutions to common local, regional, national, and international problems. Many of the problems confronting nations and people today will be resolved only with the coordinated efforts of many people. An intercultural education thus becomes more essential today than ever before in the history of the planet.

It is evident that through the various approaches to multicultural education reviewed in this volume many countries have begun to experiment with a number of ways to address the needs of diverse groups in their societies. This work is critical in helping individuals as well as nations to make a true beginning in understanding the histories, experiences, perspectives, needs, and motivations of all members of a society. Such a multicultural approach in education benefits all—majority and minority alike. For everybody to achieve their potential and become contributing members of their society, all people must feel that their contributions are welcome, that their input has impact, and that their needs are realized.

Good intercultural or multicultural education also benefits the majority culture as all have an opportunity to learn about one another, to develop empathy as well as knowledge, and to reap the benefits of collaborative effort. We must continue to teach about others from their perspective, thus transmitting the knowledge that the group itself deems important. Such an approach has been shown to have positive impact in many contexts, as is shared in some chapters in this volume.

The greatest concern from this author's perspective lies in the relative lack of attention given to the interpersonal dimension. People must feel a connectedness to other people and begin to recognize that their individual as well as collective fate is inextricably linked to that of others. Good intercultural education emphasizes the interpersonal domain, the cross-cultural dimension that lies at the root of people's ability to communicate and interact with people different from themself. It is only when people gain comfort and skill at communicating across linguistic and cultural barriers and collaborating in the resolution of common problems that our world will begin to experience a reduction of conflict and gain the benefit that can be provided when all contribute.

A pedagogy for effective intercultural education requires that we move beyond the mere identification and transmission of information at the cognitive level. Effective intercultural education demands that people have well-structured, extensive, and repeated affective and behavioral (real) encounters with others, and that the knowledge gained about others as well as the self is made evident to all parties involved in the interaction. Referred to as a cognitive booster, people must reflect on the experiences they have had, and in some cases be told what it is that they have just experienced.

Attention to this dimension requires that we rethink the manner in which we typically go about the business of schooling. Educators must reach beyond a reliance on cognitive approaches in the familiar context we know as school to include more inclusive approaches that reach into local communities and beyond. Skills learned first in the local context can then transfer to the greater whole. Educators must encourage greater opportunities for extensive interaction across cultures so that young people gain experience in cross-cultural collaboration and begin to identify with their peers across cultural boundaries at local, regional, national, and international levels.

REFERENCES

Cushner, K., & Brislin, R., (1996). *Intercultural interactions: A Practical Guide, 2e.* Thousand Oaks, CA: Sage.

Cushner, K., & Brislin, R. (1997). Key concepts in the field of cross-cultural training: An introduction. In K. Cushner & R. Brislin (Eds.), *Improving intercultural interactions: Modules for cross-cultural training programs* (Vol 2, pp. 1–20). Thousand Oaks, CA: Sage.

Cushner, K., McClelland, A., & Safford, P. (1996). *Human diversity in education: An integrative approach.* New York: McGraw-Hill.

Authors

Rod Allan is coordinator of primary teacher education at Charles Sturt University-Mitchell at Bathurst, New South Wales, Australia. Since 1976 he has variously been editor and coeditor of *Mitchell Studies*, a handbook of teaching ideas for the social studies. His research interests include multicultural education and the analysis of political processes and their impact on tertiary students, details of which have been published in Australian and British journals.

Russell Bishop is an indigenous scholar, currently senior lecturer in the Education Department at the University of Otago, New Zealand. Before taking up his present position, he taught at secondary schools in New Zealand and the Cook Islands, then trained teachers at the Wellington College of Education. His research interests include indigenous approaches to research, collaborative storytelling as research and pedagogy, institutional responses to ethnic diversity, and intercultural education. His recent book entitled *Collaborative Research Stories: Whakawhanaungagtanga* (1996), Dunmore Press, addresses these research areas.

Auxiliadora Sales Ciges is researcher on intercultural education programs and assistant professor of history of education in the Education Department of University Jaume I, Castellon, Spain. She works as a teacher trainer for several teacher centers in Spain and collaborates in research on values, attitudes, and intercultural education in the Department of Theory of Education, University of Valencia. In 1995, she received a grant to conduct research on multicultural education at Queens College of City University, New York.

Kenneth Cushner is associate dean for student life and intercultural affairs and professor of education at Kent State University, Kent, Ohio. Dr. Cushner is author of several books and articles in the field of intercultural education and training including *Intercultural Interactions: A Practical Guide* (1986, 2nd ed., 1996); *Human Diversity in Education:*

An Integrative Approach (1992, 2nd ed., 1996); and *Improving Intercultural Interactions: Modules for Cross-Cultural Training Programs, volume 2* (Sage, 1997). A former East–West Center Scholar, he is a frequent contributor to the professional development of educators through writing, workshop presentations, and travel program development. He has developed and led intercultural programs on six continents.

Resy Delnoy studied Dutch language and literature at the University of Nijmegen where she also obtained her teaching qualifications. She worked on a consultative committee for curriculum development and at the National Institute for Curriculum Development in The Netherlands. She has carried out descriptive research into language teaching and intercultural education in practice. For the past few years she has been a lecturer in intercultural education at the University of Hamburg and has produced various publications in intercultural education. She is a board member of the International Mother Tongue Education Network (IMEN).

Benjamin A. Eshun is senior lecturer of mathematics education at the University of Cape Coast, Ghana. He received his doctorate from the University of Georgia, Athens, Georgia. His interests are in curriculum development and the mathematics achievement of students. He prepared this chapter while on sabbatical leave at the Texas Tech University and is currently at Gettysburg College in Pennsylvania.

Dr. Peter Figueroa is a reader in the School of Education, University of Southampton, England. He has also been a lecturer or researcher at Oxford University, the Australian National University, and the University of the West Indies, Jamaica. His interests lie mainly in racialized and ethnicized relations and education, and in French phenomenological thought. Known internationally for his work in multicultural and antiracist education, he has also been a visiting professor at the Johann Wolfgang Goethe University of Frankfurt and the University of Dar-es-Salaam. He is a Jamaican settled in Britain.

Robert Fowler is professor of social studies education at the University of Victoria, British Columbia, Canada. He has been chair of the Department of Social and Natural Sciences as well as dean of the faculty of education at the University of Victoria. In addition to his teaching and administrative responsibilities, Dr. Fowler has served as chair of the International Assembly of the National Council for the Social Studies and has developed numerous institutes for improving university teaching for scholars from China (funded by the Canadian International Development Agency) and from Indonesia (funded by World University Service of

Canada and East Asia Bank). Dr. Fowler is author of numerous publications including *Thinking Globally About Social Studies* (1995).

Hyacinth Gaudart is professor in the Department of Language Education, Faculty of Education, Universiti Malaya, Kuala Lumpur. Her interest lies in training teachers to teach English as a second or foreign language. Dr. Gaudart currently also heads a section on cocurriculum at the university, in which one of the courses she teaches is on interculturalism.

Ted Glynn is professor of teacher education at the University if Waikato. He chairs the board of the New Zealand Council for Educational Research (NZCER). From a background of research and teaching in applied behavior analysis in education, Ted has focused recently on bicultural and bilingual issues in New Zealand education. He currently works with a team of Maori kaumatua (elders), researchers, and teachers from the Poutama Pounamu Education Research Centre in Tauranga. The team has initiated several research projects, including the effects of peer tutoring of reading in Maori on students' reading in English, a school-wide behavioral management program for parents and teachers of Maori students (with major input from the students themselves), and the use of responsive, written feedback for students learning to write in Maori.

Bob Hill teaches social education at Charles Sturt University-Mitchell at Bathurst, New South Wales, Australia. His research interests include Aboriginal education, intercultural education, citizenship education of teacher education students, and the extent and impact of overseas practicums conducted by Australian universities. He is the author of *Overcoming Inequality* and coauthor of *The First of Its Kind, Perspectives on Childhood* and *Into Asia: Australian Teaching Practicums in Asia*.

Hans Hooghoff is presently senior curriculum manager for upper secondary curriculum and project coordinator for cross-curricular issues and social and moral education at the National Institute for Curriculum Development, The Netherlands. He has studied law and sociology at the University of Utrecht and has been a social studies and civics teacher for upper secondary students. Dr. Hooghoff is currently chair of the International Assembly of the National Council for the Social Studies and a member of the executive committee of the Consortium of Institutions for Development and Research in Education in Europe (CIDREE). He is a frequent traveler to Europe and other overseas countries, and is currently working on an innovative project in South Africa. Dr. Hooghoff is the author if several curriculum publications, materials, and articles in professional journals.

Aurora Elizondo Huerta holds the post of professor at the Universidad Pedagogica Nacional, Ajusco. Under a grant from the Colegio de Mexico, she is currently director of a major trinational research project on values in teacher education programs of Canada, the United States, and Mexico. She has played a major role in the development and implementation of binational teacher education programs in Mexico and California. Dr. Elizondo has published numerous articles and delivered many presentations on values in multicultural contexts, women's issues, education innovation, and educational supervision.

Rafaela Garcia Lopez has been a professor of education at the University of Valencia since 1985. She has collaborated on several books and articles related to the study of attitudes, values, and moral education. She also has worked on the issue of compensatory education and cultural diversity in the school context. She received her undergraduate degree in psychology and her doctorate degree in pedagogy.

Dr. Steve O. Michael is currently assistant professor of higher education administration at Kent State University. Dr. Michael received part of his education in Nigeria, where he also taught at Ahmadu Bello University. He was a commonwealth scholar at the University of Alberta, Canada where he obtained his PhD. Before his appointment at Kent State University, Dr. Michael was assistant professor of education at the University of Alaska, Fairbanks. His primary research and teaching interests are in higher education finance, strategic planning, marketing of education, institutional advancement, and administration of multiculturalism. He has served as consultant of strategic planning to school districts and has made several presentations in national and international conferences. Dr. Michael is the first recipient of the Sheffield Award for the best article published in the *Journal of the Canadian Higher Education* in 1992.

Ms. Yetty A. Michael received her Bachelor's of Art as well as her Graduate Certificate of Education from Ahmadu Bello University and taught at several schools in Nigeria, including Abeokuta Grammar School, Ijebu Ode College of Education, and Katsina Ala College of Education. She received her Master's of Education from the University of Alberta, Canada. She taught at several elementary schools in Nigeria, Canada, and the United States and has extensive experience directing preschool and daycare centers in Edmonton. Ms. Michael was an executive director of Tundra Tykes Childcare Center, Anchorage, Alaska and is currently a childcare coordinator for a non-profit organization in Cleveland, Ohio.

Victor Neumann is associate professor at the West University of Timi-soara, Romania. His holds a PhD in History and Social Sciences and was councellor of the minister of culture from 1990 until 1992. A scholar, Dr. Neumann has conducted studies at the Friedrich Ebert Stiftung in Bonn, Germany; The Netherlands Institute for Advanced Study, Wassenaar, the Netherlands; Maison des Sciences de l'Homme, Paris; the International Relations and Exchange Board, Washington, D.C.; and the Institut fur Ost und Sudosteuropaforschung, University of Vienna. He has published extensively, and his works include *Culture and Society; Cultural Conver-gences: Intercultural and Political Realtions in Central and Eastern Europe, 1750– 1850; The Temptation of Homo Europaeus: The Genesis of Modern Ideas in Central and Southeastern Europe.*

Todd Rickel is a doctoral candidate in the cultural foundations program in the college and graduate school of education at Kent State University. His interests include international, cross-cultural, and multicultural edu-cation. He has completed research on education reform in the Republic of Georgia, has studied secondary achievement using race as a criterion for success, and has done student teaching in cross-cultural settings. Todd has a baccalaureate degree in biology and an Master's degree in anthro-pology. He is married to Christin and has two daughters.

Gisela Salinas Sanchez is coordinator of the Academy of the History of Ideas and Indigenous Education at the Universidad Pedagogica Nacional and also serves as director of the project for the design, evaluation and follow-up of the Licenciatura (B.A.) program for indigenous populations. She has taught in primary, secondary, upper secondary, and baccalaurete programs in indigenous education as well as in the field of social anthro-pology at the National School of Social Anthropology. Ms. Salinas Sanchez has collaborated on the development of elementary textbooks, and cur-riculum and on the production of materials for indigenous groups. She has taught various courses in the teacher education programs of different regions in Mexico and has participated in various regional, national, and international forums on the theme of indigenous education. She has published articles in a variety of educational journals.

Vilma Seeberg is assistant professor of international–intercultural edu-cation in the Graduate School of Education of Kent State University, Ohio, United States. In the area of multicultural education in the United States, she teaches courses in undergraduate teacher preparation, advises masters' and PhD students, serves as cochair of the Institute for Education That Is Multicultural at Kent State University, is a leader in local site-based multicultural school reform, and has published articles on the process of reform. She is a member of the National Association for Multicultural Education. In the international area, she teaches doctoral courses, and has authored *Literacy in China* (1989) as well as articles on Chinese higher education, maintains the Chinese Higher Education Project, has served as president of the International Studies Special Interest Group of the American Education Research Association, and has served in various capacities in the Comparative International Education Society. Vilma Seeberg was born in Hamburg Germany, received her baccalaureate degree at the University of Wisconsin, United States, and her Master's degree and PhD in comparative education at the University of Hamburg. She lives in Cleveland, Ohio, United States.

John Stonier spent 38 years working in South African mainstream education as teacher, principal, and rector of a college of education. On retiring from the latter position in 1991, he was appointed director of a small nongovernmental organization: Resource Unit for Intercultural Education in South Africa (previously known as the Open Schools Association). In this capacity he was active in helping South African schools deal with the initial stages of desegregation and subsequently, intercultural education. This was done by means of conducting workshops and seminars for teachers and principals, presenting lectures and talks with parents and students, and editing and distributing articles dealing with issues related to intercultural education.

Beth Blue Swadener is professor of teaching, leadership, curriculum studies, and early childhood education at Kent State University. Her research interests include social policy, antibias–multicultural education in early childhood settings, and preprimary education in sub-Saharan Africa. During the 1994–1995 academic year, Beth was awarded a Fulbright senior research fellowship to complete a collaborative study of changing child-rearing and community mobilization in Kenya. She has also done work with street children and their mothers in Nairobi. Beth conducted three ethnographic studies of early childhood settings, emphasizing collaborative work with teachers, and edited (with Shirley Kessler) *Reconceptualizing the Early Childhood Curriculum* (Teachers College Press, 1992), and (with Sally Lubeck), *Children and Families "At Promise": Deconstructing the Discourse of Risk* (SUNY Press, 1995). She has published numerous articles and book chapters on antibias education, social policy, and qualitative research methods. Currently, Beth is writing a book based on her Fulbright study with two Kenyan early childhood education colleagues, and recently she completed a book (with a South African colleague), *Ubuntu—A Call to Healing: Affirming Unity and Diversity in the Curriculum*. She also has guest edited a special issue of *Early Education and Development* on Children, Families and Change: International Perspectives. Beth has been active in social justice work and frequently cofacilitates Unlearning Oppression workshops for teachers and community groups.

Norma Tarrow is professor of education at California State University, Long Beach, where she teaches graduate courses in Intercultural Education and undergraduate courses in social and cultural diversity in educational settings. She has served the California State University system as resident director of the international program, and also directed the bilingual credential program at the Universidad Pedagogica Nacional in Mexico from 1994 until 1996. Dr. Tarrow was the founder and director of Semester in Mexico Program (SIM) between CSULB and Universidad Autonoma de Guadalajara. Her research interests include human rights and intercultural education, and she specializes in the education of indigenous minority groups. She is coeditor of *Multicultural and International Dimensions of American Community Colleges*, Garland, 1995; editor of *Human Rights and Education*, Pergamon, 1987; and author of *Guiding Young Children's Learning: A Comprehensive Approach to Early Childhood Education*, McGraw-Hill, 1981. She has authored numerous chapters in several recent volumes.

Marguerite Vanden-Wyngaard is a doctoral candidate in curriculum and instruction at Kent State University. She is a Holmes scholar with interests in indigenous issues, multicultural teacher education, and curriculum development. She has been a music teacher in Michigan schools.

Author Index

Subject Index

Date Due

MAR 0 6 2001			